"This book is a very important inter. .ention into the debate about 'practical wisdom.' We have long anticipated the potential of this term for scholars, educators, and practitioners alike, but this is one of the first attempts to address practical wisdom in an integrated fashion. A bold and innovative study that will enrich and revitalize practical theology."

— ELAINE GRAHAM
University of Chester

"Offering a robust and illuminating evocation of practical wisdom or know-how from a Christian theological perspective, this volume not only describes practical wisdom but also demonstrates it through the synergistic collaboration of five gifted theological educators. . . . An ideal book for anyone who wants to both study and grow in the practice of Christian wisdom."

— JOHN D. WITVLIET
Calvin Institute of
Christian Worship

CHRISTIAN PRACTICAL WISDOM

WHAT IT IS, WHY IT MATTERS

Dorothy C. Bass
Kathleen A. Cahalan
Bonnie J. Miller-McLemore
James R. Nieman
Christian B. Scharen

WILLIAM B. EERDMANS PUBLISHING COMPANY
GRAND RAPIDS, MICHIGAN

Published 2016 by
Wm. B. Eerdmans Publishing Co.
2140 Oak Industrial Drive N.E.,
Grand Rapids, Michigan 49505

Printed in the United States of America

22 21 20 19 18 17 16   7 6 5 4 3 2 1

Library of Congress Cataloging-in-Publication Data

Names: Bass, Dorothy C., author.
Title: Christian practical wisdom: what it is, why it matters / Dorothy C. Bass, Kathleen A. Cahalan,
   Bonnie J. Miller-McLemore, James R. Nieman, Christian B. Scharen.
Description: Grand Rapids, Michigan : Eerdmans Publishing Company, 2016. | Includes index.
Identifiers: LCCN 2015046915 | ISBN 9780802868732 (pbk.: alk. paper)
Subjects: LCSH: Christian life. | Wisdom. | Spiritual life — Christianity.
Classification: LCC BV4501.3 .C493 2016 | DDC 248 — dc23
   LC record available at http://lccn.loc.gov/2015046915

www.eerdmans.com

For Craig Dykstra

and with thanks to
our families and partners,
our various home institutions,
the Collegeville Institute for
Ecumenical and Cultural Research,
Saint John's Abbey,
and Lilly Endowment,
which provided financial support for
our work together through
a grant to Valparaiso University

CONTENTS

PART TWO

PART THREE

framing

ENGAGING THE INTELLIGENCE OF PRACTICE

WHY IS THE VERY KIND OF KNOWLEDGE that people need to live well — what we call *practical wisdom* — the least understood, the hardest to learn, and often the most devalued kind of knowledge?

On the one hand, this knowledge is present everywhere. A competent nurse, a good parent, a seasoned mechanic, a thoughtful congregant, a trusted daycare worker, a sage administrator — all possess such knowledge. It shows up in a kind of good judgment they are able to put into play in a particular time and place, sometimes as if by second nature. As they address the needs arising around them, they are engaged, flexible, attuned, and attentive on many levels — cognitively, emotionally, relationally, morally, and spiritually. Watch them, and you will see an intelligence of practice that fosters responsive action carried or even incarnated in their bodies — hands, facial expressions, posture, voice.

On the other hand, the importance of this kind of knowledge and the challenge of enacting it is most often not articulated or appreciated, and its features are not well understood. This disregard is no accident. Rather, it is the result of a specific understanding of knowledge dominant in the modern West that actively marginalizes embodiment and practical engagement as relevant dimensions of knowledge. This dominant sort of knowledge, called *episteme* and *theoria* in ancient Greek and Latin, undergirded the Enlightenment and its almost singular focus on objective, abstract knowledge. The rise of science and of specialized academic disciplines in the modern university greatly advanced the privileging of theoretical reasoning. This bias still exercises immense influence in the academy, including seminaries and divinity schools. The privileging of theory removed from practice is a special problem in professional schools, and theological schools in particular, because graduates need to put their accrued knowledge into action. In theological education, moreover, the subject matter itself runs far beyond what can be made available in textbooks, classroom lectures, and exams. Indeed, Christianity and religion in general contain elements that cannot be understood fully from theoretical and objective perspectives. When such perspectives outweigh other emphases, indispensable elements of Christian faith and life are obscured.

In this book, we claim that a kind of knowing resides at the core of the Christian life that is closer to practical than to abstract reason — closer, that is, to embodied, situated knowing-in-action than to disembodied, theoretical knowledge. The purpose of this book is to lift up the often unnoticed practical wisdom that is a necessary element of Christian faith and life. As we show what it is and explore why it matters, the authors seek especially to persuade the leaders of congregations, seminaries, and other religious and educational institutions of its importance. Many readers, we anticipate, will readily agree that this kind of knowledge exists, and throughout the book we cite other important efforts in theology and beyond to get at this knowledge. However, we intend to press the case beyond general agreement and prior efforts. We shall urge readers to consider both the sources of practical wisdom's marginalization and the damage done to living communities of faith as a result. Moreover, we will go beyond analyzing the problem. We will illustrate or show how practical wisdom takes shape in several arenas and explore fresh ways it might be reconceived. We will especially portray and advocate for the value of this form of knowing for Christian communities.

It is important to clarify at the outset that our purpose is to rebalance practical with theoretical wisdom, not to overthrow the latter. We note, but press against, the temptation to argue for one kind of knowing while falling into binary thinking that opposes the other. We could not write this book or practice our vocations as scholars, friends, family members, citizens, and disciples without the material benefits yielded by modern science and constant reliance on some aspects of the theoretical knowledge in which we have been formed as scholars and as members of modern civil society. Knowledge that is only contextual, local, and particular is not practical wisdom, for such knowledge too easily becomes closed, uncritical, and disengaged from larger realities and truths. Rather, practical wisdom emerges in the interplay of various realms of knowing, from the most abstract generalized theories to the most concrete, particular situations. The challenge, especially in theological education and ministerial leadership, is to see how conceptual and critical thinking stand in relationship to the concrete and particular in everyday life, and how careful thinking across domains and types of knowledge leads to fuller insight and more prudent action. As argued more fully in the chapter titled "Disciplining," we believe it is a misperception to think that lifting up one kind of knowledge requires the debasement of another. Rather, as philosopher Stephen Toulmin argues, balance between what he calls "reason" and "reasonableness," or, put differently, between theoretical knowledge and practical wisdom, was a long-held norm before the Enlightenment skewed things abruptly toward abstract reason as vastly superior.[1] We see ourselves involved in the retrieval work Toulmin and many others have undertaken, seeking a rebalancing rather than a pendulum swing toward a triumph of the practical over the theoretical.

Over the course of several years, we have worked diligently together on the questions at the heart of this book because we are acutely aware of the consequences when practical wisdom is overlooked. When Christian academic and ecclesial communities valorize theological abstraction and cognitive belief in ways that imply that practical wisdom is a second-rate, dispensable form of knowledge, Christian discipleship is undermined as a way of life and diminished as a witness in society. An important Carnegie study led by education scholar Charles Foster was sensitive to this concern. One finding was that most seminary faculty continue to privilege critical thinking as the goal of their teaching despite many efforts to reform seminary curricula and pedagogy toward the practice of ministry.[2] This suggests that efforts to reform education and honor ministry need to consider the

---

1. Stephen Toulmin, *Return to Reason* (Cambridge: Harvard University Press, 2003).

2. Charles R. Foster, Lisa E. Dahill, Lawrence A. Golemon, and Barbara Wang Tolentino, *Educating Clergy: Teaching Practices and Pastoral Imagination* (San Francisco: Jossey-Bass, 2005), p. 92. Many theological educators are influenced by Stephen Brookfield's work on critical thinking as "identifying and challenging assumptions they bring to the study of a text, situation, event or relationship as well as the contextual influences that inform their thinking." See Stephen D. Brookfield, *Teaching for Critical Thinking: Tools and Techniques to Help Students Question Their Assumptions* (San Francisco: Jossey-Bass, 2012).

"underlying epistemology," in Parker Palmer's words, embedded in teaching.[3] Education designed largely around the presentation and criticism of ideas and the inculcation of students into academic disciplines is inadequate to the richness and complexity of ministry and faith.

Christians today urgently need the embodied wisdom without which Christianity is just an idea and not a living reality in service to God and others. We write in order to encourage ministers, teachers, and leaders to notice, honor, and nurture such wisdom in communities of faith. We hope also to contribute to a wider public discussion among others who have recognized the limits of education designed primarily in relation to narrow academic ends and have called for approaches that are more attentive to practice and more attuned to the value of wisdom. Vibrant engagement with practical wisdom in long-standing religious traditions, including but going beyond Christianity, will enrich the kind of thinking and action so desperately needed in our deeply troubled global society.

Christian Practical Wisdom

In the most basic sense, by *practical wisdom* we mean what Aristotle called *phronesis* and what Aquinas called *prudentia,* notions with long, rich histories. For both Aristotle in ancient Greece and Aquinas in medieval Europe, such wisdom is the good judgment someone shows in the face of everyday dilemmas. It is the ability to render a proper assessment of a situation and to act rightly as a result.

In *Nicomachean Ethics,* Aristotle discusses this kind of wisdom at the crucial juncture where his argument turns from a consideration of the moral virtues to a discussion of the intellectual virtues. *Phronesis,* an intellectual virtue with strong moral elements, could be translated as either *wisdom* or *prudence,* though both renderings have limitations. *Wisdom* is also used to translate the Greek term *sophia,* the pursuit of the highest eternal truths, and *prudence* is often misunderstood today as narrow or selfish caution. Aristotle incorporates aspects of both *prudence* and *sophia* in his understanding of *phronesis. Phronesis* appears most clearly in his thought as an understand-

---

3. Parker J. Palmer, *To Know as We Are Known: A Spirituality of Education* (San Francisco: Harper & Row, 1983), pp. 29-30.

ing of "what sorts of things promote living well in general." *Phronesis* is different from *episteme* "because what is achievable in action admits of being otherwise" than the invariable truths of science or theory. It also differs from a third kind of knowledge, *techne* or craft knowledge, "because action and production belong to different kinds." More than either of these, *phronesis* is adaptive and engaged; it unites a knowledge of truth and reason with a concern for action related to human goods.[4] It accrues over time through experience in the world and is exemplified by good deliberation; it can discern what it means in particular situations to do the "right thing, in the right way, and at the right time."[5] This involves seeing and sustaining the connections between that which is reasonable, that which is moral, and the constraints of variable contexts. A morally virtuous person knows the good but cannot pursue it without *phronesis*. Good intentions are not enough; one must also possess practical intelligence.

Centuries later, Aquinas brought some of these claims into his own systematic development of Christian theological ethics, drawing and expanding on the patristic tradition he inherited, which had adopted the Stoic virtues of prudence, temperance, courage, and justice and combined them with the theological virtues emphasized by the apostle Paul — faith, hope, and love. Aquinas added a distinct emphasis to the discussion of prudence as a natural or moral virtue by enumerating its eight parts: memory, understanding, docility, shrewdness, reason, foresight, circumspection, and caution.[6]

Understood within this history, *phronesis* or *prudentia* denotes a kind of knowing that is morally attuned, rooted in a tradition that affirms the good, and driven toward aims that seek the good. It is not a package of pre-planned rules but stays open and adaptive to new situations. It is nimble and at times even self-critical. Most of all, this knowledge is practical, grounded in ordinary experience, and learned over time in the company of others and for the sake of others. Not surprisingly, when twentieth-century philosophers and theologians became frustrated with the state of knowledge in post-Enlightenment culture and began reconsidering practical knowledge, they returned to the concept of *phronesis* in Aristotle. We shall see examples

4. Aristotle, *Nicomachean Ethics,* trans. Robert Bartlett and Susan D. Collins (Chicago: University of Chicago Press, 2011), book VI, chapter 5, paragraphs 1, 3, and 6.

5. Aristotle, *Nicomachean Ethics,* book VI, chapter 9, paragraph 6.

6. See Thomas Aquinas, *Summa Theologica,* trans. Fathers of the English Dominican Province (New York: Benziger Brothers, 1947), I-II, qq. 55-67.

of this when we explore the use of *phronesis* in contemporary contexts later in the book.

At the beginning of our research and conversation, we frequently used the term *phronesis* to name the kind of knowledge we have witnessed within and beyond Christian communities and hoped to understand more deeply. However, we also found ourselves using other terms besides *phronesis* to capture the breadth and depth of the reality we wanted to describe — terms such as *practical knowledge, practical reason, prudence,* and *know-how.* We recognized that choosing the right words was crucial to our argument but also a complicated decision not wholly resolved by a singular term. Ultimately, we judged *phronesis* insufficient for our purposes, partly because it does not grasp the richer understandings of knowledge within Christianity. *Wisdom* comes the closest to what we are after, but it is perhaps the most complex term of all, in general but especially within Christian scriptures and traditions. Here, wisdom inhabits both the cosmic and the quotidian realms; for the wise, there is always an important interplay between the two — the living God of all that is and the temporal, embodied realities of daily life. The wise both tremble before an unknowable God (as, for example, in Job 38–41) and deal capably with others in the matters of everyday life (for example, Prov. 31:10-31).[7] Further, the parabolic wisdom of Jesus (as in Matt. 20:1-16) and Paul's influential interpretation of Jesus' death (1 Cor. 1:18-25, for example) accentuate the upside-down, paradoxical character of wisdom, which makes it seem foolish by others' standards. *Wisdom,* unmodified, opens onto a rich terrain indeed, but one on which our interest in practice might be overwhelmed by other concerns.

After struggling to find adequate words for the fluid, embodied knowledge essential to Christian living, we decided to take up the phrase *practical wisdom,* joining our voices to a long conversation that is alive in many areas of contemporary thought. There is widespread renewed interest in wisdom today beyond Christianity, a trend marked by many books, conferences, and a fascinating interdisciplinary project on wisdom sponsored by the

---

7. In *Seeing the World and Knowing God: Hebrew Wisdom and Christian Doctrine in Late-Modern Context* (Oxford: Oxford University Press, 2013), Paul S. Fiddes argues that the Hebrew wisdom tradition provides important resources for the late modern quest for "wisdom," where the term becomes "an all-purpose word to denote a way of living in the world which aims to transcend the self as a merely thinking subject." In contrast to cognitive models aimed at control, the term "indicates alternative ways of relating the self to the world" (p. 4).

University of Chicago.[8] Practical wisdom has also become a key focus in work aimed at renewing the professions — law, medicine, nursing, engineering, and ministry, among others.[9] Leaders in professional education, such as William Sullivan and Matthew Rosin, have proposed the pursuit of practical reason and wisdom as an "alternative educational agenda" and a more inclusive and important aim than the pursuit of critical reason alone. Overwhelming emphasis on critical thinking downplays the value of intuitive forms of knowing, the relevance of the concrete and particular, and the importance of moral frameworks. It "overlooks the embodied, often tacit knowledge present in skillful judgment," in Sullivan and Rosin's words, reducing knowledge to "formal or representational modes exclusively."[10] These authors do not oppose practical reason to critical thinking, recognizing the value of "developing self-awareness" and subjecting "opinions to analysis and critique." But, following the Aristotelian tradition, they see practical reason as fostering a "back-and-forth dialogue between analytical thought and the ongoing constitution of meaning" necessary for "responsive engagement in projects in the world."[11]

We have modified the phrase "practical wisdom" by adding the word *Christian*. As current research indicates, practical wisdom is not restricted

8. See, for example, the Wisdom Project, directed by Howard C. Nusbaum, professor of psychology, at the University of Chicago: http://wisdomresearch.org/, accessed September 18, 2014.

9. See, for example, Lee S. Shulman, *The Wisdom of Practice: Lessons on Teaching, Learning, and Learning to Teach* (San Francisco: Jossey-Bass, 2004). As past president of the Carnegie Foundation for the Advancement of Teaching, he also oversaw several major studies of professional education, including Foster et al., *Educating Clergy: Teaching Practices and Pastoral Imagination*. Carnegie-supported publications on engineering, law, nursing, and medicine are Sheri D. Sheppard et al., *Educating Engineers: Designing for the Future of the Field* (San Francisco: Jossey-Bass, 2008); William M. Sullivan, Anne Colby, Judith Welch Wegner, Lloyd Bond, and Lee S. Shulman, *Educating Lawyers: Preparation for the Profession of Law* (San Francisco: Jossey-Bass, 2007); Patricia E. Benner, Molly Sutphen, Victoria Leonard, and Lisa Day, *Educating Nurses: A Call for Radical Transformation* (San Francisco: Jossey-Bass, 2010); and Molly Cooke, David M. Irby, and Bridget C. O'Brien, *Educating Physicians: A Call for Reform of Medical School and Residency* (San Francisco: Jossey-Bass, 2010).

10. William M. Sullivan and Matthew S. Rosin, *A New Agenda for Higher Education: Shaping the Life of the Mind for Practice* (San Francisco: Jossey-Bass, 2008), p. 100. See also William M. Sullivan, *Work and Integrity: The Crisis and Promise of Professionalism in America*, 2nd ed. (San Francisco: Jossey-Bass, 2004).

11. Sullivan and Rosin, *A New Agenda*, p. 104.

to any particular religious tradition, and for some it has no religious content at all. And yet we see the importance of asking how a turn to religion, specifically Christianity, might provide resources for better understanding and strengthening this kind of knowing in today's world. As we inquired into the kind of practical wisdom that belongs to faithful living, we came to see that our own concern for ways of knowing that are embodied, relational, and invested in particularity grew from deep theological roots. Christian practical wisdom emerges in relation to God embodied — not only materially (the Christian belief that God "became flesh") but also purposefully, in relationship as a loving neighbor (Christ "dwelt among us," bearing "grace upon grace," John 1:14-16). Shaped by our various locations within the Christian tradition, we (re)discovered a holism in wisdom traditions informed by scripture that is missing in the hierarchical depiction of knowledge in Greek philosophy and modernity, both of which rank *theoria* and *sophia* above *phronesis* and *techne*. In Jewish and Christian scriptures the term *wisdom* belongs instead to a way of life that can emerge in many spheres, whether among the elite and educated, those who work with their hands, or children. The author of Proverbs points to multiple dimensions of "learning about wisdom" and identifies many attributes in that text's first few verses alone — expansion of understanding, instruction in righteousness, concern about justice and equity, a capacity for shrewdness, the acquisition of skill, and the art of understanding proverbs, figures, words, and riddles (1:2-7).

In biblically influenced traditions of wisdom, within which we would place our own work, wisdom is deeply located in time and place and is responsible to act rightly there, while at the same time it responds to an eternal and universal God. Wisdom can be gained and taught, but it also eludes control and always bears a certain humility cognizant of limitation. In this it incorporates not only practical wisdom but also a differently nuanced kind of wisdom, which Aristotle called *sophia* and Aquinas called *sapientia*. Such complex wisdom breathes through certain biblical books in ways Christians most often associate with the Holy Spirit. British theologian Paul S. Fiddes captures this nuance well in his account of the twofold character of ancient Hebrew wisdom, which somewhat parallels our *quotidian* and *cosmic* designations as well as the distinctions made by Aristotle and Aquinas. The "wisdom of observation," which Fiddes links to *phronesis* and *prudentia*, accrues to communities through experience and clear-eyed seeing of the world across time. The "wisdom of participation," which he links to *sophia* and *sapientia,* is attuned to "contemplative knowledge of final reality."[12] With *sapientia* or cosmic wisdom, people can only dispose themselves to receive it from God. If we grasp for it, we will fail to find it. Although our focus is on practical wisdom, sapiential wisdom also plays an important part in several chapters, as it must in any account of practical wisdom that is undertaken and understood in relationship to God.

As this suggests, Christian practical wisdom is not an end in itself but is always understood in relation to the many wider and richer ends of the abundant life that Christians believe God promises and provides. It is attuned to the love of God and neighbor, justice among peoples and nations, and care of the poor and marginalized, to name only a few of its orienting purposes. Action guided by Christian practical wisdom is therefore not something to be pondered abstractly. Rather, for Christians it is an actual, communal, embodied response to an eschatological breaking-in that provides reconciliation now, judges our failure fully to receive and embody it, and promises its future fulfillment. Therefore, such knowledge stands in close relationship to dispositions of gratitude, repentance, and hope. At the same time, Christian practical wisdom does not foreground the doctrinal claims that sharpen differences among faith communities. Rather, its engagement in concrete situations keeps it open to collaboration with wisdom from other traditions.

Ideally, Christians blessed with practical wisdom know their way around their neighborhoods not by map but as resident walkers who rely on body knowledge and all their senses.[13] There, empowered by the Spirit and joined in community with others, they discern a path that leads toward and offers foretastes of God's new creation along the way. They are attuned to the concrete and the actual, but they also cherish and yearn for what they know more generally and more abstractly. They can see what is going on, and they

---

12. Fiddes, *Seeing the World,* p. 10.

13. On this kind of knowing see "Walking in the City," a chapter in Michel de Certeau's *The Practice of Everyday Life,* trans. Steven Rendall (Berkeley: University of California Press, 1984). Making a similar point, Charles Taylor portrays the limits of modern epistemology as a preference for a formal, abstract idea of a thing (for example, a map) rather than understanding informed by practice and sense experience. See Taylor, "Overcoming Epistemology," in *Philosophical Investigations* (Cambridge: Harvard University Press, 1995). Wittgenstein's influence is evident in both of these sources. Christian Scharen's chapter "Eclipsing" in Part 2 of this book explores these epistemological issues more fully.

respond with good judgment as needed in particular situations. Of course, even the most blessed or practiced Christians do not always know their way around. Moreover, human brokenness leads even the wise to act foolishly at times, marring their ability to see what is going on and respond well. Still, by God's grace and in spite of human flaws, participation in shared practices within a way of life given by and responsive to God sometimes becomes the soil in which Christian practical wisdom grows, even while oriented toward the good of all and bearing kinship with the practical wisdom of other communities.

It is difficult to depict a complex concept like this without falling into abstract, idealistic, or even impractical language. A definition too often holds up an ideal. In fact, the authors of this book do not expect practical wisdom or any other virtue to come to full flower in this mortal life, though we do see it in play in our world in indispensable ways. For Christians, practical wisdom is oriented toward the eschatological horizon on which God's Wisdom will be all in all. Those who are wise acknowledge how infinitely short of that horizon all our practice and knowing fall. Indeed, a dynamic of unknowing — a humble and realistic sense of the limits of our knowledge of God, world, and self that emerges when we stand in relationship to God — is an unavoidable dimension of Christian practical wisdom as we understand it.

The Place and the Plight of Christian Practical Wisdom

The practical wisdom that belongs to the life of Christian faith is something that has intrigued each of this book's five authors throughout our lives as disciples, ministers, and educators, although for much of that time none of us could have named it. The need for a more fully articulated understanding of this kind of knowing became more urgently focused during our work with several other authors on the book *For Life Abundant*.[14] That book grew out of a sense that theology has failed to attend adequately to the daily tasks of leading and living the Christian life. It sought to propose to theological scholars and teachers, as well as ministry leaders and Christians

---

14. Dorothy C. Bass and Craig Dykstra, eds., *For Life Abundant: Practical Theology, Theological Education, and Christian Ministry* (Grand Rapids: Eerdmans, 2008).

more broadly, the shared *telos* toward which the work of all of them is oriented: the abundant life for all creation provided by God through the life,
death, and resurrection of Jesus Christ, which is already breaking in on the
world though it is not yet fully realized. The book reflects a conviction that
practical theological knowledge about this *telos* is needed by, and already
emerges among, many people in various settings — in daily living, ministry,
theological education, and public life.[15]

Against this horizon, contributors to *For Life Abundant* grappled with
the specific moves through which they pursue this *telos* in particular contexts of ministry and teaching. We recognized early on that the doing of
ministry demands distinctive ways of knowing, and we also perceived that
related ways of knowing are involved in participating in faith practices and
in teaching others to practice faith or to do ministry. It was evident from the
beginning that actual practice in these arenas, at its best, is not a matter of
following rules or communicating general principles or doctrines. Rather,
such practice is improvisational, highly sensitive to context, and irreducible
to verbal expression. It can never rest on certainty about what should be
done and what outcomes will result; it needs to be supple, adaptive, and as
variable as the people and places in which it operates.

As the authors sought to articulate the features of practice, we became
increasingly aware of and interested in forms of knowledge seldom described and even regularly devalued within the academy, except perhaps in
other professional schools. Craig Dykstra argued that the pastoral situation
"shapes pastors in a way of perceiving and understanding and relating to the
world that has distinctive characteristics." Bonnie Miller-McLemore articulated the "know-how" distinctive to practical theology that she brings to
teaching pastoral care and that she hopes her students will develop in their
caregiving. James Nieman described a worship class that requires future
pastors to "enact" what they are learning, because the liturgical practices
they will perform "already declare God in what they do." Chris Scharen
showed how seminarians and pastors learn ministry over the course of
several years, highlighting the importance of "embodied learning" in the
development of the "wisdom and imagination" they will need in ministry.
Kathleen Cahalan set forth the different kinds of knowledge she encourages
her ministry students to integrate as they respond to specific needs within a

---

15. Bass and Dykstra, "Introduction," in *For Life Abundant*, p. 5.

given situation. Dorothy Bass explored how ways of knowing the world that are learned through participation in Christian practices shape the faithful action of disciples. Every contributor highlighted the essential, albeit under-valued and unexamined, role practical knowledge plays in the actual living of religious faith. Bonnie and Chris both explicitly named *phronesis* as the practical wisdom needed for ministry and Christian life.

By the time *For Life Abundant* went to press, we had a heightened sense of the important role played by practical, engaged, purposive forms of knowledge in the life of faith. In a postscript to the book, the five of us, together with our *For Life Abundant* colleague Ted Smith, lifted up for further study what we called "the intelligence of practice."

> Texts and propositions alone cannot carry or communicate the knowledge of God's grace in Christ that is at the heart of Christian existence. This life-giving knowledge, which dwells in the bodies of believers and in the Body they comprise, is gained through forms of active and receptive participation that engage a wide range of human capacities. Likewise, the specific practices by which we respond to God's grace — practices such as prayer, forgiveness, and hospitality — bear knowledge of God, ourselves, and the world that cannot be reduced to words, even though words are often impor-tant in helping us to learn and participate faithfully in them. Such practices embody certain kinds of wisdom and foster certain kinds of intelligence when engaged in serious and critical ways.[16]

We returned to this statement, which we continue to affirm, at the be-ginning of our work on Christian practical wisdom. In the chapters that follow here, however, we do much more than amplify this set of claims. We provide an account of Christian practical wisdom that gets much closer to the "rough ground" of practice.[17] We set our work on a number of wider

---

16. "In Anticipation," in *For Life Abundant,* p. 358. Ted Smith was with the five of us as we drafted the statement at the end of *For Life Abundant,* and Craig Dykstra and John Witvliet made important contributions to the published version.

17. In *Philosophical Investigations,* 4th ed. (New York: Wiley-Blackwell, 2009), §107, Lud-wig Wittgenstein notes that the purity of abstract logic in linguistic analysis simply becomes empty of meaning; in order to make progress in understanding, he says, "we need friction. Back to the rough ground!" This phrase also provides the title of an important study of twentieth-century philosophy by Joseph Dunne, *Back to the Rough Ground: Practical Judgment*

disciplinary and cultural horizons. We acknowledge affection for certain people and places as wellsprings of this work. And we attempt to write in a style that is more suitable to the subject matter before us than the dense paragraph quoted above.

Among our many conversation partners — in person or through their writings — philosopher Charles Taylor was influential in a few distinctive ways. His sweeping account of the conditions of belief in the modern West, *A Secular Age,* helped us to understand the diminishment of practical wisdom in the modern West, and it also led to our adoption of a two-part structure for our book. *A Secular Age* depicts both the modern dominance of disengaged reason and the enduring possibility of an engaged knowing that is open to transcendence. Taylor's guiding question — "why is it so hard to believe in God in (many milieux of) the modern West, while in 1500 it was virtually impossible not to?" — shapes his account of the modern social imaginary, which posits disengaged reason and theoretical certainty as the obvious (to participants) qualities of genuine knowledge while simultaneously diminishing practice and embodied experience as sources of knowledge.[18] Related understandings of self, society, and nature emerged during the same period, bolstered by and contributing to social changes that made these understandings credible not only intellectually but also morally and emotionally. "The immanent frame" is Taylor's encompassing yet incisive term for how those who inhabit this imaginary conceive of reality at a lived, embodied, preconscious level. In modernity, this social imaginary provides the taken-for-granted context for living and believing (549). For those who inhabit the immanent frame, time is pervasively secular. Dovetailing "perfectly with the major theoretical transformation of Western modernity, viz., the rise of post-Galilean natural science," individuals are assumed to be "buffered, disciplined, instrumental agents" who form "societies designed for mutual benefit" within a "natural" order that can be understood and inhabited without reference to any transcendent good (542). This way of seeing the world has especially strong influence among intellectual elites, Taylor argues, but over time its diffusion into the wider society through

---

and the Lure of Technique (Notre Dame: University of Notre Dame Press, 1992). We, too, in this book, wish to turn to the concrete, the "rough ground" of practice in everyday life.

18. Charles Taylor, *A Secular Age* (Cambridge: Harvard University Press, 2007), p. 539. Hereafter, page references to this book appear in parentheses in the text.

institutions and social practices has given this account of the world and the human place in it a widely shared sense of legitimacy. As a result, the story of modern theology, including theological education, must be told in terms of theology's effort to give a legitimate rationale for itself in the face of the power of the immanent frame to define value and truth.

Even while portraying the rise to dominance of the social imaginary of the immanent frame, Taylor notices many and diverse rebellions against its terms. "The whole culture experiences cross pressures, between the draw of the narratives of closed immanence on the one side, and the sense of their inadequacy on the other" (595). Modernity has been questioned, contested, and attacked from within for centuries, he argues, pointing to forms of spirituality that emphasize poetry, art, nature, or sex; fascination with power or death; and the appeal of authentic Christian practice. "Our modern culture is restless at the barriers of the human sphere" and "very far from settling in to a comfortable unbelief," he asserts (727). While never maintaining that belief can achieve stability during this secular age — all positions, immanent and transcendent, are now mutually fragile — Taylor does argue that belief in God is both philosophically plausible and culturally and experientially alive for many thoughtful moderns, contrary to the assumptions of those who think that the stripping away of belief in the age of science is a foregone conclusion. The certainty claimed by modern despisers of religion reflects their membership in a social imaginary with specific historical roots and boundaries, Taylor insists. Secularization is not, as they suppose, the triumphant accomplishment of universally valid reason or the proof that science is more sound in every way than religion. Instead, secularization represents a shift in the "conditions of belief," which has taken place as a particular culture moved from a historical situation in which "it was virtually impossible not to believe in God" to one in which belief in God is "just one option among others" (3). Even now, however, the immanent frame can be "'spun' in ways of openness" to the transcendent, or it can be "spun" toward "closure." Although the latter spin is the dominant choice in academic culture, we choose in this book and in our lives to "spin it open" (549).

Taylor's account of the possibility of life lived "on the belief side" of modernity's cross pressures relies at several crucial points on narratives of thoughtful moderns who "broke out of the immanent frame," people who "went through a kind of self-authenticating, one might say 'epiphanic' experience," of God (730). He refers to such experiences as "places of fullness" or "conversions," noting that they seem to come as gifts from beyond the person. However, experiences of the transcendent do not establish a universal theory of a different kind, as if an epiphany could prove the inadequacy of an entire social imaginary and replace it with another. Instead, he suggests that such fullness has broken into human experience in every age and that there is room for it even in a secular age, but that it must be negotiated differently at different times in history. By way of example, Taylor describes the "itineraries" of several twentieth-century Christians whose faith took on both the fissures and the accomplishments of modernity — for example, entering into cruciform solidarity with those who suffer while also rejecting insular ecclesial stances in society and embracing the freedoms modernity has won. He calls these figures "modern civilization's 'loyal opposition'" — a party with which Taylor allies himself. As such, they live "at a critical distance from a civilization they will nevertheless defend" (745).

The five authors of this book resonate with this description. While we acknowledge the hold of "the immanent frame" on our thinking, we do not believe that this frame necessarily tells the whole truth about knowledge, action, or reality. For us, truth includes God. The kind of knowing that has been devalued under the canopy of the immanent frame is urgently needed within our own context of North American educational and religious life.

Our encounter with *A Secular Age* emboldened us to write our own "itineraries" of life beyond the immanent frame. By sharing these in the first section of this book, we hope to encourage others to articulate their own. The purpose is not to establish certainty but rather to make space for a kind of knowing that exists in the world as it is actually experienced by embodied human beings who are engaging in practices, living imaginatively before texts and traditions, aware of the limits of our knowing, and open to the beauty and the unknowing discovered in the presence of God. This kind of knowing, given by and including relationship with God, is at the heart of Christian practical wisdom. We see this wisdom as indispensable to our vocations of theological teaching and research, ministry, and living.

Amid the cross pressures of this secular age, we who live as believers do not do so because we can defend our belief within the terms of abstract universal reason. Instead, the life of faith is embodied and developed in relationship to God and others in distinctive times and places. This is what we have tried to show, in glimpses. For reasons that will become clear in Part 2 of this book, we believe that such accounts live by imagination rather than proof, and that they always leave us hauntingly aware of just how little we know about ourselves and about God.

How This Book Is Laid Out, and How We Hope It Will Be Read

In light of our emerging understanding of practical wisdom and our conversation on Taylor's work, we have endeavored to write this book in a different style than scholars in theology and religion typically use. Simply put, we write in a way that incorporates the down-to-earth flavor of Christian practical wisdom itself. We could not simply provide readers with a theory about wisdom. Thus we begin by portraying a few of the realms within which practical wisdom actually operates. In the first section of the book, each author invites readers into a set of concrete situations where the kind of engaged, embodied knowing that belongs to discipleship is visible. In portraying these situations we have drawn on our own experience. Though restricted in our social and cultural reach by who we are, we try to speak from our particularity to varied aspects of life, as the prayers of intercession do in liturgy. We write in these chapters about marriage, congregations, healing, community, culture, and much more. While acknowledging limitations — what we include only represents what each of us experiences about human and Christian knowing — we contend that this particularity also has value. We hope that readers will see the concrete specificity and personal investment evident in these chapters as positive features of the book and indications of the character of Christian practical wisdom itself. The rationalist dream of a "theory of everything" (much beloved by Descartes and other moderns, even up to Stephen Hawking) has shown itself to be a troubling detour in the history of the West, one this book contributes to moving beyond. We hope that our essays will encourage reflection, open up space for questions and practical concerns, and encourage readers to create similar stories of their own.

The chapters in the second part of the book are more discursive even though still deeply related to who we are and the culturally specific ways in which we have encountered wisdom. Where the first part "shows" Christian practical wisdom, this part "tells" how it operates.[19] The task of these chap-

19. Our choice in notation in these two sections reflects their different forms and pur-

ters is also a crucial one: to prepare the way for a revaluation of practical wisdom in Christian theology and hence within religious communities and the wider public. Before a positive case can be made, it is necessary to clear the ground by identifying and critiquing the quite different understanding of knowledge that has dominated modern Western thought. In turn, we also want to suggest fresh ways of grasping and describing reality that make greater room for Christian practical wisdom and generate creative ideas for teaching and learning as readers move through the book.

While our account is far from exhaustive, we are hopeful that these chapters will stir up discontent with the imbalance we deplore and suggest how Christian practical wisdom can amplify and serve as a corrective to other ways of knowing. Many persons in theological education and religious communities are looking for ways to engage Christian faith and practical knowledge more deeply. In fact, we see Christian practical wisdom at work in many classrooms and schools as well as churches, families, and communities. We have academic peers, students, and young faculty colleagues who exemplify this kind of knowing and are eager to attend to it. Certainly more theological teaching and learning today centers around contextual awareness, identifying and describing situational factors as well as embodied knowing that focuses on developing skilled competence through practice. Emotional attunement — the ability to identify and use awareness of feelings and affective states — and creative insight that sparks imaginative responses are more valued. And in some educational spheres beyond seminaries, practical wisdom is drawing considerable attention.

In this book, we join the effort to recognize, value, and encourage this kind of knowledge. What has been missing in theology and theological education is the capacity to talk about Christian practical wisdom — to articulate it, value it, and refine it. We portray some instances of practical knowing, but we need other people — teachers, ministers, and practitioners in other fields — to widen the pool of examples and exemplars from which we can all learn. Our audience, then, includes those interested in fostering an environment in educational institutions and religious communities where the many facets of practical wisdom are understood, valued, and cultivated.

---

poses. In Part One, we move references to the end of the chapter so as not to distract the reader or disrupt the narrative. In Part Two, we use conventional footnotes at the bottom of the page so readers can immediately follow our sources.

We intend the book to be read as a whole in which the parts require one another and do not stand satisfactorily without each other. But we also imagine that people in different settings will use the book for different purposes and will employ different reading strategies. The subheadings in individual chapters give readers a sense of each chapter's specific content. The overall arrangement of chapters proceeds from "show" (Part One) to "tell" (Part Two). Within the second part we move from identifying problems to suggesting alternative approaches. Some readers (many, we hope) will choose to follow this progression by reading the book from front to back. However, other paths can also be generative. Those eager to learn more about how problems arose for practical wisdom, how some thinkers have responded to these problems, and how certain aspects of Christian tradition offer alternatives may prefer to begin with the more analytical chapters in Part 2 before returning to Part 1, or to read Part 2 after sampling only one or two of the immersions into practical wisdom in Part 1. Those seeking immersive portraits of Christian practical wisdom should read Part 1 first, along with the Part 2 chapters "Imagining" and "Unknowing," before turning to intellectual history and recent developments in theology in "Eclipsing" and "Disciplining." Regardless of how you proceed, we hope that you will take seriously the authors' conviction that understanding Christian practical wisdom requires creative strategies like those we have tried. We hope our efforts will spark for readers not only theoretical distinctions but also fresh forms of engagement in practical wisdom.

In this regard, how we went about writing this book was crucial and an experiment in Christian practical wisdom itself. The book may appear to readers as an edited collection. It is far from it. Although we did assume tasks according to each person's gifts, and you will see individual authors named on chapters for which they bore major responsibility, none of these chapters would have come about at all without alternative means of learning and intense engagement with one another in community. We pursued more than theoretical knowledge, immersing ourselves in the subject matter rather than studying it from the outside. And we did so in close collaboration. You will hear much more about this in our final chapter. Certainly, we read, analyzed, wrote, and debated. But if we really wanted to understand, portray, and foster engagement with Christian practical wisdom, we could not go about it in the usual academic way. Among the many ways of engaging our subject, we also took field trips, watched and queried a master craftsman, shared the joys and sorrows in our lives, learned from our mistakes and limitations, spent big blocks of time together sharing work, hiked the woods surrounding the Benedictine community of Saint John's University in Minnesota, joined in its daily practice of prayer, and ate bountiful and simple meals. Thus *Christian Practical Wisdom* is not a collected work but rather a collective one, the outcome of a process that led to far more than any one of us might have imagined on our own and so, in its own way, tutored us in wisdom.

part one

spooning

HOW BODIES SHAPE KNOWLEDGE

BONNIE J. MILLER-McLEMORE

ARRIVING AT THE ABBEY CHURCH A LITTLE EARLY, I watch as the monks enter and bow toward the altar where a wooden cross is suspended from the vaulted ceiling — toward God, I suppose. God's presence seems palpable in the stained glass light and quiet. I do not know what is involved in bowing or what it means for each monk. But I seldom feel so low-church Protestant as when I don't bow before turning into the wooden pew to lower my seat and find the right page for Morning Prayer. I would feel awkard and insincere bowing. It is not a practice I have learned. It is not bodily familiar to me. I have even *incorporated* — literally taken into my body, my corporeal reper-toire — a modern bias against actions like bowing. But I also feel irreverent and careless *not* bowing, almost as if I slight God and miss a chance to mark my reverence in movement. I have gained new respect for bowing and I am curious. What does it mean to bow to God and to each other as a repeated life-long body practice for these Benedictine monks?

"This Is My Body"

This question has preoccupied me because of other worship experiences of late (and my wider interest in embodied theological knowing). A few years ago I quit attending the Christian Church (Disciples of Christ) congrega-tion where my membership resides. Sporadically I attend other Disciples churches in Nashville. More regularly I worship in an Episcopalian congregation. I am struck by body habits and postures different from those so familiar to me after a half century of faith formation among Disciples. My bodily sense of disconnect is especially acute during the Eucharist or what Disciples call communion or the Lord's Supper. What does it mean to process forward and hold out your hands to receive the Eucharist from a priest versus sitting and passing a communion plate, taking bread, and then serving your neighbor?

I am sure I am not the first to ask this. I only note it as another powerful instance in which I have felt the body and knowing theology and God come into keen play. Even if I wanted to make the Episcopalian congregation my home, compelled by its liturgy, music, preaching, and mission, my body resists, especially at communion or, in this case, Eucharist. I am not sure I will ever entirely overcome a sense that it is not quite right to process forward and exemplify in my body a theology with which I do not entirely agree — that one goes to the altar to receive, one by one, hands outstretched, Christ's body and blood from a priestly mediator of God's grace. Occasionally Disciples process forward for communion (free church worship allows for diverse practices). But when we do, the minister or congregant holds out the bread and we tear off a piece; no one places it in our hands. Even this tiny difference in bodily action is ripe with meaning.

As with bowing, I learn from and appreciate the Episcopalian practice all the more. I see meaning in cupping your hands before another. This posture overflows with potential. With your hands waiting to receive, you could be begging, pleading, hopeful, expectant, dependent, or grateful — each gesture loaded with a host of theological connotations. On more occasions than I anticipate, I am moved (to tears) when the priest or those assisting raise the bread or wine, lock their eyes on mine, and tell me, "the body of Christ, the bread of heaven," "the blood of Christ, the cup of salvation." I know I have been given a serious gift, a startling blessing, a physical taste of the intangible. I steal a sideways glance at the half circle of random adults and children around me at the front of the sanctuary, all of us standing together, waiting with empty palms awkwardly turned up as the priest and those assisting start this round of distribution. I see with a little embarrassment what a strange pose we have struck. Rarely do people display their neediness and desire to be filled (loved?) so overtly and patiently.

I make space in my pew one Sunday morning for a woman who tells me after the service how the congregation has become a good place for her husband, a lapsed Catholic, and herself, a Lutheran. I tell her how much I have been drawn myself, finding the church a home for worship, but caught and constrained somehow during Eucharist as someone raised in another tradition. She says she understands. "When my Lutheran mother visited, I had to prepare her." A little surprised, I ask, "What was so different?" I think of Lutherans as liturgically similar to Episcopalians; they go forward to receive the Eucharist after all. How could this be so disorienting? "We never drink from a common cup in my home congregation," she responds. "We use individual cups."

That this difference seems disruptive to her and so slight to me reminds me again that I am not alone in finding my faith embedded in the smallest of movements with their multiple, highly elusive, seemingly negligible meanings. Christian faith becomes deeply entangled right here, in these minute body actions and less so in the big conceptual frameworks laboriously worked out over the centuries by church leaders, scholars, and Christian denominations. We say and perceive more than we know or understand through our bodies. This might surprise theological educators who put such stock in our big words and ideas. This doesn't negate the value of systematic doctrinal reflection. But the devil, so to speak, or the divine, is in the corporeal details.

Our bodies know, our bodies remember, our bodies learn ways to embrace and be embraced by God. Bowing and eating are a small part of a whole constellation of habitual actions that make up the life of faith. Are some postures better than others? What do we confess in our small body motions? Do we lose something when we lose certain body postures in a tradition? How do we prevent ritual movements from becoming petty, trivial, or meaningless? When I join the monks for Morning and Evening Prayer, I wonder about bowing, a body movement Disciples do not practice. Monks and other Roman Catholics bow to God when they enter (or to the cross or the consecrated Host? or is it all the same?), when they praise the Trinity during worship, and when they leave. Saturday and Sunday evening, at the start and close of the Sabbath, they process in together and bow to the altar and to each other before turning to their seats. What does it mean over a lifetime to bow each time they glorify God? And what about bowing to each other? I notice some monks make eye contact; others do not. Does that matter? Some of the older monks are stooped. Is it from bowing?

Our early encounters of church and faith are remarkably sensate. When religious studies scholar Susan Ridgely Bales studied children's understanding of first communion in three Roman Catholic congregations in North Carolina, she discovered that what seven- to ten-year-old children believe and experience is not quite what adults or the wider church have in mind. One of the more striking findings from interviews and observations of African American, Anglo, and Latino/a communicants is the impact and centrality of sensory experience. To her surprise, her conversations with children in the weeks leading up to and following first communion did not center on white dresses and parties, much less transubstantiation or joining the Catholic Church universal, but on the "taste of Jesus' body," what she calls a "theology of taste." Taste preoccupies children in the days before first communion and in the hours after it. Six weeks before the service, a nine-year-old expresses a common sense of sensory anticipation: "I can't wait to taste the bread and wine." After the service, another nine-year-old remarks, "I just wanted to get the bread; that's all I wanted to do." Ryan, a communicant in the African American congregation, captures the theology "most succinctly when he explains that first communion is 'about tasting and learning about Jesus.'" Others make similar comments when asked about the meaning: "you're eating something very special from a very long time ago"; "you get to eat stuff and you get to come closer to God." One child even explains her understanding of transubstantiation through taste, saying that the real bread tastes better than the practice bread.

Taste is only one of five senses that shape bodily Christian knowing. It is perhaps the least noticed by scholars, ministers, and adult parishioners. But its power is real. The communion elements matter. A grandson of a colleague told his grandfather one Sunday visit after worship, "your bread tastes better than ours." On the day of her twins' first communion, a mother caught an incredibly poignant gasp and glance exchanged from one twin to the other when they tasted the wine. My own children moved from a church that broke freshly baked bread each week to one that passed around tiny, tasteless, mass-made wafers. They immediately saw problems with such a reduced sample of divine bounty. "Where's the bread?"

I also see what I would call a *theology of sensory movement* in Bale's account. Children yearn for inclusion in the community, but they do not see "lack of doctrinal understanding" as the cause of their disaffection. They feel separate "because they cannot perform the necessary movement." That is, they understand their separation as centering "on *action* as much as on *belief.*" They see membership as gained not through "abstract information" but by sharing in the "sensorial knowledge" that members demonstrate. So they are hyper-vigilant about movement. They want to teach "their bodies to move as the adults moved during the liturgy." While teachers hoped to convey the sacred meanings of communion, the demand of learning the gestures and actions "kept much of the children's attention on their physical bodies." In the heightened anxiety leading up to the service, their energies are directed at enacting the ritual properly, in all its physical dimensions, more than at understanding it. They want to "'get it right'" in front of the congregation. Thus, as with the theology of taste, "things which seemingly had so little to do with their initiation into the Body of Christ, in many ways, defined it."

Are these findings all that unique to children? Adults like to think we are different from children, but in many respects this desire hides important connections and deprives us of childhood wisdom. Most of us do not remember clearly our early sensory experiences, which are reshaped and reinvented through memory and later experience and learning, but our theology partly resides in body memories nonetheless. When I was in fifth grade I was baptized by immersion. I don't remember going under or coming up. Try as I might, I can't picture the minister in the baptistery or recall the temperature of the water, much less details of the baptism classes. But I do remember anticipating what new life would feel like, the weight of the white robe clinging to my body and dragging me back down as I stepped out, wet hair, a group picture, and my pondering whether I felt different. I remain convicted that Christian baptism requires visceral experience that sprinkling can hardly achieve.

We are naïve when we assume adults leave sensate experience and knowing behind, even though Western doctrinal and intellectual history implies that such detachment from bodies is possible and even admirable, even a sign of intellectual and spiritual maturity (and a mark of true science and morality). In fact, there is something to be learned from children and studies of children. Children of all ages are active rather than passive learners; they make their own interpretations right alongside those offered to them by adult teachers and parents, utilizing "information from all areas of their lives to develop their own understandings." Adults are not that different. Like the children in first communion, adult belief is grounded in sensual experience even though this escapes our notice. Sensory understandings that formed us as children linger longer than most of us realize and continue to mark our theology and knowledge of God.

Late one Sunday evening when practical theologian David Mellott was an associate pastor for a Roman Catholic parish, an elderly woman called asking if he would open the sanctuary so she could light a votive candle as promised for her granddaughter traveling across the ocean to Paris. Although he hears the voices of post–Vatican II colleagues reminding him that he should take this opportunity to educate her and discourage this "superstitious practice," he cannot bring himself to do so. Instead, he strikes a balance: he offers to light it for her while she prays at home, which should be just as efficacious. But he continues to wonder about her request and his presumptuous response about efficacy. Who was he to dictate how divine grace moves?

Despite all the education and discouragement, votive candles remain popular. Why doesn't this practice go away, as rational modern expectations would suggest? People need tangible ways to access God. When a close Jewish friend shares Shabbat with me, she lights two candles, as she did in my company once when celebrating the Mourner's Kaddish after the death of her father and another time in a hotel lobby on a visit to Nashville. Lighting candles at the end of the midnight Christmas Eve service, for Easter Vigil, at political protests, and at times of great loss constitutes a religious high point for many people. Might these tiny concrete bodily acts carry greater meaning and potential for the working of God's love than we suppose, stretching beyond a crutch for the masses, a way to get children involved, or a decorative formality?

When I was a child, a feeling of reverence immediately fell over me on entering the Gothic-style sanctuary of my home church with its limestone, red carpet, dark wood, and arched ceiling. However, directly to the right of the sanctuary's side entrance was another wooden door leading to a smaller, darker chapel that evoked even greater awe. At the front left stood the "eternal flame" flickering in its red-tinted hurricane glass atop a tall brass pedestal. When a Sunday school teacher took a group of kids in years ago, an instant hush fell over us. The chapel compelled silence. It was ostensibly for small services, but for me it was a beacon of holiness, a place of God. I learned recently that the church called the candle the *Shekinah* light based on the Hebrew word that means to settle, inhabit, or dwell, suggesting the dwelling or settling of divine presence. The term *shekinah* never made its way into lay church vocabulary, but the idea did. For me (and for many others) the candle was simply the *eternal flame*. The teacher explained that the flame stays lit forever. Or at least that's what I remember. Until this moment, I have not actually stopped to think about this. Someone must do something to refuel it; no light burns on its own. Or does my childhood knowing grasp a deeper truth that adult faith forgets about the possible, the super-rational, the inexplicable? When the church was remodeled several years ago, members decided to make better use of the space and got rid of the chapel. I can understand the pragmatic rationale, but I cannot imagine a better use of space.

Perhaps there is something of value here, Mellott speculates, "something theological" to be learned from "people who have been engaging [in votive candle lighting], often for decades." Neither Mellott nor his pastoral associates thought about asking people about their practices, he admits, because they assumed "that we knew more about [them] than they did," an attitude they might have learned, I suspect, from their theological teachers or the climate of academe. Late twentieth-century experts on faith development agreed with cognitive development theorists that concrete thinking denotes immaturity. But might this view actually harbor unwarranted prejudice against material religion, bodies, children, laity, ritual, and the knowledge within physical acts of faith?

Despite a long history of damning the body and its temptations, Christians have good reason to locate theological knowing much closer to body knowledge than has been the case as formal theology has taken shape in ecclesial and academic contexts. Incarnation, God's inhabiting a human body, is central. Redemption includes bodily resurrection. Congregations are Christ's body in the world; members are eyes, feet, hands, each with a purpose and gift. Most centrally, every week in Disciples congregations and in many churches God's presence and promise are celebrated through a partaking of Christ's body and blood. *This is my body, this is my blood.* Despite great divergence in Christian liturgical practice, people in all traditions hear these words repeated in one of the most central ritual practices of Christianity. The conclusion of each utterance varies — "which is for you" (Paul in Corinthians, prominent in many Protestant traditions, part of my own history and my theological preference), "given up for you" (the Roman Rite of the Catholic Church), "broken for you for the remission of sins" (definitely a favorite in evangelical communities and prominent as *the* interpretation of Christ's death as sacrificial). Doctrinal debates that have grown up around the interpretation of these words (e.g., sacramental and atonement theologies, Christologies, ecclesiologies) are many and complex.

For the moment, I set such argument aside. I simply want to ask what it means to encounter God through Christ's body and what our bodies teach us, if anything, in our yearning to know God. Our theology is grounded in our bodies. We have no other way to know God than through our bodies. How do bodies — bodily knowledge — inform, shape, and transform our Christian knowing? Given the main claims of Christianity, we can hardly help but wonder at the aberration of theology as a purely cognitive or intellectual exercise performed at great distance from what actual bodies know or might tell us about faith, theology, or God. There is wisdom in bodily knowing that scholars and ministers have underestimated.

Everyday Body Wisdom

"Anyway . . . she's asleep, turned away from me on her side," writes unconventional novelist Julian Barnes, author of *A History of the World in 10½ Chapters.* He has taken a break from his world saga to devote a half chapter — a "Parenthesis" — to the elusive subject that sits at the heart of history but evades scholarly accounts: love. Love appears to be entirely unnecessary as an evolutionary adaptation. It is a random historical luxury, a statistical abnormality. He lets *spooning* frame his effort, perhaps because the physical image of sleeping like spoons is vivid and suggestive: "The usual stratagems and repositionings have failed to induce narcosis in me," reports Barnes, a more restless sleeper than his wife, "so I decide to settle myself against the soft zigzag," the "map of her body," "the loose S" silhouetted beside him.

I resonate. I use the same tactic in pursuit of sleep, folding myself around my husband, Mark, curved next to his warmth and comfort, breathing these in with him. Spooning suggests a bodily knowing or wisdom that spells love and hints of God.

"This is difficult territory," Barnes recognizes. "We must be precise, and we mustn't become sentimental." And he's just talking about love. I'm trying to talk about God and the everyday body! This is even harder. I'm struck by the elusiveness of what I'm trying to show here, how hard it is to put into words, how personal it gets, and how silly it sounds. By comparison, understanding practical wisdom and the worshiping body is easy. Liturgy gives bodily knowing repetitive structure and moral parameters. Knowing God and gaining wisdom through the everyday body seems more suspect and elusive. It has wide-ranging temptations and problems. Indeed, there is something right about the Greek-influenced Christian suspicion of bodily temptation and distraction. I just reread a short but well-done overview of research on material culture in religious studies. By and large, I am encouraged by Colleen McDannell's critique of the oversight of religious objects in scholarship on religion. But she lays the ground for valuing materiality by beginning, tongue-in-cheek but wholly uncritically, with "one of America's most popular philosophers," Madonna. Try Googling the 1990s Material Girl and watch a few video clips. "I am a material girl" means sex, money, jewels, lust, and self-indulgence. Our bodies and bodily desires are incredible guides to religious knowledge. They also seriously mislead us. The plethora (and success) of body makeover shows on mid-morning TV suggests that social and religious efforts to counter warped bodily obsessions are only a blip on the screen.

To talk unsentimentally about love's power, Barnes proceeds by indirection, trying to avoid didacticism and envious of poets who get away with direct love speech. He quotes Canadian author Mavis Gallant: "The mystery of what a couple *is,* exactly, is almost the only true mystery left to us." Barnes diagrams "I love you" across multiple languages. We ought to use sparingly and carefully this unadorned sentence joining two subjects with one action verb. He dissects a heart, the organ where humans locate love. It is an elegant mess, a jungle of arteries, veins, atriums, and ventricles, twisted around each other "like drowning lovers." The brain is "complicated, to be sure," but seems sensible by comparison, "neat, segmented, divided into two halves." No wonder theologians who pursue heart knowledge get lost.

What startles Barnes, however, is how the body knows, enacts, and evokes love even in its sleep in subtleties that elude pen, history, and human understanding. "As I move and start to nestle my shin against a calf whose muscles are loosened by sleep, she senses what I'm doing, and without waking reaches up with her left hand and pulls the hair off her shoulders . . . leaving me her bare nape to nestle in." The "exactness of this sleeping courtesy" stirs in Barnes a "shudder of love." "At that moment, unconsciously, she's touched some secret fulcrum of my feelings for her." Readers are urged not to write off her act as conscious and rational, performed because she was really awake. She has done this even after cutting her hair in a hot summer, trying to "lift the lost hair." Love, he suggests, "has roots below the gum of consciousness."

I have been changed more through bodily contact with Mark and my children than through almost any other kind of experience or learning. I am not talking only about sensual and sexual pleasure, although surely they are part of this. I'm trying to get at something more basic. After thirty-plus years of sleeping with Mark, I simply do not sleep as well without him. I have gone from someone who didn't like sharing space to someone who falls asleep best entwined, leg and arm thrown over him. How has my body changed my mind? I wonder about bodily attraction and sexual intercourse too. How does our bodily chemistry secure the greater goods of love? Isn't *making love* much more than a euphemism? In my life, it has a literal impact, soothing tensions and offering relief from daily friction. My body changes my mind. Using her own sexual narrative as a key source of knowledge in Christian ethics, Cristina Traina describes sexual affection as the "glue" that holds her and her husband together, "providing refreshment in smooth times and expressing love and reassurance when words fail (or, worse, harm)." Mid–twentieth-century life-cycle theorist Erik Erikson said as much. He argues that sex allows couples to survive the irritation of living side-by-side, day in and day out. Do bodies know and evoke something of God, as they provoke family peace, that our minds forget?

Years ago while breastfeeding I saw how knowledge links mind and body indelibly as one attempts to act. "I know," I wrote about lactation and nursing, "physically through a muscular ache. Apart from the ache, I can scarcely know." Knowing involves a "mode of circular bodily reasoning, in-terweaving physical sensation, momentary cognition, behavioral reaction, and a physical sensing and intellectual reading of the results." When it works (and it can go horribly awry), this "embodied reasoned feeling" moves flu-idly between theory and practice, knows "physically the feelings of the other, because they are paradoxically both mine and not mine," knows by "affective connection that moves toward differentiation." I was disturbed but not terribly surprised to learn that Aquinas thought such tactile knowledge the least among the human senses (so close to the material, sexual, female world). This unenthusiastic view of body knowledge is typical of much of Western scholarship, certainly exemplified by Aquinas but not unique to him, taking ever new forms in modern philosophy and thought in figures such as René Descartes, as we see in other chapters of this book.

From birth, one of my sons didn't like giving in to sleep. Immediately after birth he didn't sleep, as baby books say newborns usually do for several hours. Nor did he seem to need as much sleep as my other sons. When he learned to speak, he would pull himself up on the railings of his crib in the middle of the night and yell to us across the hall, "Get me out of here." In the years to come, he invited into his twin bed, already loaded with an assortment of well-named stuffed bears, an eighty-plus-pound chocolate lab and a black-and-gold striped cat given to him on his eighth birthday in place of the second dog he really wanted. For years, awakened by dreams or just routine rhythms, he made his way from his second-story room to our first-floor bedroom to squeeze up against me. When I couldn't sleep without the room to move, I pulled a sleeping bag out on the floor beside the bed and we held hands until sleep held him securely. I complained to friends about lacking a full night's sleep in those days. But when the night visits tapered off, I missed terribly bodies curved and hands held through night terrors.

Over a decade ago I struggled to adjust to the drop-off in bodily touch as my kids grew. There is nothing like carrying a child, holding a child, and the steady skin contact between parents and younger children. How do our bodies shape our minds through physical care? What happens physiologically and in the brain through touch?

"My wife, Julie, and I sleep like spoons," reports Fergal, a friend of Christian ethicist John Giles Milhaven. Milhaven pleads for a better "phenomenology" of what makes "ordinary bodiliness" so valuable for Christian knowledge. Fergal complies.

"Not every night, nor the whole night when we do. Not in the hot weather," Fergal says. "But in the cool and cold weather most of the time. We do it automatically, taking it for granted, hardly deciding." There is pleasure here on the edge of sleep — the "pleasure of swelling desire and the pleasure of desire collapsing into satisfaction." Bodies lead; thought follows. "I don't think of Julie as I go off to sleep. She's not in my mind. But she's in my legs, torso, and arms." But there is more to it: "Only lying in touch with Julie can I count on . . . that kinesthetic sense of security," a kind of fearless trust that he takes down with him into the "abyss."

In scripture, practical wisdom is intricately connected to the abyss. Wisdom of God is bodily wisdom gained through everyday reminders of death and love. When the psalmist searches for a "heart of wisdom," he does so before life's brevity and brokenness (Ps. 90:3-6, 9-10, NRSV) *and* God's expansiveness and steadfast love (vv. 1-2, 13-17). "You turn us back to dust, and say, 'Turn back, you mortals.' For a thousand years in your sight are . . . like a watch in the night" (vv. 3-4). "So teach us to count our days that we may gain a wise heart" (v. 12). In the final verses of Psalm 90 an answer comes in God's sustaining love. "Satisfy us in the morning with your steadfast love" (v. 14). The psalmist does not seek a *mind* or *soul* of wisdom. *Heart* suggests a greater wholeness and a centered location in the body.

Spooning and sleeping together dispel night terror for Fergal, for Barnes, for me, for a son. "We know each other letting go, giving into sleep," Fergal writes. Some give in better than others, but sleeping is a "job . . . we all have to do," Barnes says, "every night, ceaselessly, until we die." Bad dreams catapult him from bed, and his wife "has to stroke the horror away from me, like sluicing down a dog that's come barking from a dirty river." He does the same for her, clutching the "gutter-muck" of her nightmares while she drifts back to sleep. For "sleep democratizes fear." In sleep a missed train is as frightening as a nuclear war.

But I think there's more to it. Sleep is like death, mirroring the body's utter vulnerability, its submission to powers greater than our own, our dependence on others. Before sleep, as before death, all of us are fearful, and only love saves. Spooning is an accompanying unto death, a molding of oneself, hinting and mimicking from one person to another in the night's deep recesses a resurrection promise of life and love beyond death. Spooning conquers death through love, and the body knows this. This "banal, undramatic, scarcely attended to, monotonously recurring moment of my life," admits Fergal, "is one I feel happiest about." "Sometimes — you may find this hard to believe — I murmur, 'God is good.'"

My mom tells me that when I was little, I didn't want to be held. I find this surprising. But from what I can glean, I wasn't an easy child. I was on the go, willful, and insistent ("I do it I do it" on tying my shoes, peddling my trike, crossing the street, etc.). I am particular about touch. I don't like to be tapped. Even so, what child doesn't like to be held? Now that I am a mother, I wonder if she had reached her limits in trying to figure out how to hold a child like me; this is not a good comparison, but perhaps kind of like our cat who wants to be petted but only just so and with clear limits. So much of love consists simply in being held and in holding literally and figuratively.

The literal and the figurative are intertwined here in complicated ways, like Barnes's messy heart. They are in fact inseparable. I do not know how one knows God's love without life's experience of physical embrace. Infants die without physical touch; adults alone without touch live off memory and hope; and many are harmed by touch imposed in the absence of love.

Compassion as a Body Posture

I walk into a sterile classroom on my first day of teaching in a university divinity school. The desks are lined up in vertical rows facing the front — the kind I hate to sit in myself, with small tops that pin you in and allow room for little more than a single notepad or computer. I try to talk myself out of my adverse reaction. After all, I took comfort in that room formation as a graduate student, appreciating the chance to hide in my row until my mind caught up with my aspirations. In addition, I know from developmental studies that "received knowledge" and rote memorization have their place in early phases of learning.

Yet on that first day this classroom bothers me. Why? What puts me off isn't exactly the hierarchical, disembodied pedagogy it presumes, or even the ugliness of the cement block and linoleum floors; I don't like these aspects but I know how much can be conveyed in such classrooms. But can pastoral care be learned in such a space? Is what I know about passion and compassion, understood via religious traditions, Christianity in particular, and supplemented by an array of social science discoveries, communicable within such confines? I have my doubts.

One semester when teaching the pastoral care course, I ask students to join together in doing "body sculptures." Small groups of students volunteer to make with their bodies a frozen tableau portraying concepts, such as "compassion" or "pain." Awkwardly, with laughter allaying discomfort and the bold leading the timid, we sculpt "pastoral," "spiritual," even "God," watching wisdom arise before our eyes — unexpected but utterly true perceptions that we harbor but cannot articulate — about how we've been hurt, what we know about healing, and what we hope for from religious communities. Portraying these ideas through arranging our bodies to show them is not the only or even best means of learning pastoral care; books and lectures have a place. But action in the classroom has a powerful effect as the semester unfolds — *and often to my surprise.* In indirect and subtle ways, this small exercise opens up the class to richer discussions and prepares students for other assignments that require body movement, such as pastoral conversation and congregational observation. In many ways, this body work is harder, takes more time and courage, requires a more sophisticated capacity for integration, and presents more challenges than reading, digesting, and writing a conceptual research paper.

I have to work against my own resistance every time I introduce embodied action into a class. Using bodies in learning goes against the grain. "We improve minds, we change others' minds, we criticize ideas, we argue positions," religious studies scholar Sam Gill observes. But we repress the body. Ironically, even writing this essay, in spite of its topic, requires a kind of bodily stasis and deprivation. There were days when I might have accomplished more by going outside to work in the yard. But academic success is all about keeping one's "butt in the chair," as well-known author Anne Lamott puts it in her typically frank way. Academicians and authors spend an enormous amount of time in restricted postures, relatively still before a desk, reading, writing, and thinking. My best writing happens when I lose track of time, place, and body. You the reader understand these words better if not distracted by bodily needs, when your five senses are reined in. The teacher and writer protagonist of Wallace Stegner's novel *Crossing to Safety* prefers his desk facing the wall while in Florence on sabbatical. It was "easier," he says, "to see what was in my head if I didn't have distractions in front of my eyes." There are good reasons why we retreat to the bowels of the library where study carrels hover in windowless stacks and why education is often designed to discipline the body to "'sit still and pay attention,'" as Gill remarks. Bodies distract us.

Bodily neglect would not be a problem if it were merely a means to sustain the attention necessary for insight, creativity, and even religious experience. However, in the history of the Western church and university there is also a deep-seated bias, as Gill says, that the "head (the mind) is superior to the rest of the body." This bias is linked to early Greek and Christian views of the physical world as "a place of transit, a temporary and dangerous place to be overcome and transcended"; these views were perpetuated by modern philosophers such as Descartes, who saw the body as a source of inaccurate information, and American Puritans, who saw the body as a source of sexual temptation. So, not surprisingly, we have come to associate "theology with thought, not with body," in Gill's words. But is knowledge conveyed at a distance from bodies sufficient for learning pastoral care?

Years ago, I put on a white clerical collar, even though nothing in my own religious tradition warrants it, because that's just what chaplains did in 1977, my senior year in college. I spent an academic quarter off-campus doing a project that exposed me for the first time to clinical pastoral education, an experiment that had emerged a quarter century earlier out of a hunch that bodies must move outside classrooms to encounter other bodies in need to understand religious knowledge more fully. I wandered in and out of hospital rooms, surprised by the multiple reactions the collar evoked and by my own sense that this work had intimations of *imitatio Dei*. And I encountered a basic first step in care: attention to bodies and their surroundings. I learned to center my attention intensely on entering a hospital room. What does the body I encounter there tell me? The facial expression, the clothes, the way of sitting? What's in the room, by the bedside, on the table? And likewise, what about my own body, where to stand, whether to close the door, whether to sit on the hospital bed or behind the office desk? What does my own body feel in this space, with this other person?

Bodies are an especially important site of practice in pastoral care. Compassion is a physical posture with basic poses of sitting, standing, looking, touching (or not — compassion must also attend to boundaries between bodies, when *not to touch*). A scholar friend whose mother had died found the action of a wise friend, who wordlessly reached out to hold her hand, surpassed the many words offered in consolation by others in the community. For Roman Catholic scholar John Carmody, dying from bone marrow cancer, the reception of anointing from a visiting priest, marking his forehead and hands with oil, was "the most moving moment" in all the care he received. "Indeed," remarks Carmody, "it has lodged itself among the half-dozen most moving religious experiences of my entire life." Compassion's close companion is pain. Attending to pain, maybe I should even say *spooning oneself around it,* is key. Pain actually deconstructs or disempowers language. It eludes meaning. Physical acts can surpass words.

To borrow one of Carmody's neologisms, cross and resurrection get *"enverbed"* in the bodies and lives of those struggling to live faithfully in the midst of pain, and in the bodies of those attempting a Christian response. Compassion or accompanying someone through pain requires a comparable *enverbed* stance, a bodily posture that speaks of God's presence and encompasses but surpasses words about care or love. This is partly why the term *holding environment,* borrowed from object relation theorist D. W. Winnicott, appears all over contemporary pastoral care literature. It captures the kind of physical space and metaphorical presence needed to shelter human fragility from inevitable wounding and to foster trust, openness, affirmation, and care. A good holding environment suggests its own kind of physical and theological spooning, the posture compassion must assume.

I had a dream while working on this chapter. I am caring for a baby; the baby seems like my third son. I have two other children standing by who seem about the same ages as my other sons when their youngest brother was born. But their identities and equation with my own sons seem hazy. What *is* memorable is the body contact of care. I mold myself around the infant in a full-bodied act of solicitude, showing the boys who admire the baby the beauty of kindness, skin on skin. It feels good, and the feeling carries over several days later when I see adults and babies swaddled tight up against each other at the farmer's market, chest to chest. The dream seemed a body sign of something I'm trying to unearth about performing bodies caught in acts of care.

There is no simple answer for how one learns compassion. But it would be silly to try to teach care to those going into ministry without showing it, requiring students to witness it, and asking them to demonstrate it through their bodies. This, of course, also means a bodily encounter with pain, something that presents one of the biggest challenges. Awkwardly, uneasily, those who teach pastoral care broker the disjuncture between academic culture and bodily encounter. I won't ever finish acquiring the necessary body knowledge for such teaching. My body suffering and practice responding to suffering remain limited, as is true for all of us; so we glean from others, like Carmody or my students or my friends.

This semester an advisee arrives for her appointment to register for the fall semester. She tells me what I had said the prior semester had given her a new lease on life, and then she describes major changes she has made, urging her husband to move and buying a home in a rural community. I remember vaguely responding to her stress but not much more. She is giving me more credit than I deserve. She has taken steps I know I didn't advise. As much as I can articulate it, I sat with her, made space for grief, held what she brought, and returned it to her as I had heard it. It was enough.

"We are never able to observe the entire surface of our bodies. Only another person can see my body all at once in relation to its environment," observes Mennonite author Julia Kasdorf. Therefore, we need others to know ourselves. She is drawing on Mikhail Bakhtin, a literary theorist and philosopher in the Eastern Orthodox tradition. She explains further, "Only an other, looking with concentrated attention, can 'consummate' me — make me whole — know me as I cannot know myself." To make her point, she includes a stunning passage from Bakhtin, from which I quote partially:

> After all it is only the other who can be embraced, clasped all around, it is only the other's boundaries that can all be touched and felt lovingly. The other's fragile finiteness, consummatedness, his here-and-now being — all are inwardly grasped by me and shaped, as it were by my embrace; in this act, the other's outward existence begins to live in a new manner, acquires some sort of new meaning, is born on a new plane of being.

In essence, only the one beholding can "overshadow" the one embraced, a term that in Russian means to "shelter, protect, and bless," as when God "overshadows" Mary in Luke 1:35 and she becomes pregnant through an "interpenetrating love so powerful it results in change." Kasdorf ignores the male sexual allusion here, and I see additional problems in English connotations of the term *overshadow* (e.g., render insignificant, cast a gloom over). But I still appreciate Bakhtin's insight into the power of bodily embrace and the unique perspective of the one who cares for others.

Body Kinesthetics and Grace

Extraordinary athletes teach us something about body knowing and grace (if not God). They astonish us with what novelist David Foster Wallace calls "Federer moments" in a feature story on the 2006 Wimbledon men's final. In a millisecond — shorter than automatic reflex but containing in its brevity incredible mental and physical gymnastics — the Swiss tennis champion returns a ball with a divine beauty that defies description and possibility "like something out of 'The Matrix.'"

What goes into such moments? An inherited kinesthetic sense, alongside repetition and hours of practice, creates new brain and body circuits, making it possible "to do by 'feel' what cannot be done by regular conscious thought." But then there's something more, something intangible in graceful performance that outruns inheritance, brawn, brain, and technological advances in tennis racquets, what Wallace in a search for words describes as "subtlety, touch and finesse," or simply "mystery." The beauty of such moments lies in their ability to reconcile us, Wallace believes, to our body's impossible, relentless, endless shortcomings — "pain, sores, odors, nausea, aging, gravity, sepsis, clumsiness, illness, limits," just to name a few.

Even ordinary athletes have a sense of such knowing. One of my sons who is an avid rock climber knows without reading a word of psychologist Mihály Csíkszentmihályi about "flow," a kind of suspended state of time and mind when body and thought merge in execution of moves that advance one up the side of a rock face. He invests huge levels of trust, not just in the safety of his equipment or the informed technique with which he installs gear into crevices, but also in his body itself and its ability to master knowledge that goes beyond anything he has thought. At an early age another son imitated with precision complicated body movements, such as swinging a bat or dribbling a ball around an orange cone. He was blessed with a kind of body elegance, what contemporary psychologists call *kinesthetic intelligence,* and a keen eye for kinesthetic brilliance around him, imitating what he witnessed, yearning to "be Michael Jordan" when he grew up. When we perceive someone who moves with beauty, we sometimes call the motion *graceful,* a word that carries within it a hint of God's presence, a sense that the movement and person are grace-filled. The person who held the hand of a friend whose mother had died moved with wisdom and grace.

You cannot really understand or have this experience without being there or without your own experience of playing the game. "The Moments are more intense if you've played enough tennis to understand the impossibility of what you just saw him do," Wallace says. He can write about this and you can watch it on TV. But it isn't like being there. Wallace's words are vivid here: "TV tennis is to live tennis pretty much as video porn is to the felt reality of human love." Witnessing such moments live is what a tournament press bus driver dubs a "'bloody near-religious experience.'"

Last week, in a church service that had otherwise thankfully downplayed Mother's Day, a small guitar group did a Paul Simon song during the offertory, "Loves Me Like a Rock." "I'm a consecrated boy, singer in a Sunday choir," the lead singer told us. *And* "my mama loves me, she loves me, she get down on her knees and hug me." In the midst of the multiple meanings loaded in the lyrics, the little kids were supposed to bring the week's offering down the aisle. Only they didn't come and they didn't come, even after an extra refrain or two (which no one minded), until the lead singer sang to the tune of "loves me like a rock," "someone send those children down . . . or we'll have to do one more refrain." He did this with ease, comfort, humor, without missing a beat, like he knew exactly what to do in awkward moments. And then the kids came. In all its ordinariness, it was a mini-Federer moment. Graceful body motions in ministry are often entirely mundane.

References

This chapter grows out of a long-term interest in lived theology that has shaped my work and is described in *Christian Theology in Practice: Discovering a Discipline* (Grand Rapids: Eerdmans, 2012), a book that offers additional bibliographical resources. I continue to work on the question of how theology is embodied in practice and have developed some of the material in this chapter in "Embodied Knowing, Embodied Theology: What Happened to the Body?" *Pastoral Psychology* 62, no. 5 (2013): 743-58 (DOI 10.1007/s11089-013-0510) and "Coming to Our Senses: Feeling and Knowledge in Theology," *Pastoral Psychology* 63, no. 5 (2014): 689-704 (DOI: 10.1007/s11089-014-0617-1). Both articles contain more resources on theology and bodies than can be included here. For reasons explored in the chapter "Disciplining," research on bodies and materiality has grown exponentially in theology and beyond in recent years.

In my search for stories (in addition to my own) showing the impact of bodies on Christian practical wisdom in worship, I turn to two ethnographies of religious communities: Susan Ridgely Bales's exploration of children's first communion in *When I Was a Child: Children's Interpretations of First Communion* (Chapel Hill: University of North Carolina Press, 2005), and David Mellott's study of the Penitentes of New Mexico in *I Was and I Am Dust: Penitent Practices as a Way of Knowing* (Collegeville, MN: Liturgical, 2009). Quotes from Bales on the "theology of taste" come from pp. 92, 99, and 100, and quotes on what I call a "theology of sensory movement" are from pp. 6, 91-92, 96, 103, 136, and 137. She discusses children making their own interpretations on p. 77. Mellott's personal reflection on lighting votive candles appears on pp. x-xi.

I found solace and confirmation of my own experience of spooning in novelist Julian Barnes's "Parenthesis" in *A History of the World in 10½ Chapters* (New York: Knopf, 1989) and in John Giles Milhaven's essay, "Sleeping Like Spoons: A Question of Embodiment," *Commonweal* 116, no. 7 (1989). Barnes turns to spooning to portray the intangible but powerful force of love in human history on pp. 224, 225, and 244. He talks about the difficulty of his subject matter on p. 231 and expounds on love, the heart, body knowledge, and fears in sleeping on pp. 223-24, 226, 236, and 242. I follow Barnes's own pattern in using present tense to talk about his wife even though she died of a brain tumor twenty years after he wrote these words. He talks about the loss in an essay in *Levels of Life* (New York: Random House, 2013). Milhaven uses spooning to explore eros and embodied knowledge. Fergal's response to Milhaven's plea for a firsthand account appears on pp. 206-7.

My comment on Thomas Aquinas's hierarchy of knowledge also relies on Milhaven's work, primarily "A Medieval Lesson on Bodily Knowing: Women's Experience and Men's Thoughts," *Journal of the American Academy of Religion* 57, no. 2 (1989), where he argues on p. 358 that for Thomas "sense knowledge is wholly inferior to the rest of human knowledge, which is rational knowledge." Milhaven also argues that

> By Thomas' epistemology, neither Mary in Bethlehem nor any other mother knows the humanity of her child by the bodily experience of Him at her breast. The senses cannot perceive distinctively human nature or any distinctively human traits as reason, will, and corresponding affections, for everything distinctively human is immaterial. Only by rising from physical experience to a higher, nonbodily kind of knowing, whether of faith or reason, can the mother attain her child as human. (p. 354)

His citations point readers to his earlier essay, "Thomas Aquinas on Sexual Pleasure," *Journal of Religious Ethics* 5 (1977): 157-81, reprinted in *Hadewijch and Her Sisters: Other Ways of Loving and Knowing* (Albany, NY: State University of New York Press, 1993), pp. 123-45 (which also includes a revised version of "Medieval Lesson on Bodily Knowing").

As an example of the ambiguity of our materiality, I couldn't pass up Madonna's well-known "Material Girl" and Colleen McDannell's uncritical reference to it as emblematic of our living today in a "material world" in her opening line (p. 371) of a journal article, "Interpreting Things: Material

Culture Studies and American Religion," *Religion* 21 (1991). I am glad to include two affirmations — theological and psychological — of the impact of sexual intercourse in long-term relationships. Cristina L. H. Traina comments on the interpersonal implications on p. 273 of her chapter, "Papal Ideals, Marital Realities: One View from the Ground," in *Sexual Diversity and Catholicism: Toward the Development of Moral Theology,* ed. Patricia Beattie Jung with Joseph Andrew Coray (Collegeville: Liturgical Press, 2001). Erik H. Erikson makes a similar remark on p. 265 of the 35th anniversary edition of his first book, *Childhood and Society* (New York: W. W. Norton, 1950, 1985). Both scholars were intellectual companions in quite different ways when I first began thinking about bodily knowledge in nursing in *Also a Mother: Work and Family as Theological Dilemma* (Nashville: Abingdon, 1994; quotes are from pp. 147 and 149) — Traina as a peer, friend, and colleague who has also written about maternal knowledge (see her *Erotic Attunement: Parenthood and the Ethics of Sexuality between Unequals* [Chicago: University of Chicago Press, 2011]) and Erikson as a long-time favorite mid–twentieth-century psychologist to whom I looked as someone who brings to his well-known theories about persons a deep desire to understand the impact of *both* culture *and* bodies.

I found religion scholar Sam Gill's provocative portrait of contemporary classrooms on pp. 81-82, 85-86, and 89 of his chapter "Embodied Theology," in *Religious Studies, Theology, and the University: Conflicting Maps, Changing Terrain,* ed. Linell E. Cady and Delwin Brown (New York: State University of New York Press, 2002). Michel Foucault hovers behind Gill's analysis of how academic settings discipline bodies, but he goes unmentioned. Other depictions of academic discipline come from a novel by author Wallace Stegner, *Crossing to Safety* (New York: Random House, 2002), pp. 249 and 253, and an interview with Anne Lamott discussing her book on writing, *Bird by Bird,* on April 29, 2011, with Kurt Andersen (Studio 360, National Public Radio, http://www.studio360.org/2011/apr/29/anne-lamott/, accessed May 10, 2011).

To show the bodily knowledge involved in care, I turn to John Carmody as cited by Ralph L. Underwood on p. 664 of "Hope in the Face of Chronic Pain and Mortality," *Pastoral Psychology* 58, no. 5/6 (December 2009). Underwood's essay is a beautiful portrait of the understanding of the body in pain (located in but not limited to the physical) as the heart of pastoral theology and ministry. D. W. Winnicott first articulates his well-known idea of a "holding environment" in "The Theory of the Parent-Infant Relationship," *The International Journal of Psychoanalysis* 41 (1960): 585-95. The words of and commentary on Mikhail Bakhtin are from pp. 83-84 of Julia Kasdorf's book, *The Body and the Book: Writing from a Mennonite Life; Essays and Poems* (University Park: Pennsylvania State University Press, 2009).

My last section refers to two general portraits of bodily wisdom. David Foster Wallace's essay on Roger Federer appeared in *The New York Times* on August 20, 2006, http://www.nytimes.com/2006/08/20/sports/play magazine/20federer.html?pagewanted=all, accessed May 18, 2011. Mihály Csíkszentmihályi's seminal work on "flow" is developed in *Flow: The Psychology of Optimal Experience* (New York: Harper & Row, 1990).

swimming

HOW THE PRACTICE OF *LECTIO DIVINA* HEALS AND TRANSFORMS

KATHLEEN A. CAHALAN

I UNDERWENT BACK SURGERY IN 2005. During the eight weeks of recovery I was allowed to sit twenty minutes a day, which included using the bathroom. I could lie down, stand, or walk. I was already an avid walker, and getting outside and moving around generally felt good. But as the days wore on I quickly succumbed to my greatest challenge: an overactive mind. When engaged in daily activities such as walking or lying on the sofa, my mind would plunge headfirst into free fall. I had a spiritual director who several years earlier had taught me that early Christians who sought solitude in the desert were plagued by their thoughts and found it difficult to pray and concentrate. I could see that my thoughts tended to run all over the place, launching into stories, conversations, arguments, and full-fledged dramas in which I held center stage.

Some thoughts, the desert monastic John Cassian (360-435 CE) taught, must be rooted out in order for God's word and presence to dwell within us. When thoughts are afflictions of the self, no other text, narrative, or reality can find space in the heart. Cassian developed the practice of attending to thoughts as they rise and replacing especially afflictive thoughts with the gospel text. For Cassian, the goal of this practice is purity of heart: one seeks to cleanse the heart of all its desires in order to mold desire and the will toward God and away from self-centered thoughts. My afflictive thoughts tended to revolve around things, anger, and vainglory, and in that vortex the ego reigns supreme.

Physical pain had brought me to a standstill, you might say. In the long recovery from the surgery (about nine months before I was pain free), I had very little energy for reading academic books or writing another paper. Rather, my free-fall thinking emerged as my dominant consciousness most of the time. Not only was I feeling trapped in a body I was not sure I was going to regain, but I was trapped in a world of thoughts that quite frankly made night-time TV dramas seem bland. I was attacked by my own inner tangles and webs. The body's vulnerability and the time required for healing became invitations to me to return to a spiritual practice that had sustained me in the past. As with most spiritual practices, I had to start over at the beginning. I had to enter back into the biblical text daily, to let the words and images sink into my consciousness and replace the noisy, annoying static on the stream of my consciousness.

"All You Who Thirst Come to the Water"

While lying on my back, I returned to reading the daily readings found in the lectionary, a practice familiar since my childhood. I would try to memorize a line or phrase and carry it with me through the day, gently replacing my thoughts of anger or vainglory with the biblical text. Repeating a line was especially helpful when I was out walking. The reading provided another narrative that gradually eased out the violence of thoughts that came rushing in at me. The traditional form of *lectio divina* involves the whole self: the words begin on the lips *(lectio),* rise to the mind *(meditatio),* sink into the heart and rise as prayer to God *(oratio),* and emerge into silence to rest in God's presence *(contemplatio).* The scriptures, then, are scripted onto and into the body as well as the mind. One narrative replaces, or roots out, another.

After the initial eight weeks of home rest, I began intensive physical therapy, which included pool therapy. I found significant pain relief from swimming. I discovered the healing quality of water, and for many months it was the only place I was pain free (in swimming aerobic style, with a waist belt, the spine is "unloaded" from all body weight and can be moved and strengthened without harm). It was springtime, and I attended the Holy Week liturgies. On Holy Saturday I listened to the seven liturgical readings that recount the grand drama of salvation history. The fourth reading, from Isaiah 55, particularly spoke to me: "All you who thirst come to the water."

I began to memorize that passage, starting one line at a time on my daily walks, and then adding more verses until I could recite the entire chapter. I had a cheat sheet, of course: I printed out the text and carried it with me on my walks so I could glance at the lines. As with any memorization I had to take it one line at a time, until I could repeat it, adding a second line and continuing with the next lines. When I went to the pool, I tried to repeat what I had memorized, but I often could not remember or lost track of the next line or jumbled the lines together. Memorizing required intense concentration, more than I realized, and I had to work hard to make progress on both sets of exercises: the bodily movements and the movements of my lips and mind. It took several months before I could recite the entire text, and only by repeated recitation could I keep it in and with me. I spent about eighteen months with Isaiah 55, and it reached a point where the text would come to me effortlessly when I woke in the morning, entered the pool, or went grocery shopping.

I had gone to the pool seeking physical relief and hoping for healing, though I had resigned myself to the reality that I might never be entirely pain free and would have to modify my life in terms of what I could do. I was surprised to find out that God was inviting me to another kind of healing. At first all I could think about was my bodily pain, but as I repeated the text on my lips it began to form my consciousness and led me to another reality: I had been immersed in the waters of baptism as an infant but I barely knew how to swim in those waters.

The opening verses of Isaiah 55 invite the thirsty and hungry to come to God's banquet, to receive wine, milk, and bread for no payment or cost (55:1-3). Spending money on what is not bread and what does not satisfy is emptiness, but Yahweh's "rich fare" is the true feast (55:2), and, like the Wisdom figure in Proverbs 8, Yahweh is luring us to a magnificent table. My problem was that I'd rather spend my money on new clothes or another book or a CD. Didn't I deserve it? Or I'd rather "sit in the seat of scoffers" (Psalm 1) and complain about how terrible my situation was. I had to spend all this time recovering, and for what? I could be doing something to make myself famous, like writing a book or giving a talk. If I didn't fully recover, I might have to give up parts of my professional life, travel, and ambition to become someone great. I might have to settle with staying home and *just* teaching.

But here was God asking me to come to the water — to "come to me heedfully, listen, that you may have life" (55:3). God had my attention: this time of recovery, painfully slow as it was, stopped me and invited me to look

SwimmingMING

at my life — my ambitions, desires, and intentions. What I found, quite honestly, was a fairly self-driven person who stood at the center of the world. Perhaps there was no other way for me to learn this lesson but by being brought low and swimming gently in the water — at Gold's Gym, no less.

But what was I to listen to? The next few verses speak of God renewing the promises of the covenant, which meant for Isaiah's audience a return from exile. For me, it meant giving myself in total and complete trust to God's goodness and mercy and not worrying about my back, a full recovery, what meetings I was missing, or how I was going to live. All of that was not important, or not as important as sitting at the rich table set for me and listening to God. Perhaps the most powerful message lay in the next few verses:

> Seek God while God may be found, call God while God is near. Let the scoundrel forsake his way, and the wicked woman her thoughts; let them turn to the Lord for mercy; to our God, who is generous in forgiving. For my thoughts are not your thoughts, nor are your ways my ways, says the Lord. As high as the heavens are above the earth, so high are my ways above your ways and my thoughts above your thoughts. (Isa. 55:6-9)

My calling was actually quite simple: to seek God, and nothing else. I had deliberately changed the text to be inclusive, and that meant I had to say the words: "the wicked woman her thoughts." I had to renounce these thoughts of self, including the vainglory that drove me to do good for others so I would look good and be praised. I had to seek mercy and forgiveness for all my self-motivated drivenness — I was not teaching, or writing, or living a life that was seeking God, but was living only for myself. And, of course, the following verses shouted to me, I was not God — not my thoughts nor my ways. God's thoughts and ways are higher, and they are unknown to me. I had to enter a pool of water and submit to daily exercises to learn what I thought I knew as a trained theologian, but clearly had never known.

The Teaching on Thoughts

When Christians left the cities of the Roman empire for the deserts of Egypt and Syria in the third and fourth centuries, they were seeking an authentic way to live the gospel, an alternative martyrdom after Christianity had become widely accepted. Their way of life would later be known as monasticism. In these early days of experimentation, lay Christians were seeking a life of prayer and virtue rooted in God. When they moved into the hills and caves of the desert, renouncing their former lives, possessions, and relationships, they discovered a startling surprise: all of these distractions came with them. The solitude of the desert, the silence and stillness of the place, opened up an inner space that instantly was filled with "thoughts" about home, longings for better food and more creature comforts, old arguments, and attractions to former friends and would-be lovers. Thoughts plagued these seekers. To combat the especially afflictive thoughts, those that came often and with intensity, they developed a set of teachings geared to transforming thoughts *before* they developed into actions or sins.

Thoughts in themselves were not understood to be sinful; rather, a thought is simply anything that appears in one's consciousness that one can consent to follow, or not. Consenting to a thought means saying "yes" to what soon becomes a trail of thoughts — one thought attaches to another and another and so on. It is when we consent to a thought and its trail that thoughts turn into intentions: a thought fuels our desire, and stirs a passion, and eventually becomes an act. For example, I recall a conversation yesterday with a colleague that makes me angry (a thought rises); I imagine telling him off today, or better yet telling other colleagues about what he did (the initial thought couples with another thought and consents to more thoughts); I get increasingly angry and imagine going to the dean and trying to get him in trouble; I imagine a scene in which I humiliate him in front of others. Before long I am so angry and fired up in my self-righteousness that I want to hurt him (desires and passions), and I end up writing an angry email to him, I have lunch with another colleague and tell her about it, and we vow to bring him down (act).

A trail of thoughts, then, begins with one simple thought but gains momentum and energy as we consent to keep thinking the thoughts. Cassian drew his insights from Evagrius Ponticus (345-399 CE), who first described the eight thoughts (which would later be revised into the seven deadly sins) — gluttony (food), fornication (sex), avarice (things), anger, dejection (sadness), acedia, vainglory, and pride. The thoughts become afflictive insofar as they take over our consciousness before we can get ahold of them. Cassian acknowledged that such thoughts are persistent in our minds but also argued that we can control whether to "permit them entry or drive them away" (*Conferences* 1.17). He counseled his followers to train the mind not to consent to the trail of thoughts but to stop the thought at its first rising. For this one must become adept at observing one's thoughts when they rise and not allowing them to attach themselves to the next thoughts that flow from them. Consenting to the thought, after all, leads the will to act, and if one can be trained not to follow a thought, one will not act upon it. The goal is to replace self-driven thoughts not of God with other thoughts, usually drawn from scripture, in order that "the thoughts deriving from all this will of necessity be spiritual and they will hold the mind where the thoughts have been." But if we let our thoughts dwell on "worldly cares and profitless worries," they will "serve as a ministry of death to our hearts" (1.18).

The training to conquer the eight thoughts was strenuous. Evagrius and Cassian both use metaphors related to athletics, warfare, and surgery to describe the power those who seek to combat afflictive thoughts must use. In these images the emphasis is on the physical strength necessary to endure, persevere, and "win" against a foe or enemy in games, war, or medicine. The body and the whole self are engaged, fully intentional and attentive to the task. In time, the strenuous effort gives way to peacefulness, since the initial struggle with the thoughts is conquered by God's grace and mercy alone. Our task is to root out the afflictive thoughts from consciousness; God's task is to pour forth the grace necessary to live a virtuous life.

Over time, desert practitioners developed practices and forms of prayer to counter afflictive thoughts, for example, keeping one's cell in order, or fasting, both "externally" from food and "internally," by practicing the guard of the heart. They also developed short prayers, one-word or one-line phrases drawn from scripture, which they called "arrows." For example, Evagrius identified nearly five hundred temptations with the same number of scripture verses that could be "thrown" against the vicious thoughts. Cassian simplified this teaching and advocated one verse to repeat at the rising of any afflictive thought: "O, God, come to my assistance; Lord, make haste to help me" (Ps. 70:1). A century later, Saint Benedict, in his Rule for monastic life, made this short prayer the opening phrase for liturgical prayer in his community.

Learning to Pray

My first memory of reading the scriptures on my own comes from the sixth grade. I somehow had the idea that I wanted to read the Bible from beginning to end. I started in but found that I knew the first few stories, so I thought it might be better to begin in another place. So I started at Ecclesiastes. I did not get far because the text was so strange and I could not understand it. My attempt faltered and I never made it all the way through either that book or the Bible. Around the same time I realized that there was such a thing as the daily lectionary. As children we planned and attended daily mass once a week with our grade level, and it is probably in this context that I was exposed to the "reading of the day." Somehow I came to understand that whole books were read over time, with a selection each day, and that if you read along every day you would eventually read a book. I mistakenly thought the whole Bible was read during the year; it was years before I learned there was a three-year cycle and that we read only a small portion of the Hebrew Bible and New Testament. Nevertheless, I decided to follow this method, but to do so I needed access to the daily readings and I needed a Bible at home. Because I was often in the church after school practicing for my organ lessons, I decided to "borrow" a missalette (a book containing the mass, readings, and hymns), take it home, and copy down the list of readings for each day, which were listed in the back pages. I would return the missalette the next day, so it was not quite stealing. I purchased *The Jerusalem Bible* at a religious bookstore in our downtown. This is how I began to pray the scriptures each day. I recognized it as a very "catholic" prayer since people all over the world were reading these same texts at the liturgy. I had "access" to God through the scriptures even though I was not present at daily Eucharist.

When I was sixteen years old, I began reading spiritual writings. I read Henri Nouwen's book, *Genessee Diary,* which is the story of his nine-month stay at a Trappist monastery. He learned to pray the liturgy of the hours and discovered the mystery of immersing himself daily in the scriptures. He learned of Thomas Merton's desire to memorize the psalms and the New Testament; Merton feared that if he were ever in a place without a Bible, such as a prison, he needed to know the text. I learned, like Nouwen, that there was a larger world of daily and liturgical prayer with scripture that shaped morning and evening. The first psalm I memorized was Psalm 4, which I began to say at bedtime.

A second influential book on prayer I read as a teenager was *You: Prayer for Beginners* by Mark Link, SJ. *You,* a little "how-to" book for beginners, demonstrated how to pray with scripture in a simple format. The method, I now know, was *lectio divina,* though Link did not use that language. He taught the reader how to read a passage slowly, savoring words or phrases and rereading the passage several times. He combined *lectio divina* with the Ignatian examen as a daily practice. I practiced this method each day, though I never told anyone I was doing so. I was very self-conscious about being religious and I never wanted anyone to know. It was definitely not cool. Of course people knew — I was very involved at school with mission trips, campus ministry, and retreats, and for one whole year I attended daily mass at lunch after a serious falling out with friends. However, I never let out what was an inner and private practice, and neither did anyone inquire.

"Human Childhood Is Infinite Openness"

I entered a Catholic grade school in Dubuque, Iowa, as the Second Vatican Council "ushered in a new era for Roman Catholics." Change was in the air, and in our small corner of the world the Council was embraced with genuine excitement and openness. The general theological milieu was saturated by an overwhelming sense of God's presence, love, and power. Our baroque church was filled with a pervasive sense of grace, with every inch of space covered in symbol and story. But aspects of the past were quickly ending — I never heard a Latin mass in that church, for instance. The Council's embrace of modernity was opening the church to the wider world, and yet for a child there was nothing about this change that seemed radical or different. It was all I knew.

I'm not aware that any of my teachers in the 1960s had read Karl Rahner on children, but they definitely believed a core element of his insight that children are able to experience the divine self-communication. For Rahner "childhood is openness. Human childhood is infinite openness." I was formed with openness toward God from an early age, primarily in school rather than at home or in the parish. School was the context for learning to be in relationship to God through worship, silence, and scripture.

At St. Columbkille's School we were a "community of practice" that focused on procedural or acquired knowledge and socialization that imitated adult behavior. Though both content and pedagogy were undergoing significant change at the time, we were taught the basics of Catholic faith and practice and we were socialized into adult forms of faith and practice. However, the school was also a community of practice that focused on identity formation through what Joyce Mercer calls "meaning-making." In my context I recall little meaning-making that addressed the broader social context, such as what *Gaudium et spes,* Vatican II's statement on the church in the modern world, was proclaiming. Instead, the world we were invited into was an interior one.

In the school I attended, we learned to pray. Traditional Catholic prayers, such as the rosary or stations-of-the-cross, were not the dominant forms at that time. As the historian Jay Dolan notes, the Council made revolutionary liturgical changes and "spelled out an agenda for reform that radically changed the way Catholics pray." The young sisters who taught us were trying out prayer forms that were new to them as well, most notably a para-liturgical form called the "prayer service." During a prayer service I recall sitting in silence, singing, praying responsively, praying spontaneously, and listening to the scriptures. In her effort to encourage adults to include children, practical theologian Jean Stairs captures well my experience. Stairs notes that ritual for children allows for a deep experience of God, not information about God. Through ritual at a young age, "children are enabled early on to read their everyday world as a life full of signs that point beyond the surface to the presence of God. In essence, by enticing children through ritual, we entice them to a habit of listening to their own souls."

In the midst of this world of ritual prayer, I learned to love silence. Somehow I had the sense that the inner life, the life of prayer and silence in sacred places, is the true and lasting life. There was a sense that the external world, filled with material things, though good, is fleeting. The true life meant not being attached to these things; it consisted in seeking God, who could be known and loved through prayer and worship. The "really real" was beyond these visible manifestations and was much larger and more important than the everyday realities of the material world. Children have an enormous capacity for silence, when given the chance. There was certainly a sense in those simple prayer services that "prayer is incomplete without a time of listening."

Of course another significant change in the 1960s was related to the liturgy, which we were now taught to enter with "full, active and conscious participation." As children, we attended liturgy once a week with the hundred-plus children in our grade, and we were not passive observers. Rather, we were engaged at all levels of planning and executing the liturgy, including selecting a theme, songs, and readings; writing prayers; making banners; and also taking on roles as readers, servers, gift-bearers, and music leaders. Of course this was a revolution compared to a few years prior, when our parents' generation, immersed in pre–Vatican II liturgy, participated primarily as observers of others' actions.

At some point, we must have begun learning about scripture, another dramatic innovation in Catholic life and education. In second grade my first communion preparation consisted of my parents attending small-group meetings in family homes, led by a parish staff member. After each meeting, parents were sent home to share scripture stories with their children, using small, simple books based on the New Testament. I vividly recall the books on the parables. In this way and others, the Bible and its stories were somehow part of my childhood formation, but it was primarily in the context of liturgy that I came to read and know them. Bible reading and study were not part of the piety of my household, nor did I feel encouraged to do this on my own.

I don't know what other children did with silence, scripture, or liturgy, but each of these became deeply rooted in my life. And my attraction to prayer and scripture was largely private, something I pursued on my own outside of school.

Formed in the Image of Christ?

I was blessed to have several excellent scripture teachers in high school and college who formed my own desire and vocation to teach scripture. I told my undergraduate scripture professor that I wanted to pursue doctoral-level training in scripture after graduation, but she told me that it was probably too late since I had not taken French, German, Hebrew, and Greek. I was about twenty-one at the time, and being quite naïve, I believed her. Perhaps she thought I could not do it, though she was allowing me to take master-level courses by my junior year since I had exhausted all the undergraduate scripture offerings. Perhaps she was discouraged by her own doctoral studies, as she returned to college teaching with an unfinished dissertation. In any case, her advice shaped my vocation. I did not pursue doctoral work in scripture; instead I pursued my other passion for studying psychology and theology.

I began graduate studies in what is commonly referred to as the "Berlin model" of university education. I was the first in my family to attend graduate school so I was naïve about the world of the research university. I had no reason to question its commitments, practices, or assumptions, and I adopted them as my own. And, for the most part, I loved graduate study: I learned everything I could. Being young, I did not have a strong sense of what it was for or where I was headed, but I trusted the system's purposes and kept moving on to the next stage.

I received my education from master teachers who stood in front of the class and spoke brilliantly for the full period. I gulped down large quantities of knowledge and gave it back in the form of exams and papers; the formation was analytical, based on mastery, and quite competitive. Not only did knowledge of the past need to be acquired, but also new knowledge, in the form of the latest book, thinker, or movement, needed to be attained. One had to keep up on all fronts. We were to hone our skills in the tradition of *Wissenschaft,* learning disciplined critical research skills that aimed to "master the truth of whatever subject is studied."

The primary formation was a critical, disciplined, and orderly epistemology, as the theologian David Kelsey describes in his reflections on the history of graduate study in the theological fields. "On this model only the results of inquiry that is *wissenschaftlich* can count as 'knowledge.'" I don't think I expected *paideia,* or personal moral and spiritual formation, from graduate school; I had already come from a long line of what could be called Catholic *paideia,* which had shaped my orientation to both God and the church. But that world of Catholic *paideia* had become a claustrophobic world intellectually and communally, and I was excited that the new knowledge I gained in graduate school breathed fresh air into my faith world. At the same time, however, the *paideia* of the Berlin model began to shape me as well. The goal of this *paideia* was to master knowledge and methods of inquiry *about* religion and to become a first-rate researcher and teacher. Mastery was clearly the telos of the Berlin model, even though I recall little direct attention given to explicit formation in becoming a researcher or teacher.

I came to graduate studies with questions about religious experience and the spiritual life. I received little encouragement to see that the questions I wanted to pursue in the academic realm were in fact deeply personal questions or connected to a community that I might serve. I had no bridge to connect all these questions and concerns. I kept them separate and hidden, perhaps even from myself.

I discovered a dissertation topic in a seminar on twentieth-century Catholic ethics. We read the first volume of Bernard Haring's *The Law of Christ,* which opens with a section on prayer. That's it, I thought with delight — that's my question: How, in fact, does prayer, the dialogue between God and human persons, form the moral life? What difference do our religious practices make in terms of what kind of people we become? I was slightly embarrassed about my topic and I pursued the research and writing without talking much to professors or classmates; I demonstrated my methodological abilities in historical and textual analysis and, in good Berlin fashion, I mastered Haring's theology.

Ironically, that dissertation is entitled *Formed in the Image of Christ.* In fact, of course, I knew very little about being formed in the image of Christ or about forming students in Christ's image. When I began teaching I taught in exactly the same way I had been taught: I was now the master of knowledge, and my job was to impart as much of that knowledge as possible to my students. Actually, I think forming students in my image was my deeper motive. Jane Tompkins writes that her obsession as a college English teacher had not been with helping students learn what they wanted and needed to know but rather with "(a) showing the students how smart I was; (b) showing them how knowledgeable I was; and (c) showing them how well prepared I was for class. I had been putting on a performance whose true goal was not to help the students learn but to act in such a way that they would have a good opinion of me." I remember one day after class a student coming up to me and asking, "Can I read the book you are reading from?"

During my first teaching job at a small college, a colleague who taught scripture was killed in an automobile accident over the Christmas break. She was teaching "Introduction to New Testament" in the upcoming spring semester, and if we canceled the course forty students would have to be reassigned to other courses. Seeing my chance to teach scripture, I volunteered to take the class. Since I lacked the doctoral training necessary, I had to immerse myself in biblical research to prepare my lectures. I was finally the teacher of scripture that I wanted to be. The truth is I loved learning about scripture in the same way I loved my studies in graduate school: I discovered a whole world *about* the text that I never knew. I found this learning inspiring, challenging, and new. I assumed its formative power, and new insights about a text, led me to pray differently in relationship to a text. I found little incongruence between learning the world of biblical scholarship and picking up these same texts in daily prayer. In fact, the strange and odd world of the biblical text became more understandable and accessible. And I wanted students to experience the same thrill of learning. But I never once taught my own practice of *lectio divina* to students; I assumed it was not my task. After several years teaching undergraduate students, I moved on to teach graduate students preparing for ministry, and this new context raised new questions about the purpose of my teaching.

"A Voice Says, 'Cry Out!' and I Said, 'What Shall I Cry?'"

After back surgery and a long recuperation, I was healed from the grinding pain. In many ways I had my life back, but now it was a new life, for not only was I given my physical life back, but I was experiencing a new calling. What I didn't realize was that this call was going to disrupt my life and teaching in significant ways. After a year's sabbatical, I returned to the classroom only to experience a much more profound loss and disorientation than my bodily ailments had imposed. I realized I had no idea why I was teaching what I was teaching.

There was something profoundly inauthentic about what I was doing. I found myself teaching what I thought was expected of me by my colleagues and would make me acceptable to them, the students, and the church. But over time, I was not even sure I believed what I was teaching! Recalling Tompkins, I had become an actor on a stage, delivering my lines with expertise. The well-known educator Parker Palmer asks a similar question: "How did it come to be that our main goal as academicians turned out to be performance?" But one day my whole performance (which was quite good) collapsed. I could not pick up the pieces and go on teaching without figuring out: What is so important to me that I cannot *not* teach it? What is my passion? And how can I teach it in a way that honors not only knowledge about something but also knowledge of God, in relationship to God, directed toward God?

During a long hiking trip with my husband that summer, I turned to Isaiah 40, the opening text of Deutero-Isaiah, and began memorizing the lines. The prophet begins with words of comfort and consolation, for he foresees that the time of exile is nearly ended and that all God's promises to restore the people to their homeland will soon be fulfilled. Yet it requires great faith to believe that this vision will come true. The prophet emphasizes that human persons are too small and inconsistent to know and understand what God knows and understands. Like grass in the field, people's faith withers and fades, in contrast to God's word that stands forever (Isa. 40:8).

I finally realized I was in exile from much of what I had embraced as a theologian in the church and as a scholar and teacher in the university. I was performing well, but it didn't matter. I did not choose exile; I just discovered I was in exile. I had been moved out, displaced from a role that had once seemed to work. Palmer recounts a similar experience in his teaching when he discovered that "the onstage show and backstage reality mirrored a great divide in my inner life." For him the outward self was projecting competence and accomplishment, while the inner self felt fearful, anxious, and fraudulent. I definitely felt like I was acting the "right" role for a post–Vatican II progressive theologian, but it was becoming increasingly false, and I questioned who I was and what I was even doing teaching at all. I found myself in exile from the Catholic community that had formed me.

My sense of myself as a *Catholic* theologian and teacher broke into a thousand pieces that year. I had experienced deep anguish over the Catholic Church's teachings in earlier years, but I always managed to regroup under the oft-spoken mantra, "It's our church too!" But this time I did not pick up the shattered pieces. I could not. As Palmer notes, "We can educate the heart by exposing it to tension-inducing ideas, relationships and experiences . . . we can help make the heart supple rather than brittle, so it breaks *open* instead of *apart* under the stresses of life. When the heart breaks apart, it breaks into a thousand pieces. But it can also break open onto larger capacity, become more open to holding the pain of the world."

I felt myself like the grass, barely able to stand in the heat of the day or through the driving wind and rain ("All people are grass . . . the grass withers, the flower fades"; Isa. 40:6-7). But like the prophet, I felt God was calling me to something different, to be some other kind of teacher, perhaps in another community. However, I had no idea what to become or where to go. As Isaiah writes, "A voice says, 'Cry out!' and I said, 'What shall I cry?'" (Isa. 40:6).

I knew the call was to teach and give witness to God, to be more true both to God's call and to myself, but I felt lost in the wilderness, exiled from the church that was part of my whole life, exiled from the doing of theology I had been trained in, and exiled from the forms of pedagogy I had mastered. "Get you up to a high mountain, O Zion, herald of good tidings, lift up your voice with strength . . . lift it up, do not fear. Say to the cities of Judah, 'Here is your God!'" (Isa. 40:9). I knew God was calling me to a high mountain, to be a herald, but why in midlife was everything coming apart — did God even want me to be a theologian and a teacher? And if so, what kind — what message was I supposed to deliver? I was too afraid to change what I thought or how I taught. If I had my body back, what was I supposed to do with my health? If reciting Isaiah 55 purged my intentions, then Isaiah 40 seemed designed to purge my vocation.

Isaiah recounts the majesty and wonder of God the creator — "Who has measured the waters in the hollow of God's hand, and marked off the heavens with a span?" — and recalls that God's ways are beyond our reach: "Whom did God consult for enlightenment, who taught God the path of justice? Who taught God knowledge, and showed God the way of understanding?" (Isa. 40:12, 14). Clearly, not me or any other human person. Who was I to claim that I knew something of this divine reality and power? The text, like Isaiah 55, pointed out that God's ways cannot be mastered by me; there is a way of understanding that surpasses all my mastery of a text or classroom. I was standing in the presence of divine holy mystery, stripped of every external support that held together my identity.

And yet Isaiah was also asking me, "Have you not known? Have you not heard? Has it not been told you from the beginning?" (Isa. 40:21). I came to see that I have known and I have heard; I've known something all my life. I've known the desire for God, even if it was distorted by my own self-serving desires or by forms of learning and teaching that distanced me from this reality. And I knew something by way of a practice that has sustained me for a long time, a practice I could claim as truly "catholic."

In the midst of these questions, I felt called to a greater sense of purpose in my life and work and to a demand for more authenticity in who I was and what I was doing. For Palmer this calling allows one to reclaim a sense of identity and integrity as a teacher. He writes, "Identity lies in the intersection of the diverse forces that make up my life, and integrity lies in relating to those forces in ways that bring me wholeness and life rather than fragmentation and death." I saw that I had to ask Isaiah's question: What have I known from the beginning? Why did I want to become a teacher? What was I passionate about teaching and how did I lose it along the way? What connects the threads of my life into a tapestry, a whole, rather than a threadbare rag?

When Evagrius left the city for the desert in the mid-fourth century, he asked Asenius, "How is it we have so much education but lack the virtues of the most simple peasant?" Over a thousand years ago illiterate men and women who were living in caves in the desert had begun to attain a knowledge far surpassing that of the day's great intellectuals and schools of learning. The connecting thread in my own life was a simple prayer born of years of practice. In most crises in my life, I found my way back to that practice and it showed me the way again.

> But be careful. You will be teaching something acquired not so much by reading as by the sweat of experience. (*Conferences* 14.17)

Parker Palmer advocates that good teaching is not based primarily on technique, but is rooted in the teacher's identity and integrity. When it came to my questions about who I was as a teacher and why I was teaching what I was teaching, I had to find an answer. I had never questioned my call to teach, one that I heard as a child, and this was not the present challenge I faced — whether I should teach or not. The challenge was something like this: What could I not *not* teach? What was I so passionate about students learning that I had to teach it and learn it again with them?

In the past few years I have had a small but steady stream of students come to me to tell me how much they dislike school. Recently a bright young man told me a story of his sadness and despair at studying theology, and another of how he had learned nothing since he had come to graduate school. Both had believed that theological study would lead them closer to God, but after three semesters, one said, he had come to see that "it is just drudgery." These conversations left me sad and a bit angry. Why were theological teachers — myself among them — continuing to conduct theological studies as if the mastery of ideas were the primary goal? Why are we not teaching out of our own practice for a life of practice? Why do our theological systems remain a set of ideal forms and not a way of life to be lived? We continue to teach a body of beliefs, and methods to interpret them, as if any of this could be grasped apart from a life of practice. What disgruntled graduate students were saying, it seemed to me, was this: "I don't want to just read theology and write papers about it. I want to read 'God' and learn how to live a life in relationship to God."

I realized that I had to become a teacher of practice and to begin teaching more out of my own practice. In that sense, Palmer does not go far enough. A teacher must have integrity and identity, but she also must have a way of life, a practice that grounds who she is and what she does. While I would agree with Palmer that good teaching cannot be reduced to technique, teaching itself is a practice that combines both skill and intention. Like a spiritual practice, it takes the will to do it and the embodied disciplined engagement to do it well. Further, as Cassian warns, it takes the whole self. "Never dare to teach someone what you have not practiced yourself," he says (*Conferences* 14.9).

The truth is that I have engaged in a practice for which I did not have a teacher or receive formal training as a young person. I was primarily taught through discovery and reading and of course through my own practice. Fortunately in the last decade I have discovered a teacher and a community of practice. What I could begin to do for students was to help them discover and ground their lives more firmly in spiritual practice — to take what was so deeply personal in my life and make it public and accessible for them.

Recently, in a course on pastoral care, I had students memorize Psalm 23 and practice sustained *lectio divina* for several weeks. They also were engaged in a set of listening-skill exercises in which they were to pray with their partner each time. They could either attempt to recite the psalm from memory or offer a spontaneous prayer in response to the issues raised during the conversation. Both methods met with varying degrees of success. Several students noted that they could not think of the right words to say in spontaneous prayer, and were quite relieved to have the memorized psalm to say (or the "Our Father," which was easier for most). Others commented that they felt freer and more open in the spontaneous prayer and could not recall the words to the psalm when they were to be uttered. In one case, a young monk, praying with a monk of fifty-plus years, completely forgot the psalm and had to be helped to finish it. How embarrassing! he told us. Here in the midst of learning to pray with others are the seeds of their own practice. But one student noted a deeper wisdom in the practice that he needed to learn: "Isn't it a matter of discerning which type of prayer is best for the person, and not so much what prayer I am best at delivering?"

It seems that this student grasped the judgment at the heart of practical wisdom. It surprised me, for I had not presented anything on practical reason or wisdom. But then I realized. In placing practice in the midst of our learning and skill building, practical wisdom began to emerge, both for me and for the students.

References

I am indebted to the teachings and writings of Sr. Mary Margaret Funk, OSB, of Our Lady of Grace Monastery, and am grateful for her many years of conversation about spiritual practice. See her books on prayer in the monastic tradition: *Thoughts Matter: The Practice of the Spiritual Life* (New York: Continuum, 1998); *Tools Matter for Practicing the Spiritual Life* (New York: Continuum, 2001); *Humility Matters for Practicing the Spiritual Life* (New York: Continuum, 2005); *Lectio Matters: Before the Burning Bush* (New York: Continuum, 2010); *Discernment Matters: Listening with the Ear of the Heart* (Collegeville: Liturgical, 2013).

For an introduction to *lectio divina* see Christine Valters Painter and Lucy Wynkoop, *Lectio Divina: Contemplative Awakening and Awareness* (Mahwah, NJ: Paulist, 2008).

In memorizing Isaiah 55 I used the New American Bible, and for Isaiah 40 the New Revised Standard Version.

For the writings of Evagrius of Ponticus and John Cassian, see *Evagrius of Ponticus: Talking Back; A Monastic Handbook for Combating Demons,* trans. David Brakke (Collegeville: Liturgical, 2009); Evagrius Ponticus, *The Praktikos and Chapters on Prayer* (Kalamazoo: Cistercian, 1972); and John Cassian, *Conferences,* trans. Colm Luibheid (New York: Paulist, 1985).

For a historian's evocative description of the early 1960s in American Catholicism, see Jay P. Dolan, *The American Catholic Experience: A History from Colonial Times to the Present* (Garden City, NY: Doubleday, 1985), quote at p. 425. Thomas F. O'Meara is eloquent about how architecture and decoration shape worshipers' sense of God's presence. See his *Theology of Ministry* (New York: Paulist, 1983), p. 120.

On Rahner's theology of childhood see Karl Rahner, "Ideas for a Theology of Childhood," in his *Theological Investigations,* vol. 8: *Further Theology of the Spiritual Life II* (London: Darton, Longman and Todd, 1971), pp. 33-50. For her appropriation of Rahner and a discussion of children's need for identity formation in communities of practice, see Joyce Mercer, *Welcoming Children: A Practical Theology of Childhood* (St. Louis: Chalice, 2005), p. 150.

Quotes by Jean Stairs are taken from her book *Listening for the Soul: Pastoral Care and Spiritual Direction* (Minneapolis: Fortress, 2000), pp. 174-75 and 184-85.

For the church's teaching on "full, active and conscious participation," see *Sacrosanctum Concilium,* in *Vatican Council II: The Conciliar and Post-Conciliar Documents,* ed. Austin Flannery (New York: Costello, 1987), p. 10.

For a study on the Berlin model of theological education, see David H. Kelsey, *Between Athens and Berlin: The Theological Education Debate* (Grand Rapids: Eerdmans, 1993), quotes at pp. 13 and 14.

For a discussion of teaching with integrity, see Parker Palmer, *The Courage to Teach: Exploring the Inner Landscape of a Teacher's Life,* 10th anniversary ed. (San Francisco: Jossey-Bass, 2007), quotes at pp. 28 and 14. Palmer's quote on an open heart was taken from an interview on his new book, *Healing the Heart of Democracy: The Courage to Create a Politics Worthy of the Human* (San Francisco: Jossey-Bass, 2011). Interview at: http://reflections.yale.edu/article/seize-day-vocation-calling-work/tension-heartbreak-and-vocation-parker-j-palmer, accessed July 8, 2014.

camping

PRACTICAL WISDOM IN EVERYDAY LIFE

DOROTHY C. BASS

ONE SUMMER NIGHT SEVERAL YEARS AGO, I perceived the reality of God's new creation. Reconciliation was evident around and within me, clear and true. Now, challenged to give an account of a kind of knowing that is embodied, engaged, and attuned to God, I return to that night. Was what I was able to know in that hour an unasked-for blessing? Yes, it was. But upon reflection, I have come to understand that I had been prepared for that mountaintop experience by many years of walking certain paths through the lowlands, where my desires were honed, my eyes and ears tutored, and my relationships expanded.

Let me tell you about that night, and then about the lowlands and the everyday people, places, and practices that prepared me to receive the blessing it bestowed. These are the places to which I soon returned and where I still make my home. We shall also follow two others who were there that night into different settings that also turned out to be located on the landscape of new creation. There all three of us have been engaged in various ways in the quotidian practices of making homes for others, the daily acts of nurture that shape where and how people live.

Seeing Creation Anew

Every year, in the middle of August, the Perseid meteor shower rains streams of light across the skies of the northern hemisphere. Most years, I forget to look or can't see anything even if I remember, as the ambient lights of the metropolitan area where I live dilute the darkness and render the fast-moving streaks of light invisible. But on this mid-August night I was in the mountains, staying in a tiny village surrounded by a vast wilderness. The moon was new, and the night was as dark as dark could be, broken only by the light of the stars.

This tiny village is named Holden, after a prospector who discovered a deposit of copper ore there at the end of the nineteenth century. Between 1937 and 1957, a mining company wrested from the mountain 212 million pounds of copper, 40 million pounds of zinc, 2 million ounces of silver, and 600 thousand ounces of gold. One day the global market in copper shifted and the miners moved away, leaving acres of machinery, dozens of furnished buildings, and a heap of tailings hundreds of feet high and nearly two miles long. Unable to sell this very remote and rapidly decaying property, the mining company ended up donating it to a Lutheran college in 1960. Eventually it became a year-round retreat center. On the night of the meteor shower, I was there as a chaperone for a group of teenagers that included my son and daughter.

Another group, hosted by my friend Ingrid, was also at Holden that week. Ingrid had raised funds to bring a dozen women from her Chicago neighborhood on a visit to this mountain village. They were residents of Genesis House, a ministry for women who are trying to regain their independence after years of tough living on the city's streets. They were poor. Most were black. Some were illiterate. Their life experiences were quite different from those of the youngsters in my charge.

When Ingrid suggested we get our groups together, I agreed. We decided to take a star hike — Holden lingo for a late-night walk beyond the village limits into star-revealing darkness. So after Vespers we rounded up a stack of yard blankets and a box of flashlights and met at the edge of the village. A few others joined us, too, including a friend of Ingrid's who plays a major and sometimes unsettling role in my life as the ex-wife of my husband and the mother of the young woman he and I think of as our oldest child. This mother's name is Ricki.

Everyone fell into comfortable pairs and trios and started to trudge up a steep incline. Though a few of the youngsters sprinted, it took a while, maybe half an hour, for everyone to reach our destination atop the tailings. Many of the Chicago women moved tentatively; the darkness, uncompromised by streetlights, seemed to disturb them, and some were worried about noises coming from the forest or were not quite in shape for the climb. But as we moved beyond the trees onto the top of the huge barren pile of wasted rock, everyone gasped. "I haven't seen this many stars since I was a little girl in Mississippi," my companion murmured in amazement. Together, we looked down from the tailings and saw the lights of the village a thousand feet below.

Moving slowly, everyone took blankets, spread them on the ground, and lay down to gaze up at the night sky. The air was crystal clear. Every now and then a meteor flared across the sky, and several times we simultaneously breathed an appreciative "ahhhhhh." Mostly, though, we were silent together as we settled one by one into our own reflective solitudes. When all were still, the voices of two women broke the silence. One voice, young and strong, bore the accents of the Pacific Northwest; the other, older, incorporated rhythms rooted in the Deep South. Alternating verse by verse, these voices lifted up a psalm to God in the hearing of this peculiar assembly.

> Sun and moon, glittering stars, sing praise, sing praise,
>> highest heavens, rain clouds, sing praise, sing praise.
> Praise God's name, whose word called you forth
>> and fixed you in place forever by eternal decree.
> God's splendor above the earth, above the heavens,
>> gives strength to the nation, glory to the faithful.
>
>> (From Psalm 148)

I'm not sure how long we all lay there under that star-streaked sky, side by side on the yard blankets. But at some point I became aware of a startling paradox. I was on top of a massive, toxic scar on the face of the earth. And I was also surrounded by a beauty beyond human imagining. A few decades before, human beings had wrecked the land beneath us; they had made money, and I had benefited too as a place of retreat became available to me. But the earth had paid a price. Fish could no longer survive in the river below, and deer could not drink from it. Even so, it was plain that God still loved this land and these creatures, including us, including me. God was somehow about the work of renewing and reclaiming it all. With the psalmist, I rejoiced: "Praise the Lord, across the heavens, from the heights!" Blessed be this strong darkness, these streaming lights, this silence, this promise of God to make all things new.

Finally an impulse to share my awe with another human being caused me to sit up and look around. What I saw overwhelmed me in a different way. My daughter Martha was lying nearby, serenely sharing her yard blanket with two women. On her right was a woman who was striving to overcome immense hardship in a city near our home. On her left was Ricki, the mother of her sister, the first wife of her dad. So much brokenness was gathered right in front of me — the failed marriage, the difficult stepfamily, the suffering long borne by a resolute woman whose name I did not know. And on the same blanket was this girl of my own heart, so fresh, so delighted by this midnight excursion, so deeply woven into my own hopes and joys and fears, and, undeniably, so vulnerable to the same kinds of brokenness the women beside her had already experienced. It was overwhelming. But I could also see, in the very same glance, that all the brokenness gathered there was being overcome, by the power of God, as these three shared an old blanket, heard some ancient words, and witnessed a display of cosmic beauty. This, too, was overwhelming.

That night has stayed with me as a foretaste of the healing of the world — the healing of creation, the healing of divisions of race and class, the healing of broken families and persons. For me this was a glimpse of the really real, a shimmering moment when the reconciliation that has already taken place in and through Christ became visible. As I have continued to ponder this vision over the years, the words of the apostle Paul have merged with the memory:

> So if anyone is in Christ, there is a new creation: everything old has passed away; see, everything has become new! All this is from God, who reconciled us to himself through Christ, and has given us the ministry of reconciliation; that is, in Christ God was reconciling the world to himself, not counting their trespasses against them, and entrusting the message of reconciliation to us. (2 Cor. 5:17-19)

Others would surely have experienced that night much differently than I did. Indeed, for most people in a secular age, the convergence of mining waste, stepfamily tensions, urban poverty, biblical poetry, maternal hope, deep darkness, and falling stars would not necessarily point to God at work in the universe, mending its brokenness and making it new. Those concerned for human flourishing would presumably endorse the longing to repair environmental and human damage that appears in my account, to be sure. And almost anyone could appreciate how beautiful the sky was that night. But to see that God was at work there? Some might concede that a private and subjective concept of "God" shaped the way I interpreted this experience in my individual mind, shaped as it was by many years of participation in worship and conversation with others who call themselves "Christian." However, to agree that a transcendent God actually made an appearance in this little drama? Not so much.

I am not trying to prove anything here about God and God's presence in the world. Rather, I am trying to show how seeing and inhabiting the world in certain ways in the company of other Christians over the years have helped me to perceive and receive the gracious presence we believe upholds, judges, and redeems all that is. In many respects, I share the worldview of those who reject this belief. Like other moderns, I see the quotidian world of production and reproduction as the primary arena of human endeavor and becoming, and I care deeply about the flourishing of all within this immanent, material world. I seek and find explanations for almost everything within the horizontal frame we call "nature," and every day I accept benefits that derive from instrumental reason's ability to manipulate nature to attain certain desirable ends, such as sustenance and health. Further, I cannot quite shake my sense that I am an autonomous individual, no matter how highly I prize my bonds with other people and that which I take to be divine. Even so, I am persuaded — by the philosopher Charles Taylor, yes, but much more by the overwhelmings that visit me in the mountains, in the lowlands, and especially at worship — that the current plausibility of the idea that there is no God does not prove that idea to be true. Together with others who have seen God making all things new in Christ and some who simply yearn to see this, I choose to "spin the immanent frame as open rather than closed" to the transcendence many modern people doubt but cannot disprove apart from rigid adherence to the conditioned assumptions of their own historical moment.

Over time, I hope to show, certain patterns of life with others prepared me to perceive and receive the God-given reconciliation that was offered to me that night. This is hard to discuss, and not only because the movements of mind, body, and spirit I'll depict feel very private, just as the prevailing social imaginary declares them to be. These things are also hard to discuss because, in keeping with the tradition within which I interpret whatever knowledge of life with God I may have, I feel awfully humble about claiming any such knowledge at all. Most days, I do not live on a mountaintop of any sort; rather, I poke along in the weeds, my eyes turned down toward my own path rather than out toward God and neighbor. Even then, of course, I retain a certain kind of knowledge of God: I can recite a long-memorized creed or summarize the views of a certain theologian. But the knowing I'm writing about here is not so readily articulated, nor is it easily lived. This kind of knowing discloses my complicity in harming land and water and charges me to repentance and restoration. It prods me to know and love those who are deemed worthless by the same society that valorizes my success, and to act for their good. It teaches me how to live in peace with my husband's first wife, the mother of our first daughter.

These last three sentences ring with obligation, as if the knowing I want to depict has to do primarily with learning to follow, and whenever possible to improve, rules regarding environmental standards, social policies, and familial behavior. And rules are an important part of the picture, to be sure. Recycle! Advocate! Observe boundaries! I take these obligations seriously and try to fulfill them. Alone, however, these lead not to healing but to fretfulness; they may uphold order and can improve conditions, but they do not bring joy or communion. Under these rubrics, I have found, I will never be able to do enough, even though I agree that I ought to do all I can, and even though I actually try to do so.

Instead, what I want to depict is a kind of knowing that allows one to recognize God's grace and healing, active in and for the world, and sometimes also to cooperate with it. Such knowing is not merely mental or even primarily moral, but rather is fueled by desire and carried in the body. Although my account of the meteor shower depicts one occasion on which I think I knew in this way, no single episode is adequate to a portrayal. The meaning of this occasion was only evident to me because it pointed to an encompassing narrative that renders a world beyond any particular moment — beyond the moment on the tailings and beyond the moment that is my entire life. I saw God at work making all things new, I believe, because I had already absorbed the story and the language of new creation. "We see images only insofar as we first hear them," the philosopher Paul Ricoeur insists. I had heard these images in the language of a community that carries a story of reconciliation between God and creation across the centuries. Moreover, this language had taken hold of me because as part of this community, the church, I had had some practice in performing it.

In the Family

When Ricki is around, I become aware of the loss that preceded the gains embodied in Mark's and my marriage and the family we have made together. When Mark and I began to date, I too had a failed marriage behind me; I knew loss even though I did not know parenthood. Our courtship involved no deception or scandal, and our marriage has been a great source of joy for both of us. At the same time, I felt then, and I continue to feel, that this is not exactly the way things should be — the parents of a little girl leaving one another and making new marriages, as both Mark and Ricki would do, confirming a rupture in which I am now implicated. In this era of widespread divorce and remarriage, some readers will think me overly scrupulous or will conclude that too many years in church have saddled me with guilt, but I hope that more charitable readers will see that some of the reconciliation looked for in this situation needs to take place, by God's grace, within me. I think that is what happened, in part, on the August night I have described, when I saw a precious child of Mark's and my marriage lying with Ricki under the stars.

But I am getting ahead of myself. My points: the situation I am describing was messy, and the practical wisdom that might allow one to know what to do, and how to do it, could never belong only to one of us. It needed to be forged in the fires of relationship.

Minimizing harm in this fraught and fragile family situation required the composure and good judgment of two estranged parents and two willing but inexperienced stepparents. Often our good intentions were expressed as rules, and (if I may say so) all four of us adults obeyed them remarkably well. As far as I can tell from my own observations and the child's behavior, none of us spoke about the others in negative terms in the presence of the child whose care we shared. (I refuse to remember or speculate on what may have been said when she was not around.) No one ever — and this is practically a miracle — failed to show up to meet a plane as our "unaccompanied minor" flew back and forth each month between Minneapolis and Chicago. Everyone fulfilled financial obligations without (audible) complaint. But it was hard, especially on our little girl, whose name is Kaethe. At six she suggested to me, in front of several neighbors, that I should marry her stepfather; then her parents could get married again, and she could come visit me and Peter one weekend each month. I realized right away that part of the meaning of her remark was that she loved me and wanted me to be in her life. Even so, her bald expression of desire for the more important thing — the reunion of her parents — shook me deeply.

How did practices of reconciliation take root in this messy family?

The short answer is that Kaethe's desire for a family that is whole overcame the adults' awkwardness about being in one another's presence. At the same time, the adults' desire to spend time at Holden created a centripetal force that pulled us all together in that place. Mark, Ricki, and their baby spent two summers together there; then Ricki and Kaethe went twice on their own. Beginning when she was four, Kaethe went to Holden each summer with first one set of parents and then the other, and soon with a growing number of siblings on each side as well. At first we made careful plans never to overlap our visits: How would that look to others? How would we manage it ourselves? Though hundreds of people are at Holden on any summer day, the village is compact; everyone lives in close quarters, eats in the same dining hall, and worships together each evening. As Kaethe grew in wisdom and stature and assertiveness, however, she insisted on a whole-family summer reunion, and soon this became an annual expectation not only for her but also for Mark's and my twins and Ricki and Peter's son, all born within months of one another and now fast friends.

Believe me, ours was no Brady Bunch: there were too many adults and too much history for that. And yet we managed, making little movements toward one another that created something new. In worship each evening, we passed the peace to one another. On Sundays, we communed together. I have a vivid memory of holding the chalice to Peter's lips and then to Ricki's, saying, "This is the blood of Christ, shed for you . . . this is the blood of Christ, shed for you," and receiving their warm, steady gazes as they drank. Once, when Mark and I canceled our trip at the last moment because forest fires were threatening the village, Ricki and Peter did the chores that would have been ours, simply filling without comment the gaps created by our absence. Though they said nothing, this became a gleeful topic of ironic village gossip when a man in the throes of a very difficult divorce realized what they were doing. "You have got to be kidding me! You are doing dish team for your ex????" This story is sometimes still told, and each of us has been asked at one time or another to counsel members of the extended Holden community who are going through divorces in which children are involved.

None of this would have happened if a little child had not led us. The practical wisdom required of me, I think, was to maintain a place for Kaethe in her father's family — which was beginning to get crowded with younger children — that allowed her the agency to lead us into the reconciliation for which she so deeply longed. Sometimes being wise meant overcoming passions that pulled me in other directions — especially my more intense, even physical, attachment to the children born to me, but also my constant awareness that Kaethe's mother could turn her against me with a word if she so chose. Perhaps I am being too pious here, but I think one crucial experience that prepared me to act wisely took place during a summer Mark and I could not go to Holden because I was pregnant with twins. After our then six-year-old returned from a journey with her mother and stepfather, she and I settled in for a summer of reading. Together we made our way through the entire Taize Picture Bible, discussing every surprising image and plot twist along the way. Discussing these stories with her, I believe, prepared me to weave them into the fabric of our even more complicated household in the years to come.

On the day our infant twins were baptized, Kaethe had a meltdown. Mark's and my attention, as well as that of the assembled aunts, uncles, and grandparents, had been diverted more than she could bear. What wisdom would bring us through this storm? First, we asked for help from dear neighbors whose daughter was the same age; as we had hoped, a break from babies and time with a friend of her own began to heal her woe. Second, we somehow got our infants fed and into their crib. And third, we put this older child, who had on that day been displaced in yet another way, at the center of attention. One of the activities she and I loved to share was cooking, and that year we had created an in-house cooking show, "Hey Good Lookin', Whatcha Got Cookin'?" We would don aprons and sing the old Hank Williams tune together, then she would cook the food I prepped and handed to her, explaining her moves to an imagined audience, pausing occasionally for commercial breaks advertising various household products. On this evening, my father was there with his video camera; the tape he shot is one of our most cherished possessions. In the background, two infants are bawling at the top of their lungs, and my mother is pleading, "Dorothy, you've got to come! Dorothy, please come feed them!" In the foreground, oblivious, a little girl is singing her heart out and showing her audience how to make English muffin pizzas, with the help of her stepmother/sous-chef and the advertising support of a line of hotpads, which she earnestly promotes during a commercial interruption. We finish our show with flair. (A few minutes later, I will confirm that the twins — and my mother — are just fine, too.)

A family is a small realm within which embodied saints and sinners repeatedly bump fists, elbows, and heads. Few families are simple, and even a cursory reading of the stories preserved by humankind across the centuries suggests that fraught and fragile families are not uncommon. Yet families are also workshops where ordinary women, men, and children can and do practice gazing with disciplined love upon those they are both stuck with and finally unable to control. Families are places where adults and kids can practice noticing resurrection, as deaths of one kind or another give way to new life. Families are places where we attempt the moves of forgiveness that we speak and perform in worship. Richard Gaillardetz, a Catholic husband, father, and theologian, says that marriage is the primary workshop in which he works out his salvation. His point could be applied, in different registers, to relationships between adults and kids; stepparents and stepchildren; exes and present partners; and siblings full, half, and step. This is "a very particular and demanding way of salvation," he writes, "a school of discipleship." The Bible is full of family stories with this kind of weight: one son is less favored by a parent than his brother is, or feels this to be so even if it is not; a woman feels slighted because she has to do all the work while her sister sits at Jesus' feet. Such stories, it turns out, tell the truths of our lives. Telling them to one another on Sundays, at bedtime, around tables, and in times of deep need is one of the practices that can help us to perceive and receive God's reconciling grace when it comes upon us. "Peace to you!" we might hear God saying to fussy kids or disgruntled spouses through one of these stories. "I have enough love for all of you, and as a result all of you have enough love for each other. There is plenty of love to go around. Now act that way. Peace to you in Jesus' name!"

In Society

Two famous biblical siblings are James and John, the sons of Zebedee, fishermen who were called from their nets to be among Jesus' first disciples. I have always pictured them as twins, though there is no warrant for this in the text. I have done this because I so identify with their mother.

Like her, I am proud of my children. And like her, I want to see them be successful: exalted, empowered, and honored by all. Oh, and close to Jesus too, of course. As Matthew's Gospel tells it, this mother adopts a humble posture; she kneels in front of Jesus while asking him for these favors. But what stands out is her ambition — ambition for her children, and perhaps indirectly for herself as well.

"What do you want?" Jesus asks her.

"Declare that these two children of mine will sit, one at your right hand and one at your left, in your kingdom," she replies.

"You do not know what you are asking," Jesus says to her. Then he turns to her two children and tells them that being with him will lead to suffering and death, without any guarantee of future glory.

In Mark's Gospel (10:35-45), James and John seek the same favors on their own behalf. (In other words, Mark, bless him, does not blame a woman for the misunderstanding of Jesus' mission that is embedded in the request.) In both versions, however, James and John gain nothing except the anger of their peers, who suspect right away that this family, whether two or three in number, is trying to grab seats of honor that they themselves desire. Jesus rebukes them all: "You know that the rulers of the Gentiles lord it over them, and their great ones are tyrants over them. It will not be so among you; but whoever wishes to be great among you must be your servant, and whoever wishes to be first among you must be your slave; just as the Son of Man came not to be served but to serve, and to give his life a ransom for many" (Matt. 20:20-28).

I identify with the mother of the sons of Zebedee because for me, as for her, one of the most challenging aspects of knowing how to live in the world that God is making new involves taking seriously the upside-down arrangements of wealth and power that Jesus announces and enacts. Sometimes I see it clearly: my privileged daughter is sharing a blanket with a woman whose life has been marred by poverty and oppression, and I know with all my mind, heart, soul, and strength that a leveling of power and possessions is how things should be, and how they are in fact when God's reconciliation is at hand: both have eaten well this day, both are with friends in a beautiful place, and both will sleep in safety this night. At other times, I can hear only the part of the story where Jesus says, "You do not know what you are asking." Infected by the zero-sum logic of my tribe — white, prosperous, and highly placed on the ladder of status and power our society upholds — I draw back, thinking of myself and my family rather than of those who have less. I don't mean to do this. It comes as if by second nature, through a knowing that integrates thought, action, and desire in pursuit of ends that are not of God. I don't know how to live in the world that God is making new because I am so comfortable, most of the time, in the world that is passing away.

And yet I also have and belong to a narrative that renders a world beyond the moment, and this narrative throws me off balance even when my grasping prevents it, for now, from shaking me off my prominent rung on that ladder. A longing to see God's reconciliation embodied in the social order has dogged me since my own teenaged years in New Jersey, when one of my pastors went off to march in Selma and another took our suburban youth group into Camden to meet with a minister and youth group there, not just once but across an entire year. Thanks to their preaching, that of others later on, and numerous teachers and peers, I have learned images I can now see embodied in the world around me: slaves forced to make bricks without straw, chariots destroyed in the sea, golden calves, widows and orphans, prophets true and false, the beggar Lazarus at a rich man's gate, a banquet hall disdained by the rich now filled with the poor. Moreover, I know that these images are meant to change me, and that some of them portray me.

Over the years, I have made sporadic, bumbling efforts to step into more active, helpful roles in these chapters of God's great story of reconciliation, though I can't say that I've so far acquired wisdom worth sharing here. My ideas, when it comes right down to it, run far ahead of where my desires are ready to propel me. Because I have shared life with others in a community that speaks often of justice and mercy for all, my mind is well stocked with images of a society ruled by servants rather than tyrants, and not infrequently I feel that my heart is breaking because this society is not yet realized. At the same time, I have to confess that I do not desire that world strongly enough to make direct participation in its realization my guiding purpose. I do not have, because I do not burn with desire for, knowledge that might sustain the sort of hands-on engagement that I eagerly bring to the care of my family.

In recent years, I have been learning not to let my terror at "You do not know what you are asking" blunt my support for those who respond more readily to Jesus' call to servanthood. I don't know how successful and exalted my son and daughter, now twenty-eight, will be in the eyes of the church or the world. However, it's pretty clear that the life they have been living in the presence of Jesus has made them more likely to be servants than potentates. Their desire for a world transformed has grown strong as they have shared conversations, homes, and meals with those who are poor over considerably longer periods than I have done. They have found freedom and mercy there.

During the year she turned twenty-three, Martha moved to a troubled neighborhood in an industrial city. As a member of the Lutheran Volunteer Corps (LVC), a national organization that places volunteers in service and advocacy jobs around the country, she lived with five other young adults in an old parsonage in Tacoma, Washington. Together, the housemates were supposed to craft a shared life shaped by LVC's three "core practices": simplicity/sustainability, community, and social justice. Five days a week — including all weekend days and holidays — she and Chad, a housemate, walked two miles to their jobs at Nativity House, a day shelter for homeless men and women founded by a Roman Catholic parish in Tacoma. I visited Martha's residence and workplace a couple of times during that year, and each time I was impressed by struggle, commitment, and early steps toward a practical wisdom attuned to justice and mercy for all.

Before moving to Tacoma, Martha and the others had to learn some rules. During a week of orientation conducted by LVC's national staff, she remembers, volunteers learned about the core practices and rehearsed embodied, specific ways of participating in them. Led by experienced activists, they practiced having "respectful conversations," staying safe in urban environments through "applied non-violence," and recognizing and combating racism. Remarkably, all six future housemates were placed in a single hotel room during orientation week — a stark initiation into communal living, and a signal of LVC's belief that the household they would share would be the community in which the core practices would be negotiated and enacted at the level of daily life, or not.

Community — negotiated around household chores and nurtured in conversations among peers encountering difficult issues at work and an unfamiliar standard of living at home — took shape as the arena (think both ancient Rome and contemporary rock music) in which the other two core practices were discussed and rehearsed. Of simplicity/sustainability, Martha recalled in response to my questioning at the end of the year, "We got $100 each for food each month, which we pooled for house meals, and less than $100 each month for personal spending, which is pretty little, as well as a bus pass. We were discouraged from bringing computers and cars. My house didn't have internet and we didn't have a car, either. This is not a particularly 'modern' way to live, and some communities probably cheat. But our community stuck it out. We all had longish commutes, which could make for long, exhausting days, but it also helped all of us to fall in love with our city — which we did. I loved bussing all around Tacoma on my days off, and I often saw people from Nativity House on the bus. This made me less separate from their reality and more of a true ally and neighbor to them. I felt so safe on the streets of Tacoma, really at any hour of night, because I knew everyone. I had a very expansive sense of family there, and I learned to trust in the power of kind words, hospitality/welcome, and nonviolent relationship, a power that extends beyond class/race divisions. I still practiced safety, don't get me wrong. . . ." (This last was clearly directed to the interviewer, her mother.)

Perhaps naïvely, perhaps wisely, Martha and her housemates tried out the upside-down quality of Christian thinking as they considered how their experiences did, or did not, embody LVC's core practice of social justice. Martha says that the rules encountered in orientation "helped everyone in my house to think critically about their workplaces. Are the people being served given an active voice in decision-making, or not? Are decisions made democratically or handed down from on high? Am I ever invited to share about myself personally with our homeless guests, or not? This was an endless topic of conversation. We also had the Catholic Worker house close by, a place with low boundaries and a lot of good authority/reputation among homeless people in Tacoma. I definitely wondered about boundaries a lot."

Struggling with rules about boundaries while entertaining a rule-defying desire for communion drew these young people onto more complicated terrain. "Should we never hang out with Nativity House guests outside of work, and never give out bus money to them from our own wallets?" Martha agonized. "This was something Chad and I and other staff puzzled over (and we did both things). It started to feel pretty inhuman to live a neatly boundaried life. It starts to seem more self-protective and limiting, rather than 'safe,' because safety is in God and in an abundance of relationships with others. We had some guests over for barbeque twice. Nevertheless, it remained confusing for many to discern how to transgress deadening boundaries, and I and others would have benefited from more serious reflection and guidance. I think so many of us at Nativity House especially were so overwhelmed by the poverty we encountered, all we wanted to do was be as close as possible because we loved the people so much." I have noticed in the years since Tacoma that Martha gives money to every homeless person she meets, wisely or unwisely but quickly, without deliberation, as if her body simply must act in this way.

What stands out to me in this report is the unexpected discovery of "love" in the midst of what would once have been alienating or scary realities — love for homeless guests and for Tacoma, both merging, upon reflection, with a strong, personal desire for the kind of realm Jesus proclaims. Something that may have been born in obligation is over time reshaped as love, the crucial virtue needed for life in this realm. Although the Lutheran Volunteer Corps did not require engagement in scripture and prayer, Martha's own temperament and training kept her close to these sources. That Nativity House was always open on Sundays and Holy Days was both a burden (she could not go to church) and a blessing (she was challenged to meet Christ there). Since her year in Tacoma, she has attended seminary while continuing to work in ministries and congregations that serve the homeless and develop housing options for the poor.

Many other experiences would be needed for the virtue and wisdom that may have been taking root in this young volunteer to develop further, including experiences of acknowledging and learning from mistakes. I observed one of these while volunteering at Nativity House one day during a visit to Tacoma. It is a minor episode, but one that demonstrates the kind of attentiveness to persons and actions that can eventually deepen into wise service. After finishing a clean-up task to which I'd been assigned, I found Martha at a lunch table and asked what I should do next. She answered me and then turned back to the man she had been talking with. He would not meet her eyes. He cursed her. He picked up the garbage bag that contained his belongings and hastened toward the door. She tried to reach him, but he refused to engage and continued out to the street and finally out of sight.

"I shouldn't have let you interrupt me," Martha remarked that evening. "He is so used to being disregarded that he took my turning away as an insult." How did she learn that? Had her supervisor taught her a rule, one she had forgotten when she made the more accustomed choice of replying to her mother? I had acted differently in a somewhat parallel situation many years before when I ignored my own mother's pleas and refused to interrupt my cooking show with Kaethe in order to feed my infant twins. But I had been thirty-six and in my own home, while Martha was twenty-three and new to her duties. Her mistake, and her prompt reflection on it, is just the sort of experience that lies along the path of developing expertise, as a novice's rational knowledge of rules becomes integrated as practical wisdom.

And what might I — a one-day volunteer — learn from this exchange? Do I know the rules that point toward justice and mercy in more than an abstract way? Am I able to integrate them into supple, wise, practical action? Is not seamlessly embodying regard for every person something all Christians need to learn to do as we wind our way through a world where so many are routinely disregarded?

Perhaps God is not finished with me yet. Consider what happens in the family of Zebedee. The nameless mother has not comprehended Jesus' message about the nature of his kingdom at the time of her request, but she will finally get it. She is one of three women specifically mentioned as those who watched from a distance as Jesus died (Matt. 27:56). After following him from Galilee and ministering to him, these three remain after all the disciples have fled, including the overconfident sons who have so recently said, "Yes, Lord, we are able to drink the cup that you drink." However, her children would return a few days later. I imagine all three — Mother, James, and John (where is Zebedee?) — among those who would soon form a new community in Jerusalem, breaking bread, praying, and holding all things in common.

In Creation

Both my story of interpersonal reconciliation after divorce and my account of learning to serve the homeless in Tacoma locate reconciliation in face-to-face relationships. However, this level of social organization is deeply entwined with other levels (macroeconomics and society-wide structures, for example), and some Christians participate in God's work of making society new in vocational settings that are less directly focused on direct service to the poor, for example in universities and seminaries. On this ground, some would say, I should be less harsh in assessing my own efforts, though I am not quite persuaded.

The account I offer next is painted on a bigger canvas. Near the center is the spot where my companions and I are gazing up at the meteor shower, around that is mountain terrain covering hundreds of square miles under a vast starry dome, and around that is the cosmos. Together, the beauty of this setting and the damage done by mineral extraction in these mountains point to a wrenching paradox that persistently disrupts my yearning for a creation that is fresh and whole. Creation's beauty is overwhelming. And the damage creation has already suffered is also overwhelming. The damage runs far beyond what was done by a mining operation across two decades of production. Climate change is melting the glaciers above Holden and contributing to the forests' infestation by deadly pests not previously seen in that region. Even in that remote location, the forces of destruction are gaining strength, while in other parts of the world destruction is far advanced. Personal efforts to resist the direction of environmental degradation — recycling, curtailing energy use, taking public transportation, and other green activities — are helpful, but scientists argue that steps of much greater scope, undertaken at the level of global energy production and use, are necessary to forestall disaster.

Ways of addressing climate change and other forms of environmental degradation are emerging through global activism, the development of alternative energy sources, and the cleanup of environmental damage (which is now under way at Holden). Meanwhile the moves most readily available to me and most of my acquaintances are of the hands-on kind, and we are gradually learning to embrace practices of care for creation at this level, incrementally reducing carbon emissions. Yet in the midst of efforts large and small, the prospect of global doom hangs over us. In this context, God's promise to make all things new is both comfort and challenge. Amid the prevailing gloom, embracing practices of care for creation as responses to God's promise can change our practices from expressions of fear into offerings of hope. What wisdom might arise from and make possible practices undertaken in this spirit?

The first time I visited Holden, one small episode evoked a love and concern for creation that have not left me. The episode centers on a Sierra cup. Back in the early 1980s, before giardia infections became common, hikers in the mountains of the American West carried these simple cups looped on our belts, where they would be close at hand to scoop cold, delicious water from each fresh stream along the trail. One sunny July day, getting where Mark and I wanted to go required a difficult passage across a field of boulders — nothing technical, but something I could just barely manage then and would not attempt at all today. Partway across, my Sierra cup dropped from my waist into the space between two boulders, where it lay like a piece of street litter in a pool of water several feet below my position. My first thought marked me as the lazy, wasteful consumer I was and am: "Oh well, it only cost a dollar, I'll get another one." But the beauty of this place, marred now by my litter, rebuked me. It took a long time and lots of hard work, but I retrieved the cup. This is a tiny example, but I remember it now when I see other places where human waste and sloth strew ugliness on the earth.

Developing eyes with which to notice creation's need, motivation to protect its beauty, and the physical strength to correct damage and waste are among the moves humankind will need to make in this century. As practices contributing to a way of life oriented to the well-being of creation develop among us, they can become sources of joy as well as obligation. I see this already among urban gardeners, bicycling commuters, and suburban composters. How much deeper and farther can such joy propel us? Can our vision and desire help our behavior catch up with our ideas, forging a way of knowing that equips us to respond to God's promise and creation's need?

While my daughter was learning to serve the poor in Tacoma, her brother, John, was learning and teaching a way of life committed to creation care as a leader of camping trips for youngsters in the mountains of Montana. During an intense period of training, he memorized hundreds of rules and regulations about everything from housekeeping on the trail (food safety, waste disposal, setting up tents) to interpersonal relations (when to touch or not touch the young campers, how to deal with injuries or misbehavior, and so on). Surrounding this instruction was a framework that encouraged the campers to notice God's presence and to grow in the life of Christian faith. Worship began and ended each day, led at first by the administrators of this Lutheran camp, then by more experienced counselors, and then by all the counselors in turn. Later, each counselor would lead his or her charges in song, reflection, and prayer. In addition, counselors-in-training engaged in close study of scripture, led by a theologian brought in to explore the summer's chosen texts, so that they in turn could lead Bible studies with their campers on the trail.

Each Sunday afternoon in July and August, groups of campers arrived, had a few rules and regulations drilled into them, piled their gear into vans, and headed into the mountains to set up their tents. On each of the next five days — rain or shine, buggy or blustery — they hiked several miles, gear on their backs, before settling in for the night. Throughout, they practiced a way of life. At the end of his second summer, John responded eagerly to my invitation to share his experiences, which interested me not only because he is my son but also because church camps are widely regarded as influential settings of faith formation. We sat at our dining room table at home as he shared vivid memories of recent experience and pondered what he and his campers had learned.

"In the wilderness," John told me, "we live simply, in ways these kids could hardly imagine before being there. You can't take much stuff at all; you are down to the basics. And you get dirty — the whole American culture of clean has to be left behind. There can't be any makeup or hairspray, because these attract bears and bugs. There is a realness, a lightness, a simplicity that turns out to be really fun and liberating. The practices of daily life are different from at home. Take food, for example. It takes a long time to prepare, most of your day, in fact. You prepare it together, eat it together, and sit around together for a long time afterwards. Then you clean up together and crawl into shared tents together. The space and the conversation are more intimate than these kids are used to. Many almost never share meals and conversation at home."

Everyday practices — deliberately embraced and reflected on — invited campers to experience themselves and their world in a recognizable but notably different way. "The way you live in time is different too. We leave clocks and watches behind and go to sleep when we are tired (and we do get tired, because we are exerting ourselves all the time). We get up when rested and eat when hungry. We find a shared rhythm. And we care for creation. We work hard to leave no trace of our presence and to do nothing that might harm the water, land, or animals we encounter."

The exigencies of life in a wilderness area required campers to relinquish, for these few days, competitive, individualistic patterns of relating to others. "Everyone has to depend on one another," John told me. "If we are going to eat and get where we are going, everyone has to pitch in. And when someone can't, when they need help, they have to ask for help." The fragmented quality of everyday life in the cities and towns from which these kids had come was also challenged. "You can't take too big a group, and the group develops cohesion and integrity: the same people are together for devotions, meals, work. These practices are not split apart like at home. So you end up talking more freely, including about the Bible. What we say in devotions is with us all day or all night. The Bible comes alive." The biblical and liturgical frame this Lutheran camp program places around each day is probably seen by some participants as the price of a great hiking experience in Glacier National Park. However, for some — and surely for the several counselors I know, John's friends — the Bible did come alive in vivid experiences of day and night under God's care, meals shared at the table of creation, and the mutual forgiveness that is necessary if life together is to flourish.

By the end of the second summer, John was still a novice in the various skills needed for this work: mountaineering, the care and discipline of teenagers, the teaching of the Bible, first aid, camp cooking, and more. What impresses me, however, is the integration of all of these into a dawning way of knowing, being, and loving that may continue to grow, in other settings all his life long, into a practical wisdom that serves abundant life. I glimpsed this at one point in particular, when he was responding to a question shaped by my own rather sentimental biblical enthusiasm. Trying to turn our conversation to God, I suggested that amazing views must be a big part of the trip, evoking awe at God's beautiful creation. "This is really not the main point theologically," John replied. "You don't want to give the impression that all that hard work is just for the sake of a reward like that. Campers' evaluations rarely mention this, or if they do it is not as a key point. You can get lots of great views quickly from an SUV; in a week's hike you might see one or two. If you talk about the trip afterwards, they will want to tell you the stories. They don't want to stay in the wilderness, but they know they have really accomplished something in being there. What really matters is not the view but the quality of life we share while getting there."

The question I had asked to evoke these reflections from a man not yet twenty-two years of age was this: "What is the difference between what you can do in ministry with young people at camp and what can be done in our home congregation in a small city in Indiana?" In the years since, it has become more clear to both of us that John's ability to see the importance of the practices he described had emerged from a long process, which began in our local congregation but also included several other communities along the way. Since this conversation, John has continued to study scripture, theology, and creation care in an M.Div. program and to work as a leader in communities of faith. Thus I want to acknowledge that his insight continues to grow and that these are not his last words on the subject.

Mortal and Yet at Home

"I can only choose within the world that I can see," Iris Murdoch declared.

"Yes," I reply. "And I can only see a world that is whole when I see it illumined and transformed by the gift and promise of God."

The huge pile of mining waste from the top of which my companions and I watched the Perseid meteor shower comprises more than 98 percent of the material extracted from Copper Mountain between 1937 and 1957. For the sake of that which was thought precious, much that was ordinary was dislodged, crushed, and left to dry in bleak orange piles. Looking at all this wasted rock, we wonder about other forms of waste: in nature, in society, in our own lives, and in the lives of others.

In the center of Holden Village stands a tree sculpted from some of the 2 percent that was carried away. Noted metal artist Paula Mary Turnbull, a Sister of the Holy Names, forged the trunk and limbs of this tree from old pipes used in the mining operations and crafted the leaves and fruit from copper produced by the mine, which she salvaged when it was torn off some rooftops in Spokane. The sculpture is a rendering of the tree of life, which grew in Eden and will flourish at the end of time in the city of God, when the new heaven and the new earth come to fulfillment here, in this world that God so loves. This is a tree whose leaves are for the healing of the nations. This is a tree whose flourishing shows forth the healing of the earth itself. The sculpture "sees" the refuse of the mine, of society, and of our lives through the lens of God's gift and promise as depicted in the book of Revelation:

> Then I saw a new heaven and a new earth; for the first heaven and the first earth had passed away, and the sea was no more. And I saw the holy city, the new Jerusalem, coming down out of heaven from God, prepared as a bride adorned for her husband. And I heard a loud voice from the throne saying,
>
> > "See, the home of God is among mortals.
> > He will dwell with them;
> > they will be his peoples,
> > and God himself will be with them;
> > he will wipe every tear from their eyes.
> > Death will be no more;

> mourning and crying and pain will be no more,
> for the first things have passed away." . . .
>
> Then the angel showed me the river of the water of life, bright as crystal, flowing from the throne of God and of the Lamb through the middle of the street of the city. On either side of the river is the tree of life with its twelve kinds of fruit, producing its fruit each month; and the leaves of the tree are for the healing of the nations. Nothing accursed will be found there any more. (Rev. 21:1-4; 22:1-3a)

John of Patmos recorded this vision during a time when the world seemed to be controlled by overwhelming evil. And yet the vision overflows with the promise of abundant life in this world, for this world. Today, when members of the community that still treasures and teaches John's book ponder this vision, we too see the world in the light of God's promises. And when we see the world in this way, we are summoned to inhabit it differently.

To perceive the promises in which God continues to wrap the world is to be invited to live in the reconciliation God already provides, even during this time when all creation — families, society, the planet — groans for fulfillment. Trusting these promises, we may recognize the homes of humankind as the habitations of God and the channels of God's grace. These habitations take shape through everyday practices, as ordinary people make space for others, responding to God who is everywhere at home. Slowly, uncertainly, we learn to pitch our tents on the ground of the one God sent to pitch his tent among us (John 1:14). Such tents provide shelter, however inadequately, for displaced six-year-olds, disregarded homeless men, and discouraged environmentalists. And they provide shelter, as well, for their imperfect hosts — the flawed and finite children of God who are called to witness to God's love. See, the home of God is among mortals.

References

The opening story is set at Holden Village, a retreat center in the North Cascade Mountains of Washington State. Holden's vision is "the love of God making new the church and world through the cross of Jesus Christ." Learn more about Holden at www.holdenvillage.org. From 2012 to 2016, the area impacted by the copper mine has been undergoing a major EPA-mandated remediation of environmental damage.

The passage from Psalm 148 read by two women on the mountaintop is from *The Psalter* as translated by the International Commission on English in the Liturgy (Chicago: Liturgy Training Publications, 1994). All other biblical quotations in this chapter are from the New Revised Standard Version.

My description of how my experience as a modern person frames my assumptions is based on Charles Taylor's account of the social imaginary of the immanent frame, as set forth in his book *A Secular Age* (Cambridge: Harvard University Press, 2007) and summarized in the chapter in the present volume entitled "Framing"; the quotation is from Taylor, *A Secular Age,* p. 550. This chapter began as an effort to depict my own "itinerary" of openness to transcendence.

In pondering "Recycle! Advocate! Observe boundaries!" I engage the distinction between rules-driven thinking and practical wisdom. See also Christian Scharen's chapter "Eclipsing" in this volume; Charles Taylor, "To Follow a Rule," in *Philosophical Arguments* (Cambridge: Harvard University Press, 1995); and work on practical wisdom by Barry Schwartz, Patricia Benner, Hubert Dreyfus, and Stuart Dreyfus. In *A Secular Age,* Taylor argues that humans cannot fully escape the nomocratic-judicialized-objectified world, but he also insists that it is terribly important to see that that is not all there is. "We should find the centre of our spiritual lives beyond the code, deeper than the code, in networks of living concern, which are not to be sacrificed to the code, which must even from time to time subvert it. This message comes out of a certain theology, but it could be heard with profit by everybody" (p. 743). Notice that I add to these interpretations of the role of rules a concern that is deeply rooted in my own Lutheran tradition, which affirms that trying to earn one's salvation through good works is not only impossible; it also undermines joy and increases dread.

The quotation from Paul Ricoeur is from "Imagination in Discourse and Action," in *From Text to Action II,* trans. Kathleen Blamey and John B. Thompson (Evanston: Northwestern University Press, 2007), p. 174. Ricoeur also emphasizes the formative power of belonging to a narrative that renders the world beyond a given moment.

For the section on the family, I thank Kaethe Schwehn, Fredrika Thompson, and Mark Schwehn for allowing me to use their stories here. My request for such permission led to rich and wonderful conversations between me and Ricki about the dynamics of step-parenting and to mutual expressions of our joy in the reconciliation we and those we love have been given amid the experiences I recount here. Kaethe (pronounced Kay-da) has published *Tailings: A Memoir* (Eugene, OR: Cascade Books, 2014) about a year she spent at Holden as a young adult. The quotation about the family as a school of discipleship is from Richard R. Gaillardetz, *A Daring Promise: A Spirituality of Christian Marriage* (New York: Crossroad, 2002), pp. 136-37.

For the section "In Society," I thank Martha Schwehn Bardwell for her thoughtful remarks and for allowing me to use them in this chapter. All of the quotations from Martha were written by her in reports or spoken to me in interviews shortly after her volunteer year ended. Her views and her wisdom have continued to grow in the years since then. For more on LVC, see www.lutheranvolunteercorps.org.

For the section on creation, I thank John Rohde Schwehn for his thoughtful remarks and for allowing me to use them in this chapter. When John and Martha were in high school, they and I were among the authors of a book that prepared us for these conversations about the practices they were engaging at this later point in their lives, Dorothy C. Bass and Don C. Richter, *Way to Live: Christian Practices for Teens* (Nashville: Upper Room, 2003).

In the final section, the Iris Murdoch quotation is from *The Sovereignty of Good* (New York: Routledge & Kegan Paul, 1970), p. 37. The NRSV translation of John 1:14 does not mention a tent, but Raymond E. Brown's commentary on this passage emphasizes the importance of the verb *skenoun* ("make a dwelling; pitch a tent") and its Old Testament associations. Israel was told to make a tent (the Tabernacle), which became the site of God's localized presence among the people; prophetic discourse drew on the image of a tent to describe a form of God's promised presence with the people; and Wisdom sang that "The Creator of all . . . chose the spot for my tent." In Brown's reading of John's Gospel, Jesus Christ is "the new Tabernacle of divine glory." See Brown, *The Gospel according to John,* vol. 1, Anchor Bible Commentary (Garden City, NY: Doubleday, 1966), pp. 32-35.

dancing

MOVES AND RHYTHMS THAT ENGAGE LOCAL WISDOM

JAMES R. NIEMAN

MY ROMANCE WITH STONEHILL LUTHERAN CHURCH began over a decade ago when I spoke at a pastoral conference hosted there. One of those picture-postcard white clapboard buildings that dot the upper Midwest landscape, it's the kind of place conjured by your memory when asked to imagine a rural church. So classic was this particular structure, delicately poised atop a scenic hilltop, that through the years its photo graced insurance agency Christmas cards, the covers of farm magazines, or the local fuel oil dealer's free calendar. The image was iconic for the best of rural life: a slower pace, simpler ways, and open spaces, all with the beloved church at the crest of it all, a beacon for what's good and true.

Such are the tender lies of any budding romance, the self-posturing that creates a strong first impression. Churches are central to rural life — why, look where they're built, atop scenic knolls the better to be admired by all. A moment's scrutiny, though, shows the implausibility of this. When Stonehill was organized in 1855 and the building constructed not long thereafter, arable land was a rare and hard-won commodity. Lacking modern machinery, farmers in those days fought to claim the earth they might till for crops by felling timber, draining bogs, dragging stones. When the time came to build a church, someone would sacrifice part of an acreage for the purpose, but it didn't have to be the most useful part. Church buildings were erected not on the best land with a prized view but in places beyond recovery, unfit for crops or livestock. Perhaps that's why such pragmatism was glossed over by ennobling a church with the lofty name of a holy mountain, as if it were a latter-day Zion or Salem or Horeb.

Stonehill's founders were at least a bit more honest. The name plainly declared its rocky perch, with land enough for a building and a modest cemetery besides. Still, it was undeniably scenic and incontestably historic, the oldest congregation among its neighbors in northern Sherman County. The charm it evoked of another era led to a deep affection for the place among Lutherans across the area, who saw the old church as their own, even though most attended elsewhere. This affection also explains why Stonehill was always first on the rotation of regular sites for convening the local pastoral conference. It was refreshing, grounding, for these pastors to return annually to this precious spot as the last snows were melting and the earth smelled rich with promise.

This is where I was invited to speak, my first acquaintance with a place so revered by all. The conference ran most of the day, starting with prayer, then two presentations by me, punctuated at the midpoint by lunch. My romance began during that lunch and without warning. That point alone is worth mentioning. When people in my line of research look at congregations, it's often with a plan in mind. That's a good thing. You might start with a hunch that a particular place would be interesting or carefully conclude that it would be especially representative and revealing. Stonehill was not like that. Common, plain, without surprise, it's not the kind of church you would choose to study, let alone develop an elaborate plan for so doing. That's surely what I thought until lunch.

As I said, the church building itself, where the main portion of the conference was held, stood on a cramped clearing. So rocky was the place that no basement had been excavated when the foundation was built. The land with any soil depth at all was reserved for the cemetery, where digging down was required. Therefore, the church lacked underground space for cooking and fellowship, essentials for any rural congregation. Stonehill worked out an alternative solution to this plight that set it apart from every other congregation in the area. It later constructed a second building on a completely separate property one-half mile from the main church. Built late in the nineteenth century, it was Stonehill's fellowship hall, kitchen, and meeting space. This was where the conference participants reassembled at midday for lunch, the place where part of its surprising story slowly unfolded.

Thirty or so pastors crowded through the doorway of this "newer" building, a massive structure perhaps forty feet wide, seventy-five feet deep, and two stories tall. Capped by a peaked roofline running front to back, the building towered thirty feet above grade, noticeably larger than the original church building itself. Guests entered directly into an open room arrayed with more than twenty long tables, each easily able to seat ten persons. Stretched along most of the left wall of the first floor was a complete commercial-grade kitchen, likely last upgraded in the mid-1950s. The implications of this scene alone were worth pondering. At the time this building was constructed, industrial America prospered mightily, but rural life faced economic catastrophe, as it often had. Why, then, would this congregation choose to build a place capable of feeding, at a single sitting, a group whose size would have exceeded its own total membership by over half?

Farmers, who predominate in the history and membership of places like Stonehill, are pragmatists and patient planners. When they expended the land, money, and personal labor to build this second structure over a century ago, they didn't accidentally miscalculate, ending up with something well beyond their membership needs. They evidently had something beyond themselves in mind — but what? My best guess at this early point was that they were thinking of the wider community, and later study confirmed that to be true. Across the decades, this place served the needs of social clubs, scout troops, township meetings, and so forth. The sheer dimensions of this outsized building underscored this church's claim to responsibility and risk, the duty one owes others coupled with a venture about a future still unseen. But was it just as simple as that, merely a question of civic-mindedness?

There was another floor above this fellowship space, and I was eager to learn what it had to tell. To reach the second story, I climbed the long stairway stretching along the kitchen side of the main floor. The top of that stairway opened directly onto a vast, unbroken meeting hall as large as the building's entire footprint. An open peaked ceiling and rafters floated above, sturdy oak floorboards stretched beneath, and tall sash windows let light stream in along each of the two longer walls. As I emerged at the top of the stairs along the left side of the room, my natural inclination was to gaze right, across to the opposite wall with its four bright windows. I shall never forget this simple, natural glance to the right, because in that one instant I knew something was wrong — or, perhaps more accurately, askew.

The floor was sloped. Judging by the modestly decreasing distance between the bottom of each window frame and the floor, there was an unmistakable slope to the floor, running from the rear of the building toward its front. It was barely perceptible, maybe two inches of drop for every ten feet of run. You could feel it immediately when stepping from the stairway onto the floor itself. I recall how quickly the pastors who also went upstairs dismissed this phenomenon. "The building settled," concluded one. "Shoddy construction," opined another. But I had repaired structures nearly as old as this one and their claims just didn't ring true. The molding joints near the floor or on the window frames were still tight and true. The plaster walls showed neither cracks nor bulges. And to stride across the floorboards was to feel something solid and sure beneath your feet, nothing springy or sagging.

I thought back to those pragmatic, patient, planning farmers who surely built this place with some sort of purpose, a story perhaps lost to us forever. It's so easy to imagine that what you cannot initially explain is the product of thoughtlessness or chance rather than a rationality you haven't yet grasped. Was it possible that this sloping floor was, in fact, intentional? "Of course," said yet another pastor, "it's built like a theater, to improve visibility." But if that were true, then visibility of what? Turning toward the front of the building, the low point of the slope, instead of an expected stage or platform was — nothing, only a blank plaster wall. There was no natural orientation or focal point in the downward direction of the sloping floor. Even if there had been, my quick inspection from several different angles showed that a slope of little more than a foot over the room's entire length failed to improve visibility. For seeing over other people, a theater's floor has a far sharper grade.

The story of the sloping floor was not unfolding easily. Why would farmers facing hard living and limited resources build far more than they'd ever need, and with a structural quirk both harder to design and costlier to build than conventional construction? More to the point, why would they do this as *church?* Just as statistical data do not self-interpret, so also artifacts, including human-designed spaces, do not speak for themselves. Such items are surely traces of human practices and the aims those practices bear, but beyond a certain point their story falls silent. They can tell their story in use, when we observe them deployed for specific tasks laden with deeper meanings. In action, we can see an ordinary chair as throne or a simple cup as chalice. But what can be learned when no active use is available, when an artifact sits mute and inert as in a museum display? What do we say about the floor of a room no longer in regular use and, judging by the accumulated dust, not having been in use for quite a while? Short of written records, informative labels, or detailed instructions, you seek an interpreter, a voice to broker past usage to present questions.

Of the handful of Stonehill members who hosted us for lunch, I found the two oldest and began to ask questions. Vern and LeRoy were in their eighties, sons of the congregation and, as it turned out, from founding families. LeRoy's great-grandfather had given the land on which the main church building and cemetery were located. Better still, Vern's grandfather actually helped to build the structure in which we now stood. Pay dirt, I thought.

"What's the story with the floor upstairs?" I asked Vern. "Oh, the slope?" he laughed, as if he expected the question. "You know why this place was built, don't ya?" I stared back, blank faced, with no idea. "Everyone today calls this the fellowship hall, but back when they put this up, it was the youth hall. Not like little kids. High school and older, young folks in their twenties, like that. They needed a place to meet and socialize, so the church thought it would be smart to build a nice place for that." So we were standing in a monument to late nineteenth- and early twentieth-century youth ministry. How odd to think of it that way, in a time when we make a cottage industry of our desperate preoccupation with appealing to young people. We evidently are not the first to be so concerned.

By this time, we had worked our way back upstairs — men in their mid-eighties don't climb stairs quickly, especially while talking. "So what's that got to do with the floor?" I pressed. "Everything," Vern shot back. "It's about dancing — as in not having any. Big space like this, young fellas and ladies, ya want 'em to mingle, but not dance. So they sloped the floor." "How does *that* matter?" I asked. "Try it," Vern said.

So I stepped toward the middle of the room and tried, wondering what sort of steps might have come naturally to late nineteenth-century bachelor farmers and their prospective belles. I opted for the sweeping circles of the waltz, holding an imaginary partner as I slowly twirled across the floor and Vern and LeRoy laughed. Almost immediately, my left hip began to hurt, followed by an occasional twinge in the right, along with the odd sense that at any moment I might just tip over or totter backward. What about something more regular and sturdy, I thought, like the mechanized routing of a square dance? Fine for a few straight steps and a do-si-do or two, but one quick turn or backing step and the floor made it clear that this dance wouldn't be for long. After a few other attempts, I quickly exhausted my already impoverished repertoire of pre–Second World War dance moves, and yet not one worked with ease or grace in this unconventional room. Only standing, walking, or sitting would happen here without a second thought. "Y'see?" said Vern. "T'ain't pretty. Problem solved." "What problem?" I wondered aloud. Not answering me directly, Vern moved to what really mattered. "Ya know, we're Norwegians here. Folks back then was just following Hauge."

Vern's thickly encoded remark was meant as rationale for the whole quirk of the sloping floor: Hauge — a name symbolically significant for congregations founded by immigrant Norwegian Lutherans. It was a code I was meant to understand immediately or remain confounded forever. Whether in Norway or America, Haugeans were a pietistic lay movement comprised of those who read and affirmed the writings of lay preacher Hans Nielsen Hauge (1771-1824). On this side of the Atlantic, Hauge's name was associated with a brand of moral strictness and personal severity. Hard work, spiritual devotion, and abstemiousness were the creed of the movement. Haugeans represented a kind of Puritanism on the prairie, orderly and controlled. I was supposed to grasp that this would have naturally also included a prohibition on dancing. Thus, the sloping floor. "Ahh," I sighed, "Hauge."

Satisfied that I had finally absorbed the point, Vern sauntered away to speak with other pastors exploring the anti-ballroom. In the next moment, though, LeRoy, who had been silent up until now, moved close to me and said in lowered, conspiratorial tones, "It wasn't quite that way." A bit older than Vern, LeRoy was a retired pastor, one of several this tiny congregation had produced over a century and a half. In fact, LeRoy had served as a military chaplain during the Second World War, followed by fourteen years as a missionary in Japan, and finally as pastor of several different congregations stateside. This unassuming, mustachioed old man with twinkling blue eyes, who always appeared on the verge of telling a joke or giving a compliment, had seen the world during his ministry. Only later did I learn that he was personally responsible for translating the hymnal used by the fledgling Japanese Lutheran church.

LeRoy continued to unravel his little secret. "When I was living in Japan, one time I was at the Lutheran school there. A couple of Norwegian missionaries were teaching there at the time, so we got together one evening to talk about where we were from, our homes and churches, like that. Of course I had to tell 'em about this floor here and the Haugeans, but those fellas started laughing. 'You Americans always blame Hauge,' they said, 'but he was a businessman! He smoked, he drank, he even danced! He wasn't against those things. Your story must be wrong.' Well, I didn't know what to say," LeRoy concluded, "but I found out they were right."

Indeed they were. Hauge's main concern in late eighteenth-century Norway was not moral strictness but the state church and its abuse of power. He called for greater lay authority, spoke openly in congregations about the need for such reform, and for his efforts spent over a decade in prison, convicted of preaching without ordination. The moral dimensions of his work did not focus on specific activities, whether dancing or anything else, but on a call for spiritual awakening and individual faithfulness. In larger frame, the real threat that Hauge evidently represented was economic, in his call for personal productivity and communally shared wealth that could also provide for the sick and destitute. To be sure, his name was later used among some immigrants to appeal for heightened moral strictness, but that was never part of Hauge's program of reform. Even had it been, though, the "Haugean influence" theory of the sloping floor didn't work for a more basic reason: no such faction was ever part of Stonehill's history.

So what was the real story here? I soon realized that most attempts to account for the floor were internally focused, as if the congregation were simply its own self-contained processes, membership, and resources. Was a wider picture needed? Purely by coincidence, I was at the time studying a small Methodist congregation elsewhere in Sherman County. During that work, I learned how Methodism spread through this part of Wisconsin, starting with gatherings of Welsh immigrant lead miners in the southern part of the county, and spreading eventually to a flood of churches across the county's northern reaches as well. In the early generations of the Stonehill church, then, their closest church neighbors were these Wesleyans, including rather strict groups of Primitive Methodists. Turning wider still, by the 1870s statewide and national conventions of Methodists voiced opposition to various "immoral" public activities. They joined forces with anti-saloon leagues and, of special interest, objected to "social dancing." If this was the religious milieu in which the farmers of Stonehill planned and built their youth hall, did it offer at least some rationale for the sloping floor?

In the end, there was no way to know for sure. It had become clear that these Lutherans had told themselves an acceptable internal story to account for this eccentric construction decision. It was about devotion, control of the body for the sake of the soul, a theology that seemed to fit with what Haugeans were supposed to believe. As already noted, the story didn't hold water because Hauge never espoused such beliefs and Haugeans had never been a force within the congregation, but that was a minor inconvenience. The accepted story served another purpose, to reinforce an appropriate ethnic and religious identity during the risky transmission of that identity to a new generation in changing times. After all, the sloping floor was in a building constructed for the *youth*. The durability of this account, despite LeRoy's counter-narrative, proved how effective the sloping floor and its accompanying explanation had been at conveying what it meant to be a good Lutheran.

What was lost along the way, though, may have been an alternative story that was just as revealing about the practical wisdom of the Stonehill church. If you're going to expend the energy and resources to build a much-needed second structure, you might as well venture a risk and make it valuable to as many people as possible. That's pragmatism coupled with community spirit. But if your larger community mainly consists of strict Wesleyans worried about moral laxity, they won't use the building you've offered, at least not without a few adjustments. Is it such a loss to incorporate their concerns about social dancing and, in a subtle but ingenious way, control against a dreaded outcome? It's easy to see this today in suspicious terms as a devious regime of constraint or capitulation to an outside ideology of control. But if you're a nineteenth-century farmer, maybe the landscape looks a little different. The folks to whom you sell your livestock, the ones who help you during the harvest, these are people with whom you've spent a lot of time, hearing their thoughts and dreams, not to mention their anxieties about a world gone awry. Is it so implausible to imagine the sloping floor as a kind of gift, a sign of mercy to worried Methodists? Maybe the deeper story of that floor is the willingness to set aside your own needs for the sake of your neighbor. Or maybe that's just a fanciful tale.

It would take more exposure at Stonehill to test which theological story was true. In the end, I came to see both accounts as fundamental to the congregation's deepest beliefs. On the one side, they were clear about their identity, sometimes even using an implausible history to assert who they were and what they believed as Lutherans. Yet, on the other hand, they had learned the art of holding that identity lightly, equally concerned to pay attention to their neighbors near and far. These two theological stories — clarity about one's faith and embrace of the surrounding world — played out far beyond the long forgotten construction of a youth hall and its peculiar sloping floor. They surfaced in other times and arenas as well: preparing young people to become pastors and missionaries, deploying rich song and homespun rituals when burying the dead, advocating on county boards for various causes, and choosing a certain altar painting to dominate the sanctuary. Gradually, I learned that while these two stories cannot encompass all there is to say about Stonehill, they do resound as guiding tones throughout this congregation's ordinary existence, carriers of its own special practical wisdom.

Recognizing Wisdom in Faith Communities

After seeing the practical wisdom embedded in congregations, it's only natural to wonder how this wisdom arises. While sometimes we can eventually know this in rather sketchy form, my experience is that these origins usually remain remote and forgotten. It is instead more important simply to recognize *that* this wisdom exists in congregations in the first place, since we are familiar with the idea of wise *individuals* but strain to imagine how a *community* can have that same capacity. Though we may never uncover the longer history of shared wisdom, what really matters is to highlight it in action, not least of all so a congregation can recover a potent resource to navigate its own times of change and stress. But in order to do this, a new challenge arises: cultivating wisdom among those who look at churches so they can discern and explore communal wisdom when it appears. Just how does that investigative wisdom happen?

To answer this, let me interrupt my narratives of practical wisdom in congregations with something atypical: a few briefer accounts of how I came to recognize communal wisdom. These are simply my stories alone, of course, but they bear strong similarities to what I have heard from others who study congregational life. Sometimes you start to look at these communities like a formal researcher, using tools refined in disciplined social research. In other cases, you may lack all such preparation, plunged instead into church life for other reasons entirely (such as pastoral leadership, which was my case). Either way, though, there tend to be breakthrough moments where your assumptions about a congregation, whether drawn from a dominant social theory or a treasured ministry model, are broken open in surprising ways. From then on, these breakthroughs (and over time there are many) evolve into a kind of pattern language. Later on, in an unfamiliar situation, you recognize again *not exactly* what first surprised you long ago but *something like* it, a pattern of practices that alerts your senses and impels you to explore further. This pattern is then subjected to wider investigation, often in concert with those refined tools and pastoral skills, until the local practical wisdom of a place finally comes into greater clarity.

But that's all fairly abstract. How did that happen for me with Stonehill? Though I couldn't say so at the time, I know now that an incident in a congregation that I once served as pastor generated a pattern that prepared me much later to raise questions about the sloping floor of the fellowship hall. That incident involved a hymnal. My second call was to an urban church comprised almost entirely of Alaskan Natives, and their historic, preferred hymnal consisted of four-part, shape-note gospel harmonies and texts from the late nineteenth and early twentieth centuries. These hymns were tilted decidedly toward end-times imagery, derided by outsiders for their "pie in the sky by and by" theology, with language and melodies that sounded quite at odds with the Lutheran roots of the congregation. Denominational officials were blunt with me that, as soon as possible, I should replace this hymnal with one more attuned to the orthodoxies and ethnicities predominant in American Lutheranism. Clearly, they argued, the members didn't know how inappropriate and retrograde these hymns really were. When given a better option, they would surely become more spiritually sound and faithful.

Fortunately the replacement never happened. To some degree, this was because I was subsumed in the pastoral urgencies of a congregation mired in poverty, dysfunction, alcohol, and violence. In larger measure, though, the weekly worship itself exposed the flaws in those assertions about the hymnal and its use. For example, while the style and details of Sunday worship were more casual and flexible than those of other nearby Lutheran churches, the congregation still followed the form of the historic Western eucharistic *ordo*. The hymns might have been unusual for this denomination, but the overall worship patterns were not. That's because the members were mainly third- and fourth-generation Lutherans introduced to the faith long ago in their rural, home villages. They thoroughly knew Luther's *Small Catechism* but were also quite comfortable speaking to the spirit of the salmon they dip-netted from the local streams. And it wasn't just religiously that these members negotiated a dual reality. Every day at work, in stores and businesses, during public encounters, they were treated with a corrosive disregard that reduced them to living as non-persons in a white-dominated world.

Far from being unaware, these members were deeply attuned to their setting and their traditions, operating with delicate nuance in nearly every facet of their lives. The same was true of the hymns they sang during worship. By holding onto songs first taught to their ancestors, music with a striking similarity to the tones and harmonies in Native Alaskan chants, they preserved a heritage that gave stability and strength in difficult times. The end-time images of these hymns offered not escapism but expression: a cry for justice, an eschatological longing, a hope for something more. For people who tread carefully between dominant and subordinate cultures in order not to succumb to the former or abandon the latter, the hymns gave an alternate worldview of assurance and guidance. No wonder their use was especially intense on difficult occasions, times of acute loss or tragedy. And this larger awareness helped me recognize just how much was packed into an apparently backwards relic from generations gone by. It opened me to see a pattern later reflected in Stonehill's peculiar sloping floor.

Whenever we encounter something in a congregation (or really any group) that makes no sense to us, it's easy to conclude it makes no sense at all. Far more difficult is to retain an open posture toward such practices, to await an alternate rationality that may be driving the strange thing we have only newly encountered. For me, this has been a powerful insight essential to recognizing the wisdom of a faith community. Even when local ways of being have become unhealthy or unsustainable, that rarely means they are senseless or stupid. It's more likely that I just don't understand yet as the locals do, and so it will call for patience to await the embedded meanings. That's the insight that gave me pause when I set foot on the second floor of Stonehill's fellowship hall. Was there something more going on than first met my eye? Were the initial stories I heard conveying the full account? Only time would tell.

Noticing Local Patterns and Variations

When you sleuth around a congregation, sometimes a financial statement is just that. As important as such a report may be for tracking a church's resources, many people would assume that it isn't soaked with further significance. Funds come in and funds go out, nothing less and nothing more. But sometimes, such seemingly flat and factual records are actually a window into a congregation's soul, unintentionally revealing its deeper wishes and worries. About twenty years ago, that's what I discovered in the early days of looking at Zion Lutheran Church, established in 1858 in Laurenton, Iowa. Although Zion's membership by then had become only half of what it had been early in the twentieth century, recent decades had seen its worship attendance stabilize at between fifty and sixty persons. All that seemed a good sign, even promising for the longer term. It was the financial statement, though, that told a different story.

Like most churches of its scale, Zion was increasingly strained to gather the revenue it needed for its common life. Its membership was relatively older than the population in the surrounding area and its average household income somewhat poorer. Even so, it had long prided itself on living within its means, embodying a frugality found in the lives of members who often needed several part-time jobs to make ends meet. What the financial statements revealed, though, was that Zion's modest budget for expenses was not even close to being met by the Sunday contributions of its members. Annual donations represented only about 65-70 percent of needed income, a considerable shortfall. Yet every year for the past thirty, year-end reports showed the congregation either breaking even or with only minor losses. What could possibly have made up the difference? Was the congregation the regular beneficiary of a series of wills? Had some other kind of windfall magically filled the gap?

It didn't take long to discover the explanation, a surprise of another type. While many similar congregations rely on increased charitable giving at Christmas or Easter, it turned out that Zion's finances were ruled by October. This one month garnered a wildly disproportionate share of the church's annual revenue. It wasn't the Sunday giving that made such a difference, either, since this was at or below the level received in other months. Instead, I stumbled on the answer through a simple bookkeeping entry. Early every October, under the modest notation "Auction," the church recorded a single infusion of cash that represented nearly one-quarter of Zion's annual income. This simple entry in the financial records soon led me into a richer set of stories, not the typical tales of strapped resources but the delicate negotiations about how the congregation might truly thrive and what its character would be.

To understand these negotiations, you have to grasp something of the congregation's longer history. Since its founding, Zion underwent four phases, each spanning several decades. After a difficult initial period of becoming established as a congregation through the efforts of many visiting pastors and missionaries, the next three decades after 1878 were a time of consolidation under the unbroken tenure of the much-revered Pastor Leonhard. Many central elements of the congregation finally came together, including core organizations, patterns, and practices, as well as the construction of the church building itself. A third phase spanned the first half of the twentieth century until the late 1950s and consisted of filling in the broad forms Leonhard had arranged. Written records and a few elderly parishioners remembered facility improvements and repairs, equipment for worship and education, and a general catalogue of what was purchased when, by whom, and for how much. But since those days, Zion had endured a time of instability where the taken-for-granted was far less steady. Pastoral services could now be had only in partnership with other nearby congregations, and pastoral tenure that once averaged over a decade dropped to around three years. Challenges mounted, several of Zion's long-standing groups and activities were often on the verge of collapse, and for the first time the church's financial condition was mentioned as a serious concern.

It was during this last, unstable period that the fall auction, whose proceeds I noticed in the financial records, first came into existence back in 1963. Of course, it didn't appear out of thin air but resulted from Zion's informal patterns of organization. As it turned out, much of the important work at Zion had little to do with the elected forms of governance, such as the church council or its few committees. It happened instead through grassroots groups of three kinds. One involved people with similar traits, like the youth group, couples club, or women's circles. Another set of groups that could get things done involved relationships, especially the potent and pervasive extended family clans. Of the eighty-five households that constituted Zion's total membership, three-fourths were interwoven into six clans of varying sizes, with the very largest incorporating twenty-three households on its own, and thus one-third of all the members. The remaining type of group was focused on programs, like a congregational task or activity. The education committee, responsible for the Sunday school, was one example, as was the parish life committee, attending to events and anniversaries. This was also the character of the auction committee, a handful of volunteers who organized and operated the fall auction. Because of the financial significance of this event for Zion, its work was closely watched by all. Its members also shared similar traits, since it consisted entirely of women, as well as deep relationships, since it drew from the very largest of the family clans — that is, until lately.

The work of this committee far exceeded the day of the fall auction itself and included the many elaborate rituals of planning and execution, not to mention the complexities faced by those charged with these responsibilities. Arrangements actually began with selecting the committee at the semiannual congregational meeting the preceding July. Work then intensified during the late summer and early fall with advertising, soliciting donated goods, and other logistical arrangements to prepare for the event. Work ended only when final administrative tasks were completed weeks after the auction, such as record-keeping, applying for matching funds from local charitable agencies, and so forth.

While I was learning about Zion, the selection of committee members underwent a significant change with consequences no one dreamed. Prior to this, the auction had been guided by a handful of women now sixty years old and above, and the congregation always affirmed their selection. For the first time, though, these women now began to express a deep concern that they no longer had the energy for the job. When a trio of younger women immediately volunteered to plan the event, their offer was gladly accepted by all, including those who now stepped down from their duties in weary relief. Nobody I later interviewed about this change of guard noted at the time that these younger women were not from any of the six central family clans at Zion. What was more, all were from "in town," a code phrase that meant they didn't live in Laurenton or its adjacent townships but, like many younger members, resided in the nearby communities of Freeburg and Poweshiek. Trivial as these differences may seem, they eventually proved decisive for how their efforts were received, opening up an unexpected debate about the purpose of the auction itself.

What the new members of the auction committee kept to themselves, and only disclosed to me in the weeks after the event, was a commitment to three strategic changes. First, they would decrease the overall time span of the event from six hours to three or four at the most. Second, they would limit the bake sale, one of two revenue sources for the auction, to only a few of the most popular kinds of goods. Third and most daringly, they would replace the traditional sit-down dinner for the entire community with a simple refreshment stand from which participants could purchase lunch. Their plans were not hastily conceived changes but instead drew upon careful observations of the event made over the years, an event to which they had often given their own baked goods, meal assistance, and willing help. Through these changes, they focused on one simple aim: to make the auction more efficient in terms of time and money. Upon hearing of the innovations, previous members of the auction committee quickly criticized their younger counterparts for not consulting them. Surely, they said, such changes would lead to fewer participants and lower receipts.

At long last, the first Saturday in October arrived, time for the auction, to be held at the Laurenton community center, located one-half mile south of Zion on the main north-south road that led into town. Converted from its earlier use as a creamery, this block structure measured about seventy-five by seventy-five feet overall and was divided into two parallel rooms running east to west. The northern room was about twenty-five feet wide and was entered directly from the outside at its east end, while the southern room was twice as wide, three feet higher than the parallel room, and accessible from it by means of several wide interior entryways with steps. The space was arranged and stocked starting at 9:00 a.m. and, evidently by long-established precedent, divided into four quadrants that I was able to walk in a clockwise rotation: craft tables to the northeast, auction seating and stage to the northwest, bake sale tables to the southwest, and the refreshment stand to the southeast. The public began to arrive around 10:00 a.m. for the craft and bake sale, which lasted roughly an hour. A shifting crowd of about forty persons inspected and purchased various homemade articles and baked goods during this time, visiting with one another and Zion members. During this same period and the next, the refreshment stand sold food and beverages to attendees. The climactic phase, of course, was the auction itself, conducted by Tiny, a retired professional auctioneer and long-time member of Zion, who called for bids on articles and services ranging from the valuable to the ridiculous. The crowd, which now numbered over seventy persons, used the auction more for casual conversation and loud joking with one another and with Tiny than for any serious bidding on goods. When the auction ended, those who set up the event turned to cleaning the facility.

It would be simplistic to treat the disagreements about how to plan and run this event as just another petty power struggle over a tedious and trivial slice of church life. When people expend surprising personal energy and emotions on something as apparently small as this, I sense that something far more urgent is usually at stake. In this case, the underlying issue can't be reduced merely to resisting change. After all, in its nearly century and a half of existence, Zion had seen plenty of change, often far more tumultuous than this. Instead, I think it's more fitting for the contested space of Zion's fall auction to be thought of as a dispute over how to perform a script.

Though it rarely receives comment, value-driven groups (like churches) often freely submit to a prescribed sequence of words or events — a script. This is really rather remarkable. To submit to a script means that a group somehow affirms what it represents: its values, the content of its message, or the togetherness it requires. For example, when church members agree to meet early on the same day each week to say prayers or sing hymns, all within a larger pattern of performance that remains quite similar from week to week, this script not only says something potent about their beliefs but even looks a bit countercultural, a commitment likely not shared by many of their neighbors. At the same time, though, even the most tightly held script has variations in its performance. These variations in what is chosen or how it is done typically bear local values and meanings. Again, the script of Christian worship allows such variations, like which prayers are recited on what days or which hymns are sung with particular gusto. The wider bonds that a script creates are thereby attuned to quite local interests and needs.

The fall auction was just this kind of script performance, a patterned series of events and roles, a ritualized choreography whose sequence had deep meaning. Up until the period I've described, the annual and unvaried repetition of this script meant its "goods" were simply reinforced, subsumed, and accepted. In particular, the fall auction was freighted with values strongly affirmed by the older women from the main family clans at Zion. Above all, for them it represented a public sign of commitment to the church, not just by members but also by those in the wider community whose participation signified their support. This was why the auction was always held on the same weekend every year, lasted the better part of a day, and included a meal comparable to what you might offer in your home. Through all these signs and others besides, Zion was showing the kind of place it truly was: reliable, lavish, cordial, where time spent with others was inherently valuable. Orderly script performance was essential for this public witness.

It's not that the younger women who now planned the auction were unaware of these values. Instead, they varied from this received script in order to foreground other values and alternative goods. For them, the event mainly served an important pragmatic aim of garnering the needed financial resources for Zion to survive. This was, after all, why the fall auction first ended up on the calendar in early October, at just the point each year when the congregation's savings were depleted but seasonal expenses, like utilities or program needs, were growing. These new volunteer planners were acutely aware of these meanings and also saw the timing as a fundraising opportunity to tap into the overall harvest-time mood of generosity and good cheer. As it turned out, their instincts were right. When the receipts were tallied and all final reports assembled, the fall auction conducted in their new way proved to be better attended than ever before and vastly more profitable.

Embedded within this seemingly innocent example of script and variation was, therefore, a basic question of what it meant to be church, a local wisdom about being a community of faith, worked out in particular practices and behaviors. I came to see that the real dispute was whether faithfulness to Zion was better shown through a script that stressed participation or productivity, relationships or revenue. By claiming to be more attentive to building community, the older women accused their younger counterparts of not caring about the congregation and its deeper values. Stung by these remarks, the younger women retorted that they did all they could for Zion in light of their busy schedules, and that planning the event carried with it the authority to make needed if not long-overdue changes. Jackie, one of the trio of new planners, said of the older women, "They see we're not doing things the way they did, so they say we're not as committed. They say we're making excuses — but I think we're having to make choices." Such was the *grand pas de deux* between the generations at Zion, a basic struggle to work out who would take the lead and who would follow.

Learning to Expect Something More

The temptation with a struggle like the one surrounding Zion's fall auction is to simplify its terms and thus discount its meaning. The dispute between the older and younger women was just a bald-faced power struggle, some might conclude, with pious activity masking profane motivations. Of course, power was at stake in this incident, but why didn't I just stop there? What led to my eventual claim that there were actually contrasting forms of faithfulness involved in this incident and alternative traditions of how to be church? Sorting these out as traditions lodged in different generations required a wisdom to see beyond the apparent, but in my case that capacity to see had rather foolish origins. Long before my time with Zion, a pastoral experience included a breakthrough moment that I now recall to my chagrin. I learned to read the "something more" in the fall auction because, many years earlier, I so thoroughly misread another situation, regarding it as something less.

The first parish I ever served as pastor was a rural congregation not unlike Zion. After the long and benumbing tenure of my predecessor, it seemed to me that my task was to do a fair bit of cleanup, revitalizing local practices with up-to-date ideas. For reasons that now elude me, I began with the handling of the collection during worship. As in many Lutheran congregations, the usual procedure in this congregation was that, following the sermon and petitions, ushers distributed the offering plates row by row through the assembly. At the end of this process, the offering was brought forward along with the bread and wine in preparation for the eucharistic rite. It was this latter half of the collection that I wanted to eliminate, that of returning the plates to the chancel along with the communion elements. I had all sorts of supposedly sensible reasons to support this change, a mixture of pragmatic, ritual, and theological claims. The procession of gifts would thereby be simpler and their presentation neater. The focus would properly remain on the meal, not on the money. It would allow me to remove from an overcrowded chancel the side-table on which the offering plates rested. And after all, wasn't the collection just a functional matter that could be done in other ways? Wasn't it even a bit unseemly?

The pushback to what seemed to me a perfectly reasonable, modest change was swift and sustained. Most vocally opposed were Art and Irene, he the high school janitor and she an aide on the swing shift at a nursing home, who still shared their simple house with their daughter, Ann, a young adult who could not fully care for herself due to Down syndrome. As a team, Art and Irene could be personally difficult on even a good day, and within weeks of my liturgical change they insisted I meet them at home in order to set me straight. That meeting went just as badly as I expected, a barrage of loud accusations to which I could only offer feeble, awkward replies. Wasn't their money good enough to be brought forward during worship? Why wasn't the side-table, which Art personally helped to build, worth having in the chancel? And just who did I think I was imposing my ideas on folks like them who had been members of this church for their whole lives and surely would outlast me besides? Good points, one and all, and so a natural temptation was to conclude that this was nothing but a power play.

After a while, the volume and volatility subsided, but Art and Irene weren't finished yet. Suddenly, though, they were no longer talking about last week's offering but about the church's Christmas pageant back in 1962. Such events are often steeped in long-held traditions, and one of this congregation's rituals was always to have the lead role of Mary played by one of the girls who had just turned six. By received practice, then, 1962 would have been Ann's turn. Fighting back tears that coupled humiliation with rage, Irene recounted in quiet, electric tones how the church matrons had visited her privately that November to say that this year someone else would take the lead in the pageant. Ann was a little "different," after all, and they didn't want to embarrass her. The blatant disregard toward Ann, a treasured only child, was still fresh for Art and Irene. And though they never directly said so, it was utterly clear that I had shown the same disregard with the collection. It was all about whether gifts are received with dignity, and what that says in turn about basic human value.

A month or so later, the same point was driven home in another way. The congregation produced an elaborate annual report detailing all its programs and activities. On the first page of the report was something I had never seen before and found shocking. Each and every donor to the congregation was explicitly listed by name, ranked from the highest annual contribution to the lowest. At first, I could only conceive that such a practice elicited either pride or shame, neither being exactly Christian virtues. Surely this was beyond the pale, I thought, another candidate for cleanup. After a few days, though, I reviewed the list and began to notice who was included where. At the very top was the single mother of one of my confirmation students, a woman whose days were spent at the local dairy plant wrapping cheese on a production line. Next was her brother, a married father of three girls who supervised one of the county road crews for near minimum wage. Art and Irene were number five on the list, remarkable in light of their spare means, let alone how Ann had been treated. In fact, the top ten names included only one of the wealthier members, while most of the poorer households gave a far higher proportion of their income than the well-to-do. This donor list resembled how the offering was handled in worship: like a procession of gifts, a dignifying practice that conveyed worth.

These pastoral mistakes early in my vocation interrupted me just long enough to see that something more was happening. But by "something more," I don't mean just strong feelings or social status. One of the challenges with congregations is not to become jaded but seriously to imagine that religious impulses may actually drive a group's practices, and not just sometimes. The emotion expended in my first parish on the collection and contributions signaled a deeper faith-claim at work — in this case, one about giving, grace, and what we confess through how we spend. It may not represent a very sophisticated or complete stewardship theology, but it was a local theology all the same. Over time, this congregation had developed its own practical wisdom. It knew something about what it meant to give. And these kinds of breakthroughs helped me much later to perceive at Zion something more than merely a power struggle between old and young. At heart was a kind of nascent, undeveloped ecclesiology, the previously unstated claim that to be church demands energy and effort, sometimes even disagreement.

Sensing Depth in the Ordinary

"Y'know, we're not *Mayberry R.F.D.* here," drawled Steve. A lifelong member of Emanuel Lutheran Church in rural Illinois, he was married, the father of four children, and worked as an engineer at a nearby electronics firm. His accent, though, was purely a ruse. Steve was deeply committed to his church's survival, and one way he showed that commitment was by mocking the caricatures others held of Emanuel and rural residents like him. Though he lived far from any major city, Steve's work representing his company regularly sent him to international centers of commerce. His daily life therefore encompassed a complexity that outsiders might not expect. Nor was he the only one, for others in the church and community also nimbly negotiated such differences. The drawling remark about an old television show indicated Steve's awareness that Emanuel was not always what it seemed. "Folks think we're some peaceful little farming town.

We're a small church, sure, but we're also diverse — many different walks of life, lots of different personalities, some in this group and some in that." As I came to learn, this variety and adaptation were found not only among other members, but also in how they nurtured the faith of their children.

If you wanted to see Emanuel's wisdom at work, then its Sunday morning educational program was a prime example. This was where a treasure was being handed on. The care devoted to formative processes was as great as that given to any decisions about content. I saw the centrality of this one program revealed in many ways. For example, the annual cycle of educational activities was firmly set and well known. September marked the formal start of the weekly program, with each of the four Sundays that month highlighting some aspect of the program: Rally Sunday, which launched the entire year; Promotion Sunday, for attendance pins and moving to the next grade; Teacher Installation Sunday; and Investiture Sunday, for inducting students into the confirmation program and giving each a new Bible. The Sunday school Christmas pageant was held on the second Sunday in December, after at least a month of rehearsals, and the year closed with confirmation on Pentecost Sunday. Weekly programming then lay dormant until the next autumn, except for the Vacation Bible School program each June.

The value of Christian education was reinforced in ways beyond the calendar. It was the only program at Emanuel with a standing committee mandated in the by-laws and a cycle of administrative oversight that stretched throughout the year. The church council reinforced the status of this work by refusing to cut the Sunday school budget during times of financial hardship and even approving its requests for additional funds. Finally, there were subtle visual reminders of the depth of member support for the program. The walls next to the organ in the southeast corner of the worship space enshrined a gallery of confirmation photos stretching back for decades, including those of even the oldest living members. Hanging on the west wall of that same room to the left of the pulpit was a hymn board, modified from its original purpose to display the weekly attendance and offering at Sunday school compared with figures from the previous year. All told, Emanuel's scheduling, governance, resources, and artifacts made clear just how serious the congregation was about forming their young people.

Atop his already full family life and work duties, Steve was also the much-respected superintendent of the Sunday school, a role he had held since just after he and Becky were married. Since his daily work was demanding and intense, he relied on a self-imposed regime involving day planners and Gantt charts to keep various projects straight. In turn, he managed Emanuel's tiny Sunday school the very same way, with its own extensive schedules and diagrams. There was good reason for such organizational sophistication. The entire program integrated a short-term plan of regular weekly Sunday school gatherings into a long-term one involving eight full years of confirmation studies. Staying organized was a perennial challenge.

During the Sunday morning hour before worship, five adults and twenty to thirty youth, from preschool through tenth grade, gathered in the large basement room of the church for the weekly instructional program. Events began with a five- to seven-minute tightly scripted period using memorized prayers and songs in an unvaried pattern. After an opening prayer said in unison, birthdays were acknowledged and the offering received, followed by an offering song and offering prayer. Only one of the teachers led this event, but I found it fascinating that the uninvolved teachers rather absently recited all the songs and prayers to themselves while still setting up their classroom areas. It wasn't hard to understand why, since ten to thirty years earlier these same songs and prayers were recited when *they* were Sunday school students. The morning then continued with forty-five minutes of age-segregated instruction held in five classroom areas created by pulling curtain dividers across the room. Each class used printed curricular resources from a Lutheran publisher and focused on biblical themes and texts. I never saw that these resources were ever completely followed, but they instead set the basis for the main classroom work of oral storytelling, question-and-answer, and conversation. The entire weekly program concluded shortly before the scheduled Sunday worship by gathering students and teachers again for a few minutes of closing songs and prayers.

Stop to consider the range of resources Emanuel mobilized every week in order to hand on something it treasured. Besides the obvious physical and financial resources, the program used the ritual resources of songs, prayers, and patterns of time, as well as social and human resources, like gathering with others. The last of these was especially important. In the records I read that covered several generations, intimate, small-group encounters between a handful of students and an adult member were the preferred way Emanuel showed concern for its youth and their growth in the Christian faith. And this wasn't a relationship with just any adult member, either. Across several measures, all of the teachers were very active members of Emanuel, holding multiple leadership roles and types of involvement. More significant still, all but one of them had the highest level of formal education in the congregation. Indeed, education was nearly the only factor they had in common, since their participation in other church activities rarely overlapped and they often differed widely in their opinions of the congregation.

Aligned with this, the committee also wanted the pastor directly involved in the Sunday school rather than other activities scheduled during the same time period (including adult education). Steve claimed that, historically, "When the most educated person in church taught these kids, someone they saw up front every Sunday, they got real excited about it," and years later they would speak of close relationships with previous pastors. It was all the more interesting, then, to contrast the teachers' higher levels of participation and education with the young people they actually taught. As for these students, only about half were from active member families. Indeed, having a child in the Sunday school was one of the few ways that many of these inactive families ever participated at Emanuel. That fact was not lost upon Steve, the education committee, or the teachers as they planned teaching methods and objectives.

What made this program still more complex and revealing about Emanuel is that weekly Sunday school was not an end in itself but fit into an eight-year plan of confirmation studies. On Investiture Sunday near the end of each September, third graders were formally enrolled in confirmation through a ceremony of promise-making and gift-giving. The promise, specified in a contract signed by student, superintendent, and pastor and filed in the church office, called for regular worship attendance, taking on additional mid-week instruction starting in seventh grade, and reading the Bible. The gift, awarded when the contract was publicly submitted, was the very Bible the students agreed to read. Confirmation Sunday came at the other end of the eight-year program and occurred at the festival of Pentecost. I found it striking that this ceremony again paired promise-making with gift-giving: the promises specified in the confirmation rite, followed by the gift of a hand-made quilt for each confirmand. In between these bracketing rituals were the eight years of weekly instruction organized within a plan of annual themes and learning goals, such as studying the historic creeds, Old Testament history, or Luther's *Small Catechism.*

This tight integration of weekly Sunday school with the multiyear confirmation program revealed the deeper purposes of Christian education at

Emanuel. One could cynically claim that the main intent was merely to preserve membership from one generation to the next, but this fails to account for the elaborate structure of the program, its main rituals, the lavish use of resources of all types, and the importance it held for adult and youth participants. Instead, I came to see that this program had much more to do with incorporating the youth into Emanuel's values so they could take on its future work. A closer look at the two occasions of gift-giving at the beginning and end of the program makes this clear.

When third-grade enrollees received their Bibles, their teacher, Jean, admonished, "This Bible is to start you on the road to success. You're not worshiping this book. It's a learning tool — so use it!" Emanuel's parish education often referred to scripture as a tool, a move that embedded students in the congregation in several ways. Each student's Bible had one verse secretly marked within it, chosen specifically for that child, who was then to find it and discuss it in a private meeting with the teacher. Not only did this open up an intimate conversation with an active adult member, but it also signaled that marking these new Bibles was desirable. As Wayne, the Sunday school teacher for the seventh- through tenth-grade class, once said to his students, "Look at the tools in your dad's workshop. How do you know which ones are his favorites? They're the ones that are all worn out. That's how your Bible should be, too — worn out with lots of use." Most of the teachers used their own third-grade Bibles in the classroom to show students that they were now part of a larger set of practices at Emanuel. These gift Bibles rooted the students in the congregation in another way, since the version distributed was exactly the same as that found in sanctuary pew racks. The education committee successfully resisted one former pastor's efforts to change the Bible given to third graders to a more up-to-date version simply because it would disrupt this direct link to worship. The chance for these students, like others before them, to follow along with the assigned Sunday readings in an already familiar version of the Bible outweighed all other considerations.

When, years later, the confirmands received their hand-made quilts, this practice was also freighted with symbolism. As many as ten older members, all at least seventy years old, were active in making the quilts. Very involved in leadership and various groups, they represented an ample cross-section of the membership. These persons also presented the quilts on Confirmation Sunday, adding their own personal comments, like "This is to cover you with Emanuel" and "This is a sign of the work you're now part of." During later interviews, the parents and teachers of the confirmands emphasized to me how important it was that these admired, long-term members gave such a gift to this new generation of members. But beyond this, these older members also produced exactly the same kind of quilts for distribution to overseas refugees through an international Lutheran relief agency. More remarkable still was that this fact was well known even among the confirmands. In an important sense, then, these quilts were signs of work not just at Emanuel but beyond it as well, and so reminded confirmands that they now needed to take up their place in that broader labor.

Maybe to some this all seems rather ordinary, quaint, or even overblown. Education in this place was just a well-planned program able to deliver the cognitive goods. But it seemed to me that, just as Steve said earlier, Emanuel was not always what it seemed. When it came to handing on the faith, something extraordinary was at work. Program focus and instructional content surely mattered, but these were more the backdrop than the main event, the score and notes for a melody supporting a vastly more inventive and sophisticated series of movements. In the end, the people, their rituals, and their spare resources were part of an exchange of symbols, a handoff that bore Emanuel's real treasure. Across manifold layers and in multiple forms, that treasure could be found in the depth of relationships and mentoring, the meaning of responsibility and discovery, the openness to give lavishly and receive gratefully, and the commitment to people and places beyond yourself. When paired with educational content, the result was then this wider waltz that coupled *what* would be taught with *how* that would best be done.

Developing Wisdom about Congregational Wisdom

The intervening accounts of how I began to recognize communal wisdom may leave the wrong impression of a one-to-one correspondence between what I later saw in congregations and some previous experience in my life. It's more accurate to say that family resemblances developed over time, and common themes and features gradually became recognizable — a kind of pattern language, as I said earlier. My personal accounts have simply lifted up one of many previous instances that contributed to noticing a resemblance. It would also be wrong to conclude that, at least for me, these accounts always originated strictly from within my research interests. In the case of Emanuel's educational program, my sensitivity to its extraordinary undercurrents was surely awakened by events quite early in my life, even in childhood. Indeed, I have been reassured to learn that many of us who study congregations can recall incidents from family or early upbringing that first ignited our deeper curiosity.

When I began elementary school, our family belonged to a prosperous downtown church that was largely German in ethnicity and Pietistic in theology. Its newly expanded facility was a massive monument to the rapid growth such congregations enjoyed in America during the 1950s, though never again. To enter this church's main facility required going through a wide narthex, where people first greeted one another on Sundays, and then proceeding into the sanctuary itself, a vast worship space that could be viewed from the narthex through large glass walls. This separation of spaces, visible to one another, was important.

Every Sunday morning, starting about thirty minutes before the scheduled worship time, elderly men began to enter the still-empty and silent sanctuary, one after another. It wasn't a coordinated, orderly procession but more of a random yet dignified entrance, with each one heading his own way to an accustomed place of seating for the worship to come. But when the men reached those places, they remained standing. So picture this: roughly twenty tall, gaunt, white-haired men, all in their seventies and eighties, usually attired in severe blue serge suits, standing at scattered points throughout the room. And there they remained for the next half hour, like motionless pillars. Everyone else waited outside in the narthex, occasionally glancing into the sanctuary. No one entered and no noise or activity interrupted the space until, with no prior signal, one after another, each man would sit down. The organ prelude then began and the rest of the members would finally enter the room for worship.

What's hard to convey about this odd ritual is just how ordinary and unexceptional it was to the rest of us. I never recall anyone remarking about the practice or considering unusual our delayed entrance into the sanctuary. When I was around six years old and exasperated with the waiting, I turned to my grandmother, who stood in the narthex visiting with friends. Tilting my head toward the men in the blue serge suits, I blurted out, "What are they *doing* in there anyway?" With a look of mild surprise, she simply said, "Praying, of course." "But praying for *what?*" I demanded. She paused, glanced at the men, then slowly answered, "Well, *for us*," using both senses of that prepositional phrase: "on our behalf" and "to our benefit." For me, this incident captures the striking convergence of embodied pattern with exceptional purpose. What happened was more than a pious display by a few old geezers, but the collective practice that everyone, whether central or peripheral to its unfolding, tacitly affirmed. Through this collective wisdom, a faith community publicly witnessed to what matters most, to persistent fidelity across the years, and to waiting as an inherently worthwhile endeavor. With that kind of formative experience, no wonder I paused with Emanuel's education program to look at its extraordinary commitments borne through patterned practices.

Throughout this essay, I have lifted up congregational stories evoked by significant if often overlooked spaces, scripts, and symbols. Alongside each, of course, I also offered another kind of story, the account of my discovery process. These underlying stories are as multi-stranded and wandering as the main ones, hard to summarize neatly or present in an orderly fashion. So much of what I have encountered has been accidental: what I happened to see, who I chanced to meet, the other research I was coincidentally conducting. It was essential to remain open to the moment, not reaching premature conclusions but retaining an inquisitive stance. Of special importance, this openness included appreciation for the theological realities of Stonehill, Zion, and Emanuel. Many studies of congregations fall flat on this very point, deficient because they betray a basic doubt that people ever think and act for truly faithful reasons. By comparison, I wasn't naïve or credulous about every pious assertion, but was simply willing to venture that religious practices might sometimes be driven by more than secular motivations.

That said, my own story of discovery was also highly iterative, moving back and forth between looking closely and posing questions, then stepping back to gauge significance and interpret meanings before venturing forward again with new insights and inquiries. Similarly iterative was my use of research methods and tools, from basic observation to structured interviews, then consulting historical documents or even testing a hunch with my own body. A student of congregations moves fluidly among various sources and informing approaches. Equally important, this work requires multiple perspectives to confirm or complicate what has been learned *en route*. And all through the process, your discovery is guided by what Howard Becker, in the field of qualitative social research, once called "tricks of the trade" —

simple moves that resolve a conceptual problem or find the path around a common, persistent difficulty. When looking at congregations, many such tricks emerged from my prior, personal experience, a kind of cumulative "wisdom literature" about faith communities, such as these:

- Notice the distinctive wrinkles and ruptures in a setting, and seek out the underlying reasoning, the alternative explanations you don't yet grasp.
- Even as you attune yourself to those matters that don't make sense, on the other hand avoid becoming infatuated by what appears exotic.
- Appreciate the ordinary, the mundane and regular in a setting, and seek out the important variations, the ways a broad pattern is locally adapted.
- For any explanation you are offered, regularly and repeatedly ask the sociologist's main investigative question, "Is that really so?"
- Seek religious work in typical places — where it focuses energy, provides a worldview, supplies an aesthetic, explains a limit, or justifies atypical behavior.
- Approach the study of congregations with caring discernment rather than cynicism, a spirit of love that seeks their benefit, even when they are dysfunctional.
- No one story sufficiently expresses the wisdom of a congregation, so listen for many accounts, each with an angle on the wider picture.

This final insight bears closer attention. Because the foregoing accounts of congregations resulted in stories to be shared, they were surely neater than the reality of the events they depict. I plotted my ever-deeper understanding with a natural logic, but in each case you can also sense the shifts between present and past, action and reflection, description and theory. That's because these narratives inevitably are fictional. I don't mean by that the common distortion of this term, as if what I wrote were false or invented. Instead, it's simply that any effort to account for the reality as complex as in these congregations is still the product of a narrator's convictions and decisions, including what to foreground or include and what to suppress or omit. These narrative decisions may seem a limitation or disadvantage, but in fact they hold the potential for an account that conveys detail, evokes interaction, and stimulates imagination, and I pray they might even deepen local wisdom. By considering such an account of itself, a congregation can gain a potent and enriching resource, a perspective that holds the critical potential for change. In this way as well, congregational stories can enrich local practical wisdom to make new judgments and to plan what might happen next.

References

The main congregational narratives in this chapter about Stonehill, Zion, and Emanuel derive from previously unpublished fieldwork, part of research I have conducted in scores of congregations during the past twenty years. Particular details about these groups are found only in my confidential fieldnotes. Proper names, locations, and other identifying features have been masked in accord with the agreements negotiated for the research, but in a way that preserves for the reader accurate substantive portrayals of these actual faith communities.

My own research has been nourished and guided by the wealth of materials that have developed since the early 1980s in the field of congregational studies. Early examples of guides for such research include the pioneering work of James F. Hopewell, *Congregation: Stories and Structures* (Philadelphia: Fortress, 1987), and Carl S. Dudley, ed., *Building Effective Ministry: Theory and Practice in the Local Church* (San Francisco: Harper & Row, 1983). The first general guidebook in the field was Jackson W. Carroll, Carl S. Dudley, and William McKinney, eds., *Handbook for Congregational Studies* (Nashville: Abingdon, 1986), which was significantly revised a decade later in Nancy T. Ammerman, Jackson W. Carroll, Carl S. Dudley, and William McKinney, eds., *Studying Congregations: A New Handbook* (Nashville: Abingdon, 1998). The work of the "Congregational Studies Project Team," a mainstay in providing these guides, can now be found in an interactive website at http://studyingcongregations.org/. This group, with which I have been personally connected for the past decade, has been profoundly influential on my work.

For further overview, those interested in the wider situation of American congregations should consult James P. Wind and James W. Lewis, eds., *American Congregations,* vol. 2: *New Perspectives in the Study of Congregations* (Chicago: University of Chicago Press, 1994), and the broad sociological research of Mark Chaves, *Congregations in America* (Cambridge: Harvard

University Press, 2004). A different way to gain perspective on the range of issues facing faith communities is to look at comparative research on multiple congregations. Two significant examples of such studies are by Nancy Tatom Ammerman with Arthur E. Farnsley II et al., *Congregation and Community* (New Brunswick: Rutgers University Press, 1997), and by Penny Edgell Becker, *Congregations in Conflict: Cultural Models of Local Religious Life* (New York: Cambridge University Press, 1999).

Without a doubt, though, the best way to learn how to study congregations comes through reading accounts of responsible research on particular communities. Three that have been the most helpful for me are the longitudinal study of a single congregation by R. Stephen Warner, *New Wine in Old Wineskins: Evangelicals and Liberals in a Small-Town Church* (Berkeley: University of California Press, 1988), the deeply sensitive and appreciative exploration of an evangelical congregation by Nancy Tatom Ammerman, *Bible Believers: Fundamentalists in the Modern World* (New Brunswick: Rutgers University Press, 1987), and the remarkable community-wide study of three congregations by Nancy L. Eiesland, *A Particular Place: Urban Restructuring and Religious Ecology in a Southern Exurb* (New Brunswick: Rutgers University Press, 2000).

Given the vast diversity of religious gatherings in America, several other studies deepen your awareness of ethnically or racially distinctive congregations. One of the earliest studies about African American congregations, still gripping in its detail, was conducted by Melvin D. Williams, *Community in a Black Pentecostal Church: An Anthropological Study* (Prospect Heights, IL: Waveland, 1974), while a more current example is the neighborhood-encompassing work of Omar M. McRoberts, *Streets of Glory: Church and Community in a Black Urban Neighborhood* (Chicago: University of Chicago Press, 2003). Other ethnic-specific research has been conducted by Charles W. Dahm, *Parish Ministry in a Hispanic Community* (Mahwah, NJ: Paulist, 2004), and the innovative efforts toward a multiethnic ministry are recounted in Gerardo Marti, *A Mosaic of Believers: Diversity and Innovation in a Multiethnic Church* (Bloomington: Indiana University Press, 2005).

For those interested in my own view on approaching congregations, I refer you to three resources. My more theoretically oriented overview about appreciating the theological ways of faith communities is recounted in "Attending Locally: Theologies in Congregations," *International Journal of Practical Theology* 6, no. 2 (2002): 198-225. Though written with an eye toward homiletics, a good summary of the methodologies for exploring congregations can be found in chapters 2-4 (text and notes) of *Knowing the Context: Frames, Tools, and Signs for Preaching,* ed. O. Wesley Allen Jr., Fortress Elements of Preaching (Minneapolis: Fortress, 2008). Finally, those interested in the relationship between congregational studies and practical theology that undergirds this chapter should consult "Congregational Studies," in *The Blackwell Companion to Practical Theology,* ed. Bonnie Miller-McLemore (Oxford: Blackwell, 2011), pp. 133-42.

rocking

PRACTICAL WISDOM AT WORK IN POP CULTURE
CHRISTIAN B. SCHAREN

I ADMIT IT. I PAID A SCALPER a lot of money to see the Alabama Shakes and Jack White play the Ryman Auditorium in Nashville. The combination of the three presented an overwhelming temptation. I've wanted to see a show at the Ryman for a long time. The Ryman is well known as a cathedral of popular music. Built as the Union Gospel Tabernacle, and for many years host of the Grand Ole Opry, its gracefully curved wood pews on the main floor and balcony immediately suggest to music-goers they are in for something beyond mere entertainment. The stage now betrays its long use as a performance venue, but the curved back wall hosts a riot of beautiful stained-glass windows, bathing the room in otherworldly light. The Alabama Shakes, a young band from Athens, Alabama, got their start as high school students in the mid-2000s. After being touted on the *Aquarium Drunkard,* an influential L.A. music blog, they have taken the music world by storm. Led by the amazing voice of singer/guitarist Brittany Howard, who styles herself after gospel blues pioneer Sister Rosetta Tharpe, they offer a tight sound honed by years playing covers of classic rock songs in rowdy small-town bars. Alabama Shakes are a worthy band to warm up for Jack White, as both draw inspiration from the delta soil that gave birth to the blues and rock 'n' roll a century ago.

But nearly everyone in the sold-out auditorium was there to rock out with White, celebrating his first solo album's debut at number one on the Billboard top-selling album chart. If you've never heard of Jack White, or The White Stripes, the band he made his name with (literally: born John

Anthony Gillis, White took his band name and surname from his first wife and band-mate, Meg White), stop reading this now and look up their performance of "Seven Nation Army" and "Death Letter Blues" at the forty-sixth Grammy Awards (http://www.youtube.com/watch?v=H1_cg9hFSVE& feature=fvwrel). Turn up the volume. Click play. Hold on to your chair. White's simple aesthetic scheme of three primary colors (black, white, and red) and basic musical set-up (Meg on drums and Jack singing and playing electric guitar) has an energy that would serve as case in point for a college course on rock 'n' roll, hitting the body with a frightening yet absolutely compelling force, immediately both visceral and transcendent in impact.

This show, this particular Wednesday night in Nashville, was a rock and roll show, and it seemed like church. Holy moments unfolded with the heartbeat of a thumping drum and a screaming electric guitar. And I don't mean only that rock and its pantheon of guitar gods, of whom White is one, *function* like religion. No, I mean that as a Christian disciple, pastor, and theologian, I see "more" there. Yet a few weeks after the concert, reading a highly regarded book of essays on pop culture, I was reminded of why so many don't, or can't, see what I see: the author writes, "rock 'n' roll is always on some level a move away from God into the devil's music." The view that rock 'n' roll is the devil's music is a powerful trope in U.S. culture. It is also wrong. You might be skeptical of this bald opposition, but the music keeps teaching me otherwise. I'd like to invite you along as I try to show how I learned the wisdom to hear God's presence and voice speaking through pop music, even when the music *is* talking about the devil (which it mostly doesn't anyway).

Away from God?

While on vacation together, I noticed my friend was consumed with a book of pop culture essays about Christian rock music, Michael Jackson, Bob Marley and The Wailers, and, of all things, the infamous Guns N' Roses' lead singer, Axl Rose. During our week together, he was staying up late reading John Jeremiah Sullivan's *Pulphead*. I had never heard of Sullivan, but then even now, with a Ph.D. in theology, I'm still not very savvy when it comes to what's hot in literature. I was raised in rural Montana with little appreciation for cosmopolitan literary magazines like the *Paris Review* (where Sullivan is listed as Southern editor). I grew up reading classics of the American Western: Louis L'Amour, Jack London, and Hemingway's short stories. I loved the terse sentences and gut-hardened heroes. I played junior high football with Hemingway's grandsons, the legacy of his love of (and roots in) the Paradise Valley north of Livingston, Montana. However, I took notice when the *New York Times* lauded Sullivan as among "the best young nonfiction writers in English." While writing for highbrow journals like the *Paris Review,* Sullivan also writes regularly for *GQ,* a decidedly more popular venue. And when, nursing a late-night beer, my friend burst out laughing at Sullivan's fantastic portrayal of Axl Rose, the lead singer of 1980s rock band Guns N' Roses, I knew I'd have to dive into Sullivan's portrayal of pop culture and music.

I flipped through haphazardly, taking stock. No surprise: I landed on the chapter titled "The Last Wailer." For me as for most white college men in the 1980s, Bob Marley was a staple of my music collection. Mostly it was party music, although I personally never got the sophomoric attraction to Bob Marley as a justification for smoking joints. I knew guys who liked the joints, but they certainly didn't understand the religious context of marijuana for Rastafarianism. Sullivan's experience is similar. "It had long been a dream of mine to meet Bunny Wailer — a pipe dream, sometimes a literal one in the sense that I dreamed it while holding a pipe." For Rastas, smoking weed is like the bread and wine of Holy Communion for Christians: partaking of a holy and life-altering substance. Having spent a semester of college in Kingston, Jamaica, living with a family and working near Half Way Tree in the center of the city, I resonated with Sullivan's desire to find the deeper spiritual and political logic of Marley's music. To pursue his questions, he sought out the last living member of Bob's famous band, The Wailers. Bunny Wailer, a.k.a. Neville O'Riley Livingston or Jah B, still lives in Kingston. Bunny and Bob were stepbrothers, growing up together, being shaped by the same religious and political climate in the 1950s and 1960s. On the basis of one phone call promising an interview, Sullivan got on a plane to Jamaica.

On the plane to the island, Sullivan muses on why he is pursuing the story. The fact that it was first published in *GQ* magazine explains part of it — I presume their readership is like me, those Baby Boomers and Gen-Xers who came of age partying to Bob Marley's music. But Sullivan presses deeper — and this is surely part of his attraction as an essayist. He argues that some pop music catches you up and makes you dance in the moment, but fades away with time. It is not worth returning to; in fact, it never occurs to you to return to it save in a moment of nostalgia. (Like, for instance, seeing the 1980s band Journey at the 2013 Minnesota State Fair. Yes, I really did. My teenage son unexpectedly loves them.) A fading away, stemmed by infrequent bouts of nostalgia, does not happen with Jamaican music. Sullivan suggests that the reason it "deepens over time, over years, not with nostalgia but with meaning and nuance, is that it's a spiritual music." His caveat: not spiritual as in the hyper-produced and theologically boxed-in music sold under the "Christian" label. "Right," I thought. "Exactly." I was totally with him to this point. But then he lost me. After reading the next sentence, I tossed the book onto the coffee table in disgust. "In the States, rock and roll is always on some level a move away from God into the devil's music, but in Jamaica the cultural conditions were different. Pop grew towards Jah." This view seems hopelessly naïve — both about Jamaica and about the USA. Sullivan, in rehearsing that old saw about rock as the devil's music, masks the shared spiritual roots in the spirituals and blues.

But to tell the whole story, I have to admit that I was shaped by that same cultural trope, that rock and roll equaled the devil's music. I remember vividly the weekend our church youth group took a van trip to Hamilton, not quite all the way to Billings, for a regional youth event. It was supposed to be fun, and I guess it was. The bus ride was fun because I sat in the back listening to jokes the older boys were telling. We got there in the afternoon and played those embarrassing group-bonding games, like the one where you get in a circle and all turn sideways and sit, so that every person is a chair for everyone else. Of course we all fell down, a tangled pile of people half laughing and half grossed out by being much too close to people we didn't want to be close to at all. We may (as they said) be one body of Christ, but as a teen I liked having my own body, separately.

The main event was after dinner. The speaker was a hip guy who had played in a rock band and had been saved from that by Jesus. He told us horrible stories about how rock music is Satanic and makes you take drugs and bite the heads off of bats as part of bizarre rituals. (This made us all curious about who he had in mind. It turned out to be Ozzy Osbourne from the British metal band Black Sabbath. At a January 20, 1982, gig in Des Moines, Iowa, a fan threw a live bat on stage. Thinking it was a toy, Ozzy bit the head off.) Satan uses rock music to tempt us, he said, to draw us away from God.

He didn't say it exactly, but I think he was suggesting that if we listened to rock music *we'd* be brainwashed into taking drugs and having sex and biting the heads off of bats, too. He said that some bands even recorded secret Satanic messages on their albums, and if you played them slowly backwards on the record player you would hear the message. The worst example was Led Zeppelin's song "Stairway to Heaven" since it seemed Christian on the surface but had Satanic messages encoded in the song.

We tried to laugh about it at the time, but looking back on it, we were susceptible to the intended scare tactics. The presentation was frightening. The speaker said there were some new Christian bands offering wholesome alternatives (Petra, an early pioneer in Christian rock, was his prime example). He encouraged us to choose wisely when we listened to pop music because our souls were in danger. I asked my mom about it later and she told me a story about how when she was a teen in the 1950s, Grandpa Victor, a Lutheran pastor, forbade her from listening to Elvis. Instead, she put the radio under her pillow, listening late at night to "Blue Suede Shoes" and "Heartbreak Hotel," imagining those famously dangerous gyrating hips. Choosing wisely is indeed the challenge, yet fear and rules lead to rigid obedience or else rebellion. Did I choose wisely after the youth retreat by shying away from pop music, or feeling guilty when I sang along, as my mom did to Elvis under her pillow?

Choosing wisely, in part, means attending to something carefully enough to make a wise judgment. Yet such a description sounds too conscious, too rational; in fact, apprenticeship in Christian faith and life can tutor one to simply know how to receive the popular arts and discern their depth and meaning in light of faith. Perhaps I can show how this happens as I describe further the concert I saw at the Ryman.

Blue for the Blues

The excitement of the crowds is palpable as I walk up Fifth Street toward the Ryman. I reach the imposing red-brick building, step up through the arched doorway, and float through the foyer on a buzz of anticipation. The seats are in the balcony, so I head past the merchandise tables, past the mob at the bar, and up curving stairs toward the second floor. The stairs are graceful, covered in a crushed velvet carpet, and bordered by white-metal and dark-walnut rails that invite a hand just to feel their elegance. About halfway up, I pick up a muffled song over the rumble of conversation filling the foyer and stairs. Its insistent, mid-tempo beat and slight wail of guitar accompanied the crying voice, singing, "You got to hoooooold on, Hey, you got to hoooooold on." In a panic, I realize the Alabama Shakes are playing my favorite song, "Hold On," the lead single from their debut album *Boys and Girls*. I head straight in, walking what seemed like the endless arc of the back pew to the far side, section 9, with a reserved seat about midway down. Along the way to the seat I have a sinking feeling. I realize I have an emotional investment in their pulling off a good showing in this classic venue, in a high-profile gig, surrounded (undoubtedly) with music business people as thick as bees on a hive.

The auditorium is only about half full at this point, and the band members are all standing in their spots as if glued to the floor. Lead singer Brittany Howard describes their live shows as "like the Baptist church, except it's real loud and there's cussing. It's just like going to a rock 'n' roll church." Yeah, I think, except now you are in one of the cathedrals of pop music looking like deer in headlights. "Hold On" is a plea, a pop psalm that alternates between a person flailing around ("don't know where I'm gonna go, don't know what I'm gonna do") and the voice of the Almighty ("come on, Brittany, you got to get back up, you got to hold on"). The intensity of the dialog reaches a fever as she sings, in the voice of the Almighty, "Yeah! You've got to wait, Yeah, you've got to . . . wait." And answering in her own voice, now nearing a full-throated scream, "But I don't wanna wait! no I don't wanna wait!" Polite applause greets the band as they finish "Hold On." After a rockabilly song and a couple slow tunes, the crowd has filled in a bit but still seem pretty stand-offish.

Admittedly, the audience is a hip crowd: they know the trend, and the Shakes' style of retro-soul is in full revival. Before her tragic death, British soul diva Amy Winehouse set the bar. In the last few years, Adele, also British, earned a shelf of Grammy awards (for her 2010 album *21*), further establishing the revival. Adele's pasty-white look belies a style that owes boatloads to Aretha Franklin and other soul divas. But Brittany plays the soul card naturally and yet doesn't even want it. She name checks Bon Scott, the original lead singer for the Australian hard rock band AC/DC, as a major influence, shocking music journalists. In the same breath, she credits sitting between aunts in the pew at church, belting out the hymns. Ironically, she claims she was never in the choir because she was too shy. Such surprising unself-conscious honesty led Justin Gage to claim in his influential post about Alabama Shakes on *Aquarium Drunkard* that the band's music is the sort of "stuff that can't be faked." They are, he wrote, "a slice of the real." The hype built from there.

As the audience at the Ryman continues its sleepy response to the band, I grit my teeth. Perhaps Jack White is the slice of the real and the Shakes are merely pretenders. I don't want to admit I've misjudged the depth and significance of this young band. Then, finally, I feel a surge of electricity move through the room. Heath Fogg, their steady and talented lead guitarist, hits a clean G sharp chord and Brittany uncoils the microphone cord from the stand, taking it into her hand. She looks down at the floor and almost whispers, "All the world, can't hold a candle to you." Steve Johnson, the drummer, comes in with a tisha tisha, tisha tisha, on the ride cymbal. Zac Cockrell, the understated but outstanding bassist, throws his head back, smiling under his shrubby beard, as if he knows just where the song is going to take us. And he is dead right. The song unfolds like a switchblade, a screed of fighting words from a lover to all who might try to steal her man. Wham. Watch out. Holding her hand out, palm open to the audience, flying to her upper range, Brittany claims, "All them girls, they don't know you like I do," then runs to the edge of the stage, leaning over into the mike, saying, "what I want to know is, will you be mine?" The band then picks up speed, moving from slow groove to racing train as she howls, "be mine, be mine, be mine, always be mine." With this, the crowd returns the band's level of energy, the man in front of me shouting out, as if in church, "That's right, now. Preach, Sister!" I relax. They have gotten over, and the crowd is with them through the last soulful, searing rendition of "You Ain't Alone," a song that stretches the band from hushed tenderness to a rousing and raspy ferocity. By the time they walk off stage, the nearly full auditorium jumps to their feet, an honest effort at an encore that isn't to be. Even before the Shakes get off stage, smartly dressed roadies step on stage to transform the visual aesthetic to blue and black, Jack White's chosen style for his tour.

The intermission affords the chance to get a beer. After seeing the long line at the foyer bar, I settle for a plastic bottle of Bud Lite from a cart in the back of the balcony. I glance into the building's historical display cabinets, which are set at intervals between the stained glass windows. The era of its life as a church seems absent, but I learn some of the key moments of the

Opry, including the night in the summer of 1949 when a twenty-five-year-old Hank Williams played his famous tune "Lovesick Blues" for the first time on stage at the Opry. He was called back for six encores — a record that stands to this day.

Down in front, the new stage being set glows in a blueish hue under the spotlights. The back of the stage is floor-to-ceiling blueish-white fabric with three distinct black strips, also floor to ceiling, in the center of the stage. I realize this is a subtle but stylish reference to Jack White's adoption of "III" at the end of his name. He loves the number three, a feature of the strict stylistic conventions he adopted from the Dutch art school *De Stijl* (The Style). The White Stripes' second album, *De Stijl,* was dedicated to Gerrit Rietveld, a furniture designer at the heart of the movement in the Netherlands. In a recent interview, Jack White described why he loves the number three: "It sort of means perfection to me . . . in art, it keeps me confined at all times. I need to confine myself in order to create things, so I try to base most of the things that I do off of that number, even in secretive ways and ways that people would never notice." The White Stripes consistently used this rubric, as White explains: "I always return to the number three. Red, white, black. Vocals, guitar, drums. Storytelling, rhythm, melody. . . . The Holy Trinity, that's the big one." The White Stripes used a three-fold color scheme (red, white, and black) for all their albums, stage clothing, and album art. Asked in an interview about the meaning of his new blue aesthetic marking his debut as a solo artist, White said in a matter-of-fact way that he recorded the album on a pale blue Telecaster and an old blue amplifier. He began to wonder: "What if blues musicians like Robert Johnson and Blind Willie McTell actually wore blue clothes?" Then he laughed. Of course: blue for the blues.

As the lights go down, I quickly reenter my pew. Shortly, Jack White strides out, wearing a smart powder-blue country suit with a black wide-collar shirt and black boots. For this record and tour, he is working with two distinct bands: one male and one female (called Los Buzzardos and The Peacocks, respectively). This night The Peacocks play, which was my hope all along because of the haunting backup vocals by Ghana-born singer Ruby Amanfu and a fierce punk drummer, Carla Azar, known for her work with the band Autolux. They are all smartly dressed in various vintage gowns. Yet their formal demeanor immediately crashes into a fast and furious rendition of the first two songs from White's first solo album, *Blunderbuss:* "Missing

Pieces" and "Sixteen Saltines," followed by an equally rocking White Stripes tune, "Black Math." Each builds upon White's signature simplicity: vocals, guitar, and drums. The audience is on its feet immediately, with a kind of intensity of focus rare in concerts I've attended. Perhaps it is the venue, or perhaps it is that White has adopted Nashville as a hometown, creating a special bond between audience and performer, or perhaps it is just the intensity of the music itself. White's style of garage rock–influenced blues can do that to an audience.

There are signs aplenty that White wants to send a message of love to his new hometown, however. His Western-style light-blue suit pays homage to the country spirit of the Opry, and mid-set he brings out a surprise. Little known to most fans, White contributed a song to an unusual album made up of Hank Williams song lyrics that Williams himself had never set to music, titled *The Lost Notebooks of Hank Williams*. White's twanging tune, "You Know That I Know," pulls in the full band, including Maggie Björkland's beautifully wavering pedal steel guitar. The next song, "Hotel Yorba," draws again on The White Stripes catalog but here shines in new glory as if it had always been a barely concealed country song. About a dive hotel in Detroit, the song with its ironic chorus, ending "all they've got inside is vacancies," becomes the first full-throated sing-along of the night, an eager crowd shouting along as the band plays.

Jack White's deep musical love, however, is not country but the country *blues* — the early masters like Eddie James "Son" House, Robert Johnson, and William Samuel "Blind Willie" McTell. Unlike so many shallow white blues players, White seems to have always known he'll never quite have that something that makes the blues completely authentic. "The blues is from such a different time period and culture than where I'm from. Being a white kid from Detroit who was born in the '70s is a long way from being born black in Mississippi in the '20s. I'm always worried that playing the blues is going to be misconstrued as me trying to cultivate an image, or that it's going to come across fake." Unlike rock 'n' roll musicians in the generation before him (most famously Led Zeppelin, who were successfully sued for unacknowledged use of existing blues songs), White owns the truth that he is both borrowing from and honoring the blues as music that fundamentally belongs to others. A humorous case in point: After *L.A. Times* music critic Linda Leseman placed White at number twelve on "The Top Twenty Whitest Musicians of All Time," he featured her derisive comments on his website's homepage, as if the comment nicely summarized his sense of indebtedness to the blues players he so admires. She wrote: "His songs are often little more than de-fanged blues, lacking the passion and grizzled realness that makes the genre speak to so many people." Actually, given the number one record and sold-out show I am attending, his revival of the blues indeed speaks to many people. But ironically his deferential attitude and desire to honor the depth and power of the blues tradition contribute to making his own adoption of the blues vital.

While the concert ranges widely in musical style, dynamics, and influence, the final songs are pure Jack White blues. When he comes out for the encore without his coat, a drumbeat picks up the tempo from "The Hardest Button to Button" and the crowd claps along. Boom, boom, boom, boom. White, with his blue Telecaster, joins in with a pulsing grhange, grhange, grhange, grhange, matching beat for beat with the drum. From The White Stripes' major label debut, *Elephant* (2003), the song is what I call a "classic head-bobber." My head is bobbing, my body rocking slightly back and forth. It is a lament blues, a song about being a little brother and not fitting in. All the members of the family are buttoned up, but not this boy — he's the hardest button to button. The final song, voted far and away the favorite Jack White song in a poll by *Rolling Stone* magazine, is a classic twelve-bar blues song titled "Ball and Biscuit." His voice half spits, half begs: "It is possible I'm your third man, baby, but it's a fact I'm the seventh son." The lyric draws on lore about the superhuman strength of the "seventh son" (surely referencing Bluesman Willie Dixon's song of that name), and White is, as it turns out, the seventh son of ten children. The song describes the efforts of a man courting a woman, bemoaning the fact that he's only her "third man." Of course, "third man" also has overtones since White's Detroit upholstery business, where he got his start many years ago, and now his Nashville record label as well, are both named "Third Man." But here, he's singing the blues because he's only her third man, daring her to take a chance on him. Interspersed in between the verses, White breaks loose in guitar solos, a fuzzy melding of man and instrument in a desperate electric plea, head down, hair shaking, body twisting, lunging toward and, during the last solo, *into* Azar, who keeps pounding on the few parts of her drum kit that don't fall over. As the musicians bow and depart from the stage, the auditorium roars its appreciation. The whole crowd is caught up with me in a kind of ecstatic unity with the intensity of the songs. As the crowd cheers and the house lights come up, I think to myself: I've just had rock-and-roll communion.

As I file out of the auditorium, I ponder what I've just seen and heard. I know I intend to write about the concert, showing how such concerts are holy ground. But how can I make the claim, either of holy ground, or communion, or whatever? What predisposes me, or better, what accounts for a practical Christian wisdom with which I can see such depth in the music of Jack White (and the Alabama Shakes, for that matter) when the culture seems predisposed not to? In 2005, Mike Wallace did a CBS *60 Minutes* special featuring White. During the interview, White told Wallace his life could have turned out differently. "I'd got accepted to the seminary in Wisconsin, and I was gonna become a priest, but [at] the last second I thought, 'I'll just go to public school,'" says White. Wallace asks White, "What drove you from church?" White replies with a wry smile, "I had just gotten a new amplifier in my bedroom, and I didn't think I was allowed to take it with me." Why does Wallace imply that White was driven from church? Perhaps he is also working with the trope that "rock 'n' roll is always on some level a move away from God into the devil's music." The title of the CBS show was, not surprisingly, "Choosing Music over Religion."

White doesn't at all report choosing music over religion. His older brother, Ray Gillis, recently died unexpectedly. White and his brother were very close, and *Blunderbuss,* White's new album, is dedicated to him. Ray Gillis, too, felt a call to seminary and in fact served for a time as a Redemptorist priest. Both of White's parents, Gorman and Theresa, worked for the Catholic Archdiocese of Detroit. Recently asked if a relationship with God influences his music, White was articulate about his beliefs. It is not surprising to hear him claim, as a man of his generation, that he's not all that religious. He believes in God, and yet, he says, there are times you have to admit "there's a good chance [God] might not exist." Yet, White admits, "in a bigger sense, [believing in God] can influence everything, because if you try to create a song, or try to create something like an album, it pales in comparison to what God could create: a universe." A theologically informed humility is attractive, especially in a man regularly called a "rock god."

The God-influence shows in obvious ways. White's favorite bluesman, Son House, was a Baptist preacher who, like most early blues musicians, melds blues and gospel in his songs. The White Stripes' first album includes a cover of Son House's song "John, the Revelator." Their fourth album's title, *Get Behind Me Satan,* is a direct quote from Jesus, first speaking to the devil during his temptation in the wilderness, and then again speaking to his disciple Peter. Various songs include theological or scriptural allusions, including the tender closing lines of The White Stripes' song of love lost, "Dead Leaves and the Dirty Ground": "You know why you love at all if you're thinking of the Holy Ghost." The devil's music? It would be hard to make the case, actually.

The Scatological and the Theological

It is one thing to critique the categorization of rock and roll as the devil's music. It is another thing altogether to defend the claim that God is in pop music, to see in it a theological depth that shouldn't be ignored and might be formative of faithful Christian living. As soon as I make such a claim, friendly critics offer an example of some song or band that in their mind clearly shows what is "godforsaken" or at least tasteless in pop music. Black Sabbath, as I've already mentioned above, has such a profile. Yet in one of their first and most enduring hits, "Paranoid," guitarist Tony Iommi's charging guitar carries Ozzy Osborne along as he belts out lyrics like, "People think I'm insane because I'm frowning all the time." The lyric is weak, but then again, they wrote it in twenty minutes in the studio. Black Sabbath started as Earth Blues Band, covering such classics as Sonny Boy Williamson's "Early One Morning (Blues Fell Down)." After modest success, they realized that they could capitalize on the same cultural energy that drives the horror movie genre. After seeing fans lined up to see the Boris Karloff horror film *Black Sabbath,* they changed their name from Earth to Black Sabbath, becoming hugely successful and defining the sound of a new rock genre, heavy metal. They developed a reputation for massive drug and alcohol abuse and occult music, making use of the tritone, called a "flattened fifth" or "the Devil's Interval," in their songs. Yet they turned this in surprising directions, too, for instance claiming that war is demonic, caused by power-hungry politicians they label "War Pigs." The ironic ending of the song gives a fairly traditional biblical account of Judgment Day, when "no more war pigs have the power/hand of God has struck the hour/ Day of Judgment, God is calling." Even their supposedly most satanic song, "Black Sabbath," the first to feature the evil-sounding tritone, feels like a

Halloween song that goes "boo." After all, at the end of each verse, Ozzy sings, "Oh nooo!"

But one doesn't need heavy metal bands to argue for the view that there are "godforsaken" places in popular music. One could simply list some flatulent pop song that merely fills the air and leaves a bad odor. I'm thinking of the summer 2012 hit single by rapper Flo Rida titled "Whistle." The song starts (and mostly continues all the way through with) "Can you blow my whistle baby, whistle baby." Critics panned the song, a thinly veiled euphemism for oral sex, as "the least subtle song ever." Of course, such a song would never have a chance without a catchy tune, including a simple whistled melody.

Lots of other songs are equally bawdy, and always have been. Mozart famously wrote "Leck mich im Arsch," a canon in B flat for six voices, thought to have been composed in Vienna in 1782 as a party song. While literally the title means "lick me in the ass," a colloquial translation today would likely be "kiss my ass." Mozart had such a penchant for scatological references (in song, speech, and letters) that some medical historians suggest he suffered from Tourette's syndrome. At the least, he had a fairly crude sense of humor, something largely suppressed by his more cultured defenders. One feels their pain when listening to the juxtaposition of Mozart's sublime classical music, displayed even here in this canon, with accompanying lyrics imploring, "Lick me in the ass, quickly, quickly."

The story of how I found Mozart's song offers a perfect storm of bad taste in pop music. I had asked a friend what I should use as an example to test my arguments about the theological value of pop music. Her response: Insane Clown Posse (ICP). I knew nothing about them, but a quick search filled in details. Described as "horrorcore rap," the Detroit duo unknowingly stole a page from Black Sabbath. Originally known as Inner City Posse, rappers Violent J (Joseph Bruce) and Shaggy 2 Dope (Joseph Utsler) achieved only modest local success. They adopted a supernatural- and horror-themed style — including dark carnival and evil clown personae — as their means of creating a distinctive style. Widely dismissed as musically terrible and lyrically offensive, they have nonetheless found a loyal following over more than twenty years in part through their carnivalesque live shows.

Apparently, Jack White saw carnivalesque potential when he discovered the bad-boy side of Mozart. Recorded for his Third Man Records "Blues Series Single," the video announcing the single flashes "the collaboration you have all been waiting for . . . 230 years in the making." The words "Insane Clown Posse and" appear while a wheel of names cycles by on the other side of the screen: Gershwin, Bacharach, Presley, Dylan, Saarinen, and finally Mozart. The song, according to White's Third Man Record's press release, "marries Mozart's melody (and lyrics sung in operatic German) with ICP's poignant lyrical addition in English and Jeff the Brotherhood's monster-riffs, letting the whole thing tie together in the most beautiful of ways." While the ICP lyrics are difficult to find, one source lists the opening rap lyrics as: "Ahhh . . . Mozart, dope for the most part/Respected cuz he knows art/ . . . He wrote this, don't sugarcoat this:/'To get your ass licked off is the dopest'/Call it a fetish, call him a freak/Call him in need of a tongue on his butt cheek." In my view, this moves beyond disgusting to blatantly offensive. I have a knee-jerk reaction, and I doubt the good of even including the quote. Yet it represents the end of the spectrum that begins with explicitly religious or sacred song. In between, there are examples of explicit or implicit religious references, and nonreligious music that is not, however, offensive. Mozart and ICP (and Jack White, as the producer) deliberately seek to offend. Is this music then outside the theological pale? And if we say it is so, have we made an unwise decision that may lead to claiming categories of people (the Jews, African Americans, the mentally ill, and any number of other examples) are also somehow less than fully God's beloved?

On one level, of course, it makes sense to be discerning. Pop music is not all profound, of the sort that repays careful listening. Practical judgment helps see what is soul food, what is ear candy, and what is not worth eating at all. Yet too quick a judgment can be just as harmful. What helps me along the way when I first meet a new artist or, in this case, encounter a new song? When I first hear a new artist, I pay attention to a couple of key things in order to make a judgment about pop music's depth and significance. First, regardless of the obvious signs that may be telling me what sort of entrée the artist offers onto holy ground, I assume the artist *does* offer a way onto holy ground, even though it is cracked and broken at the same time. A vital doctrine of creation helps save me from thinking there is such a thing as unholy ground. Jesus, as my best theological teachers insisted, taught about a God who gives the best: "the sun and the rain to nourish — to everyone, regardless: the good and the bad, the nice and the nasty" (Matt. 5:45, The Message). This prodigal God holds the world in being each moment, and not one spark of life, not one flash of artistic insight, even if it is crude, happens outside of this creative presence. Rowan Williams uses the simple analogy of electricity keeping the lights on once the switch is flicked. The light is constantly held on by the flow of electricity. God's creative power is like that: the world was not created long ago and then God went away on holiday. Rather, God is present, with us, close as our breath, holding all things in being. Yet despite this, what does happen, and often, is that people deny or forget this holy presence. The reality, then, is that I see every work of art, every song or singer, as full of God. This conviction all by itself means I can't give rock and roll over to some realm outside of God's reach, as if it is territory ceded to the devil. Even if it is Flo Rida or ICP, I listen with openness to the presence of God's creative power at work. To avoid this would be only to see brokenness in their music, and not the creative power that produces their particular forms of pop art.

Further, then, I believe that in music that shows its brokenness, its self-imposed exile from God, God is especially attentive and engaged. While many people might grant me the generic "God made everything" argument above, this preferential option for the "sick and twisted" might be harder to accept. Let me explain. Martin Luther, the late medieval German theologian, argued for a category of theologian he called a "theologian of the cross." He meant by this to point to the undeniable fact that God's embodied action in reconciling love for the world shows up in the most surprising places: not just in the expected version of the Almighty parting the clouds, but as Jesus whom Christians call Immanuel — God with us. Jesus was born to an unwed teenage mother in a stable, surrounded by animals and straw. The gospels describe Jesus eating with the outcast, healing the impure, criticizing the religious leaders. In the end, he died in a place of shame, outside the city gate, side by side with condemned criminals. Believing in the God shown in Jesus teaches me to see that what many would consider "godforsaken" is exactly the precinct of the holy work of God. If this theological vision of Christian faith is true, wouldn't the Holy Spirit's work regularly surprise us in the midst of broken lives, outside the pale of properly religious music? Despite itself, even the most broken music finds itself caught up in larger purposes of which it knows not.

Still, after these core theological perspectives that help position me as a curious and attentive listener, it does help to know something of the religious background that shapes a musician's perspectives. Many more musicians sing out of faith convictions than actually sing explicitly faith-based music. Many of these, I've come to see, consider it a calling, as Jack White does, to use the creative gifts they've been given. They are driven to create, to give their talent away for the sake of the life of the world. As I say "give their talent away," I am also aware that many make a lot of money from their talents. However, for some at least money is not the driving force. Not only the music they make but the life they live tells a truth about what matters most. Here, the deep commitments can't ultimately be hidden. As Jesus put it, "Let anyone with ears listen!" (Matt. 11:15). This or that song can't be judged on principle (because it contains profanity or whatever other offense you might highlight). Instead, theological commitments lead to practical wisdom, listening for the character of the art and artists, and not just to see if I like it on first blush. I learned to listen this way, trying to hear the subtlety of artists' callings, their way of living their values through their art, by serving a long apprenticeship to the Irish rock band U2.

In the School of U2

It was the fall of 1985, my freshman year in college. I drove up to see Nick, a high school friend, who was attending a Christian college in Seattle. I was at a Lutheran college, and we had some rules (no drinking on campus, for instance), but it was different from Nick's school, where they had to sign a contract saying they'd abide by a much longer set of rules — no cards, dancing, drinking, drugs, premarital sex, and on and on. Code morality undergirding their rules was to apply as long as they were students, whether on campus or not. Had I thought about it, I would have been expecting to find only the "heavenly" side of my musical "heaven and hell" experience. That night, as we sat in Nick's dorm room, his roommate Joe clicked a cassette tape into his stereo. He turned up the volume knob and turned back to me. Slowly the sound of drums and a man yelling "Gloria" emerged from the silence, pushing into the room, insistent in its energy. Then the classic "2, 3, 4" count-off by the singer brought in the whole band with pulsating bass and chiming, echo-y guitar. When the singer started to sing, the lyric almost stuttered: "I try, I try to speak up/but only in you I'm complete." Before I could even think, "Oh, a sappy love song," the singer — whose odd name, Bono, stuck with me — sang chant, holy sounding chant, which I later learned was called Gregorian chant. He sang, "*Gloria, in te domine/Gloria, exultate/Gloria, Gloria*/O Lord, loosen my lips."

Joe then told me the album, *October,* was by the band U2, that it was their second album, and that they were Christian. Not a Christian rock band, he said. They are legit — a straight rock band. But Christians *as* a legit rock band. I didn't know you could do that. But the first time through the album I was totally sold. I'd never heard something so completely hold together the passion of full-on rock and roll and yet take the passion beyond the stereo-typical sex, violence, and drugs to a another place — to holy ground. I asked Joe if he'd make a copy for me and I listened to it all the way home in the car. I'm listening to it now, as I write this. The title track, "October," still haunts me to this day. It is a track with simple piano and only two or three lines for a lyric. Bono now calls it "unfinished." At the time, he so strongly believed in the inspiration of the Holy Spirit that he often went into the studio with no lyrics written, or only outlined ideas. The simple lyric of "October" basically says that while kingdoms rise and fall, "you" go on. I remember wondering, "Who is the 'you' that makes me complete? Who is the 'you' that goes on, beyond all the crazy power trips offered by the kingdoms of this world? Could he mean God?" Over time it seemed clear that he did. It was the band's way of making the lyric mean what they meant but also be open to many listeners, and to the others those listeners wished to imagine as the "you." Joe also slipped me a copy of the band's subsequent album, titled *War.* Its first song, "Sunday, Bloody Sunday," powerfully juxtaposed the shallow victories achieved by the Northern Ireland terrorist groups and the British soldiers, turning again and again to their guns and bombs, and the powerful victory won by Jesus' willingness to die on the cross for the sake of another vision: life over death, peace over war. The final song on the album, "40," is a simple rendition of Psalm 40, taking its chorus from Psalm 6: "How long to sing this song? How long?" It was a poignant ending to the album, in effect asking, how long do we wait for hope and history to rhyme?

The last line, about waiting for hope and history to rhyme, is language I learned from U2. It actually comes from *The Cure at Troy,* Seamus Heaney's adaptation of Sophocles' play *Philoctetes.* Bono quotes it in what is perhaps my favorite U2 song: "Peace on Earth." Let me explain. A decade ago, I'd just finished my doctoral studies in theology and culture at Emory University and had taken a call to an old Swedish congregation in downtown New Britain, Connecticut. My daughter, Grace, had just been born, and at her birth in the fall of 2000 I'd received a gift copy of U2's album *All That You Can't Leave Behind* from a dear friend. The album was for many fans the perfect pop album, an irony since the band's previous (and least popular) album was in fact titled *Pop!* The lead song from *All That You Can't Leave Behind*, "Beautiful Day," was number one on the pop charts and won three Grammy awards. Yet it was the song "Peace on Earth," a song never heard on the radio, which really spoke to me. I started the call in June of 2001. Within the first six months, I'd had thirty-two funerals, thirteen baptisms, seven weddings, and a patriotic fervor wash over the congregation in the wake of the attacks of September 11th. The worship committee chair took it upon himself to lead a congregational charge to install the U.S. flag in the front of the sanctuary, just left of the pulpit. I was overwhelmed!

One late fall Sunday, I was sitting in my car in the church parking lot. I'd arrived to teach confirmation for the seventh and eighth graders. Among North American Lutherans, confirmation typically requires two years studying the Scriptures and the Lutheran Confessions, leading in effect to a functional graduation ceremony that releases youth from churchly obligations. Cynical, I know, but all too true in the habits of many churches, this one included. Desperately trying to make a connection with the youth, I'd stumbled onto the practice of asking them to bring a favorite song to play, and I'd improvise a conversation on the basis of the song, connecting somehow to the Bible, church history, or doctrine. A few weeks before I'd listened to a hip-hop song brought in by one of the boys. It was Coolio's "Gangster's Paradise," and it begins with the lyric, "As I walk through the valley of the shadow of death/I take a look at my life and realize there's not much left." I asked the group to turn to Psalm 23 in their Bibles. I had no preparation for their reaction, which, to a person, expressed surprise and delight to find Coolio, a famous rapper, quoted in the Bible! Their interest in the Bible momentarily shot up until I calmly suggested that Coolio was sampling lyrics from the Bible, that Psalm 23, attributed to King David, was thousands of years old and is one of the most well-known and beloved psalms. Whatever else it was, they were engaged, and I went away feeling like we'd done something that connected, that mattered to them. So that became our catechetical pattern: songs leading into discussions of faith.

That night in early December, however, sitting in my car in the parking lot, the weight of the world lay heavily upon me. As I looked at the world beyond our small city, I felt a total loss of control. The war in Afghanistan, now a month into a major bombing campaign, seemed to me a huge mistake as a response to the September 11th attacks. Yet it was welcomed with raucous support by what seemed to be a unanimous response locally: lock-step patriotic flag-waving. I wanted to believe in the Lord who came as Prince of Peace, whose life was the inauguration of the new creation where lamb could lie down with wolf, where every tear would be wiped away (Isa. 11:6; 25:8). Yet the creation I was living amidst was eye for an eye, and that, as Mahatma Gandhi sharply put it, makes the whole world blind. As I sat, blankly staring out the front window, the song "Peace on Earth" came on. "Heaven on Earth/We need it now," Bono sings. The song was written in response to a terrible bombing in Northern Ireland just months after the Good Friday peace accords had been signed. The bomb, set off in the commercial center of Omagh on August 15, 1998, killed twenty-nine people and injured 220. Men, women, children, all out doing their Saturday shopping. Bono almost chokes on the lyrics, "sick of the sorrow/sick of the pain/sick of hearing again and again/that there's gonna be peace on Earth."

In a very touching, bitter, and difficult moment in the song, Bono recalls hearing of the bombing on Irish radio as name after name was read: "They're reading names out over the radio/All the folks the rest of us won't get to know/Sean and Julia, Gareth, Ann and Breda/Their lives are bigger than any big idea." The line honors the dead while offering a none-too-subtle critique of the "big ideas" that provide fuel for the long-standing "troubles" in Northern Ireland. The less subtle critique of the song, its most bitter cry, comes in the form of Bono's complaint against Jesus. The lament centers on the song of the angels sung at Jesus' birth, "Peace on earth and good will to all people" (Luke 2:14). "Jesus, sing a song you wrote/The words are sticking in my throat/Peace on Earth." He's sick of hearing these words, and faced with the utter evil of the violence in Omagh, he can't say them either. The harsh ending recalls hearing the phrase "every Christmas time/ But hope and history won't rhyme/So what's it worth/This peace on Earth."

"What peace on earth," I remember saying, tears welling up in my eyes, not at all prepared to face the teens soon to arrive for their confirmation class. This band was able to articulate with profound truth what it felt like just then to have one foot firmly planted in faith and the other firmly planted in the midst of a nation torn apart by war. U2's lives as men of faith were put to the test as men of action in the world, seeking peace, seeking to wrestle down a world where "hope and history rhyme." Stolen as though by a magpie, the famous line runs a bit different in Seamus Heaney's version of the ancient Greek play: "History says, Don't hope/On this side of the grave,/But then, once in a lifetime/The longed-for tidal wave/Of justice can rise up/And hope and history rhyme." Yet even in the engagement with the song, on my own and then with the confirmation class (that's right, I brought the song that night), U2 were tutoring me in what it looks like to live faith daily, and to sing it through one's music. This, I've come to see, is like night and day compared to Flo Rida singing about his whistle or Jack White and ICP sinking to the level of Mozart's scatology.

References

Engagement with pop culture requires digging in soil scholars rarely explore. Christian practical wisdom regarding pop culture is cobbled together from wide influences — friends and mentors, of course, and simply from my own experiences over time. That is the reason for telling stories from my own life, as do my coauthors in these opening chapters of our book. Perhaps because of the enduring assumption about the deep divide between people of faith and popular music, which is a leitmotif of the chapter, much of the best writing on pop music is not theological in any explicit sense. Of course there are exceptions, but whether because of its fleeting nature as a subject or because of its perceived taint as a realm obsessed with sex and drugs (the phrase "sex, drugs, and rock and roll" is common shorthand for the culture of popular music), few theologians have ventured to take up pop music as a theologically serious topic.

A couple of foundational texts have been important in framing my perspectives here, although I do not quote them explicitly. First, and perhaps most profoundly, I have learned from a slim volume by C. S. Lewis titled *An Experiment in Criticism* (Cambridge: Cambridge University Press, 1961). It is a rich resource not only in its main area of literary criticism, but also in making sense of how to engage in any of culture's popular arts, music included. Gordon Lynch offers a solid and helpful introduction to the field of studies in his *Understanding Theology and Popular Culture* (Oxford: Blackwell, 2005). Likewise, William D. Romanowski has worked this territory for many years, and his book *Eyes Wide Open: Looking for God in Popular Culture,* now in a revised and expanded edition, is a standard (Grand Rapids: Brazos, 2007).

Lynch and Romanowski introduce interested readers to a much wider range of related literature. My own thinking in this area has been developed in a book on theology and popular music: *Broken Hallelujahs: Why Popular Music Matters to Those Seeking God* (Grand Rapids: Brazos, 2011).

Given the relative dearth of good theological writing on pop music, it makes sense, then, that my first sources in the chapter are music blogs and essays. I begin my explorations here drawing on the well-regarded music blog *Aquarium Drunkard,* which first sang the praises of the Alabama Shakes, raising their profile considerably. The post about the Shakes was found at http://www.aquariumdrunkard.com/2011/07/25/the-shakes-you-aint-alone/, accessed September 7, 2012. Another source for pop culture fact and lore comes in the form of the long essay, and of this genre John Jeremiah Sullivan is an acknowledged master. I benefited from and quote his *Pulphead: Essays* (New York: Farrar, Straus and Giroux, 2011), p. 280. His essay "The Last Wailer" was originally published in *GQ,* January 2011. In sorting out my reactions to Sullivan's essay, I drew on a couple of critical resources, including Ennis Barrington Edmonds's excellent book on Rastafarianism, *Rastafari: From Outcasts to Culture Bearers* (New York: Oxford University Press, 2003), p. 75, and James Cone's *The Spirituals and the Blues* (New York: Seabury, 1972), one of the best books on the blues, bar none.

Another major source of information is the artists' albums themselves — the music but also the cover art and liner notes, and the accompanying music videos. All tell stories about artists and are worth consulting. Music references of this sort are noted in the chapter and can be readily found through a quick Internet search. Nearly any song you could imagine is now available for your listening pleasure on YouTube or numerous streaming music services including iTunes Radio, Spotify, Grooveshark, or Pandora.

Along the way in the chapter, I quote specific journalists who cover the artists I discuss, including the comparison of Alabama Shakes concerts to a rock-and-roll church (Sheena Barnett, "Alabama Shakes on a Wave of Success," *Northeast Mississippi Daily Journal,* December 2, 2011, http://djournal.com/view/full_story/16550136/article-Alabama-Shakes-on-a-wave-of-success?instance=home_news_bullets, accessed September 15, 2012). I include a set of quotes helping to unpack Jack White's creative use of the number three and his current use of the color blue, from a strange interview with NASA astronaut Buzz Aldrin, http://www.interviewmagazine.com/music/jack-white/print/, accessed September 8, 2012; Scott Frampton's en-

gaging conversation with Meg and Jack in *Esquire* magazine, http://www
.esquire.com/features/what-ive-learned/whitestripes0707; and Jake Coyle's
review of Jack White's first solo album, *Blunderbuss*, "In first solo album,
Jack White taps a blue vein," *The Washington Post,* May 3, 2012, http://www
.washingtontimes.com/news/2012/may/3/in-first-solo-album-jack-white
-taps-a-blue-vein/?page=all, accessed July 12, 2013. In a thoughtful dialog
with Darrin Fox, Jack owns the truth of his "borrowing" the blues, and in
the process shows his great respect for the history and context of the blues
in African American culture. "Jack White," in Mike Molenda, *The Guitar
Player Book* (New York: Backbeat Books, 2007), p. 92. The funny blog post
about Jack White being one of the whitest musicians is found at: http://
blogs.laweekly.com/westcoastsound/2012/05/top_20_whitest_of_all-time
_com.php?page=3, accessed September 9, 2012. The CBS special about Jack
White is from Rebecca Leung, "Choosing Music over Religion," http://
www.cbsnews.com/stories/2005/02/08/60ii/main672415.shtml, accessed
on September 9, 2012. Comments about Jack White's priest brother come
from Josh Eells's excellent biographical article in the *New York Times Magazine:* Josh Eells, "Jack White Is the Coolest, Weirdest, Savviest Rock Star of
Our Time," *New York Times Magazine,* April 5, 2012, http://www.nytimes
.com/2012/04/08/magazine/jack-white-is-the-savviest-rock-star-of-our
-time.html, accessed September 10, 2012.

There is a large literature on Mozart's scatological compositions and
the various letters showing similar tastes. The particular piece Jack White
recorded with ICP was Mozart K. 231. You can hear it, for example, in Chorus Viennensis, disc 8, in *Mozart: Complete Edition Vol. 12: Arias, Lieder Etc.*
(10 CDs; New York: Decca Music Group, 2006). This YouTube version includes the sheet music along with the Chorus Viennensis version: http://
www.youtube.com/watch?v=S9MN2WeqFY8, accessed July 5, 2013. Some
authors think Mozart suffered from Tourette's syndrome — on this see Benjamin Simkin, "Mozart's Scatological Disorder," *British Medical Journal* 305
(1992): 1563-67.

The theological references near the end of the chapter draw most especially on Rowan Williams's quite sophisticated and yet accessible theology of
creation found in his book on the creeds: *Tokens of Trust: An Introduction to
Christian Belief* (Louisville: Westminster/John Knox, 2010), p. 35. I also use a
phrase, "close as our breath," which is borrowed from Martin Laird, an outstanding patristics scholar and expert on Christian traditions on the practice

of contemplative prayer. See especially his *Into the Silent Land* (New York: Oxford University Press, 2006). For an excellent introduction to Luther's idea about being a theologian of the cross, see Gerhard O. Forde, *On Being a Theologian of the Cross: Reflections on Luther's Heidelberg Disputation, 1518* (Grand Rapids: Eerdmans, 1997). A longer and deeper exposition of this tradition that has influenced my writing here is Jürgen Moltmann, *The Crucified God: The Cross of Christ as the Foundation and Criticism of Christian Theology* (Minneapolis: Fortress, 1993).

I wrote about my ministry experiences in Connecticut in a previous book to which the authors of this present volume contributed some years ago. See Christian Scharen, "Learning Ministry over Time: Embodying Practical Wisdom," in *For Life Abundant: Practical Theology, Theological Education, and Christian Ministry,* ed. Dorothy C. Bass and Craig Dykstra (Grand Rapids: Eerdmans 2008), pp. 265-88.

My little book on U2, *One Step Closer: Why U2 Matters to Those Seeking God* (Grand Rapids: Brazos, 2006), seeks to depict how the band members draw on scripture and theology in their popular art, not only in songs but also in concerts, in videos, and in their social activism — a major component of their shared work as a band and in each of their individual lives. While their lead singer, Bono, is most known for this sort of activism, he is supported and often joined by the band in his work for those Jesus called "the least of these." U2's quote about hope and history is, as I note, from *The Cure at Troy,* translated by their fellow Irishman, the Nobel Prize–winning poet Seamus Heaney, whose adaptation of Sophocles' play *Philoctetes* is simply a literary marvel (New York: Farrar, Straus and Giroux, 1991).

part two

eclipsing

THE LOSS AND RECOVERY OF PRACTICAL WISDOM IN THE MODERN WEST

CHRISTIAN B. SCHAREN

NEAR THE END OF *DESCARTES,* his masterful study of the French Enlighten-ment philosopher René Descartes, John Cottingham writes, "Though Des-cartes' contribution to the philosophy of knowledge can scarcely be exag-gerated, his contribution to the philosophy of practice is generally regarded as negligible."[1] In this chapter, I press Cottingham's observation further by arguing that Descartes led the modern West on a trajectory that prized abstract reason and universal truth over practical wisdom and embodied judgment. God, for Descartes, is a brilliant creator who placed in humans the spark of reason, allowing our own rational search for the laws of nature and of human life. Yet Descartes's picture of a distant, rational God does not have a place for the peculiar story of a God who becomes flesh and blood, who dies and rises to new life, who sends the Spirit into the world. A practi-cal wisdom for the Christian life requires God incarnate, whose Spirit calls us to discern faithful lives in response to the needs of God's beloved world.

A clear challenge, therefore, in working out the proper role of practical wisdom within a practical theological account of the Christian life derives from the fact that modernity, following Descartes, has so clearly prized theory and abstract reason. The move to privilege abstract reason and the-oretical certainty, then, demotes practice and embodied experience as valid sources of knowledge. Underneath this persistent privileging of theoretical reason is a drive for certainty, a cultural and historical as much as philosoph-

1. John Cottingham, *Descartes* (New York: Blackwell, 1985), p. 152.

ical development in the West. On Stephen Toulmin's persuasive account, this drive for certainty emerged in response to the Thirty Years' War (1618-1648), fought at least formally across the religious divide between Roman Catholics and Protestants in Europe.[2] Until this point, Toulmin argues, both reason or abstract theory and reasonableness or practical wisdom coexisted as important if distinct kinds of knowing crucial for self and society. The descent into the horror of wars of religion, while not causing the vindication of Cartesian rationalism, at least produced a fertile ground for its reception during the seventeenth century. By the end of the eighteenth century, reason had won a clear victory over reasonableness (to name it differently: abstract reason over practical reason).

In this chapter, I seek to accomplish three things. First, I account for the central claim of this book that the kind of knowing at the core of the Christian life is closer to practical than to theoretical reason — closer, that is, to embodied, situated knowing-in-action than to disembodied, universal knowledge. Second, I describe how modernity in the West has been dominated by the desire for certainty, a dream of universal reason as the solvent for every knotty problem of human life or the natural world. As a result, modernity bequeaths us an impoverished understanding of the very kind of knowing by which we know and love God truly and love one another and the world rightly. I develop the second point by considering the remarkable philosophical and theological correspondence between René Descartes and the Bohemian Princess Elisabeth of the Palatinate. While not widely read until recent decades, their extended correspondence sheds considerable light on questions of the character of the good life, Christian responsibility, and practical judgment. Their theological and philosophical discussion of ways of knowing and their consequences offers a compelling case study of the limits of theoretical reason and the crucial place of prudence *(phronesis)* in the Christian life. Third, I sketch the long shadow of the victory of Cartesian rationalism in philosophy and theology, which continues to be strong but was challenged significantly by twentieth-century philosophers such as Martin Heidegger, Maurice Merleau-Ponty, and Ludwig Wittgenstein. The vital returns to "the rough ground" of practice forged by these philosophers and others have revalued practical wisdom and set the stage for a revitalized practical theology.

2. Stephen Toulmin, *Cosmopolis: The Hidden Agenda of Modernity* (Chicago: University of Chicago Press, 1992).

The Primacy of Disengaged Reason: Plato, Lipsius, and Descartes

In the West, Plato set the trajectory of seeking and privileging universal rules over the judgment of wisdom in particular cases, a trajectory Descartes in part followed. In fact, one can read the whole history of the West as a tension between two basic conceptions of knowledge, what Toulmin named reason and reasonableness. In a classic example of this tension, one of Plato's dialogs portrays Euthyphro as arguing for piety based on his own and similar particular cases. Socrates rejects these as "mere instances" and instead argues for a general definition that can be applied in any case.[3] In his discussion of Plato on this point, Aristotle contests the move to the universal, suggesting that the complexity of individual cases means that our right criterion is situated perception tutored by experience *(phronesis)*, not universal rules.[4] The trajectories of both Plato and Aristotle have a long history as influential ways of understanding Christian life and thought, but with the rise of the modern age the more Platonic alternative, abstract reason, became the dominant intellectual position.

Below, I rehearse a crucial moment in the turn to abstract reason in the West. The temptation might be to see this turn as merely scientific and philosophical or as the result of Descartes's own idiosyncratic brilliance. Yet this turn was a decidedly theological turn, with roots prior to Descartes and with lasting theological consequences. To set the context of Descartes's dialog with Princess Elisabeth, I begin with a preliminary discussion of the social and intellectual precursors of Descartes's position. The history of the concept of abstract reason as a privileged mode of knowledge helps to show why Descartes's conceptions of God and the Christian life would prevail in the West despite the fact that the arguments of his interlocutor clearly showed that the kind of knowing at the core of the Christian life is closer to practical than to theoretical reason, closer, that is, to embodied, situated "knowing how" than to disembodied, abstract "knowing that."

In setting the stage for Descartes's own developments in this direction, Charles Taylor emphasizes the role of Christianized Stoicism. Justus Lipsius (1547-1606) developed a vital and influential revision of traditional Chris-

---

3. Plato, *Euthyphro.* "Universal," from the Latin *universalis,* "of or belonging to all," was a translation of the Greek *katholou,* meaning "on the whole."

4. Aristotle, *Nicomachean Ethics,* book VI, chapter 9, paragraph 6.

tian ideas in two central respects. First, Lipsius replaced grace with reason. While traditional Christianity sees human beings as dependent upon God's grace to liberate our potential for good, Stoicism depends upon our innate power of reason. Grace comes to be seen as irrational, counter to how God (and those creatures made in God's image) act rather than integral to it. Second, Lipsius replaced *agape* with *apatheia*. While the pinnacle of Christian life is to be transformed by grace into Christ-like persons who love others unconditionally and give themselves away for the needs of the other, Stoicism views wisdom as a withdrawal from love, pity, compassion, or other strong emotions. Self-giving love becomes irrational, a sign of lesser moral and spiritual achievement. Using reason to know and obey God, then, a wise person is not buffeted about by winds of chaos or change; rather, a wise person in Stoic terms finds peace by inner firmness or constancy of mind.[5]

Why did this neo-Stoic voice have such an impact in the sixteenth and seventeenth centuries? First, of course, many members of the elite were appalled that religious divisions stemming from the Protestant Reformation had brought not greater peace but rather instability and war. The neo-Stoic revision of orthodoxy pulled back from the obsession with confessional differences and found common ground in Providence above and reason here below.[6] Second, these same elites wanted not just a new religious framework but also a new social order likewise based on reason. If God were the source of reason, in following reason we are following God's image placed in us, what Descartes would later call "the Maker's mark."[7]

The general contours of Lipsius's position had a profound influence on Descartes, who, while not adopting all his teachings *tout court,* still adopted a posture of neo-Stoic detachment and determined to seek inner truth

5. I'm drawing from Charles Taylor's excellent discussion of Lipsius in *A Secular Age* (Cambridge: Harvard University Press, 2007), pp. 114-20.

6. This Enlightenment hallmark is summed up in Kant's conclusion to *Critique of Practical Reason:* "Two things fill the mind with ever new and increasing admiration and reverence, the more often and more steadily one reflects on them: the starry heavens above me and the moral law within me." Immanuel Kant, *Critique of Practical Reason,* in *Practical Philosophy,* The Cambridge Edition of the Works of Immanuel Kant (New York: Cambridge University Press, 1996), p. 269. This quote was engraved on his tombstone.

7. Descartes, *Discourse on Method (Discours de la Méthode),* trans. John Cottingham, Robert Stoothoff, and Dugald Murdoch, in *The Philosophical Writings of Descartes,* vol. 1 (Cambridge: Cambridge University Press, 1985), p. 127.

through reason. One's deepest joy comes not from externalities, but from an inner joy arising from obedience to one's own reason and will. To hear Descartes pose the issue at its most theological shows the distance his views departed from the orthodoxy of prior centuries: obeying one's own reason "makes us in a certain matter equal to God and exempts us from being his subjects" because to do so is to be "like" God.[8]

In places, Taylor calls the inward turn that Descartes's position represents a "form of disengaged reason." The theological revision setting the "immanentization" of Divine Providence then separates the mind from the world, abstracted from its surroundings but with ideas "in" us corresponding to what is "out" there.[9] This has a similarity of sorts to the old paradigm of Platonic ideas, but the crucial difference is the collapse of these ideas into the mind, which has the effect of objectifying the world and at the same time withdrawing from it. Thinking in this way, we withdraw even from our own bodies and from all we experience in common with others, whether tradition or culture or family; we must find the truth of things by inquiring of our own mind and reason. Here we have not only "the eclipse of God" but the eclipse of our own bodies — with our desires and emotions — as sources for wisdom about daily living.[10]

The obvious theological difficulty with such a position is that it has done away with the crucial fact of Christian life: Jesus Christ, who calls disciples to follow him in loving God and neighbor. As Taylor points out, "Christ in the Gospels is portrayed as being moved 'in the bowels' by compassion (*splangnizesthai*)," which can hardly be followed by dispassionate and disembodied reason determining the right action.[11] The impulse of Descartes's attempt to determine right principles for action through dispassionate reason echoes through Kant's categorical imperative to Habermas's ideal speech situation.[12] This impulse, Taylor notes, can be described as a modern West-

8. Descartes, letter to Queen Christina of Sweden, November 20, 1647, trans. John Cottingham, Robert Stoothoff, and Dugald Murdoch, in *The Philosophical Writings of Descartes*, vol. 3: *The Corespondence* (Cambridge: Cambridge University Press, 1991), p. 325.

9. Taylor, *A Secular Age*, pp. 257-58.

10. Taylor, *A Secular Age*, p. 288.

11. Taylor, *A Secular Age*, p. 115.

12. Immanuel Kant, *Groundwork for a Metaphysics of Morals*, trans. Mary Gregor and Jens Timmermann (New York: Cambridge University Press, 2012); Jürgen Habermas, "Discourse Ethics: Notes on a Program of Philosophical Justification," in *Moral Consciousness and*

ern "code fetishism," which is to say we imbue sets of abstract rules with a kind of artificial power ("fetish" derives from the Latin *facticius,* "artificial," and *facere,* "to make") and universal applicability.

Taylor's contrast between the code fetishism of the modern West and the example of embodied knowing leading to right judgment for the neighbor that emerges in the Gospels' accounts of Jesus' compassion points to the privileged distinctions between abstract reason and practical knowing that are the focus of this chapter. The conviction that disengaged reason is the proper means for determining wise action — in everyday living as well as in the rarified space of scientific research — took on the artificial power of a universal code in the wake of Descartes's life and work. At the time, however, his position was relatively new and not yet culturally secure. Re-membering this, let us return to his correspondence, asking if Descartes's arguments in defense of abstract reason are as decisive as the later influence of his position would lead us to expect.

Debating Practical Wisdom:
René Descartes and Elisabeth of Bohemia

While not widely known until recent decades, the extended correspondence between René Descartes and the Bohemian Princess Elisabeth of the Palat-inate centers upon the crucial issue of the relation between mind and body as it pertains to Christian responsibility and practical judgment in daily life. Their debate captures in stark relief how modernity's privileging of theo-retical reason eclipses practical wisdom as a legitimate source of knowledge and ground for right action. However, thanks to Elisabeth's sharp mind and deep faith, their theological and philosophical debate offers a compel-ling case study for the limits of theoretical reason and the crucial place of practical wisdom or *phronesis* derived from experience in the Christian life, realities we are only now fully recovering nearly four hundred years later. The work of feminist historians in recovering Elisabeth's voice as part of the tradition of Western philosophy points to how the privileging of theory entailed eclipsing not just the embodied knowing of practical wisdom but

---

Communicative Action, trans. Christian Lenhardt and Shierry Weber Nicholsen (Cambridge: MIT Press, 1990), pp. 43-115.

also those whose bodies led them to be viewed as less rational — women and people of color especially. So one must name the fact that a whole history of domination and oppression accompanies this primarily privileged Western story of the "life of the mind."[13]

Brief Biographies

Descartes was not the first to spark the cultural and intellectual shift from the medieval to the modern world. After all, fifty years before his birth in 1596, Nicolaus Copernicus published his revolutionary conclusion that the earth rotates daily on its axis and revolves yearly around the sun.[14] While still a schoolboy, Descartes heard of Galileo Galilei's discovery of the moons of Jupiter.[15] Copernicus, Galileo, Johannes Kepler, Francis Bacon, and others set a context for Descartes's own path-breaking work in what he called "natural philosophy." As an area of inquiry, natural philosophy doesn't translate well, but it represents an early modern ambition to develop a method by which to explain all phenomena according to the light of reason. Of course, to do this one must assume human life works according to logic in the same way that gravity holds moons in orbit or levers move cogs in a machine. In this frame, nature and bodies become objects of manipulation and use, opening the way to ills of our time including oppression of women and people of color and, with similar logic, the earth itself. While Descartes was not alone in this theory fever, his work was then and remains of singular importance to the shape modernity would take in the West.

The basic facts of his life include his birth in La Haye, France. His mother died shortly after, and he was raised by his grandmother until the age of ten, when he was sent to "one of the most famous schools in Europe," the Jesuit college of La Flèche in Anjou, France.[16] He followed his years of formal

---

13. See on this Manuel Vasquez, *More Than Belief: A Materialist Theory of Religion* (New York: Oxford University Press, 2010), and Willie Jennings, *The Christian Imagination: Theology and the Origins of Race* (New Haven: Yale University Press, 2010).

14. Copernicus, *De Revolutionibus Orbium Celestium.*

15. Galileo, *Siderius Nuncius.* Stephen Toulmin gives an account of the events at La Flèche in *Cosmopolis,* pp. 56-61.

16. Descartes, *Discourse on Method,* in *The Philosophical Writings of Descartes,* 1:113. This same college trained many of the Jesuit explorers who, in the name of missionary expansion

education with worldly exploration, during which he famously vowed to "seek no knowledge other than that which could be found in myself or else in the great book of the world."[17] With a small pension from inherited lands, Descartes took a law degree and continued to travel and study through his twenties. After a time in Paris, he moved to Holland to find solitude for his work. Save for occasional travels to France and his last months in Stockholm tutoring the Queen of Sweden, he remained in Holland. As early as 1629, he envisioned a project that placed mathematical certainty at the center and took the knowledge of "all the phenomena of nature" as its scope.[18] Rejecting the perspectives of theologians (whom he accused of merely mastering "the art of denigration" by their quibbles, reminding him no doubt of the Thirty Years' War then raging), Descartes sought to develop a method for certain knowledge.

Descartes's famous method is outlined in his *Discourse on Method, Principles of Philosophy,* and elsewhere. The basic procedure begins when we are able to "lay aside all our preconceived opinions," "lead the mind away from the senses," and "give our attention in an orderly way to the notions that we have within us."[19] Essential to these moves is the "turning inwards" to innate notions that we find within our minds, first of which is his famous claim that "I am thinking, therefore I exist."[20] While he can doubt the truth of everything around him, even the reality of his own body, he cannot doubt that he exists — to doubt, he must be thinking, and therefore must exist. So the foundation for true knowledge is that he, Descartes, exists as a *res cogitans,* a thinking thing. A second truth, following from the first, is his ability to imagine God, an infinite being who created him. By this claim, then, Descartes builds a bridge from sure knowledge of his own thinking to sure knowledge of the world. The "Maker's mark," implanted in humans,

---

for Christianity, also subjugated whole peoples to European monarchs under colonial rule. See Willie Jennings's depiction of Jesuit theologian (and contemporary of Descartes) José de Acosta in *The Christian Imagination,* ch. 2.

17. Descartes, *Discourse on Method,* in *The Philosophical Writings of Descartes,* 1:115.

18. Descartes's book *Le Monde (The World)* remained unpublished after he heard that Galileo's book, *Dialogo sopra i due massimi sistemi del mondo, Ptolemaico e Copernicano* (1632), was condemned by the Congregation of the Holy Office in 1633. He recounts this in his *Discourse on Method,* in *The Philosophical Writings of Descartes,* 1:141-42.

19. Descartes, *Principles of Philosophy,* in *The Philosophical Writings of Descartes,* 1:224.

20. *Discourse on Method,* in *The Philosophical Writings of Descartes,* 1:127.

allows us to know true things about the world. Ironically, then, to have true knowledge about the world, we must turn away from it, distrust our senses, and rely on the truths God has implanted in our minds.[21] Descartes echoes here the Western tradition of Plato, Plotinus, and Augustine in turning "away from visible light — the ordinary world perceived by the senses — to the innate *lux rationalis,* the intellectual light implanted in our minds by the creator."[22]

For Descartes, soul and mind are equivalent. In prior medieval thinking, the soul was understood to be one with the body; the soul was understood as the substance and the body as the form, the soul "animating" the body.[23] For Descartes, Platonic forms collapse into the substance; persons are not merely forms, but distinct and created substances, the difference being the body's extension (having matter). Since the "I" Descartes can be sure of is the "mind," a non-extended substance, he can claim, "it is certain that I am really distinct from my body and can exist without it."[24] "The body," Descartes argues, "is always a hindrance to the mind in thinking."[25] He recognizes that passions (emotions or feelings) are not rational, not derived from the will, but arise unbidden from the conditions of life. "Why," he writes, "should that curious tugging in the stomach which I call hunger tell me that I should eat?"[26] While the question shows that he clearly recognizes the complicated question of the relation of body and soul, he never successfully resolves it.

We know something of Elisabeth's intelligence and character from the fact that she picked the most neuralgic problem — how the soul relates to the body — to begin her correspondence with the famous philosopher.[27] Elisabeth was of noble birth, the third child and eldest daughter

21. *Discourse on Method,* in *The Philosophical Writings of Descartes,* 1:127.

22. Cottingham, *Descartes,* p. 148.

23. Cottingham, *Descartes,* pp. 110-11.

24. *The Philosophical Writings of Descartes,* 2:54.

25. *Descartes' Conversation with Burman,* trans. with introduction and commentary by J. Cottingham (Oxford: Clarendon, 1976), p. 8.

26. *The Philosophical Writings of Descartes,* 2:53.

27. In academic convention, René Descartes is referenced by his surname; yet the equivalent is not available for Elisabeth since she is known by the noble house to which she belonged (alternatively Bohemia or The Palatinate). I have chosen here to follow the pattern of the correspondents themselves, which was to use "Descartes" and "Elisabeth," despite its obvious limitations.

of Frederick V, Elector Palatine and later King of Bohemia, and Elizabeth Stuart, daughter of James I of England. Born in 1618, she lived her sixty-two years amid the politics of religion in the seventeenth century. Her parents' marriage was hailed as a union of English and continental Protestantism. Her father's ascension to the throne of Bohemia in Prague was the result of a revolt against the emperor of the Holy Roman Empire, Ferdinand II, and one marker of the start of the Thirty Years' War. It was not long before Ferdinand rallied his forces and deposed Frederick after only a five-month reign, which earned Frederick the (unflattering) title "Winter King" (he was king only for the duration of the winter). The family fled to Germany, and then, with Ferdinand's troops advancing, to The Hague. Elisabeth, who had been living with her grandmother in Brandenburg during these years, finally was brought to The Hague in 1629, two years before her father was killed in battle. Elisabeth pursued studies in Holland during these years, and over time became active in managing family affairs. Although the character of her education is mostly unknown, her siblings gave Elisabeth the nickname "La Grecque" for her intellectual achievements. She remained in Holland through the 1640s; after the Peace of Westphalia in 1648 she returned to Germany, where she lived out her last decades as abbess of a large Lutheran convent at Herford.[28]

The Correspondence, 1643-1646

It seems that Elisabeth had tried to meet Descartes prior to the start of their correspondence, which she began after reading *Meditations on First Philosophy* in 1643. She opens an early letter in their correspondence by noting her "joy and regret": joy in Descartes's "charity in willing to share yourself with an ignorant and intractable person" and regret for "the bad luck that robbed me of such profitable conversation." She thanks him for sending "solutions" to some problems she had encountered in reading a book on physics and physiology. Their go-between was Alphonse Pollot (referred to in the correspondence as M. Palotti), a French gentleman-in-waiting in

28. This brief biographical sketch is drawn from Lisa Shapiro, trans. and ed., *The Correspondence between Princess Elisabeth of Bohemia and René Descartes* (Chicago: University of Chicago Press, 2007), pp. 7-16.

the court of her uncle and benefactor in the Netherlands, the Prince of Orange. Claiming M. Palotti had assured her of Descartes's goodwill, she charges into her pressing question: "I ask you please to tell me how the soul of a human being (it being only a thinking substance) can determine the bodily spirits, in order to bring about voluntary actions."[29] This first letter shows her humility, a virtue that seems in many cases to pave the way for her incisive questions. And in one way or another, her questions continue to return to this fundamental issue at the heart of Descartes's problematic construal of the mind's independence from the body.

Descartes's reply admits the problem Elisabeth has pointed out regarding the relationship of the body and the soul, but doesn't take the question seriously. He says, as if it were transparently obvious, that the soul[30] thinks, and being united with the body, can act on and be acted upon by it. His work up to this point has said nothing about this, as his "principal aim was to prove the distinction between the soul and the body" (*Correspondence*, 65). In her reply, Elisabeth first mentions her social and political obligations, "the interests of my house, which I must not neglect" (67). She notes that these responsibilities weary her, keeping her from being able to understand at all how a non-extended and immaterial soul can move the body. She admits finding it easier to "concede matter and extension to the soul than to concede the capacity to move a body and to be moved by it to an immaterial thing" (68). Elisabeth's engagement in practical affairs and her sense of Christian duty to serve the needs of others funds her critical reading of Descartes's position.

Descartes portrays himself as withdrawn from social and political affairs: he moved to the country to have quiet, and he works on his studies only a few hours a day, resting and gardening otherwise. Given this, he admires the fact that Elisabeth can attend to the issues in his *Meditations* in the midst of all that her position requires. She should, Descartes encouragingly notes, "feel free to attribute this matter and this extension to the soul, for to do this is to do nothing but conceive it as united with the body" (71). Those readers who caricature Descartes will be caught up short here: he does in fact argue

29. Shapiro, trans. and ed., *Correspondence*, p. 62. In what follows, page references from this work will be given in parentheses in the text.

30. Remember, for Descartes and Elisabeth, "soul" and "mind" are synonymous terms, pertaining to the non-extended created substance, the *res cogitans*.

for a kind of union of body and soul, but also for "the distinction between the soul and the body" (71). This admission, here undeveloped and sketchy, later becomes the motivation for developing his theory of the passions as a way to account for how passions seem to mediate between body and soul, coordinated, so Descartes thought, through the pineal gland in the brain.[31] In her reply, Elisabeth makes clear that Descartes's claim is not at all satisfactory — she presses Descartes, saying her experience shows her that the soul moves the body, and his writing teaches nothing of *the way* in which it does so (72). She wonders if perhaps there are "properties of the soul, unknown to us," which could perhaps overturn his claim about the non-extendedness of the soul. This first flurry of letters takes place over six weeks in the summer of 1643. Descartes does not write again until mid-November, and their correspondence turns to problems in geometry and algebra.

Nearly two years pass with little correspondence. Then, in May of 1645, Descartes's letter laments that "your Highness has been ill for a long time, and I rue my solitude, for it is the reason I did not know anything sooner. . . . I am so removed from the world that I do not learn anything at all about what happens" (85). He attributes her persistent illness to "sadness, and the stubbornness of fortune in persecuting your house continually" (86). The impact of the Thirty Years' War had already cost her family their ancestral lands and her father the throne of Bohemia, and now the outbreak of civil war in England was threatening her uncle, King Charles I, who had helped support her family since their exile to The Netherlands.[32] Descartes commends her for personally feeling so deeply the misfortune of those she loves. But he goes on, drawing on Lipsius's neo-Stoic teaching, to describe the difference between vulgar and noble souls. Vulgar souls are happy or sad in equal measure to agreeable or unpleasant events, whereas others, those he calls the great souls, "have reasoning so strong and so powerful that, even though they too have passions, their reason nevertheless remains mistress and makes it such that even afflictions serve them and contribute to the perfect felicity which they can enjoy in this life" (87). With this recommendation, Descartes sets up a conversation about what constitutes the

---

31. Descartes, *Les Passions de L'Ame (The Passions of the Soul)*, in *The Philosophical Writings of Descartes*, 1:340.

32. Charles I of England was the brother of Elisabeth's mother, Elizabeth Stuart. Charles was King of England, Scotland, and Ireland from March 1625 until his execution in 1649.

good life, a question that runs along the lines of how embodied experience ought to relate to one's reason and judgment.

Elisabeth laments that it is impossible to mimic the great souls Descartes speaks of who put mind over matter, for just as she calms herself, another disaster befalls her. For such anxiety, Descartes suggests, there is but one remedy: to divert one's imagination and one's senses and employ only one's understanding "when one is obliged to by prudence" (91). Descartes counsels that he "makes contentment depend upon myself alone" (92). Elisabeth, seemingly horrified, regards such a position as unfaithful: to so divert her attention from her imagination and senses to focus on false contentment was no less than "sinning against my duty" (93). Descartes believes he has Elisabeth's health and well-being in mind when he argues that there are no events so disastrous that one cannot find a favorable angle. His frustration shows in his voice when he says, "I have tried before to recommend carefreeness to your Highness" (95). A fundamental divide begins to show itself here: Descartes's neo-Stoic ethic of reason over passion, of mind over matter, and of inner contentment cut off from worldly events, clashes with Elisabeth's practical connection of her bodily passions and her moral duty for the well-being of others. To put it more sharply: the world is an object to Descartes, a thing he can control and rise above in order to live the good life, whereas Elisabeth inhabits a world filled with subjects about whom she feels passionately and toward whom she must act compassionately, for to her acting such is synonymous with what it is to live a Christian life.

Sure that Elisabeth has not been convinced by his own arguments, Descartes writes suggesting that they read and discuss Seneca's *De Vita Beata*. Seneca, a Roman Stoic philosopher, allows Descartes the vehicle for pressing his position that "to live happily is nothing but to have a mind that is perfectly content and satisfied" (97). This does not come, he argues, from external events fortune brings to us, but from internal satisfaction. It comes through reason and the will, and not the passions, bound as they are to the senses and bodily experience. "The greatest felicity of man," Descartes writes, "depends on the right usage of reason" (99). To Descartes's surprise, Elisabeth appreciates Seneca's rhetoric but considers his instruction unhelpful. One cannot, she argues, arrive at true happiness by will alone. She pointedly raises the example of Epicurus, who while he "was struggling to convince his friends that he felt no pain from his kidney stones, instead of crying out like the vulgar, was leading the life of a philosopher and not that of a prince or a captain" (100). Her point, subtly put as always, is this: unless a person is as withdrawn as Descartes, not engaged in affairs of the world, one can hardly afford such mind games. Politely thanking him for his explication of Seneca, Elisabeth pointedly encourages him to continue onward, especially in teaching her how to strengthen her understanding so that she can "judge the best in all the actions of life" (106). She wants, in other words, to learn *prudentia* rather than Seneca's (and Descartes's) offer of *contemplatio*.[33]

In his next letters, Descartes begins to sketch a theory of the passions, suggesting to Elisabeth that he has control of mind over body and has no upsetting dreams, nor even any sad thoughts (107)! In a strong reply, Elisabeth refocuses from inner life to public life. Given the many accidents that surprise us, Elisabeth argues, persons governing the public do not always have time to examine all possible responses, and so (no matter how virtuous they are) they perform actions that they might later repent of, something Descartes had advised her one should never do if one has acted with right reason. True, she argues, judging by reason, without passion, will help protect one from numerous faults, but "in order to esteem these goods in this way, one must know them perfectly. And in order to know all those goods among which one must choose in an active life, one would need to possess an infinite science" (110). This is a devastating critique, one prefiguring the twentieth-century philosophical critiques of code fetishism and the dream of artificial intelligence based upon it. As contemporary philosophers such as Hubert Dreyfus have shown, even supercomputers cannot achieve results that rise to the level of human practical wisdom in making accurate situational judgments.[34] Elisabeth is fully aware that one cannot know every

33. Seneca argues, as does Descartes, for transcending the body and its limitations in order to find the good life. He wrote: "Just as skilled workmen, who have been engaged upon some delicate piece of work which wearies their eyes with straining, if the light which they have is meager or uncertain, go forth into the open air and in some park devoted to the people's recreation delight their eyes in the generous light of day; so the soul, imprisoned as it has been in this gloomy and darkened house, seeks the open sky whenever it can, and in the contemplation of the universe finds rest. The wise man, the seeker after wisdom, is bound closely, indeed, to his body, but he is an absentee so far as his better self is concerned, and he concentrates his thoughts upon lofty things." Seneca, *Volume IV, Epistles 1-65,* Loeb Classical Library 75 (Edinburgh: Hunter & Foulis, 1917), p. 455.

34. Hubert Dreyfus, *What Computers Still Can't Do* (Boston: MIT Press, 1992).

situation in all its complexity in order to know how reasoned positions or principles would apply in each case. For her, passionate engagement and practical judgment are required.

Descartes's response is theological: one needs only knowledge of the truth and the habit of remembering and acquiescing to this knowledge. Again, Descartes betrays his neo-Stoic revision of Christian conceptions. The key to this knowledge, he says, is knowledge of the God upon whom all things depend, including our immortal souls. The vastness of the universe God has made sets our human desires and pleasures in perspective, causing us to seek what is pleasing not to us but to God. Being disposed to "judge well," Descartes believes, comes from "long and frequent meditation" on knowledge of the truth, thus "imprinting it sufficiently in our mind so that it turns into habit." In what seems like an acknowledgment of her point, Descartes admits that knowing this truth about God by reason is not enough. "In this sense, the Schools are right to say that the virtues are habits, for one rarely makes a mistake because one doesn't have the theoretical knowledge of what to do, but only because one doesn't have the practical knowledge, that is to say, because one doesn't have a firm habit of believing it" (113).

Elisabeth worries about this theological position, a view of God that she thinks "separates the particular providence, which is the foundation of theology, from the idea we have of God" (115). She insinuates that his separation of the idea of God from particular revelation in Jesus Christ relates to his rejection of the importance of experience and understanding arising from concrete particulars of Jesus' life, death, and resurrection.[35] She gives an example: prudence, which, in her view, suggests that wise action does not always consist of *ignoring* circumstances but of *directly engaging* them: "In observing the customs of the countries where we are, we sometimes find some very unreasonable ones that it is necessary to follow in order to avoid even greater inconveniences. . . . I am constrained to abide by the impertinent established laws of civility so that I do not acquire enemies. Since I began writing this letter, I have been interrupted more than seven times by these annoying visits" (124). Prudence, Elisabeth seems to say, means acting

---

35. In a later letter, Elisabeth expands on the term "particular providence": "By that special providence which is the foundation of theology, I understand that by which God has for all eternity prescribed means so strange as His incarnation. . . ." Shapiro, trans. and ed., *Correspondence*, p. 124.

in response to the particulars of the situation. Descartes firmly disagrees, suggesting that even if we do not have the "infinite science" Elisabeth says she requires to act rightly by reason, one can still be confident and not regret one's actions if one has basic principles to follow. Fundamental among these, Descartes argues, is that God is infinite and has ordered all things in the world such that "even if each person related only to himself, and had no charity for others, he would not ordinarily fail to work for them in everything" (122).

Exasperated at not getting the sort of help she desires for practical ethics, Elisabeth clarifies that she would really like to hear Descartes's maxims for civic life rather than his pontifications about relating only to himself. In laying out her challenge, she suggests that for guidance in public life she has "always found it better to avail myself of experience rather than reason" (134). In their prior letters, Descartes had admitted to Elisabeth his own need for solitude, and some of her pointed replies suggest her frustration that his replies to her do not relate to a life of public duty such as she finds herself living. Descartes, to his credit, admits that he has been unhelpful. Because he "lives a life so retired, and . . . distant from the management of affairs," he does not feel able to advise her on maxims to observe in civil life. Here he makes an extraordinary concession, countering his own arguments thus far in their correspondence: it is "better to regulate oneself in this regard according to experience rather than reason since we have rarely come across people who are as perfectly rational as all men ought to be, to the extent that one could judge what they will do solely by considering what they ought to do" (137). Encouraged by this reply, and unhappy with the practical help provided by their discussion of Seneca, Elisabeth asks Descartes to read and comment upon Machiavelli's *The Prince*. Here, finally, she has an angle for discussing prudence and practical ethics in civic life. Unfortunately, but not surprisingly, Descartes has a strong negative reaction to the book.

While Descartes admits to finding some good precepts in Machiavelli's famous treatise on political leadership, he objects strongly to the argument overall. How, he wonders, can a good house be built on a bad foundation? Machiavelli builds his main case from the perspective of a usurper and how he must rule. Still, Descartes demurs from giving advice, claiming that the imagination required to judge effective political leadership requires intimate knowledge of particular circumstances, something he admits he lacks. "I would deserve to be mocked if I thought myself able to teach something to your Highness on this matter" (143). As if to retreat to territory where he feels more comfortable, Descartes returns to Seneca, hoping Elisabeth is willing to practice maxims teaching that one's felicity depends only on oneself.

By the time Elisabeth receives Descartes's comments on *The Prince,* political events have caused her to move to Berlin, and she admits "a thousand regrets" for not bringing her copy of the book with her on the trip (145). Yet she disputes Descartes's position anyway, suggesting that Machiavelli simply uses the usurper as the most extreme case in order to examine how to govern under more complex circumstances than most will face, thereby dealing with the most difficult challenges to his argument. Descartes does not pick up this thread, instead continuing his theme of seeking inner happiness, following one's "interior joy" (148). One almost feels that he is unable to cope with the inapplicability of his own position, yet unwilling to admit the need to plunge into the difficulties of right judgment in complex circumstances of civic life. He cites Socrates, who calls interior inclinations to joy or contentment his "daemon," and recommends such a focus for Elisabeth as well, rather than dwelling on the difficulties raised by her "Physician of Princes" (149).

While the letters continue sporadically for another three years (up until Descartes's death in February of 1650), Elisabeth's reply in late 1646 seems to be the last word on the relation of body and soul to knowledge and practical judgment. Descartes had encouraged the example of Socrates, perhaps trying to dislodge her attention from the discussion of Machiavelli's view of practical judgment for rulers. Her tart rejoinder to Descartes suggests she's having none of it: "one would have to have a greater daemon than Socrates to succeed in that matter, for since he was not able to avoid either imprisonment or death, he has no reason to brag about it very much" (151). She goes on to affirm the value of her own experience in public life, asserting that "those matters where I follow my own inclinations succeed better than those where I let myself be guided by the advice of those more sage than I am." Without arrogance, she simply states her matter-of-fact view: "I have examined the paths," she writes, "better than those on whose judgments I rely" (151).

The character of the friendship is warm, yet the overall character of the debate is more heated than warm. Descartes said that, of all his colleagues and acquaintances, Elisabeth was the only one who understood everything he wrote. While we have only her letters as a theological and philosophical window into her thought, it is an extended and impressive view. Particularly given the larger story of the rise of theoretical reason and abstract principle as the authoritative mode of knowledge in the West, it is telling here to see the fragility of Descartes's position, and even its failings. Over the course of only a few years, a rather focused debate on the formal issue of the mind-body relation gave way to debate about abstract reason versus embodied wisdom in the Christian life, raising theological questions leading in quite different directions. While others might judge differently, in my view Elisabeth's argument for embodied and contextual judgment, prudence, and practical wisdom learned over time gains the upper hand in their debate, despite the fact that Descartes's position would eventually take precedence.

It is instructive to take account of the outlines of what happened subsequent to their correspondence. In part as an effort to gain support for Elisabeth's family, scholars believe, Descartes accepted an appointment tutoring the Queen of Sweden. Unfortunately for him, she required the lessons at 5:00 in the morning, while his pattern throughout his life had been to remain in bed until at least 10:00 a.m. Within a year, Descartes became ill and died. His body was returned to France, and in a ritual borrowed from festivals for the saints, he was buried with full rites of the Catholic Church.[36] This served the agenda of his friends who were seeking legitimacy for Cartesianism.

The victory for Cartesianism was won. By the time Immanuel Kant wrote his three critiques, he was ignoring the whole Western tradition of using distinct words to differentiate theoretical reason from practical reason (in Greek: *theoria* and *phronesis,* or what Toulmin calls reason and reasonableness). Kant used the same word for pure and practical reason: *Vernunft* (reason).[37] Why did he not use something else, like *praktische Verstand* (practical understanding), for the second critique?[38] One might say, among other things, that Descartes's position won among intellectual elites, including increasingly influential scientists, but also among theologians who were working out conceptions of God and the Christian life in his wake.

Elisabeth charted a quite different course after the end of her corre-

36. This fascinating story is chronicled in Russell Shorto, *Descartes' Bones: A Skeletal History of the Conflict between Faith and Reason* (New York: Doubleday, 2008).

37. Immanuel Kant, *Critique of Practical Reason.*

38. A point made by Stephen Toulmin, *Return to Reason* (Cambridge: Harvard University Press, 2003), p. 24.

spondence with Descartes. Her family regained modest land holdings, but a number of the men in the family had died in the war, including her father. Seeking a place of refuge and service, Elisabeth joined a large Protestant monastery at Herford, Westphalia. Within a few years, she was exercising her practical wisdom as abbess of the monastery, overseeing an enterprise that included about seven thousand people and the abbey farms, vineyards, mills, and factories. She offered hospitality to religious dissenters, including William Penn, Robert Barclay, and others.[39]

Even though the dominant forces of Elisabeth's age were the rise of abstract reason *(episteme)* and related advances in technical production in the rising capitalist economy *(techne),* her story shows that practical wisdom *(phronesis)* did not go away but remained as vital to everyday Christian life as ever. One might say, then, that the work to overcome Descartes's subject-object split and the disengaged, disembodied reasoning it entails, a move that gained substantial energy in philosophy and culture only in the twentieth century, simply aims to articulate something already there, suppressed and ignored, and to advocate for its importance. This is also our main work in this volume. In the correspondence, as in Christian life generally in the modern era, practical wisdom was eclipsed but never went away. Descartes was simply unable to see its place and power, despite Elisabeth's ability to force him to recognize this blind spot in his arguments.

Returning to the Rough Ground

The victory of Cartesian rationalism in philosophy and theology held sway until the twentieth century, when philosophers such as Wittgenstein and Heidegger forged vital returns to "the rough ground" of practice and practical wisdom, setting the stage for the revitalized practical theology this volume as a whole seeks to develop and encourage.[40] But the long-standing influence of Cartesian rationalism, Scottish theologian Fergus Kerr writes,

39. Shapiro, trans. and ed., *Correspondence,* p. 214.

40. Wittgenstein distinguishes the "crystalline purity of logic" from the "rough ground" of what we actually say and do. See *Philosophical Investigations,* trans. G. E. M. Anscombe (Englewood Cliffs: Prentice Hall, 1953), §107. See also Joseph Dunne, *Back to the Rough Ground: "Phronesis" and "Techne" in Modern Philosophy and in Aristotle* (Notre Dame: University of Notre Dame Press, 1992).

impacts much work in theology up to today.[41] All along, the social and natural sciences, and increasingly the humanities as well, have been dominated by modern conceptions of an individual mind thinking through reasoned laws or principles that supposedly make sense of the world.

Yet, as Kerr points out, these "modern conceptions of the self sprang from explicitly theological concerns." Descartes, from whose work these characteristic "modern conceptions" issued forth, subtitled his famous *Meditations* (1641) thus: "in which are demonstrated the existence of God and the immortality of the soul."[42] The work was dedicated to the theology faculty in Paris. As we have seen above, Descartes's understanding of mind and world is based on a new method rooted in skepticism. Kerr claims theology and spirituality in the modern era have been "permeated with Cartesian assumptions" that have often gone unrecognized. Kant, writing in the famous *Groundwork of the Metaphysic of Morals* (1785), shows us the Enlightenment man "who confronted even with Christ turns away to consider the judgment of his own conscience and to hear the voice of his own reason." Here, Kerr concludes, we have "the picture of the self-conscious and self-reliant, self-transparent and all-responsible individual" inherited from Descartes.[43]

While Kerr's focus is not practical judgment *(phronesis)*, his argument about the Cartesian influence on modern theology's conception of the self has direct implications for it. Among his examples, Kerr engages Hans Küng, one of the most widely read theological writers in the English-speaking world. His many books — including the classic *Does God Exist?* — stake out a basic argument rooted self-consciously in modern epistemological categories.[44] Küng's overall argument is set over against the modern legacy of radical skepticism (Descartes) and nihilism (Nietzsche); he characterizes both thinkers as apostles of "mistrust." But he will not accept the critique

41. Fergus Kerr, *Theology after Wittgenstein,* 2nd ed. (London: SPCK, 1997), p. 3.

42. René Descartes, *Meditations on First Philosophy,* in *The Philosophical Writings of René Descartes,* 2:12.

43. Kerr, *Theology after Wittgenstein,* p. 5. Of course, it is remarkable to consider how obviously male this conception is, a factor Descartes's debate with Elisabeth brings into stark relief. The intertwining of such abstract conceptions of knowledge with male dominance, not only over women but also over people of color and, one has to add, over the earth itself, is only widely noted in the various literatures of liberation after 1960. See the next chapter in this book, "Disciplining."

44. Hans Küng, *Does God Exist? Answers for Today* (New York: Doubleday, 1978).

that faith is an irrational alternative. To bolster his eventual claim for faith in God, Küng argues that one must make a conscious decision to trust any fact of reality at all, which he claims even the natural sciences must do. Thus, he claims, if "there is no logically conclusive proof for the reality of reality, neither is there one for the reality of God."[45] As Kerr summarizes, Küng ironically pictures the self in very Cartesian style as an individual who must decide to trust that God exists and is intelligible, more or less in the same way one must decide to trust or not that the world exists and is intelligible. This impulse to describe our plight so, Kerr argues, seems reasonable because we are creatures of a society formed within Cartesian assumptions. We find "objective" and "principled" points of view as more trustworthy, more valid somehow. But in order to achieve this perspective, it has to be (as Bernard Williams put it) "the absolute conception of reality" rather than a contextual, situated, and embodied conception more characteristic of day-to-day human life.[46] Kerr convincingly shows how taken-for-granted this conception of reality is, such that we very often cannot even see the extent to which we work within it. Descartes's legacy, Kerr surmises, taints everything we see.

Sarah Coakley, while agreeing on the whole with the critique, wonders if Kerr's version of Descartes is quite as accurate, and therefore as devastating, a critique as Kerr maintains. She notes how Descartes plays for Kerr the "veritable anti-hero," as a thinker who reduces himself to a solitary, detached, objective, and disembodied ego. Further, Coakley notes, these characteristics are all lumped under the term "individualism." Without making a project of exonerating Descartes, Coakley argues — as does this chapter, following her move — that Descartes does look rather more complicated when one reads beyond "selected purple passages, especially the 'peeling back' maneuvers of Meditation II."[47] In pursuing her argument, Coakley turns to the correspondence between Descartes and Elisabeth to show how in actual fact the relation of body and soul in Descartes is "often badly misunderstood." Descartes shows himself to have a notion of quite close interaction of body and soul, as we noted above, despite still claiming

45. Küng, *Does God Exist?* p. 475.

46. Kerr, *Theology after Wittgenstein*, p. 23.

47. Sarah Coakley, *Powers and Submissions: Spirituality, Philosophy, and Gender* (Malden, MA: Blackwell, 2002), p. 76.

a distinction one from another. Coakley's argument is in part to show how, by careful historical work, one can discover much more nuance in Descartes, raising questions for us about the taken-for-granted notions we live by.

Genetic Histories

My point in rehearsing the Kerr-Coakley debate over Descartes's legacy is to display two modes of responding to the question: What are the historical roots of our present modes of living? In Kerr's version, Descartes becomes a straw man who sets up Kerr's exposition of a theological alternative that draws on the work of Wittgenstein's philosophy. Here, no careful historical work is done; but, on the basis of a critical summary of the problem Descartes's legacy imparts to us, Kerr shows the Cartesian influence over various contemporary theologians (Küng among them). Coakley's example of a more careful historical analysis offers another way.

Similarly, in a previous volume my coauthors and I shared in writing, *For Life Abundant,* our colleague Ted Smith described this other way of asking about the history of the present.[48] He calls for doing theological histories of practice in order to understand the stakes in our patterns of living and articulate theological reasons for living differently. While Kerr and Coakley agree that the Cartesian legacy is problematic, following Coakley and Smith leads to a subtler and ultimately more powerful critique that shows how the very history Kerr rejects as unhelpful contains hints of exactly what we need for developing contemporary philosophical and theological alternatives. Spelling out a bit more carefully how this second historical way unfolds will set up my concluding comments about a return to situated or embodied cognition and its dependence on *phronesis.*

Theological histories of practice entail three moves. A first move focuses on practices — on the embodied habits of daily living. Smith means by this widely shared actions, and therefore not exceptional actions. A second move entails what Smith, borrowing from Charles Taylor, calls "genetic history."[49]

---

48. Ted A. Smith, "Teaching History in a Practical Class," in *For Life Abundant: Practical Theology, Theological Education, and Christian Ministry,* ed. Dorothy C. Bass and Craig Dykstra (Grand Rapids: Eerdmans, 2008), pp. 211-23.
49. Smith, "Teaching History," p. 213.

These histories explicitly look back to discover how patterns of thought and action developed and moved from radical innovation to established norm. These are not case studies, however, which tend to remain within one historical moment. Rather, in a third move, genetic histories have a theological (or better: eschatological) horizon, and they try to connect the dots across time and into the present. For Christians, God is at work in history. Thus, despite the brokenness of practices and processes that establish themselves as natural, Christians believe the Holy Spirit is indeed at work in and through them, working redemption.

Such histories have enormous critical power. I chose to highlight the Descartes-Elisabeth dialog exactly for this reason. Close attention to the practice of thinking about how one lives rightly invites us beyond Kerr's dismissal of Descartes and shows the alternative contained in their dialog, which was suppressed and forgotten in the course of time. Why such history is powerful for practical living becomes clear when we listen to Charles Taylor's basic claim for philosophy in developing his argument for genetic history.[50] One could, I think, make the same argument for theology. "Philosophy is an activity which essentially involves, among other things, the redescription of what we are doing, thinking, believing, assuming, in such a way that we bring our reasons to light more perspicuously, or else make the alternatives more apparent, or in some way or other are better enabled to take a justified stand on our action, thought, belief, assumption. Philosophy involves a great deal of articulation of what is initially inarticulated."[51] Why, one might ask, does history — rather than, say, social analysis or constructive theoretical argument — play an essential role here? Taylor continues: "successful articulation frequently requires — though it never simply reduces to — recovering previous articulations which have been lost."[52]

What is lost in the West with Descartes's victory for disengaged, abstract reason and the search for universal principles? His dialog with Elisabeth

---

50. It is worth noting the similarity of this notion to Foucault's genealogy, a perspective Taylor gestures to as similar but nihilistic, given its dependence on Nietzsche, a characteristic Taylor obviously wants to avoid. See Michel Foucault, "Nietzsche, Genealogy, History," in *Language, Counter-Memory, Practice: Selected Essays and Interviews,* ed. D. F. Bouchard (Ithaca: Cornell University Press, 1977), pp. 139-64.

51. Charles Taylor, "Philosophy and Its History," in *Philosophy in History* (Cambridge: Cambridge University Press, 1984), p. 18.

52. Taylor, "Philosophy and Its History," p. 18.

makes clear what is lost: her argument for the validity and importance of embodied experience as a mode of knowing required for living wisely. As the case with Princess Elisabeth shows, there are at least three reasons why Descartes's disengaged reason alone cannot guide us well in making practical decisions.[53]

First, as Elisabeth clearly argues, events are underdetermined; no rule can ever capture all the variety of circumstances in which one has to act. In a perhaps sarcastic tone, she pokes at Descartes's arguments, saying one would need an "infinite science" to know how to act rightly in every case. Anticipating a point made much later by Ludwig Wittgenstein, Elisabeth means that rules help only when one knows how to follow a rule in the midst of this or that specific situation, with all of its messy complexity.[54] In her example of balancing the rules of civility, she argues that wise action does not consist of *ignoring* circumstances but of *directly engaging* them. To follow a rule, therefore, means to follow *here,* in *this* moment. To follow a rule is a practice, something Descartes finally acknowledges but does not have space for within his method of disengagement. Taylor summarizes it this way: "the good person with *phronesis* really operates on a deep sense of the goods concerned, plus a flexible ability to discern what the new situation requires."[55]

Second, there are almost always multiple goods; more importantly, these goods conflict. Descartes advocates withdrawal, even from the senses and the body, in coming to right judgment. His lifestyle, disconnected from the world, shows the result of his conviction. Elisabeth presses her claim that one must judge between conflicting claims by plunging into the conflicted space of leadership, where actions cannot always be wholly pure and one must face regret as well as satisfaction. Her offering of *The Prince* for conversation underscores this view. Descartes acknowledges this point, agreeing with Elisabeth regarding the necessity of "regulating oneself according to experience," something he admits not having, given his withdrawal from social and political life.

Third, the complications of competing goods block the ability of codes

53. Taylor, *A Secular Age,* p. 704, outlines these three reasons that I adapt to summarize the strength of Elisabeth's arguments.

54. Wittgenstein, *Philosophical Investigations,* §202; Charles Taylor, "To Follow a Rule," in *Philosophical Arguments* (Cambridge: Harvard University Press, 1991), p. 167.

55. Taylor, *A Secular Age,* p. 704.

or abstract rules to exactly fit any given circumstance, heightening the need for practical wisdom. Add to this the Christian perspective of discerning the situational need of the neighbor we are called to love, and one sees, as Taylor puts it, "how Christian faith can never be decanted into a fixed code." Right judgment in a particular situation, from a Christian perspective, always includes "more" than the situation in its materiality. The situation also opens to an eschatological dimension: grace is fundamentally arational, by which I mean that it gives itself over to other logic (mercy, not rigid law). Elisabeth clearly sees how she owes others her best concern and care, and she feels it would be a sin against her neighbor (and, by extension, God) to follow Descartes's advice to seek only a decontextualized attitude of "carefreeness." The general rule of seeking "carefreeness" for oneself regardless of circumstance could not possibly make sense in situations to which Elisabeth is called to respond.

Taylor shows the problem of reliance on decontextualized codes or rules in relation to Jesus' parable of the vineyard workers. The owner of the vineyard invites workers to come and work at the harvest for the price of the "usual daily wage," regardless of how far into the day they begin work. To consider this arrangement a generalized rule for a society would validate the protests of those workers who began at the start of the day. Yet the overwhelming, undeserved mercy offered to those who come late to the labor defines the character of the vineyard owner, a figure for the God revealed in Jesus Christ. Such cannot be determined in advance, by dissociation from engagement in the rough-and-tumble of daily life. Here, then, is the place for what Elisabeth calls prudence, or practical wisdom, in making judgments about daily life.[56] It is for her, as Taylor describes, a particularly Christian practical wisdom: seeking the complex, situational good of the neighbor.

Articulating Practical Wisdom

Despite how the privileging of abstract reason and universal principle eclipsed practical reason and situated or embodied judgment, such a central mode of knowing and acting has always been present on the level of daily life. Yet it took until the early twentieth century for a recovery of

56. Taylor, *A Secular Age,* pp. 704-7.

embodied practical wisdom to find a renewed prominence. With such thinkers as Dewey, Heidegger, Merleau-Ponty, and Wittgenstein, the importance of practical, embodied knowing and action has become central to academic thought, growing in its impact on practical theology, as Bonnie Miller-McLemore's chapter "Disciplining" shows.[57] Briefly sketching how two of these thinkers — Heidegger and Merleau-Ponty — open up space for reconsideration of practical, embodied wisdom shows recent efforts to vindicate the arguments by which Elisabeth prevailed against Descartes.

As we have seen thus far in this chapter, the dominant modern theory for connecting mind and world, rooted in the ancient philosophy of Plato, developed in Descartes, and further explored by Immanuel Kant in the eighteenth century and Edmund Husserl in the twentieth, argues that the mind is given shape by ideas or essences, allowing the mind to make sense of material objects in the world.[58] This "mentalist approach" requires my mind to consciously have the idea of a child, a door, and a school, along with their meanings as external realities, in order to aid the child in going out the door and off to school for the day.[59] In order to clarify the nature of the mind and the character of things in the world, Husserl developed a method for bracketing preconceived notions and attending to the phenomenon, the thing itself, in order to understand its thing-ness.[60] In doing so, he felt he could identify the essence of the child, the door, and the school as a way to understand how the mind recognizes the world and directs our apprehension of it as we figure out how to act day to day. The result, however, is an account of everyday life ordered by the mind and its rules for how to interact with objects in the world. This philosophical perspective fits hand in glove with the rational and technological emphases synonymous with the modern age.[61]

57. In the following paragraphs I draw on Shaun Gallagher's excellent article, "Philosophical Antecedents of Situated Cognition," in *The Cambridge Handbook of Situated Cognition,* ed. Philip Robbins and Murat Aydede (New York: Cambridge University Press, 2009), pp. 35-51.

58. Plato, *The Republic* (New York: Penguin Classics, 2012), 514a-520a.

59. Hubert Dreyfus outlines the "mentalist approach" in "Overcoming the Myth of the Mental," *Topoi* 25 (2006): 43-49.

60. Edmund Husserl, *Ideas: General Introduction to Pure Phenomenology* (New York: Routledge, 1931).

61. Charles Taylor, "Overcoming Epistemology," in *Philosophical Arguments,* pp. 1-19.

Husserl's student, Martin Heidegger, through his study of another ancient philosopher, Aristotle, began to develop a version of phenomenology quite distinct from his teacher's. Heidegger's key shift was to acknowledge that in ordinary daily living, one does not think about what one is doing as the Platonic-Cartesian-Husserlian view would have it. Rather, Heidegger describes the way a child is "given" a world through a kind of embodied apprenticeship — learning language and practices to cope with the world as one finds it. In this view, phenomenology is not so much about minds trying to understand the world (maintaining the subject-object split introduced by Descartes) as it is about beings who have a world, in an immediate sort of way (collapsing the subject-object split, as Heidegger's term for this — "being-in-the-world" — articulates).[62]

In Heidegger's perspective, when a parent is busy getting a child ready to go out the door and off to school, the flow of action simply unfolds. Carefully attending to the phenomena shows us *how* the door is available as the way out to school and *that* the child is a beloved other sent to learn. One does not need to consciously recognize the child and figure out how to use the door to send the child off to school. It all unfolds naturally, as we act in the world we have been given.[63] Were this everyday coping to break down, say the school was closed because of a snowstorm, we would briefly pause to deliberate, but even so the deliberation would be of a different sort than rational calculation. The obvious and available options of sledding in the fresh snow or making hot cocoa and playing a game would present themselves exactly because the available practices of life within which we have been raised give us ways of having a world and moving through it skillfully day to day.[64]

What Elisabeth articulates, and Descartes grudgingly admits to, is the importance of the kind of situatedness Heidegger describes. Descartes wants to begin by withdrawing from being-in-the-world, constituting the subject as observing the world as an object of analysis, about which one can determine rules for understanding (laws of gravity and so on). While Heidegger readily admits this is helpful in mathematics or physics, such knowing is always predicated upon a more basic knowing, a situated,

62. Martin Heidegger, *Being and Time* (New York: Harper & Row, 1962), p. 59.
63. Heidegger, *Being and Time*, p. 67.
64. Heidegger, *Being and Time*, p. 133.

embodied knowing in the world we depend upon to live wisely in our local communities. Heidegger does not discuss the role of the body in such knowing, however, despite how obviously important a factor it is. This was the task taken up by Merleau-Ponty, who, though French, read both Heidegger and Husserl. He was influenced by Husserl's later writings, especially unpublished lectures distinguishing between Descartes's concept of the objective body (body as extended substance) and the "lived body," by which Husserl meant the body I experience and with which I act.[65] The lived body offered Merleau-Ponty a way to describe how experience accumulates in the body. "My body, in a familiar surrounding," he writes, "finds its orientation and makes its way among objects without my needing to have them expressly in mind."[66]

In addition to this social orientation of perceptual ability, one tends to act in ways deeply shaped by what Merleau-Ponty calls "situational values" that are present "intercorporeally."[67] Whereas Descartes considered others a detriment to good judgment, Elisabeth found it hard to imagine how one could know how to judge wisely without embodied experience in community — exactly there, she says, she finds the challenge of acting wisely. Likewise, Merleau-Ponty argues that the body of the other is not interference with my knowledge of how to act but rather necessary, through direct interrelation with the other, to my perception of what good action is.[68] His example is language: "I learn language as I learn to use a tool, by seeing it used in the context of a certain situation."[69] Here, one recalls Elisabeth's desire to read *The Prince* and to discuss very practical consequences of wise action in challenging circumstances. Descartes both accedes to her point and withdraws from debate, not being willing to, as Merleau-Ponty puts it, "plunge in" as a body "being in the world."[70]

65. Gallagher, "Philosophical Antecedents," p. 42.

66. Maurice Merleau-Ponty, *Phenomenology of Perception,* trans. C. Smith (London: Routledge & Kegan Paul, 1962), p. 369.

67. Merleau-Ponty, *Phenomenology,* p. 379.

68. One can see here why Merleau-Ponty became a key partner to feminist scholars a generation later. See, for example, Judith Butler, "Merleau-Ponty and the Touch of Malebranche," in *The Cambridge Companion to Merleau-Ponty,* ed. Taylor Carman and Mark B. N. Hansen (Cambridge: Cambridge University Press, 2004), pp. 181-205.

69. Merleau-Ponty, *Phenomenology,* p. 403.

70. Merleau-Ponty, *Phenomenology,* p. 403.

Practical Wisdom Recovered

At the beginning of this chapter, I noted the context of the Thirty Years' War as an influence on the drive to disengaged theory and universal reason in science particularly and in "natural philosophy" generally. I also rooted this perspective in a long tradition in the West going back to Plato. As Stephen Toulmin notes, Plato was responding to similar circumstances of cultural upheaval — war, political crisis, moral confusion — when making his appeal to abstract universal theory against the Sophists, who thought there was no abstract truth to guide us but rather only acts based on a judgment regarding "the right thing at the right time."[71] Sophists were caricatured as those who could argue for this or that action regardless of any more foundational or objective warrant, which made their approach vulnerable to abuse by the most persuasive voice. Instead, Plato shifted from the timely to the timeless, from the particular to the general, rendering ethics as a theoretical science, like geometry.

In doing so, Plato necessarily downplayed practical knowledge. His famous student, Aristotle, determined that both theoretical and practical knowledge are necessary, theoretical for formal and analytic arguments as in geometry *(theoria)* and practical for generic ways of doing things *(techne)* and ways of doing things specific to each case *(phronesis)*. A radiation or MRI technologist, for example, is a technician since she interprets X-ray photos on the basis of predetermined formulae. A clinical physician, on the other hand, has to go beyond predetermined formulae from which to judge and must deal perceptively and in a timely way with whatever the patient presents. Any account of practical wisdom as *phronesis* considered procedurally implies the first step of identifying the situation, which according to Aristotle has certain features that must be considered: who did it, what was done, to what or in what context it was done, using what, to what end, in what manner, and so on. Therefore, theoretical precision is something even brilliant youths can display, but practical wisdom requires richness of experience for the sake of being able to perceive and weigh the significance of the details of particular cases.[72]

71. Albert R. Jonsen and Stephen Toulmin, *The Abuse of Casuistry: A History of Moral Reasoning* (Berkeley: University of California Press, 1990), p. 60.

72. Jonsen and Toulmin, *The Abuse of Casuistry,* p. 72. This is what Patricia Benner calls

If *phronesis* is fundamentally about perception, judgment, and action, then in some sense it is always moral action in that it entails acting appropriately to one's calling. To operate, then, *phronesis* requires embodied knowledge (what is implied by the equation "time + experience"). In Merleau-Ponty's sense, experiences layer as sedimentation in one's body so that one gains the sense of salience with which one can read a situation and see what it is that needs to be done here, now, within the horizon of one's calling. It does not follow that all embodied knowledge is *phronesis;* for example, one can become so skilled at hitting a nail with a hammer that one can deftly drive a 16d nail in a few blows, but such embodied skill is closer to *techne,* a kind of embodied generic knowing that does not require the perception of situational complexity, such as a physician would need when encountering a person with a smashed thumb. That situation requires, to be sure, knowledge of anatomy and physiology, but (as I note above) such theoretical knowledge only begins to point to the right action in the moment.

This is the bottom line for the sake of this book's larger project: in the Christian life, we need exactly this kind of knowing — concrete, as well as universal; timely, as well as timeless; a kind of knowing rooted in a capacity to understand situations with reference to their type and to hear their call, that is, the need to which one's action responds. This kind of knowing is fundamental to ministry and to the Christian life. It is the kind of knowing indigenous to practical theology. It is a kind of knowing that suffers under the dream that abstract theory can show what ought to be in general and thus here and now.

Practical theology has always traded in this coin of practical wisdom, although it has usually not been theology's main voice; at times it has even been suppressed as unreliable and dangerous. Practical theology has been working to revive this kind of practical wisdom over the past few generations, and in some sense you might say such a revival has been under way since Heidegger, Merleau-Ponty, Wittgenstein, and others set the stage for recovering a practical, embodied way of knowing.

"learning a sense of salience." See Patricia Benner, Molly Sutphen, Victoria Leonard, and Lisa Day, *Educating Nurses: A Call for Radical Transformation* (San Francisco: Jossey-Bass, 2010), p. 49.

disciplining

ACADEMIC THEOLOGY AND PRACTICAL KNOWLEDGE

BONNIE J. MILLER-McLEMORE

IN THE LAST CENTURY, as Christian Scharen's chapter "Eclipsing" suggests, scholars inside and outside academic theology have challenged the modern view of knowledge as located internal to the mind disengaged from bodies and society — what Canadian philosopher Charles Taylor dubs the "thrall of intellectualism."[1] Taylor names G. W. F. Hegel, Martin Heidegger, Maurice Merleau-Ponty, and Ludwig Wittgenstein as key figures unsettling this mind-centered epistemology. Much contemporary theology bears their influence, as well as the influence of a myriad of feminist and critical theorists whom Taylor fails to acknowledge but who also question ways of knowing that displace and disparage bodies, emotion, and social relationships. Impatience with theology done within the immanent frame of "mind over matter" has marked Christian scholarship since at least the mid-twentieth century. However, few theological disciplines have pursued the epistemological questions that Taylor and others raise as persistently as practical theology. As an academic area of study, it stands out for its relentless, even if inadequately recognized and evaluated, exploration of practical knowledge and the intelligence within practice.

This book as a whole has worked to "show" and "tell about" a kind of theological knowing that arises within practice and makes good practice possible. Our telling (Part 2) draws on age-old deliberations and contem-

---

1. Charles Taylor, *Philosophical Arguments* (Cambridge: Harvard University Press, 1995), p. 180.

porary scholarship to gain a better grasp of the knowledge displayed in our showing (Part 1). This chapter contributes to this effort by asking about epistemological trends of the last half-century and developments in practical theology whose reemergence as a discipline capitalized on and contributed to these trends. It asks: What important shifts in ways of knowing have occurred and how have contemporary theology and practical theology in particular sought fresh ways of knowing essential to theology and Christian life? It argues that an important epistemological reorientation stands at the core of practical theology's twentieth-century revival, even though this has received little notice or analysis. Instead, in the effort to establish the discipline, practical theologians have emphasized our contributions to methodology or how to go about doing theology. In fact, many scholars reduce practical theology to method, defining the discipline either around empirical study, as in the Netherlands where empirical research is central, or around the movement from description to interpretation to normative and pragmatic response, as in the United States where the discipline hopes to guide ministers and others in the practice of faith.[2] Of course, appreciation for practical theology's diverse methodologies is important. But this focus has inadvertently led us to slight what is offered not just methodologically but substantively to theology itself through practical theology's epistemological efforts.

This chapter addresses this oversight by bringing to the surface the steady interest in theological knowledge itself that has been a powerful undercurrent running beneath practical theology's better known interest in how to do theology. I proceed by describing general shifts toward greater interest in materiality and practice across disciplines and then investigating and assessing developments in practical theology primarily in the United States, focusing on a sampling of scholarship in which questions of theological knowing come to the fore both in the 1980s revival of the discipline and in a second generation of literature since the mid-1990s.[3] Reimaging

2. In the Netherlands, the work of Johannes A. van der Ven has been influential. See his *Practical Theology: An Empirical Approach* (Kampen: Kok, 1993). In the United States, many examples could be offered, but the most recent iteration is Richard R. Osmer, *Practical Theology: An Introduction* (Grand Rapids: Eerdmans, 2008).

3. When I discuss the "academy," my focus is the self-standing seminary and divinity school within the wider university. I do not explore how other university professional schools, such as law, education, and medicine, have broached the challenges of practical knowledge,

theological epistemology has certainly not been practical theology's only or even primary disciplinary aim. But, as this chapter demonstrates, it comprises one of its most important contributions. Through its close attention to practice and lived experience in the last several decades, practical theology stands among the most recent and most sustained efforts to recover, honor, articulate, refine, and advance forms of practical knowledge, whether pursued under the guise of *practical reason, wisdom, phronesis, pastoral imagination, theological know-how, poesis,* or *embodied knowing.*

Epistemological Trends: Philosophical and Theological Reappraisals

In 1863, when British geologist Sir Charles Lyell, a close friend of Charles Darwin, first uttered the phrase *mind over matter,* it probably seemed inconsequential.[4] His words extolling the upward ascent of life from "sensation" and "instinct" to the "improvable reason of Man himself" and the "ever-increasing dominion of mind over matter" merely echoed an age-old conviction running back to Greek antiquity that elevated spirit and intellectual virtue over nature, bodies, women, and sexuality. His phrase also fell neatly in line with the century of Western expansionism and imperialism that immediately preceded him. Seventeenth-century father of modern philosophy René Descartes put it simply: "I am truly distinct from my body, and can exist without it," an idea that goes along with his infamous epistemological claim, "I think, therefore I am."[5] Of course, as Scharen points out in "Eclipsing," we must take care not to misrepresent or exaggerate Descartes's intent. Descartes is not divorcing body and soul here. Rather, he is privileging the

---

generally with more success than theological education. The latter has been in thrall of the arts and sciences and has tried to earn a place within the humanities when, in fact, we might have learned quite a lot by turning to other professional schools. Further research and conversation are needed here, and I look forward to exploring this in future work.

4. Sir Charles Lyell, *The Geological Evidence of the Antiquity of Man* (1863), cited by Wikipedia, http://en.wikipedia.org/wiki/Mind_over_matter, accessed October 2010.

5. René Descartes, *Meditations on First Philosophy (with Objections and Replies),* in *The Philosophical Writings of Descartes,* vol. 2, trans. J. Cottingham, R. Stoothoff, and D. Murdoch (1641; Cambridge: Cambridge University Press, 1984), p. 54.

mind and emphasizing the distance from bodies that is required of thinking. Thinking requires withdrawal from bodies.

In the century after Lyell, however, and in the wake of Descartes's legacy, the phrase *mind over matter* assumed a place beyond their imagining, encapsulating in shorthand the modern hope in the mind's mastery over the body and the world around it. It also aligned well with an array of other binaries that shaped Western discourse, including theological talk about God and Christian faith, such as intellect over emotion, theory over practice, men over women, white over black, colonizer over colonized, and adult over child.

Today, this phrase and the assumptions behind it have been disrupted, even turned upside down, in a new leaning toward *matter over mind* — with *matter* standing in for a host of new interests in bodies, everyday life, practice, materiality, ethnography, childhood studies, brain studies, and so on. The reversal partly coincides with democratization and liberation movements that have given voice to those unable, for complicated political and economic reasons, to distance themselves from their bodies to the same extent as Descartes and the like, either because their bodies are marked as different by gender, race, sexual orientation, nationality, age, disability, and so forth, or because they bear acute responsibility for the care of bodies within the many dependencies of the extended family and beyond. Either way, the return of *matter* as a valid source of knowledge has parallels to the rise of subjugated knowledges of all sorts.

Examples of new ways of studying religion and theology, more attentive to its materiality, appear across all areas of religious and theological study. Only a few decades ago a prominent dictionary defined systematic theology as that "form of specialism which seeks . . . a rational and orderly account of the content of Christian belief."[6] Today, by contrast, one can buy a whole series of books on theology as practiced with gerunds as titles (*traveling, working, playing, shopping,* etc.).[7] In the 1980s, it was "difficult to think of a theologian interested in describing a congregation," according to

6. S. W. Sykes, "Systematic Theology," in *Westminster Dictionary of Christian Theology,* ed. Alan Richardson and John Bowden (Philadelphia: Westminster, 1983), p. 567.

7. See, for example, Elizabeth Groppe, *Eating and Drinking* (Minneapolis: Fortress, 2010), David H. Jensen, *Parenting* (Minneapolis: Fortress, 2011), and Darby Kathleen Ray, *Working* (Minneapolis: Fortress, 2011), among the first books in the series Christian Explorations in Daily Living, edited by Jensen.

Carl Dudley, well known for his contributions in congregational studies.[8] Today, ethnography, a social-science tool for studying living people, has gained incredible prominence, with scholars describing "ethnography as dogmatics," "ethnography as theology and ethics," and "ethnography as a pastoral practice."[9] To take one more instance, sociologist of religion Peter Berger contrasts the "very abstract" and "remote" research typical of his discipline's early reliance on survey data with a new interest in "how religion is experienced by living human beings in their actual lives," exemplified in recent books such as *Everyday Religion*.[10] The list of examples could go on to include instances from subject areas that might seem even more unexpected, such as biblical and historical studies.[11]

Scholars within and beyond theology differ in their assessments of the changes afoot, and these differences reflect the power struggles inherent in making epistemological claims. Within philosophy, for example, Stephen Toulmin describes what is happening as a "pendulum swing."[12] He talks more about a "recovery" of practical philosophy than about a win-lose battle. The value of practical knowledge has a long history, he argues, with origins in early tensions between Plato's theory-centered approach and Aristotle's more practical concerns. In his account, there are two major turning points. Although a kind of "practical philosophy" reigned from antiquity

8. Carl Dudley in informal conversation, as depicted by Don Browning, *A Fundamental Practical Theology: Descriptive and Strategic Proposals* (Minneapolis: Fortress, 1991), p. xii.

9. Nicholas Adams and Charles Elliott, "Ethnography Is Dogmatics: Making Description Central to Systematic Theology," *Scottish Journal of Theology* 53, no. 3 (2000): 339-64; Christian Scharen and Aana Marie Vigen, eds., *Ethnography as Christian Theology and Ethics* (New York: Continuum, 2011); and Mary Clark Moschella, *Ethnography as a Pastoral Practice: An Introduction* (Cleveland: Pilgrim, 2008).

10. Peter L. Berger, "Foreword," in *Everyday Religion: Observing Modern Religious Lives,* ed. Nancy T. Ammerman (Oxford: Oxford University Press, 2007), p. vi.

11. My immediate examples come from my own Vanderbilt University faculty colleagues, whom I do not see as unique on this score: James Hudnut-Beumler, *In Pursuit of the Almighty Dollar: A History of Money and American Protestantism* (Chapel Hill: University of North Carolina Press, 2007); J. Patout Burns and Robin Jensen, *Christianity in Roman Africa: The Development of Its Practices and Beliefs* (Grand Rapids: Eerdmans, 2014); and David A. Michelson, *The Practical Christology of Philoxenos of Mabbug* (Oxford: Oxford University Press, 2015). For an example in biblical studies, see Ferdinand Deist, *Material Culture of the Bible: An Introduction* (New York: Bloomsbury T&T Clark, 2000).

12. Stephen Toulmin, "The Recovery of Practical Philosophy," *American Scholar* 57 (1988): 349.

to the Renaissance, cataclysmic crises in the 1600s made people impatient with the more modest occasional Aristotelian reasoning and hungry for the assurance of timeless truths; in turn, today's challenges, such as nuclear war, the environment, and medical technology, have swung philosophy back to knowledge attuned to particular cases in specific situations. Neither style exhausts the scope of knowledge in Toulmin's eyes. Now is simply the time for the ascension of practical reason as a "neglected half of the philosophical field."[13]

Taylor has a darker and, in my view, more penetrating take on epistemological trends, enhanced by his keen religious sensitivities. He is less sanguine about modern epistemology and its anthropological assumptions. Descartes's "reflexive turn" or the idea that truth lies in the internal contents of one's own mind, abstracted from "what they 'represent,'" dramatically distorts both understanding and subjectivity, he argues, by presuming the possibility of a *disengaged self* distinguished from natural and social worlds (even from one's own body); a *punctual self* free to improve the self and world; and *atomism* or a view of society as built around such instrumental purposes.[14] Modern reason in this view is indelibly associated with some of the "most controversial and questionable" and "most important moral and spiritual ideas of our civilization." One cannot alter ways of knowing without "sooner or later" running up against the "force of this tradition" and some of its misperceptions of selves, bodies, and society that are inextricably interwoven into modern conceptions of knowledge.[15] Rather than waiting on a pendulum swing, Taylor sees a need to "overcome" modern Cartesian epistemology, replacing a pernicious representational model of knowing, where one depicts the known in one's mind, with a participational model in which one participates in the known. But his use of the term *overcome* is quite specific. He is not ruling out *theoria* nor imagining its destruction. Like Toulmin, he recognizes the value of critical reason and scientific examination of general truth-claims as "a very old" practice indeed.[16] Rather, he critiques modernistic distortions and argues for greater inclusion of alternative kinds of knowing. An Aristotelian-like *phronesis* is needed to close the gap

13. Toulmin, "The Recovery of Practical Philosophy," pp. 338, 345.
14. Taylor, *Philosophical Arguments,* pp. 5, 7.
15. Taylor, *Philosophical Arguments,* p. 8.
16. Taylor, *Philosophical Arguments,* p. 4.

between a general rule and its practice, a reality ignored in epistemologies that give "primacy to the rule-as-represented."[17]

Scholars in theology offer similar overviews of trends but with limited awareness of the effects of the fresh interest in materiality on conceptions of theological knowledge and with strikingly varied assessments of practical theology's contributions. In the early 1990s, historical theologian Randy Maddox wrote a succinct and comprehensive survey of the "various stimuli pushing for a recovered practical theology."[18] Although his essay predates the lively interest in material practices of the last two decades, it is singular in grasping the deeper historical roots behind the elevation of theory-centered theology, the epistemological problems this created, and the range of alternative ways of knowing now reshaping the discussion.

The title of Maddox's essay mirrors Toulmin's own title and essay, which Maddox cites in the footnotes. Maddox also reflects a comparable view that theology was inherently practical in its own early history. Rather than naming major turning points, however, he tells the story as one of gradual demise, parallel to Edward Farley's classic 1983 *Theologia,* from theology as a lively *habitus* or disposition toward God to a "functional-specialty discipline," a purely theoretical science devoted to systematic coherence.[19] Distinct from the tendency among many people in theological education to locate the problem in the nineteenth-century establishment of theology as a university science, where Farley focuses much of his attention, Maddox locates the decline several centuries earlier. In contrast to impugning Friedrich Schleiermacher with the creation of the theological encyclopedia that sequestered practice to one corner of the curriculum and reduced education to clergy training, problems arose in thirteenth-century debates between monastic leader Bonaventure and university scholar Aquinas over whether theology is a practical discipline devoted to what humans do or a speculative science aimed at contemplating God. Aquinas prevailed, Maddox argues, and the relation between the logical arguments of comprehensive *summae* and lived realities has been problematic ever since. In both the thirteenth and nineteenth centuries, the shifting social location

17. Taylor, *Philosophical Arguments,* p. 177.

18. Randy L. Maddox, "The Recovery of Theology as a Practical Discipline," *Theological Studies* 51 (1990): 650.

19. Maddox, "The Recovery of Theology," p. 657. See Edward Farley, *Theologia: The Fragmentation and Unity of Theological Education* (Philadelphia: Fortress, 1983).

of theology had a significant impact. As cathedral universities grew in the medieval era, with knowledge pursued for its own sake, a more practically inclined theology became "increasingly marginalized," located near monasteries and "only tangentially related to Christian life in the world" even in this context.[20] The Reformation reacted against this but without major effect. Instead of intellect and practice being reconnected, the two became further polarized. Protestant Orthodoxy, focused on faith as a "set of intellectual affirmations," adopted the university model of theology as science, while Pietists reacted by devaluing theoretical reflection and promoting spiritual theology.[21]

In his narrative, Maddox is both attentive to and ambivalent about practical theology as a discipline, partly because he was writing as its reconstitution gathered momentum in the late 1980s (he says in his article that it is hard to imagine a topic that has received so much attention). He gives notable space in a second article to divergent definitions of its subject matter and tasks. But he remains uncertain about its academic role, stressing its disciplinary confusion rather than its innovation. He concludes both essays with the same worry about theology's cohesion: if practical theology is defined broadly as mediating "praxis and the normative convictions of Christian faith," then, he asks, "What remains for systematic theology?" Yet, if we return to understanding Christian theology as practical (seemingly, his preference), the need for a "specialty-discipline Practical Theology is called into question." Notably, he seems unsure about whether practical theologians offer anything of long-lasting value, and he does not anticipate a promising future. The "prospects" of a renewed practical theology (as an academic discipline) overcoming the "split between doctrinal reflection and . . . Christian life are surely dim." What is needed instead is the "recovery of a model of theology per se as a practical discipline."[22] Of course, the matter of social location surfaces again, raising the question of whether it is possible to sustain theology as practical when its primary or most highly recognized location is the university and academy.

Two decades later, in a retrospective commemorating the twenty-fifth

20. Maddox, "The Recovery of Theology," pp. 652, 654.
21. Maddox, "The Recovery of Theology," p. 655.
22. Maddox, "The Recovery of Theology," pp. 658, 660; and Randy L. Maddox, "Practical Theology: A Discipline in Search of a Definition," *Perspectives in Religious Studies* 18 (Summer 1991): 168-69.

anniversary of *Modern Theology,* systematic theologian Kathryn Tanner is not pessimistic about practical theology; instead, she is curiously negligent. She does not include it in her review of major trends, even though she lifts up as central a new investment in practical matters. She says anxiety about theology's validity vis-à-vis modernity — the tired Chicago/Yale methodological debates over whether religious thought and language stand up to public criteria or have other purposes entirely — has given way to more substantive and grounded concerns. She offers a long list of contributing theologies, such as liberation, pragmatist, and radical orthodoxy.[23] Practical theology is conspicuously absent from the inventory. Because she was schooled at Yale, where practical theology has had little disciplinary visibility, her oversight should not surprise us.

Nevertheless, when Tanner assesses the journal's track record — what is "less commonly treated within its covers" — she faults the journal, and by implication modern (systematic) theology more widely, for its inattention to everyday theology. In the process, she unknowingly names a concern at the heart of practical theology's reemergence as a discipline in the 1980s:

> [A] theology, if genuinely concerned at the end of the day not just with academic matters but Christian living, would also benefit from seeing beyond elite forms of theological expression, in written texts primarily, to the popular theologies of everyday life: how people without specialized theological training go about trying to live in accord with their Christian commitments.[24]

Here and elsewhere, Tanner helpfully resituates what she calls "academic theology" as a Christian social practice on a continuum with other social practices and not as a second-order theory standing above "everyday theology."[25] But regrettably she says nothing about a discipline with longstanding interest in the latter. Shaping Christian living, learning from everyday theology, influencing thought and action — all these require a kind of practical knowledge that modern theology has largely disregarded and

23. Kathryn Tanner, "Shifts in Theology over the Last Quarter Century," *Modern Theology* 26, no. 1 (January 2010): 39-40, 42.

24. Tanner, "Shifts in Theology," p. 42.

25. Kathryn Tanner, *Theories of Culture: A New Agenda for Theology* (Minneapolis: Augsburg Fortress, 1997), ch. 4.

that practical theology has pursued. Greater familiarity on her part with practical theology's interest in *phronesis* or what James Fowler calls a "theology *habitus*" might have especially enriched her final conclusions, in which the term *judgment* appears repeatedly.[26] If academic theology is to make a full turn to more "substantive theological judgments and their practical ramifications," she concludes, "what is really necessary" is "an often more difficult and nuanced discernment about particulars . . . how to read the situation in a Christian light."[27] Such thinking is "messy, ambiguous, and porous" — something "disciplines such as sociology and anthropology reveal." And perhaps practical theology also?

Tanner might have learned a different approach from colleagues at Chicago, where she spent several years in mid-career before returning to Yale. Her University of Chicago predecessor, David Tracy, was considerably more cognizant and appreciative of practical theology, especially in its early 1980s efforts to resituate itself as a valuable university discipline. He arranged types of academic theology on a "logical spectrum" from the "relatively abstract (fundamental theology) to the concrete (practical theology)" in their efforts to correlate Christianity and everyday realities.[28] He is seen as a major contributor to this early movement, and when the International Academy of Practical Theology hosted its ninth biennial conference in Chicago in 2009, he returned as a celebrated guest speaker. He reiterated a conviction that had emerged for him in the intervening years on the essential place of spiritual exercises both in ancient philosophy and in today's theology, sparked by his reading of French philosopher Pierre Hadot.[29] In this light, he strongly affirms practical theology's unique position as a dis-

26. James Fowler, "The Emerging New Shape of Practical Theology," in *Practical Theology: International Perspectives,* ed. Friedrich Schweiter and Johannes A. van der Ven (Frankfurt: Peter Lang, 1999), p. 88.

27. Tanner, "Shifts in Theology," pp. 40, 43.

28. David Tracy, "The Foundations of Practical Theology," in *Practical Theology: The Emerging Field in Theology, Church, and World,* ed. Don S. Browning (San Francisco: Harper & Row, 1983), p. 62. The same threefold "portrait of the theologian" appears in chapter 2 of the second and last book of what he originally intended as a trilogy based on this same typology, *The Analogical Imagination: Christian Theology and the Culture of Pluralism* (New York: Crossroad, 1981).

29. Pierre Hadot, *Philosophy as a Way of Life: Spiritual Exercises from Socrates to Foucault,* ed. Arnold I. Davidson, trans. Michael Chase (Oxford/Cambridge, MA: Blackwell, 1995).

cipline sympathetic to the exercises necessary for the practical living out of religious convictions.[30]

Although Mary McClintock Fulkerson is Tanner's contemporary, she by contrast joins Tracy in giving significant credit to practical theology, even as she highlights the discipline's institutional instability and elusive definition.[31] In one of the best accounts of the new "lure of the practical," she traces a Protestant lineage familiar to practical theologians, from Anton Boisen's 1950s declaration that the "living human document" possesses qualities comparable to scripture and history as a valued text and source for theological construction, to his student Seward Hiltner's understanding of pastoral theology as "generating theology, not simply exploring a particular practice," to Hiltner's student Don Browning's use of German philosophy to argue for a reconceptualization of all of theology as practical. Only within this context, shaped also by liberation and recent pastoral theologies, does scholarship in systematic theology finally follow suit, late to the party, according to Fulkerson, moving away from "a (useless) kind of theory relevant only to academicians" toward making practice more central to its work. Interestingly, she describes this development as a "dispersion" of practical theology across the specialties.[32]

It is problematic when scholars, such as those influenced by Alasdair MacIntyre's virtue ethics, reclaim theology as practice while "virtually ignoring . . . the work of the so-called 'practical field'" — a critique of Fulkerson's that might also apply to Tanner and others influenced by George Lindbeck's postliberalism. Such patterns reflect hierarchies in the production of knowledge internal to theological studies, with scholars as members of a "professional managerial class," that beg for further analysis.[33] In addition, and in contrast to Fulkerson's own leaning, the turn to practice in itself

30. David Tracy, "A Correlational Model of Practical Theology Revisited," in *Religion, Diversity, and Conflict,* ed. Edward Foley (Berlin: Lit Verlag, 2011), pp. 52, 56-57. See also earlier essays by Tracy that express similar ideas: "Traditions of Spiritual Practice and the Practice of Theology," *Theology Today* 55, no. 2 (1998): 235-41; and "Reasons for Hope for Reform: An Interview with David Tracy," *America* 173, no. 11 (October 14, 1995): 12-18.

31. Mary McClintock Fulkerson, "Theology and the Lure of the Practical: An Overview," *Religion Compass* 1, no. 2 (2007): 302.

32. Fulkerson, "Theology and the Lure of the Practical," pp. 297-99.

33. Fulkerson, "Theology and the Lure of the Practical," p. 300. See Bonnie J. Miller-McLemore, "The Hegemony of Theory and the Politics of Practical Knowledge," in *Conundrums in Practial Theology,* ed. Bonnie J. Miller-McLemore and Joyce Ann Mercer (Leiden: Brill, 2016).

does not guarantee appreciation for the epistemological value of practice or positive reappraisal of and engagement with laity and clergy engaged in religious practices. Scholars can turn to practice in a completely theoretical way. Equally important, highly theoretical research in theology and beyond has its necessary and valued place and so is not by definition entirely "useless," as our book as a whole hopes to affirm.

Maddox concludes his historical summary by enumerating factors that have led to the recovery of theology as a practical discipline, with the specialty discipline of practical theology as only one of many. Nonetheless, the items he lists feature prominently in practical theological scholarship. Criticism of Western scientific rationality is key (e.g., the dislocation of knowledge from community and tradition, equation of knowledge with the universal and absolute, and disconnection between theory and practice). In addition, he names the rejection of professional elitism, new interest in doctrine's practical function in forming ethical communities and character, attention to social and political realities in political and liberation theologies, and renewed interest in liturgy, hymns, and care as theological activities. He suggests that these characteristics cohere around a common epistemological theme: "In large degree the move toward recovering theology as a practical discipline could also be seen as the move toward recognizing that theological reflection, in its most primary sense, is . . . *phronesis*" or the "wisdom for interrelating the universal with the particular."[34] Such reclamation of *phronesis* is actually a key feature of practical theology's revival as a discipline in the 1980s and 1990s, even though few scholars, Maddox included, have examined its appearance, evolution, and diverse conceptualizations in the discipline, a task to which I now turn.

Phronesis and the 1980s Revival of Practical Theology

Rodney Hunter, Emory University emeritus professor in pastoral theology, is best known for editing the preeminent *Dictionary of Pastoral Care and Counseling*. Even though he does not use the term *phronesis*, he was the first to argue that pastoral theologians pursue a distinct kind of how-to knowledge that they need to spell out more clearly. His depiction of "pastoral

34. Maddox, "The Recovery of Theology," p. 669.

theology as practical knowledge" in his 1980 essay in *Pastoral Psychology,* a leading U.S. journal of theology and psychology, is such a pivotal piece that it is surprising that others, such as Browning and Thomas Groome, do not refer to it at all. Hunter had studied with Hiltner, and his review of themes in the essay from a colloquy in Hiltner's honor reveals the growing pains of a relatively new academic area that, at that time, lacked the usual qualifications as a discipline, such as a professional society and journal. Hunter identifies in particular a tension between Hiltner's reorientation of theology as "operation-centered" (which Hunter calls an "ill-chosen" phrase likely adopted from John Dewey) and Browning's effort to turn pastoral theology toward a more theoretical kind of normative inquiry.[35] In contrast to the Hiltnerians, Browning's "more abstract and systematic moral reasoning" downplays the value of the particular or the "'idiosyncratic truth of the case,'" giving his approach at least the "appearance" (if not the reality) of a return to "logic-centered" knowledge.[36] Hunter sides with Hiltner on this issue and locates the discipline's future in its reclamation of theological knowledge linked to practice. But if academic status depends on the ability to "create *knowledge* of some kind," and if case analysis is the "center of our heritage," as pastoral theologian John Patton insists, then Hunter argues that more work is needed on the kind of knowledge made available through cases — "how the operations of ministry . . . disclose anything . . . theological."[37] This significant request — a plea really — stands at the heart of Hunter's essay and still cries out for further exploration.

In an essay published five years later, Hunter expresses his frustration that Hiltner's proposal that practice shapes theological knowledge has fallen on deaf ears. In 1958 Hiltner argued in *Preface to Pastoral Theology* — which Hunter also sees as unappreciated and misunderstood — that the "proper study of practice" has the potential to "illuminate theological understanding itself."[38] Did *Preface* fall into a gap between audiences, he asks, too difficult for ministers and not rigorous enough for scholarly peers? He ultimately concludes:

35. Rodney J. Hunter, "A Perspectival View of Pastoral Theology: A Critique of Hiltner's Theory," *Journal of Pastoral Care* 4, no. 4 (1985): 20.

36. Rodney J. Hunter, "The Future of Pastoral Theology," *Pastoral Psychology* 29, no. 1 (1980): 64. See also Hunter, "A Perspectival View," pp. 32-33.

37. Hunter, "The Future of Pastoral Theology," pp. 62 (emphasis in original text), 65.

38. Seward Hiltner, *Preface to Pastoral Theology* (Nashville: Abingdon, 1958), p. 47.

> [T]he book meets resistance precisely at the point of its central thesis. The idea that anything truly fundamental can be learned about the Christian faith by examining the concrete work of pastors or other Christian "practitioners" with hurting people, presents a double challenge. It challenges theology to consider the possibility that something of truly theological (and not merely psychological) significance can be learned by studying carefully the experiences of ordinary people.... At the same time Hiltner challenges theology to reflect on the potential importance of practical skills and knowledge as a source of theological understanding.[39]

Provoked by the dismissal of pastoral theology as merely concerned with "how-to" knowledge and inspired by Michael Polanyi's *Personal Knowledge,* Hunter is bent on redeeming the notion of such knowledge as far richer and more complicated than such views presuppose. For Boisen, who followed William James in his pragmatist interest in *"documents humains,"* and Hiltner, who followed Dewey, thinking is never static or disembodied.[40] It exists in action or, in Hunter's words, as a "contextually embodied, forward-moving problem-solving activity."[41] This kind of knowing stands behind a seemingly endless variety of activities — how to be a friend, how to be creative with a sermon, how to make a decision, how to be a leader or a follower, how to have sex, how to play classical music. Nonetheless, as he admits, Hiltner unfortunately does not "clarify the full epistemological import" of his claim.[42] In what way do such documents provide knowledge and what are the limits? How does practical knowledge compare and relate to other forms? Is there any such thing as practical *theological* knowledge?

39. Hunter, "A Perspectival View," p. 19.

40. Neither Boisen nor Hiltner explicitly identified or traced such roots. But Robert C. Dykstra points out Boisen's reliance on James in *Images of Pastoral Care: Classic Examples* (St. Louis: Chalice, 2005), p. 229 n. 4. See Anton Boisen, *The Exploration of the Inner World: A Study of Mental Disorder and Religious Experience* (New York: Willet, Clark & Co., 1936), and William James, *The Varieties of Religious Experience: A Study of Human Nature* (1902; reprint, New York: Penguin Books, 1982), pp. 10-11. For the influence of Dewey on Hiltner, see Hunter, "A Perspectival View," pp. 28-30. Hunter refers to earlier works on Hiltner's pragmatism (with which he only partially agrees) by Thomas Oden, *Contemporary Theology and Psychotherapy* (Philadelphia: Westminster, 1967), pp. 81-85, and Alastair Campbell, "Is Practical Theology Possible?" *Scottish Journal of Theology* 25 (1972): 223.

41. Hunter, "A Perspectival View," p. 29.

42. Hunter, "A Perspectival View," p. 20.

And how does one generate "theological knowledge that does *not* surrender its practical character"?[43]

Hunter's constructive effort to answer such questions is the heart of his earlier 1980 essay. There he describes the dynamics of practical knowledge, its location and development, and then attempts to elucidate characteristics distinct to theological knowledge in particular. Practical knowledge involves more than the "rational-technical forms of . . . manipulation" typical of the "advanced industrial world" — what those in the Frankfurt School and others since label *technical rationality* or *instrumental reason.* Doing brain surgery, raising children, or preaching all illustrate how practical knowledge emerges amid contingencies that require a different order of "logical complexity" sometimes described as the "wisdom of experience." Although he does not try to define *wisdom,* by *experience* he means a more expansive reflection than the usual individualistic connotations of personal or private encounter. It is a "form of knowledge that has accrued and matured through a history of practical contingent events," comparable to wisdom literature in the Bible.[44] What appears within this literature as merely a collection of maxims actually embodies deeper theological intuitions about faithful living that have evolved over time through religious traditions.

As this suggests, practical knowledge is acquired in communities of practice through apprenticeship. Unlike "products of a consumer society, simply there for the taking," it takes time and work. In a sense, "one must be an insider, a practitioner oneself, disciplined by the practice." At the same time, such knowledge is "not utterly esoteric" or out of reach, even if it cannot be reduced to general principles. It is communicated and learned in a movement between "precept and example," it requires "considerable intuition and interpretation on the part of the one who is learning," and it is most evident in the routine activity of expert practitioners or, as he says succinctly in his later article, in the "ordinary instances of highly developed expertise."[45] Finally, it requires a certain "authenticity" on the part of the learner. One imitates the master, but ultimately one must discover one's own gifts and style.

Is there anything distinctive, however, about practical *theological* knowl-

---

43. Hunter, "A Perspectival View," pp. 31, 32; emphasis in original text.
44. Hunter, "The Future of Pastoral Theology," pp. 66-67.
45. Hunter, "The Future of Pastoral Theology," p. 67; "A Perspectival View," p. 33.

edge? Here I struggle to do justice to Hunter's prose as he tries to get at the demanding and yet grace-filled character of such knowledge, analyzing what we decided in this book is sometimes better shown. Of course, as we have said, practical knowledge as theological wisdom is not something any-one should blithely profess to have acquired. So, not surprisingly, Hunter turns to Proverbs to speak about the "dangers of failing to take these lim-itations seriously": "'The fear of the Lord is the beginning of wisdom,'" he observes, and "also its end." Here the "end" of theological knowledge is understood both chronologically (our finitude) and teleologically (God as telos) — fulfilled only eschatologically.

The final paragraphs of the essay unpack this pithy proverbial saying by making two essential points on the unique "complications" of religious prac-tical knowledge. First, theological forms of practical knowledge hover at the "limits of human agency," engaging questions such as "how to be saved from death and sin, the ultimate practical religious questions, or how to facilitate the salvation of others," or, for pastoral theologians, how to care for others and support their faith in and knowledge of God.[46] It is presumptuous and unwise to presume mastery here, although even faithful professionals and laity are tempted toward trite "manipulations of the divine." (Here I think of uncritical claims about answered prayers or comments to the ill or be-reaved that suffering or loss is God's will.) Can "anything at all," he asks, "be learned about these things, that is, about how to live with that which transcends even life and death?"

Second and related, religious forms of practical knowledge ultimately mean a paradoxical transcendence of self and an alliance with the wider wisdom within God's created world. All practical knowledge by definition seeks to influence the world and ends up changing the actor. But in reli-gious practical knowledge, the self is not only changed but also transcended. "For practical religious learning must in some sense entail a learning about how to live with life's transcending limits themselves — moral evil, death, meaninglessness — as destructive of the self yet not ultimate." This means "learning something like how to receive one's existence from God" or "how to live transcendently as a child of God." And this requires not just receiving grace, but practicing and even becoming "experienced" in "living in grace."[47]

46. Hunter, "The Future of Pastoral Theology," p. 68.
47. Hunter, "The Future of Pastoral Theology," p. 69.

Wisdom, then, means participation in the life of God, the doing of God, God as a verb. People who are wise have a sense of how the world works and strive to align themselves with the wisdom within the world — what he describes in his later article as "wisdom about the totality of life experience as theological narrative or drama."[48] The telos is to live within the life of God, leaning toward a convergence between our knowing and God's knowing.

When Hunter wrote these words in the 1980s, the discipline had not made much headway on the distinctive nature of such knowledge because of intellectual prejudice, as Hunter himself notes, and because of the absence of serious exploration. His own reflection would have been deepened by books that came out in the ensuing decade, such as Donald Schön's *The Reflective Practitioner,* Joseph Dunne's *Back to the Rough Ground,* Albert Jonsen and Stephen Toulmin's *The Abuse of Casuistry,* and Alasdair MacIntyre's widely read *After Virtue.* Even so, Hunter lays out in barebones fashion some key ideas that gained wider recognition through these later works and that anticipate work to come in practical theology. Although he never wrote the book on practical knowledge toward which he aspired, he structured the *Dictionary of Pastoral Care and Counseling* around his notion of the knowledge distinct to pastoral theology, choosing entries such as those on wisdom, casuistry, and prudence and asking authors to organize their writing accordingly.[49] For Hunter, pastoral theology is a "form of religious wisdom about how to live, specialized by its focus on the question of how to care for others."[50]

Hunter is singular, nevertheless, in his efforts to capture some of the elusive qualities of specifically *theological* practical knowledge. His comments in this regard suggest the curious intellectual distrust of such knowledge, es-

---

48. Hunter, "A Perspectival View," p. 33.

49. See Rodney J. Hunter, ed., *The Dictionary of Pastoral Care and Counseling* (Nashville: Abingdon, 1990). This interpretation of *The Dictionary* arose in personal conversation with Rodney Hunter, June 26, 2013. He himself contributed entries on wisdom and prudence, both of which reflect arguments laid out in this chapter. So, for example, he defines *wisdom* as a "deep or insightful understanding of life achieved through experience" and *practical knowledge* as "knowledge about how to do things or how to proceed in certain situations, also achieved through experience" (p. 1325). Pastoral theology can be "best understood as a form of wisdom and practical knowledge rather than as formal theology, philosophy, or science" (p. 1326), and "one of the aims of pastoral counseling is the cultivation of 'practical wisdom' or 'prudence'" (p. 969).

50. Hunter, "A Perspectival View," p. 33.

pecially its confessional leanings. Writing around the same time but apparently unaware of Hunter's efforts, although they were colleagues at Emory, James Fowler raises two concerns at the end of an essay otherwise devoted to singing practical theology's praises: practical theologians fail to account for divine initiative, and they remain enthralled by Enlightenment rationality. Almost as soon as he has uttered this critique, he retracts it, worrying that his peers will misperceive his comments as "anti-intellectual" and "ungrateful."[51] As it turns out, his worry was for naught because his ideas went almost entirely unmentioned and unnoticed until Thomas Hastings retrieved them over twenty years later. Hastings sees Fowler's critique as a bright spot in his own effort to disrupt what he feels is a modern rationality that permeates the university, even its post-Kantian critics. This way of thinking holds North American practical theology captive by an intellectual protocol that censors depictions of the divine.[52] Both Fowler and Hastings see the way forward as requiring practical theologians, in Fowler's words, "to place more radical trust in God's self-disclosure . . . ; more radical investment in . . . the in-breaking . . . of Love; and more radical engagement, through present action and prayer, . . . in God's work of creation, governance, and liberation/redemption."[53] No easy tasks.

Phronesis *as Practical Reason*

About a decade after Hunter's plea for greater clarity on practical knowledge, Browning and Catholic religious educator Thomas Groome each published a major book and Protestant religious educator Craig Dykstra wrote a pivotal article that at least partly answered Hunter's wish. What is often seen as Browning's magnum opus, *Fundamental Practical Theology,* is in essence a book on the practical nature of all theological reasoning. Examining what he accomplishes both confirms the concerns of Hunter, Fowler, and Hastings and shows where Browning may have benefited from Hunter's own Hiltnerian promotion of practical knowledge.

51. James W. Fowler, "Practical Theology and Theological Education: Some Models and Questions," *Theology Today* 42, no. 1 (April 1985): 57.

52. Thomas John Hastings, *Practical Theology and the One Body of Christ: Toward a Missional-Ecumenical Model* (Grand Rapids: Eerdmans, 2007), pp. 4-6.

53. Fowler, "Practical Theology and Theological Education," p. 58.

Fundamental Practical Theology begins with what seems like a straight-forward question: How do religious communities exercise practical reason? But Browning's answer is anything but simple. The complexity is a result of the subject matter itself and a consequence of the broader agenda he pursues on his way to answering his question. Brief mention of his broader agenda will help situate the contributions and limitation of his work on *phronesis.*

Most important, drawing on the momentum of the rebirth of practical philosophy in a manner reminiscent of Toulmin and Maddox, Browning insists that all theology is fundamentally practical — "through and through and at its heart."[54] This claim, which builds indirectly on ethicist Thomas Ogletree's remarks to the Association for Professional Education for Minis-try in 1980, goes beyond merely calling academic theology a social practice on a par with everyday theology, as Tanner suggests.[55] To identify all the-ology as practical re-embeds the disciplinary pursuits of historical, ethical, and systematic scholars in a larger practical sphere, insisting that they grow out of practical interests and are ultimately shaped by practical aims. In one sense, Browning simply adds his voice to a common refrain heard nation-ally and internationally, rejecting the parochial view of practical theology as merely a "technical discipline" that applies in practice truths developed with greater sophistication elsewhere, a claim that follows naturally on the heels of Hiltner's and even Schleiermacher's attempts to resituate pastoral or practical theology.[56] But by calling all disciplines practical at heart, he levels the playing field more radically. This puts high-level doctrinal treatises on a continuum with everyday activities, similar to Tanner's cultural argument several years later but shaped conceptually by German philosophy and re-visionist theology instead of a postliberal cultural turn to Pierre Bourdieu

54. Browning, *Fundamental Practical Theology,* pp. xi, 7.

55. Ogletree's society paper is reprinted as "Dimensions of Practical Theology: Meaning, Action, Self," in the first edited volume of the renewed movement, Browning, ed., *Practical Theology,* pp. 83-101. Ogletree says, "My aim . . . is to contribute to a reconstruction of the principal features of theological study in relation to one another. *The guiding thesis is that all theology, properly conceived, is practical theology.* . . . Thus, practical theology is not one of the branches of theology; the term practical rather characterizes the central intent of theology treated as a whole." Historical and philosophical theology are "dimensions" of an encom-passing practical theology (pp. 84-85; emphasis added). Oddly, Browning includes the paper in the volume "because of the importance of his statement" (p. 2), but he does not credit Ogletree as a source of his main thesis in *Fundamental Practical Theology.*

56. Browning, *Fundamental Practical Theology,* p. 56.

and postmodern anthropology. Essentially, Christians struggling with crises in religious communities and academicians engaging in theoretical debates all move from practice to theory back to practice — a model Browning juxtaposes to what he depicts, fairly or not, as the classic Barthian revelation-centered theory-to-practice model.[57]

As a natural consequence of this reorientation of all disciplines around practice, theological education is reordered, with "fundamental practical theology" enfolding within it four sub-moments of descriptive, historical, systematic, and strategic knowledge. In fact, Browning believes rather idealistically that if theological education would only embrace this model, then the "problems for theological students who wonder about the relation of their theological education" to ministry would be solved. He even envisions these four emphases as constituting the "practical *habitus* of theological education" despite their formulaic and abstract quality.[58] More persuasive is his emphasis on descriptive theology as the starting place for all theology. Although many scholars now see descriptive research on material religious practices as essential — itself a reflection of changes since his 1991 comments — Browning is still distinctive in his understanding of the qualities that comprise adequate description, shaped by his reading of Hans-Georg Gadamer. One must examine through concerted self-reflection what Gadamer calls one's "effective history," or pre-understandings, and how these biases shape what one sees. One must also assess critically the dialectic between explanatory and interpretive knowledge inherent within the human sciences used in description. Most important, one must recognize and evaluate the religious and moral horizons implicit in all description in a public fashion accessible to those outside one's community, a task reminiscent of Cartesian aspirations for personal detachment and universal principles understood by everyone.

So how does Browning understand practical knowledge itself? In a way, the kind of knowledge we are trying to capture in our book is everywhere and nowhere in his book. The mega-structures he creates — the fourfold movement within fundamental practical theology and what he identifies as five levels or dimensions of practical reason that guide description and diagnosis in descriptive theology and that establish norms for practice in strategic theology — are intended to define the *habitus* of ministry and the

57. Browning, *Fundamental Practical Theology,* p. 7.
58. Browning, *Fundamental Practical Theology,* pp. 58-59.

practical reason of religious communities. Broadly speaking, therefore, practical reason involves a movement from situational description to historical analysis to systematic and normative construction to strategic practical action. And it includes questions at five levels — *visional, obligational, tendency-need, environmental-social,* and *rule-role.* So, one asks within any situation or text: What are the dominant narratives or visions of ultimacy, the guiding moral norms, the key human needs and tendencies, the social and environmental pressures, and the basic rules and roles for behavior? These questions characterize all "conventional practical thinking," he contends, even if "uncritically assumed and unthematized." And it is precisely the task of "critical practical thinking" as distinct from "conventional thinking" to make them "conscious."[59]

Why then say that practical knowledge is *nowhere* in Browning's book? There are positive insights here. Browning's strong desire to systematize and create typologies that capture the "intuitive experience of what goes into practical moral thinking" provides helpful categories that students, ministers, and others can use to guide analysis and action.[60] And he makes some helpful claims about how human thought works. Practical thinking is more central than either theoretical or technical thinking, which he describes as "abstractions from practical thinking." Even the most abstract theory is "always embedded in practice."[61] Practical knowledge is deeply conversational; it exists only in and through conversation within time and across history. Finally, he adeptly redefines the nature of theology itself.

Nevertheless, what has Browning really said about practical knowledge as practiced on the ground? On at least two accounts, he misses some of the richer dimensions and hidden mysteries that characterize the *phronesis* and wisdom we seek to elucidate. My use of the terms *thought* and *thinking* in the previous paragraph was purposive. Browning views knowledge largely as a mental process located internal to the mind. Even though he uses a number of terms interchangeably to describe his subject — practical wisdom, *phronesis,* practical reason, and practical moral thinking — a close reading reveals that he favors practical *reason,* practical *thinking,* what he

---

59. Browning, *Fundamental Practical Theology,* p. 108. These five dimensions "interpenetrate so smoothly that we are unaware of them as differentiated aspects of experience."

60. Browning, *Fundamental Practical Theology,* p. 108.

61. Browning, *Fundamental Practical Theology,* pp. 8, 9.

sometimes calls practical *rationality,* and, most important, practical *moral* thinking. In contrast to postliberal theologians who, he believes, overemphasize tradition and community, he prefers to give "more weight to the reason in practical reason."[62]

> Reason as *phronesis* [asks] the questions, What should we do? and How should we live? It can be distinguished from *theoria* or theoretical reason, which is often thought to ask the more dispassionate, objective, or scientific question of What is the case? or What is the nature of things? It is also distinguishable from technical reason or *techne,* which asks the question, What are the most effective means to a given end?[63]

Here he defines (and truncates) the Aristotelian categories entirely in terms of reason and describes *phronesis* primarily in terms of moral deliberation. Practical reason and practical moral thinking are largely one and the same, constricting practical knowledge to cognition, verbal interpretation, and morality. In fact, in an early article, Browning puts *practical reason* in parentheses when he defines *practical moral thinking.*[64] It is worth noting that his road to Aristotle and *phronesis* comes through Gadamer, and Gadamer is most worried about the understanding that occurs in textual interpretation. Gadamer turns to Aristotle because he sees, in Browning's words, "important analogies between the interpretive process that he calls hermeneutics and Aristotle's understanding of *phronesis* or practical reason."[65] In Browning's reading of Gadamer, therefore, practical reason or *phronesis* is an "interpretative and reinterpretative process" for discerning truth within text-oriented traditions more than a practice-bound wisdom internal to action that sometimes eludes and runs beyond reasoned interpretation of texts.

There is a second problem to which Hunter points. Even though Browning says he follows Tracy in revising Paul Tillich's correlation model in a more dialectical fashion, he does not pay that much attention to the knowledge *within* practice. This devaluation of contextual and embodied knowl-

---

62. Browning, *Fundamental Practical Theology,* p. 180.

63. Browning, *Fundamental Practical Theology,* p. 10.

64. Don S. Browning, "The Revival of Practical Theology," *Christian Century,* February 1-8, 1984, p. 134.

65. Browning, *Fundamental Practical Theology,* pp. 10-11. He says elsewhere, "understanding as interpretation and *phronesis* as practical wisdom interpenetrate" (p. 39).

edge is apparent in both of his grand theories or portraits of practical reason — the four movements of fundamental practical theology and the five levels of practical reason. Even in the practice-theory-practice movement, practice learns more from theory than theory gains from practice. Practices "form the questions we bring to the historical sources," not the answers. Strategic practical theology "builds on the accomplishment of the first three movements." When practice does "play back" on the entire structure, it is primarily to "engender new questions."[66] Christian communities are "carriers and implementers of practical rationality" more than sources or sites of theological activity. Even his illustrative pedagogical exercise that converts the "four movements of theology into a simple course assignment" is focused on rendering theological "resources" or the "Christian classics" relevant to a practical issue and not on discerning theological dimensions of lived practices.[67] This turns the hermeneutical circle into an arch, an advance over previous patterns but still an insufficient model for practical knowledge.

A similar dynamic appears in the five dimensions of practical reason. In one of his first statements of the model, Browning argues that "situations themselves do not provide us with the metaphors, theories of obligations and indices of needs that are required to address them normatively."[68] Two decades later, but without explicit acknowledgment of criticism about the hierarchical structure of his model, he drops the term *levels,* avoids beginning with the "highest levels" of vision and norms, and replaces what he previously called "rules and roles" with "practices" with reference to MacIntyre and Bourdieu.[69] Nonetheless, although he uses "dimensions" as well as "levels" and modifies his model over time, the reasoning generally moves from abstract to concrete. "Metaphors" and "principles" are the top tiers, and they shape the contextual particularities of social context and bodily habits that fall below them. On the bottom are the "rules and roles of life" that are the "settled results of reflection at the higher levels."[70] In Weberian fashion, big ideas shape action and not the other way around.

In the end, epistemology — the desire to understand how people know

---

66. Browning, *Fundamental Practical Theology,* pp. 10, 43, 55, 58.

67. Browning, *Fundamental Practical Theology,* p. x.

68. Browning, "The Revival of Practical Theology," p. 134.

69. Browning, *Christian Ethics and the Moral Psychologies* (Grand Rapids: Eerdmans, 2006), pp. 23-27.

70. Browning, *Fundamental Practical Theology,* p. 107.

what they know — is rendered procedural and bled a little dry.[71] He recognizes the "analytical austerity" that his abstractions create, destroying the "art and grace" of the knowledge he wants to portray.[72] But he does not know how to avoid this. There is something strangely unsatisfying about his abstract exposé of *habitus* and *phronesis*. Ironically, when he tries to include everything, practical wisdom's inconclusive, fluid character is contained, controlled, and spelled out, and the concepts themselves are emptied of meaning. Ultimately, he leaves unanswered one of the tricky problems Hunter foresaw: How does one generate "theological knowledge that does *not* surrender its practical character"?[73] Or perhaps Browning's answer is clear. In his introduction to *Practical Theology: The Emerging Field in Theology, Church, and World*, a conference book that marks the beginning of practical theology's 1980s rejuvenation, Browning states, "we will never have an adequate practical theology unless we first learn to reflect critically and think abstractly."[74] This view is not unique to Browning but characterizes the general tenor of the effort to invigorate practical theology's academic position.

Two More Holistic Models of Knowledge and Practice

Although not apparent in his book title *Sharing Faith: A Comprehensive Approach to Religious Education and Pastoral Ministry*, Groome tackles queries

71. At one point, Browning says, "By epistemology I mean what Gadamer meant by method, that is, the procedure for gaining knowledge" (*Fundamental Practical Theology*, p. 82).

72. Offering an analogy, he says looking at a film frame by frame does not do justice to the "rich, thick, and dense . . . multidimensional fabric of practical reason" (*Fundamental Practical Theology*, p. 135).

73. Hunter, "The Future of Pastoral Theology," p. 32; emphasis in original text.

74. Don S. Browning, "Introduction," in Browning, ed., *Practical Theology*, p. 6. In summarizing the contents of each chapter, he attributes this idea to Tracy, although I do not think this is an entirely accurate reading of Tracy's chapter. But later in the introduction, Browning suggests again that Tracy "sees the theoretical as far more important and far more complicated than Ogletree" and, by implication, other authors in the volume. The "more abstract features of theory are more determinative than the less abstract and more concrete features." So, ultimately, practical theology must "consider some of the remotest of metaphysical principles" (p. 14).

that Browning skirts. Published the same year as *Fundamental Practical Theology,* Groome's book pays significant attention to epistemology, the only such treatment in contemporary U.S. practical theology. As a teacher and writer for Christian educators, he faces even more regularly than Browning questions about what comprises Christian knowledge and how one forms people in it. Most important, from page one his book is shaped by a critical assessment of modern epistemology seldom questioned by Browning. Groome has known "for some time," he says, "that the 'learning outcome' of Christian religious education should be more than what the Western world typically means by 'knowledge.'"[75]

A one-chapter historical overview assesses the "mixed heritage" of Western epistemology from Plato through the mid-twentieth century. In Groome's reading, there is no golden age. Even early debates between sophists and skeptics in the fifth to fourth centuries BCE reflect divisions over whether reason or sense experience is the source of reliable knowledge, leading to two general schools in antiquity still recognizable today as *rationalism* and *empiricism.* Hence, long before medieval *summas,* Cartesian science, or the modern university, one can discern what Groome identifies as three persistent patterns: the quest for rational certainty; the dichotomy between thought and life that denigrates the "praxis of ordinary people as a reliable way of knowing"; and, finally, a patriarchal hierarchy of "mind, ideas, and men over body, nature, and women" as well documented by feminist theorists such as Sandra Harding and Evelyn Fox-Keller.[76]

In his review of Plato, Aristotle, Augustine, Aquinas, Descartes, Locke, and Kant, Groome's hermeneutic is to deconstruct and reconstruct, at once respecting and challenging the high valuation of mental cognition. On the one hand, "critical rationality should be a constitutive dimension" of faith. Western philosophy has honed its operation in beneficial ways. But, on the other hand, if the aim is to help people *know* faith, then "we cannot settle for engaging 'the mind alone.'" We "must unlearn much of what this tradition has bequeathed to educators."[77] To challenge the hegemony of a narrow

---

75. Thomas H. Groome, *Sharing Faith: A Comprehensive Approach to Religious Education and Pastoral Ministry* (New York: Harper Collins, 1991), p. 2. Epistemological concerns are also apparent in his prior book, *Christian Religious Education: Sharing Our Story and Vision* (San Francisco: Jossey-Bass, 1980), pp. 152-83.

76. Groome, *Sharing Faith,* p. 37.

77. Groome, *Sharing Faith,* pp. 7, 32-33.

scientific rationality, he engages many of the same figures that appear in other efforts in practical theology and beyond — Marx, Husserl, Heidegger, Dewey, and James.

Of particular interest here is his rereading of Aristotle's tripartite understanding of knowledge or ways of life as *episteme/theoria* (theoretical knowing as an end in itself), *praxis/phronesis* (practical knowing of how to live), and *techne/poesis* (productive knowing of how to make things). Groome's account is distinguished from similar references to these modes of knowing in Browning, Bernard Lee, and others by a twofold reconstruction.[78] First, he names the classist and sexist biases behind the hierarchy of *theoria* as the most valuable form of knowledge and *poesis* as the "lowest and least reliable," at least for the knowledge necessary for Christian life, and tries to subsume both underneath a richer understanding of *phronesis*. Second, he insists on their integral interconnection as "co-constitutive" in contrast to what he sees as Aristotle's "trichotomization" of each one from the other.[79]

In his effort to clarify what is lost in modern views of knowledge, Groome revives a term, *conation,* that has fallen into disuse. As he attests in a footnote, he borrows the idea from Sara Little, who became the first female professor at Union Theological Seminary in Richmond in 1973. She uses it to describe the participatory knowledge that emerges from Paulo Freire's revolutionary pedagogical theory. "The knowledge that resulted," Little says, "might be called conative, with will and desire united in action that in turn developed the freedom of sense, power, and understanding."[80] Groome downplays the emphasis on liberation and uses the term largely to underscore knowledge as a holistic activity that includes but goes beyond cognition: "conative activity engages people's corporeal, mental, and volitional capacities, their heads, hearts, and overt behaviors, their cognition, desire, and will."[81]

For those "who find the term too strange," Groome uses *wisdom* as a

---

78. Bernard J. Lee wrote two key papers on the Aristotelian categories: "Practical Theology: Its Character and Possible Implications for Higher Education," *Current Issues in Catholic Higher Education* 14, no. 2 (1994): 25-36, and "Practical Theology as Phronetic: A Working Paper from/for Those in Ministry Education," *APT Occasional Papers* 1 (Winter 1998): 1-19.

79. Groome, *Sharing Faith,* p. 46.

80. Sara Little, *To Set One's Heart: Belief and Teaching in the Church* (Atlanta: John Knox, 1983), p. 82, cited by Groome, *Sharing Faith,* p. 456 n. 33.

81. Groome, *Sharing Faith,* p. 30.

synonym. However, when he gives a brief overview of wisdom in the biblical tradition it is clear that wisdom contains some non-synonymous elements. *Wisdom* is a "plenitudinous term," and the wisdom literature is complex and idiosyncratic. He describes a loose biblical trajectory from its definition as "a technical skill, to a practical mode of living, to an ethic of life, to person-ification as a divine partner and something truly of God."[82] Ultimately, in both Jewish and Christian contexts, wisdom is a "gift of God's spirit that leads people to know, desire, and live in right relationship with God, self, others, and creation" — surely an idea and ideal that far outrun the term *conation,* however helpful. Groome prefers *conation* when trying to get at the "critical/theoretical" dimensions, perhaps hoping for greater academic credibility.[83] Occasionally, his use of *conation* starts to sound interchange-able with the idea of human potentiality in general (e.g., a "style of being"). There is also an essentialist dimension to his definition that likely evolves out of a Catholic orientation toward natural law: conation is a "constant cohesive structure at the heart of human existence . . . an innate ethical disposition" toward the good. Despite these questionable theoretical moves, he at least underscores the bodily, sensate, volitional, and action-oriented di-mensions as well as the practices of judgment, discernment, and "reflective-ness" essential to practical knowledge.[84] Equally noteworthy, he is the most attuned among his peers to sexism and feminist theorists such as Harding and Keller. His overall intent is to move education "beyond simply cogni-tion," even beyond epistemology, and resituate knowing as a way of being or an ontological matter.

Unfortunately, although there is a great deal of value in the first part of *Sharing Faith,* epistemological reflection is only the first section of a book whose primary intent is to expand what was so well received in a previous book, *Christian Religious Education* — a five-step method for theological reflection that Groome calls "shared praxis."[85] So, like Browning, Groome waxes procedural. The second and third parts of *Sharing Faith* lay out chap-ter by chapter each movement of an approach that received only one chapter before and then illustrate its use in several ecclesial venues. The "epistemo-

82. Groome, *Sharing Faith,* p. 31.
83. Groome, *Sharing Faith,* p. 30.
84. Groome, *Sharing Faith,* p. 32.
85. Thomas Groome, *Christian Religious Education: Sharing Our Story and Vision* (San Francisco: Harper & Row, 1980).

logical underpinnings" of this approach, although in the foreground initially, are actually subsidiary to the book as a whole.[86] The connection of the first part to the rest of the book is not clear, apart from a generic emphasis on holistic knowledge. Its accomplishments only indirectly impact the movements of shared praxis and its implementation in ministry, where, oddly enough, Groome does not return to questions about the nature of ministerial knowledge, the dynamics of *conation,* or the development of expertise or wisdom. As in Browning, the method of "shared praxis" emphasizes what the Christian "story and vision" say to practice more than the reverse.

Had Groome published his part I as a separate book, it would have stood out as a distinct argument and had greater impact. As it is, there has been little discussion of what he accomplishes, and the book repeats a common pattern. An opportunity to foreground practical theology's substantive challenge to theological knowledge gives way to the promotion of practical theology as a method. Method becomes again, as Fowler worried, the "fulcrum" on which the challenge to the Enlightenment rests while the limits of critical reason and the "rationally self-grounded subject of the Enlightenment" go unaddressed.[87] Perhaps it seems more acceptable to figure out a method for being knowledgeable than to focus on what practical theology actually knows about practical knowledge itself.

In his lead chapter in an edited book on theological education, Dykstra fundamentally shifts the subject from method to the malformation of modern conceptions of practice. A Presbyterian and a graduate of Princeton Theological Seminary like Hunter, and a faculty member in religious education at two seminaries, he is best known for his contributions as vice president of religion at Lilly Endowment. He had just begun a long, accomplished tenure there when he laid the conceptual infrastructure for two decades of growth around the study of practices in an essay on "reconceiving practice."

Like Hiltner and Hunter, although without explicit reference to either, Dykstra believes "engagement in certain practices may give rise to new knowledge." Indeed, "certain practices are in fact conditions to the possibility of 'recognizing the risen Lord.'"[88] However, distinct from both of

86. Groome, *Sharing Faith,* p. 2.
87. Fowler, "Practical Theology and Theological Education," p. 57.
88. Craig Dykstra, "Reconceiving Practice in Theological Inquiry and Education," in *Virtues and Practices in the Christian Tradition,* ed. Nancey Murphy, Brad J. Kallenberg, and Mark Thiessen Nation (Notre Dame: University of Notre Dame, 1997), pp. 172-73. This

them, he sharpens a diagnosis only latent in their arguments. Practice itself has been misconstrued in theological education not only in practical theology but also across the disciplines. His opening sentence reads: "Theology and theological education has been burdened by a picture of practice that is harmfully individualistic, technological, ahistorical, and abstract." Practice is mistakenly understood as something individuals perform to achieve technical ends in the present moment guided by theoretical principles. This distorted view even characterizes the so-called theoretical disciplines where "practice has no intrinsic place." But when practice is relegated to practical theology, "certain features intrinsic to the 'academic' theological fields are [also] hidden." Failing to recognize their own inherent dependence on and intricate relationship to Christian practices, they "become distorted, fragmented, and overly dependent upon and conformed" to secular university standards.[89]

Like several others, Dykstra harkens back to Aristotle, but instead of focusing on his conception of practical reason or intellectual virtues, such as *phronesis* or *techne,* he offers an alternative reading of practice built significantly on MacIntyre's reclamation of Aristotelian virtue ethics as a more encompassing way of life: in its fullness, practice entails "participation in a co-operatively formed pattern of activity that emerges out of a complex tradition of interactions among many people sustained over a long period of time."[90]

This redefinition has had a reverberating influence through Dykstra's leadership at Lilly on research and programs revitalizing ministry and education. It spawned several later publications, such as *Practicing Our Faith* edited by Dorothy Bass, and paved the way for our own interest in the wide-ranging complexities of practical knowledge. Of additional note, Dykstra moves beyond MacIntyre's "historical-moral claim" to make "epistemological-theological suggestions" that resemble Taylor's insight about the intimate connections between how we understand knowledge and how we understand the nature of persons and their social worlds. "Our identities as persons are constituted by practices and the knowledge and

---

article first appeared in 1991 in *Shifting Boundaries: Contextual Approaches to the Structure of Theological Education,* ed. Barbara G. Wheeler and Edward Farley (Louisville: Westminster John Knox), pp. 35-66. References below are from the 1997 reprint.

89. Dykstra, "Reconceiving Practice," pp. 163-64.

90. Dykstra, "Reconceiving Practice," p. 170.

relationships they mediate," Dykstra observes. "Correlatively, communal life is constituted by practices. Communities do not just engage in practices; in a sense, they *are* practices."[91]

Ultimately, if practices are so constitutive of Christian faith as well as human subjectivity and community, then they must occupy a more central place in the theological curriculum. Dykstra refers to Farley's own recovery of theology as *habitus* — a "cognitive disposition and orientation of the soul"[92] — but he enriches it by locating this knowledge within a "profound, life-orienting, identity-shaping participation" in practices of the gospel and by including an array of human intelligences in addition to linguistic and logical reason. "Theology as wisdom . . . includes," in his view, "not only insight and understanding but also the kind of judgment, skill, commitment, and character that full participation in practices both requires and nurtures."[93] His use of Jeffrey Stout's example of baseball makes especially clear that "some of this knowledge is entirely somatic."[94]

Only a few lone voices rise up to question whether anything is amiss in the considerable progress made in reappraising *phronesis,* practice, and practical reason during the late 1980s and early 1990s. Rebecca Chopp, the only woman in two early anthologies behind practical theology's academic reestablishment, foreshadows Fulkerson's and Tanner's recap and critical assessment twenty years later. Influenced by liberation theology, she argues that this young movement has already missed the boat in its modernist anxiety about the "crisis of cognitive claims" among an intellectual nonbelieving elite rather than addressing more pressing practical problems among the world's marginalized.[95] And, as I have already noted, Fowler believes these theologies follow critics of Enlightenment rationality like Gadamer, Heidegger, and Wittgenstein, only to become, along with the critics themselves,

---

91. Dykstra, "Reconceiving Practice," p. 173.

92. Farley, *Theologia,* p. 35.

93. Dykstra, "Reconceiving Practice," p. 176.

94. Dykstra, "Reconceiving Practice," p. 176 n. 28. See also p. 177 n. 29.

95. Rebecca S. Chopp, "Practical Theology and Liberation," in *Formation and Reflection: The Promise of Practical Theology,* ed. Lewis S. Mudge and James N. Poling (Philadelphia: Fortress, 1987), p. 126. Her second article is "When the Center Cannot Contain the Margins," in *The Education of the Practical Theologian: Responses to Joseph Hough and John Cobb's Christian Identity and Theological Education,* ed. Don S. Browning, David Polk, and Ian S. Evison (Atlanta: Scholars, 1989), pp. 63-76.

"trapped in a dialectic in which critical reason tries to overcome the limits of critical reasoning by the mediation of reason alone."[96] Chopp's inclusion among the early inner core is partly token, however, and Fowler's concern comes like a cry in the dark at the tail end of an essay otherwise devoted to holding up the progress made thus far.

Giving Credit Where Long Overdue: Liberation Theology

As Chopp implies, there is a major oversight in this body of 1980s literature: the credit owed liberation theories and theologies, especially when it comes to epistemology. In some ways, this slight is not surprising. Practical theology's U.S. revival centered around major universities where white male scholars such as Browning and Farley hosted conferences and wrote grant-supported volumes on practical theology. Publication of the first major edited book, *Practical Theology,* resulted from a conference, partly sponsored by the Lilly Endowment and hosted by Browning, at the University of Chicago while I was a doctoral student there. Browning's editorial introduction makes clear that this university context as well as the involvement of scholars from areas beyond the arts of ministry was essential to earning academic respect.[97] I remember vaguely the conceptually abstract presentations by established white and mostly Protestant men (except for Catholic scholars David Tracy and Dennis McCann). Apart from one sentence in Browning's introduction, none of these scholars credits liberation theology for practical theology's resurgence, an omission that seems notable in retrospect. McCann devotes the most space to liberationist theory, and his approach is largely one of disenchantment and critique of what he sees as its excessive and uncritical Marxist "politicization."[98]

Practical theology's revival had many causes, but epistemological unrest — the "irrelevance of contemporary theology," in Browning's words — was among the most important factors, and liberation theology's early influence

---

96. Fowler, "Practical Theology and Theological Education," pp. 56-57.

97. Browning, "Introduction," in Browning, ed., *Practical Theology,* p. 3.

98. Dennis P. McCann, "Practical Theology and Social Action: Or What Can the 1980s Learn from the 1960s?" in Browning, ed., *Practical Theology,* pp. 105, 109, and Browning, "Introduction," p. 3. See also McCann's book, *Christian Realism and Liberation Theology* (Maryknoll, NY: Orbis, 1981).

played a crucial, although almost entirely submerged, role on this front.[99] By and large, leading intellectuals give only an occasional nod in this direction — Chopp and Bernard Lee are the exceptions — even though liberation theology's influence is apparent in remarks on connecting theory and practice, social location, material interests, power, poverty, class, and so forth. Early publications, such as one of the first coauthored books, James Poling and Donald Miller's *Foundations for a Practical Theology of Ministry,* exemplify this pattern. They mention early Latin American theologians, feminists, and black theologians in aggregate, not as specific scholars, and even then mostly in footnotes, all the while claiming some of the key ideas and giving greater attention to white men and women who draw on liberation theology, such as Matthew Lamb, Francis Fiorenza, and Chopp.[100]

Of course, liberation theology received a chilly reception more generally, a turbulent history that is easily forgotten today. In a mid-1970s essay, before Fiorenza later declared himself a proponent, he weighs the contributions of political and liberation theologies against criticisms he describes as "so massive that one wonders how any intelligent person or decent theologian could possibly advocate" such theology.[101] But by the late 1980s Fiorenza has changed sides. He identifies the Marxist tradition as one of four prominent models for reconnecting theory and practice, alongside hermeneutical, linguistic, and pragmatist. Whereas the hermeneutical and linguistic models remain bound to text, language, and tradition, the Marxist and pragmatist models locate knowledge within practice itself. In Fiorenza's words, practice "conditions" and transforms knowledge in Marxism and "aids in clarifying and assessing ideas" in pragmatism. The Marxist model is the most explicit in its critique of a purely theoretical view of reality and its support of knowledge as political and not just social or personal.

Drawing on Marxism, Latin American liberation theology is one of the earliest and most provocative efforts to redefine theological knowledge as radically practical. From its inception, it was not just an effort to give voice to the poor but to liberate theology as an academic discipline, as Juan Luis

99. Browning, "Introduction," p. 1.

100. See, for example, pp. 14-15 in James N. Poling and Donald Miller, *Foundations for a Practical Theology of Ministry* (Nashville: Abingdon, 1985).

101. Francis P. Fiorenza, "Political Theology and Liberation Theology: An Inquiry into Their Fundamental Meaning," in *Liberation, Revolution, and Freedom: Theological Perspectives,* ed. Thomas M. McFadden (New York: Seabury, 1975), p. 4.

Segundo's book title, *The Liberation of Theology,* captures so well. Indeed, these two aims are inextricably bound together. Giving the poor theological priority demands a radical alteration in how and where theology is done.

Just as no one escapes Aristotle, neither do contemporary scholars evade Marx, as Segundo observes, especially when it comes to the political construction of knowledge.[102] Although many people challenge Marx's identification of the economy as the sole force behind all belief structures, his idea of the "material basis" of ideology — that ideas are formed by "material practice" and so undone not by "intellectual criticism" but by "revolution" — has permeated intellectual culture. Even though Marx's original ideal of revolution is quelled and redefined, his view that interpretation of the world (the philosopher's task) does not suffice, that the "point is to change it," foreshadows or even paves the way for a theological discipline oriented toward transformation in the 1980s.[103]

Segundo's concerns about a "certain type of academicism" removed from suffering are sprinkled throughout his book and hint at the kind of altered epistemology he envisions. Theology as an "academic profession" practiced by those secure from risk is distinguished from "theology as a revolutionary activity."[104] One cannot begin theology "with certitudes deduced from revelation." Such theology is a "second step," as liberation theology's preeminent founder Gustavo Gutiérrez said. Practical and political commitment is, in Segundo's words, "necessary for any and all authentic knowledge of the gospel message and its demands." As is evident in Gospel narratives of Jesus' life, theology starts with "what is good for people" at the "level where human beings make their most critical and decisive options: i.e., the heart."[105]

Would the practical theology movement of the 1980s have found the particular, the local, and the communal so compelling without such the-

102. Juan Luis Segundo, *The Liberation of Theology* (Maryknoll, NY: Orbis, 1976), p. 35 n. 10.

103. *Writings of the Young Marx on Philosophy and Society,* ed. Loyd D. Easton and Kurt H. Guddat (New York: Doubleday, 1967), pp. 400-402, cited by Francis Schüssler Fiorenza, "Theory and Practice: Theological Education as a Reconstructive, Hermeneutical, and Practical Task," *Theological Education* 23, no. 3 (1987): 18.

104. Segundo, *The Liberation of Theology,* p. 27.

105. Segundo, *The Liberation of Theology,* pp. 78-79, 84. See also Gustavo Gutiérrez, *The Theology of Liberation: History, Politics, and Salvation,* trans. and ed. Caridad Inda and John Eagleson (Maryknoll, NY: Orbis, 1973, 1988), p. 11.

ories? It is hard not to wonder if the 1980s revival of practical theology emerged partly out of a desire to recapture some of the energy emerging at this time among minorities in church, academy, society, and world (e.g., base communities, people of color, women, Southern Hemisphere) and harness it to reestablish the social interests of the privileged, as Segundo himself forewarns. It is worth noting that the numerical and influential decline of the U.S. Christian largely white mainline goes virtually unmentioned in much of the early practical theology literature, even though it looms like a dark cloud on the horizon and is partly what motivates Lilly Endowment's support of the academic books and conferences behind practical theology's revival.

At the same time, liberation theology faced adversities of its own that tempered its success in reclaiming practical knowledge. As early as 1976, when Segundo published his book, and within its first pages, he worries about trends that threaten liberation theology's reception and future. On the one hand, it is persecuted as dangerous because it unsettles the political status quo of economic inequity, while on the other hand its terms are readily "adopted in watered-down form" for all sorts of causes, emptying the language of liberation "of all real meaning."[106]

Most important for our purposes is an additional problem with which practical theologians are familiar, rooted in the institutional infrastructures that govern theology. The effort to liberate theology is threatened by what Segundo describes as "academic disdain" for a "theology rising out of the urgent problems of real life" as "naïve and uncritical." He says it is time to "frontally attack" this tendency, "a challenge that is authentically and constructively theological in nature" and that requires one to "get down to epistemology." Unfortunately, he moves away from this effort both here and in his book more generally, turning rather quickly to methodology. He means, he says, that it is "time to get down to analyzing not so much the content of Latin American theology but rather its methodological approach and its connection with liberation."[107] Most of the book revolves around method, beginning with his revision of Bultmann's hermeneutical circle, describing

106. Segundo, *The Liberation of Theology*, p. 4.

107. Segundo, *The Liberation of Theology*, p. 5. Later he says, the "only thing that can maintain the liberative character of any theology is not its content but its methodology" (p. 40).

a movement from political critique to experience to revised interpretation and practice. Both here and in the practical theology literature of the 1980s a kind of Cartesian rationalism creeps in and forces a turn from content to methodology by grounding epistemology in methodology. As in Descartes, one knows something is true because one has followed a clear method of directing one's reason. So, "getting down to epistemology" is primarily a matter of defending one's method, as Segundo tries to do.

As troubling, beyond Segundo's work, liberation theologians in a variety of spheres recognize the academic disdain Segundo identifies and shy away from self-identifying as practical theologians or pursuing studies in the discipline precisely because it might jeopardize their intellectual status, recognition, and position. People talk about this fear, but they seldom put it in writing. In a recent notable exception, Carmen Nanko-Fernandez names "academic second-class citizenship" as one reason why so few Latino/a scholars contribute to practical and pastoral theologies. Those who "already experience marginalization" find little advantage in such affiliation, "especially when others seek to classify our theologies as practical as a means of dismissing" their value.[108]

There is a further problem, implied in McCann's critique of liberation theology as lacking "middle axioms" necessary to connecting sweeping principles, such as solidarity with the poor and critical reflection on praxis, with concrete practices.[109] People's lives are a source of knowledge, but there is less interest in practice. Few Latin American liberation theologians come full circle and return to practice. For the most part, they do not concretize their global ideals, and they do not design ways of living out the claims they assert. Of course, these are broad generalizations, and there are important exceptions.[110] Still, we must wonder whether occupying university

108. Carmen Nanko-Fernandez, *Theologizing en Espanglish: Context, Community, and Ministry* (Maryknoll, NY: Orbis, 2010), p. 22.

109. McCann, "Practical Theology and Social Action," pp. 115-16. He relies on Christian ethicist John C. Bennett's definition of "middle axioms" as lying between guiding principles and particular programs. They suggest "strategies that remain 'more concrete than a universal ethical principle and less specific than a program that includes legislation.'" See Bennett, *Christian Ethics and Social Policy* (New York: Charles Scribner's Sons, 1946), pp. 77, 79.

110. See, for example, a study of Gutiérrez's pastoral involvement in Peru by Olle Kristenson, *Pastor in the Shadow of Violence: Gustavo Gutiérrez as a Public Pastoral Theologian in Peru in the 1980s and 1990s* (Uppsala: Uppsala Universitet, 2009).

positions and inheriting intellectual presuppositions from Catholic education in Western Europe at least indirectly created a distance from concrete
ministerial and faith practices.

In a wonderful essay on "little moves against destructiveness," professor of applied theology Nancy Bedford offers a strong antidote to the
problem of a too-abstract liberation theology. Her work foreshadows
and participates in the development of a new body of practices-oriented
literature. In contrast to pronouncements of revolutionary change by
1970s liberation theologians endowed with a "sense of an impending and
triumphal Exodus," today's situation of continued and even worsening
structural injustice requires a more nuanced and complicated response.
Recognizing the enormity of the problems and the "tenuous, ambiguous" nature of theology, she argues that the practice of discernment or
"figuring out what to do, all together as a church, with the help of God's
Spirit" provides at least a small but important step forward.[111] In her small
urban congregation in Buenos Aires, it is no longer a matter of the wealthy
encountering the poor. Rather, church members must determine how to
live with "their own near-poverty or poverty." The story of how the community began to take steps — "small moves" — to address local problems
demonstrates the role of a different kind of discourse. Theology has, in
her words, "no alternative but to deal with the [hellish] facts presented so
graphically by reality" by becoming involved on the ground in practices
of discernment.[112]

A New Generation of Literature: Place, Body, Stuff, Know-How

The 1980s practical theology literature is rich in understanding practical
knowing through conceptual frameworks of philosophy and language but
weak in nonverbal, aesthetic, narrative, symbolic, and embodied dimensions. For all the discussion of *phronesis,* conation, and practical reason,
there is still little sense that theological knowledge actually arises within

111. Nancy E. Bedford, "Little Moves against Destructiveness: Theology and the Practice
of Discernment," in *Practicing Theology: Beliefs and Practices in Christian Life,* ed. Miroslav
Volf and Dorothy C. Bass (Grand Rapids: Eerdmans, 2001), pp. 158-59.
112. Bedford, "Little Moves against Destructiveness," pp. 159, 164, 173.

practice, with the exception of isolated essays such as those of Hunter and Dykstra. Nor is there much development of the kind of theological knowing that makes good practice possible. Few people grapple with the knowledge embedded in material realities of bodies, stuff, place, and communities in action.

What important epistemological shifts have occurred in recent years and what further work is needed? When placed in this genealogy, literature of the last fifteen years stands out for its pursuit of what can be learned within practice itself, funded partly by interest in materiality and context. Elaine Graham's *Transforming Practice,* published in 1996, represents an apt turning point. The double entendre of the title itself announces an appreciation not just for how the Christian tradition or minister might change practice but also for the power of practice to transform. Neither singular in her efforts nor especially innovative — the book is largely a dissertation-style analysis of literature guided by the question of ethical norms in postmodernity — she finds fresh ways to develop ideas that we have seen in Hiltner, Hunter, and Dykstra. With the help of social theorists such as Bourdieu, Judith Butler, and Donna Haraway, she insists on theology as a "performative discipline" and pastoral action as a "generator of theological disclosure." If theology is "enacted and embodied in Christian practice," then practical theology must become a kind of *"critical phenomenology"* devoted to "excavating" the "norms which inhabit pastoral *praxis.*"[113]

These are fairly high-level formulaic claims. Graham also receives criticism from British scholars, such as Nigel Biggar, Robin Gill, and Jeremy Law, for collapsing theory into practice.[114] I do not believe Graham is as adamant that practice is *the* singular fount of knowledge, exclusive of theory, or as negligent or disparaging of theory as she is accused of being. Other scholars, such as Mary Clark Moshcella and Carrie Doehring, have given her global claims about the epistemological value of practice greater nu-

113. Elaine Graham, *Transforming Practice: Pastoral Theology in an Age of Uncertainty* (London: Mowbray, 1996), pp. 3, 7, 10, 140; emphasis in original text. She is also among the first to raise questions about whether Browning is "truly listening to the embodied, incarnational practical wisdom of the congregations" he studies (p. 90).

114. Nigel Biggar, "Should Pastoral Theology Become Postmodern?" *Contact* 126 (1998): 25; Robin Gill, Review of *Transforming Practice: Pastoral Theology in an Age of Uncertainty* by Elaine L. Graham, *Theology* 100 (May 1997): 228; Jeremy Law, Review, *Expository Times* 108, no. 8 (1997): 252.

ance and richer illustration.[115] Understanding the kind of knowledge that emerges within action, practice, materiality, location, particularity, and so forth has been on the minds of practical theologians in the intervening years since 1996.

Trying to capture what is happening is a little like describing the water in which we swim, including developments that lead right up to this book. My solution is simply to provide a sampling of emerging insights on the nature of practical knowledge in three spheres: appreciation for *techne* and *poesis;* work on bodies and place; and study of congregations as enacting theology. I underscore the term *sampling:* for each scholar I lift up there are others to whom I might have just as readily turned for illustration (more than I can name in footnotes without creating a bibliographical nightmare regarding who deserves mention).[116] It is also important to mention, even if I cannot go into expository detail, the many intellectual developments outside theology that stand behind the reorientation in each of these spheres: critical race and gender theories; practice, place, and performance theories; theories of learning; and ethnographical methods. None of these theories and methods is entirely new to the last few decades, but they enjoy heightened popularity and refinement. In particular, Michel Foucault's exposé of the intricate link between power regimes, discourse, and the discipline of bodies has deepened arguments already implied in liberation, race, gender, and sexuality theories. Even though only a few scholars, such as Tom Beaudoin and Susan Dunlap, explicitly reference and analyze his work, his ideas pervade all three realms that I explore, absorbed as much by osmosis through general and secondary scholarship as through intentional analysis (e.g., Graham reads Butler and Jane Flax, both of whom build on Foucault).[117]

115. See, for example, Moschella, *Ethnography as a Pastoral Practice,* and Carrie Doehring, *The Practice of Pastoral Care: A Postmodern Approach,* revised and expanded ed. (Louisville: Westminster John Knox, 2015), both of whom refer to Graham's work (Doehring turns to Moschella's use of Graham).

116. For a sense of the expanding body of scholarship, see the authors and bibliographies included in Bonnie J. Miller-McLemore, ed., *The Wiley-Blackwell Companion to Practical Theology* (London: Wiley/Blackwell, 2012).

117. See Tom Beaudoin, *Witness to Dispossession: The Vocation of a Post-Modern Theologian* (Maryknoll, NY: Orbis, 2008); Susan J. Dunlap, *Counseling Depressed Women* (Louisville: Westminster John Knox, 1997).

Know-How, Poesis, *and Stuff*

In the 1980s, practical theologians sought to redeem *praxis* and *phronesis* and a few explored problems with Western conceptions of *theoria* and *episteme;* but as a general rule, almost everyone except Groome neglected *poesis* and *techne* as potentially valuable realms of knowledge (Graham included). Using feminist theorists such as Hilary Rose who have insisted on the value of domestic and caring labor, Groome boldly insists that "we must reject Aristotle's debasement" of *poesis* as "the lowest and least reliable way of knowing" as "class biased and sexist" and we must "reject his separating of praxis from productive and creative labor."[118] But, for nearly everyone else, this third Aristotelian mode of knowing and living was often seen instead as *the* problem. Scholars consistently equate *techne* (or the art and craft of making) with technical rationality or an obsession with technique, efficiency, instrumentality, and means-end reasoning. And they rarely mention *poesis* or the life of creating transient goods. Browning, for example, defines *techne* flatly (and always in contrast to the other two) as concerned simply with the question, "What are the most effective means to a given end?"[119] *Techne* and *poesis* remain at the bottom of the knowledge hierarchy as the kinds of knowing to be avoided or, if not avoided, then given the briefest of mention, even in Groome's design for a more equal and interconnected relationship between *theoria, praxis,* and *poesis.*

There has been fresh interest in *techne* and *poesis* in recent years. My own work questioning the clerical paradigm or the focus on ministerial skills as an adequate interpretation of all that is wrong with theological education is motivated by what I perceive as an oversight of the complexity and value of the skills of artful ministry and a revaluation of maternal and material knowledge.[120] Although I agree that education should not be reduced to clergy training and technique, lost in this analysis is appreciation for the knowledge one must have to sustain good practice. When I teach pastoral care, entering seminary students find helpful basic rules of the very sort that the critique of the clerical paradigm seems to negate, not as the only or

118. Groome, *Sharing Faith,* pp. 46, 47; see also p. 48.

119. Browning, *Fundamental Practical Theology,* p. 10; see also p. 34.

120. See Bonnie J. Miller-McLemore, *Christian Theology in Practice: Discovering a Discipline* (Grand Rapids: Eerdmans, 2012), part II. See especially ch. 7, "The Clerical *and* the Academic Paradigm."

even primary goal of learning but as a necessary means to the bigger aim of discipleship and ministry. I tell them, for example, to refrain from talking about their own personal problems or from immediately offering solutions as small steps toward the kind of practical wisdom that characterizes the larger practices of empathy and compassion.

Other colleagues describe the complex relationship between *techne* and *phronesis* as requisite for teaching subjects such as religious education and worship, which require ways of knowing that often go unrecognized in academic contexts, except perhaps in professional schools (e.g., law, education, and medicine). In addition to the textual and interpretative knowledge of Christian sources for which scholars such as Groome and Browning developed methods of practical engagement, one needs knowledge that puts theology into action through movement, exercise, accumulated trial-and-error experience, and so forth. To understand the place of *techne,* scholars draw on analogies with practices such as playing an instrument, learning a sport, and nursing. John Witvliet, for example, likens skill acquisition in teaching worship to doing scales in learning to sing or play an instrument. Scales maintain "muscle memory," and such memory is part of theological knowledge.[121] Even virtuosi do not quit doing scales. People learn in Witvliet's classroom by "encountering actual practices: concrete examples of gestures, symbols, sermons, songs, images, and environments."[122] To understand the learning of ministry, Christian Scharen and Kathleen Cahalan turn to nursing scholar Patricia Benner, who studies how nurses move from novice to expert through bodily "sedimentation" of skills, a kind of "embodied know-how" also examined by Stuart Dreyfus and Hubert Dreyfus.[123]

121. John D. Witvliet, "Teaching Worship as a Christian Practice," in *For Life Abundant: Practical Theology, Theological Education, and Christian Ministry,* ed. Dorothy C. Bass and Craig Dykstra (Grand Rapids: Eerdmans, 2008), p. 140. See also the six essays on teaching by authors in different disciplines in Kathleen Cahalan, Carol Lakey Hess, and Bonnie Miller-McLemore, "Teaching Practical Theology: Introducing Six Perspectives," *International Journal of Practical Theology* 12, no. 1 (2008): 35-87.

122. Witvliet, "Teaching Worship," p. 130.

123. Christian Scharen, "Learning Ministry over Time: Embodying Practical Wisdom," in Bass and Dykstra, eds., *For Life Abundant,* p. 267 (and the chapter as a whole); Kathleen A. Cahalan, *Introducing the Practice of Ministry* (Collegeville: Liturgical, 2010), pp. 137-41. Scharen and Cahalan cite Patricia Benner, "Using the Dreyfus Model of Skill Acquisition to Describe and Interpret Skill Acquisition and Clinical Judgment in Nursing Practice and Education," *Bulletin of Science, Technology, and Society* 24, no. 3 (June 2004): 188-99, and *From*

All this modifies the epistemological bias that we think our way into acting, giving greater weight to the influence of body and action on thought.

Alongside appreciation for *techne* lies a revaluation of stuff — or, in the words of British scholar Heather Walton, the "power of things in human life" — to inscribe our worlds and create and sustain meaning. "Things matter to people" in ways that Christian- and Marxist-influenced critiques of capitalism and consumerism have not adequately comprehended. This interest in materiality seems especially characteristic of practical theologians who are pushing back against a harsh Calvinist- or Puritan-influenced Protestant aversion to the sacramentality of everyday life, a sacredness many Catholics already presume, although these scholars seldom recognize the influence of their Protestant context. Walton questions the hierarchy of values that has led to an "unthinking subordination" of *poesis*. She traces an emerging materialism on the edge of contemporary theory that suggests love of or delight in objects as not wrong in itself, especially when approached critically and without romanticization.[124] Another British colleague, Stephen Pattison, also probes the modern proclivity to see material artifacts, even in our ostensibly materialistic society, as occupying a radically inferior position. He contrasts the "scopic regime of the 'arrogant eye,'" which regards materiality from a disengaged distance, with "haptic vision" connected to the body and other senses. He argues for a more complex, even person-like treatment of the inanimate world for its power to shape us and as an ethical requisite for ecological care.[125] In the United States, pastoral theologians such as Robert Dykstra and Jaco Hamman, both influenced by Princeton pastoral theologian Don Capps, try to make a place for aesthetic imagination and "artistic abandon" — that "capacity to recognize and delight in the beauty around us," in Dykstra's words. He argues that this capacity has been repressed and displaced by "linguistic body-checks" or language patterns that shame people into mistrusting what we know

Novice to Expert: Excellence and Power in Clinical Nursing Practice (Menlo Park, NJ: Addison-Wesley, 1984); and Hubert L. Dreyfus and Stuart E. Dreyfus, *Mind over Machine: The Power of Human Intuition and Expertise in the Era of the Computer* (New York: Free Press, 1986).

124. Heather Walton, "Desiring Things: Practical Theology and the New Materialisms," in *City of Desires — a Place for God? Practical Theological Perspectives,* ed. R. Ruard Ganzevoort, Rein Brouwer, and Bonnie Miller-McLemore (Berlin: Lit Verlag, 2013), pp. 130-32, 138.

125. Stephen Pattison, *Seeing Things: Deepening Relations with Visual Artifacts* (London: SCM, 2011), p. 19.

through child-like intuition, including our earliest sense of God's beauty. "What if we were to write theology with our left hands, our non-dominant hands, our child-hands?" he asks. Would we then speak the truth, theology at its "most relevant, sensual, and heroic," desisting "for once from habits of questioning our questions and instead articulate aspects of ourselves that we didn't know we knew . . . to become once again a child before they took the poetry away"?[126]

Although high regard for the everyday seems as if it would be a priority in practical theology, the pragmatic orientation of the discipline toward change has made it difficult to appreciate the more fleeting and elusive value of the creative arts. In beautiful evocative prose, Dykstra and Walton help us see how much we miss as we rush by. Whereas Browning's influential work "reinscribes" the Aristotelian separation of *phronesis* and *poesis,* John Wall, Browning's own student and now an ethics professor, uses Martha Nussbaum and Paul Ricoeur to argue for their integral connection. A "poetic phronesis," in Wall's words, is not supplementary to knowledge but absolutely essential to "making" or constructing meaning.[127] For Walton, a turn to poetics and the creative facilities demanded by art forms such as literature engages the emotions, ignites our imagination, invigorates our perception of the particular, and tempers an epistemological over-reliance on moral philosophy, hermeneutics, and the social sciences.[128]

Full Bodied and in Place

Few participants in the 1980s revival of practical theology note the Western history of disparagement of the body. Even fewer connect this with patriar-

126. Robert C. Dykstra, "Unrepressing the Kingdom: Pastoral Theology as Aesthetic Imagination," *Pastoral Psychology* 61 (2012): 393, 408; see also Jaco Hamman, "Seeing Things Differently and Not Being Looked At," *Pastoral Psychology* 58 (2009): 551-62; and Donald E. Capps, "The Lessons of Art Theory for Pastoral Theology," *Pastoral Psychology* 47, no. 5 (1999): 321-46.

127. John Wall, "Phronesis, Poetics and Moral Creativity," *Ethical Theory and Moral Practice* 6 (2003): 337, as cited by Heather Walton, "Poetics," in Miller-McLemore, ed., *The Wiley-Blackwell Companion to Practical Theology,* p. 179.

128. Walton, "Poetics," p. 174. See also Heather Walton, "Seeking Wisdom in Practical Theology: *Phronesis,* Poetics, and Everyday Life," *Practical Theology* 7, no. 1 (2014): 5-18.

chy, misogyny, racism, colonialism, and the political construction of knowledge in relationship to particular bodies. Yet the rise of modern science and the epistemology of "mind over matter" coincides with the Western colonization of peoples in the Southern Hemisphere, the idealization of white womanhood, and the industrial exploitation of the natural world, all of which rest on a certain disdain for place, earth, nature, and our mammalian bodies as well as the knowledge gained through them. Part of the thrall of intellectualism is its very relief from entanglement with situated bodies.

Scholars in recent years have become acutely aware of such connections. Examples of the reappraisal of the impact of place and bodies on knowledge abound within theology in general and practical theology in particular, including my own work on maternal knowing and everyday knowledge.[129] These developments reflect wider intellectual trends. My claims about how a mother knows through her body, in undulating movements, of reason, feeling, response, and recalculation or about the spiritual meaning within the chaos of everyday care for those dependent on us rest on prior feminist efforts to reconstruct knowledge. Many feminist scientists and philosophers as well as theologians tried to undermine dualisms of mind (man) over body (woman) and articulate patterns of knowing suppressed within modern intellectual abstraction.

Comparable interest in bodies and place has arisen around race and the distortion of both bodies and place by racism and colonialism. Scholars who engaged the Aristotelian categories in the 1980s mostly ignored their origin within a hierarchical class system in which women, slaves, children, artisans, and others close to material production and reproduction held inferior status. Only Greek, free, aristocratic males had the capacity to pursue the highest good, as British scholar Robert Smith points out. He criticizes Browning for failing to address the "exclusive nature" of Aristotelian *phronesis* — a problem not unique to Browning — and, as a result, misconstruing the Christian telos. Beyond declaring all theology practical, Smith wants to show "how *phronesis* is contextually located" in its racially influenced particularities and nuances.[130] The telos within black faith history is not a

---

129. See Miller-McLemore, *Christian Theology in Practice,* part II; *Also a Mother: Work and Family as Theological Dilemma* (Nashville: Abingdon, 1994); and *In the Midst of Chaos: Care of Children as Spiritual Practice* (San Francisco: Jossey-Bass, 2007).

130. Robert L. Smith Jr., "Black *Phronesis* as Theological Resource: Recovering the Practical Wisdom of Black Faith Communities," *Black Theology: An International Journal* 6, no. 2

Kantian categorical imperative of equal regard, as in Browning, but God's redemption from bondage to evil — violence and racism in the case of slavery. Smith makes a case — in the most general of terms — for "black *phronesis*" or practical wisdom within the "history and experiences of Blacks in America." Even black theology itself requires a "redirection" or "shift" in this direction from its more abstract "systematic approach."[131]

In an evocative account, told partly through narratives from the slave trade across several continents, black church scholar Willie Jennings creatively answers this need. His book, *The Christian Imagination,* is not overtly on epistemology, but its implications for understanding Christian wisdom are extensive. He makes epistemological contributions on two levels — through his writing style itself and through one of several narrated stories in particular, that of José de Acosta Porres.

To take a step back first and briefly explain the project, Jennings shows how our colonial and slave history distorts Christian imagination, making it almost impossible to recognize the compassionate intimacy that lies at the heart of the gospel. Colonialism and slavery operated through destruction of bodies and displacement of peoples from native lands and sacred places that bind communities, sustain livelihood, and define identity. Schemas for sorting and ranking people by race, endorsed by Christian theology, arose as a means to enforce the destruction and displacement. Once the identity grounded in the land is destroyed, "you have no alternative but racial identity."[132] Unfortunately, Jennings does not address the obvious link between white supremacy and hyper-masculinity even though the displacement of female and children's bodies by male and adult bodies is woven into, and is as disturbing as, the displacement Jennings describes (whether through mundane practices such as domestic submission or horrific acts such as rape). However, he does offer pointed criticisms of the Christian academy and its "highly refined process of socialization" as a site where the distortion of the Christian social imagination is perpetuated.[133]

José de Acosta Porres, the first well-trained Jesuit priest from Spain to

(2008): 178-79. See also his book, *From Strength to Strength: Shaping a Black Practical Theology for the 21st Century* (New York: Peter Lang, 2007).

131. Smith, "Black *Phronesis*," pp. 176-77.

132. Willie James Jennings, *The Christian Imagination: Theology and the Origins of Race* (New Haven: Yale University Press, 2010), p. 58.

133. Jennings, *The Christian Imagination*, p. 7.

disembark as teacher, missionary, and resident theologian in Lima, Peru, in 1572, is seldom included in standard theological texts precisely because he "exposes the imperialist matrix" of contemporary Christianity.[134] Jennings shows the problems with this omission, including the artificial and even morally indefensible construction of modern systematic theology as wholly separate from missiology and practical theology. Only in light of Acosta can we grasp the full import (and limitations) of Gutiérrez's *Theology of Liberation,* published in Lima centuries later, as well as modern theology's plight more generally, "floating above land, landscape, animals, place, and space." Acosta "marks an epistemological crisis in the history of Christian theology," a pivotal point when theology is forged through a denial of certain kinds of authority, including native knowledge.[135] He simply cannot comprehend the logic of native convictions about land and divine action, much less accord them any value because they are seen as innately inferior or even demonic in an ordering of creation and providence in which the "body of the European" is the "compass marking divine election." Jennings offers an especially pithy characterization of the crisis in how scholars define and understand theology: theology as *"faith seeking understanding* mutates into *faith judging intelligence"* or faith that ranks peoples and their intelligence by the color of their skin.[136]

As key as the substance of Jennings's argument, his account also displays a different way of doing theology, one he knows his readers may not recognize but one I wager people like Walton and Pattison would appreciate. Rather than offering an analysis of classic doctrine more typical of systematic theology, he analyzes theology's social performances "in order to capture the social condition of Christianity itself." Like a "film director," he recounts untold tales of people whose lives are paradigmatic in their particularity, attending to "things only now entering the horizon of theological reflection, questions of race, space, place, geography, and identity."[137] The problem in academic theological knowledge, therefore, is not its split of theory from practice, classical from practical disciplines, academy from church, or even abstract from situated thinking but its "complex process of

134. Jennings, *The Christian Imagination,* p. 115.
135. Jennings, *The Christian Imagination,* pp. 293, 70.
136. Jennings, *The Christian Imagination,* pp. 33, 108.
137. Jennings, *The Christian Imagination,* pp. 9, 10.

disassociation and dislocation" from our bodies, place, and the incarnate life of Christ. Theology is done from the "commanding heights" that require of the colonized an "adaptability, fluidity, formation, and reformation of being" not required of those in charge. In the end, Jennings's book is a wonderfully fertile exegesis of its first line and the stories behind it: "Mary, my mother, taught me to respect the dirt."[138]

Fulkerson, Jennings's colleague at Duke, is also adamant about naming theology's cognitive captivity and even more intentional than Jennings about pursuing fresh avenues for reconstruction, including through practical theology. Like him, she talks powerfully about bodies and place. In contrast to his sweeping panorama of distant times and communities, she immerses herself in a local congregation where finely tuned ethnographic sensitivities reveal a troubling disjuncture between professed beliefs about Christian inclusivity and her own immediate visceral reactions to those disabled and of other skin colors. She writes of her first encounter:

> While I am expecting a mixed-race group, I am surprised at my own response to all the dark skin in the room. . . . I find myself aware of the paleness of my skin. . . . Next I notice a thin white man sitting twisted in a wheelchair. . . . As I approach . . . , my body feels suddenly awkward and unnatural. . . . I do not know where to place myself. My height feels excessive and ungainly.[139]

Of greater significance than self-disclosure, she recognizes that her body- and memory-shaped knowledge is not unique to her but operative in the embedded life of the congregation as a whole, even if invisible and unarticulated. Even more important, she uses this awareness to point to the gross limitations of systematic theology in comprehending theological formation at this level. Its individualistic and highly cognitive frame cannot comprehend theology as shaped by "habituated bodies with desires and . . . affective and visceral reactions," especially when bodily memory produces messages at odds with stated convictions and intentions.[140] In particular, linguistically oriented accounts of practice, such as that of MacIntyre, fail to account for

138. Jennings, *The Christian Imagination,* pp. 7, 8, 1.
139. Mary McClintock Fulkerson, *Places of Redemption: Theology for a Worldly Church* (Oxford: Oxford University Press, 2007), pp. 4-5.
140. Fulkerson, *Places of Redemption,* p. 11.

"bodied traditioning" — the "distinctive communicative force of bodies" — and the ways in which a great deal of the wisdom of tradition evolves not just through teaching or proclamation but through situational competence and improvisation.[141]

To take seriously such knowledge, one needs nontextual modes of analysis. Fulkerson's own search for understanding leads her to sociology and place theory, where she explores aversive forms of response: how people substitute stigma for knowledge; how obliviousness functions as a form of "not-seeing"; how such oblivion is viscerally and reflexively determined by fear, anxiety, and disgust; and how place itself is "truly fundamental in generating knowledge." Place signifies *"bodied ingression into the world."* Place theory surpasses appreciation for the lived body by respecting the "density of location," extending the site of knowledge both geographically and chronologically. It suggests both synchronic and diachronic meanings. That is, place is a "kind of *gathering*" that takes place at one point in time, and place is also a "territory of meaning" that evolves over time.[142]

Sociologist Paul Connerton's distinction between "inscription" and "incorporation" proves especially fruitful here. Inscribing practices, such as creating an alphabet and writing, record meaning in order to convey it across the passage of time, long after the body's involvement. In practices of a non-inscribed kind, what Connerton calls incorporating practices, the body conveys its message in real time. Whereas inscribing is two-dimensional and time and space are obscured, incorporating is three-dimensional and operates through nontextual, nonverbal means. Incorporating practices involve, for example, the "memorisation of culturally specific postures" for men and women, for ceremonies and everyday occasions, for people in positions of authority and subordination, and so forth.[143] Knowing happens through "commemorative" acts or rituals. But these "prove to be commemorative only in so far as they are performative; performativity cannot be thought without a concept of habit; and habit cannot be thought without a notion of bodily automatism."[144] Once again,

---

141. Fulkerson, *Places of Redemption,* p. 49.

142. Fulkerson, *Places of Redemption,* pp. 25, 27-28; emphasis in original text.

143. Paul Connerton, *How Societies Remember* (Cambridge: Cambridge University Press, 1989), pp. 72-73.

144. Connerton, *How Societies Remember,* p. 5.

the idea of sedimentation appears: "In habitual memory the past is, as it were, sedimented in the body."[145]

So bodies are not mere mediums; they are sources of knowledge. They do not just convey meanings; they contain and create them. In one of Fulkerson's more important qualifications, she argues that Connerton goes beyond Bourdieu's notion of *habitus* by arguing that "certain long-established bodily *habitus* merit the status of tradition" because "'incorporative' practices *convey their own meaning in the performance.*" Bodies are not "simply *expressing* or *enacting* the values of a community in a secondary way." Bodily activity "is itself the communication."[146] She concludes by reiterating what now seems obvious: faith practices are more than cognitive, require consideration of bodies and practical competencies, and create tradition through incorporation, not just inscription.

The Local: More Than a Recipient, More Than Token Representation

On first blush, developments in the study of local congregations seem the least remarkable of the three areas I identify for innovations in practical knowing. After all, congregational studies has been a vital enterprise at least since the 1970s when a group of scholars, including Carl Dudley and James Hopewell, received Lilly funding for concentrated research.[147] Influenced by this development, Browning builds his masterwork *Fundamental Practical Theology* around case studies of three congregations. In fact, interest in challenges faced by parishes and churches arose long before this in the early twentieth century and continues today among sociologists such as Nancy Ammerman and Penny Becker.

However, since the mid-1990s there has been a notable epistemological shift. For Browning and his peers, the focus was mostly on the congregation as object of study and recipient of the expert knowledge gained through such study. Moreover, social science researchers were hesitant to venture into theological territory. Browning himself notes this problem. When he

---

145. Connerton, *How Societies Remember*, p. 72.

146. Fulkerson, *Places of Redemption*, p. 46; emphasis in original text.

147. See Carl Dudley, ed., *Building Effective Ministry* (San Francisco: Harper & Row, 1983), and James F. Hopewell, *Congregations: Stories and Structures* (Philadelphia: Fortress, 1987).

joined a team to study Wiltshire Church in 1981, the "leaders had invited no one to represent a theological or biblical perspective." They assumed that "theology had nothing to contribute" and understanding was "largely a matter for the social sciences."[148] Browning sees the impediment as hermeneutical: those in the sciences do not recognize all disciplines as embedded in normative histories. His solution, therefore, is to delve into the philosophy of science, redefine science so that it sees its own norms, reorganize the academic study of theology, and, finally, correlate resources in the longer tradition with the local situation to clarify central norms for Christian communities. All notable contributions, but his rationale for studying local congregations is restrained: they touch lives, they have been ignored, they are interesting, and they keep his project practical.[149] He suggests a "new way of thinking about theology" by challenging the wooden theory-applied-to-practice habits of his peers.[150] But in the end theology is still *brought to* more than *evident within* congregations. Mostly, the three case studies "illustrate my points."[151]

There are epistemological exceptions, of course. Walton suggests we have missed a novelty in our admiration for Hopewell's work in congregational studies — his insistence that creative aesthetic work, such as narrative, accompany other forms of knowledge, such as empirical resources. She describes his classic *Congregation: Stories and Structures* as "a very unusual, 'poetic' text." Because congregations are corporate works of art, they require aesthetic tools for full comprehension. He "does not set poetics apart from other forms of knowledge . . . but he presents imaginative work as essential to grasping the fullness of Christian practice."[152]

Hopewell's world is still a far stretch from the contemporary scene where scholars like Fulkerson immerse themselves in local contexts expecting to learn within them. Mary Clark Moschella, the first to introduce ethnography to pastoral care, spent many hours in an Italian Catholic immigrant community in San Pedro, California, "piecing together . . . bits of theological wisdom" in artifacts of food, prayer, and home décor and in practices

---

148. Browning, *Fundamental Practical Theology*, p. 78.

149. Browning, *Fundamental Practical Theology*, pp. 3, 15.

150. Browning, *Fundamental Practical Theology*, p. x.

151. Browning, *Fundamental Practical Theology*, p. 12; see also pp. 16, 18.

152. Walton, "Poetics," pp. 175-77.

of feeding, fishing, and celebrating.[153] Later, in a guidebook for using ethnography as a pastoral practice, she contrasts theology as "special knowledge" that teachers and leaders should impart with theology as "wisdom . . . already there in the congregation," waiting to be "excavated," borrowing Graham's metaphor.[154] In Moschella's words, "By studying over time the repeated actions and interactions of people in a particular group, one can catch a glimpse of theology as it is lived out in the life of the group."[155]

Years ago Chopp warned against romanticizing the knowledge of congregations. She did so in light of her overall concern about the bourgeois nature of practical theology's 1980s revival and its liberal bent toward elite questions of intellectual credibility. She is right that theologians will find "no gnostic formulas" in congregations and that churches often echo the same individualistic worries about God language and cognitive claims as the theological academy, with Browning's study of Wiltshire Church as a prime example.[156] However, researchers such as Moschella and Fulkerson reveal that Chopp underestimated what might be learned.

On this front, James Nieman stands out for his efforts in essays and lectures to redefine theology in such a way that it becomes visible in congregational contexts. Understanding theology in context is critical for scholars in congregational studies who remain nervous about theology's validity as part of their descriptive and interpretative research, but it also has implications beyond this sphere for understanding Christian practical wisdom. Theology's modern self-perception as second- or third-order reflection, perpetuated by modern theologians, including liberation theologians such as Segundo, has not served us particularly well in this respect.[157] A primary task of practical theology, as Nieman states succinctly, is to correct the "misperception that theology is reducible to being a secondary reflective or regulative enterprise dominated by experts." Instead, a "view of theology as a primary, performative religious activity that happens in and through

153. Mary Clark Moschella, *Living Devotions: Reflections on Immigration, Identity, and Religious Imagination* (Eugene, OR: Pickwick, 2008), book cover.

154. Moschella, *Ethnography as a Pastoral Practice,* pp. 38, 40.

155. Moschella, *Ethnography as a Pastoral Practice,* p. 47.

156. Chopp, "Practical Theology and Liberation," pp. 124-25.

157. Segundo, *The Liberation of Theology,* pp. 75-76; see also Theodore Jennings's oft-cited entry "Pastoral Theological Methodology," in *The Dictionary of Pastoral Care and Counseling,* ed. Rodney J. Hunter (Nashville: Abingdon, 1990), p. 862.

ordinary adherents, and often by means of their practices" deserves further elaboration and understanding.[158]

In a fine essay entitled "Attending Locally," Nieman develops rubrics by which religious leaders can discern theology in their midst. In addition to theology's "speculative" function (as a kind of thinking rightly about God or "thought project") and "regulative" function (as a device for maintaining order or a "normative strategy"), he shows "basic mechanisms by which theology operates discursively" or in the midst of local practices. The challenge is "to define theology broadly and flexibly enough to be recognizable across different times and places."[159] Within local communities, theology's primary intent is "dynamic."[160] The term suggests that theological knowing in local communities "seeks to do something, even to create a significant outcome for its users." These distinctions allow us "to acknowledge that practices as disparate as customary attire, financial management, or hymn performance may also be assertions of theology."[161]

Elsewhere Nieman describes the way of knowing needed by leaders trying to grasp the theological dynamics within religious communities as "a personalized, empathetic kind of knowledge" rather than that of a naturalist, statistician, or even anthropologist.[162] In another essay, he works alongside Jesuit theologian Roger Haight to develop a more nuanced depiction of theology's various forms within historical and contemporary communities of faith. Since churches are oriented toward both God and world, we can only fully understand them when we connect formal doctrinal confessions with living realities. The intention, as Nieman clarifies, is "neither to restrict theology to church life nor to denigrate the value of academic theological insight, but instead to ensure an attitude attuned to the ecclesial purposes

158. James R. Nieman, "Congregational Studies," in Miller-McLemore, ed., *The Wiley-Blackwell Companion to Practical Theology,* p. 140.

159. James Nieman, "Attending Locally: Theologies in Congregations," *International Journal of Practical Theology* 6, no. 2 (2002): 200-202.

160. The use of the term *dynamics* actually harkens back to Hiltner's attempt to identify theological dynamics in a book by that title: Seward Hiltner, *Theological Dynamics* (Nashville: Abingdon, 1972). He, of course, was partly borrowing the term from Sigmund Freud's "dynamic psychology" or psychology focused on the mind as itself a lively interaction between various forces.

161. Nieman, "Attending Locally," pp. 205-6.

162. James R. Nieman, *Knowing the Context: Frames, Tools, and Signs for Preaching* (Minneapolis: Fortress, 2008), p. 35.

of theology enacted by its basic users — a commitment that does challenge some scholars to revise their perceptions of what counts as theology."[163]

So What Next? *Disciplining* as Ultimately Insufficient to the Cause

Amid all the interest in material religion today, there is an unasked question. What does this heightened attention, dispersed across the disciplines, mean for theological knowledge and education? Does it suggest anything new about the nature of such knowledge? Indeed, how does one come to "know theology" when religious traditions themselves insist on "particular formative regimes and disciplines if transformative truth is to be known and understood," as comparative theologian John Thatamanil suggests? If religious knowledge is cultivated through formative practices such as prayer and liturgy, then this seems to suggest that religious knowledge differs from "knowledge *about* religious traditions." It is much more akin to knowledge within the "arts of dance and acting," he says. If this is true, then its knowledge "can be gained only by somatic teaching and learning . . . [it] requires embodied knowing."[164]

Thatamanil's suggestions are not new for practical theologians who teach in an area frequently designated "arts of ministry." But this view distinguishes Thatamanil from his theological predecessors. It also reflects a growing awareness of the complicated relationship between practices, formation, *and* theological knowledge — a relationship the ensuing chapters on scriptural imagination and spiritual disciplines explore in more detail.

As Tracy argues, the "three great separations of modern Western culture" — feeling and thought, form and content, and theory and practice — have been devastating for theology and theological education. If education and knowledge are about formation, then there must be a rejoining of theological theories and spiritual exercises, which are inextricably linked in ancient and medieval theology and philosophy and "analogous to the exercise employed by an athlete for the body." Practical theology has

163. Roger Haight and James Nieman, "On the Dynamic Relation between Ecclesiology and Congregational Studies," *Theological Studies* 70 (2009): 589.

164. John Thatamanil, "Comparative Theology and the Question of Formation," *Teaching Theology and Religion* 14, no. 4 (October 2011): 368-69; emphasis added.

an essential role as the discipline "best placed" to recover the fragmented way theological knowledge enters everyday modern life partly because, in Tracy's words, it "explicitly and brilliantly corresponds to the ancient insistence on the role of practical exercises for personal and communal living," something Kathleen Cahalan demonstrates in her chapter "Unknowing." Its ability to "cultivate moments of tact, silence, attentiveness to the world outside ourselves" can ward off our proclivity to curve in on ourselves and "help us recover . . . the great artistic, metaphysical and mystical fragments," the "'hints and guesses'" of the "something more" in life.[165]

When it comes to practical knowledge, however, there is another unsettled question that Fulkerson names but few have considered.[166] How will we adjudicate what she calls the "intersection of knowledges" or the plural knowledges requisite for good theology — biblical truth, scientific finding, critical inquiry, wisdom, and so forth? Recovery of *paideia* or spiritual exercises does not dispel the need for critical thinking. My play on words of *matter over mind* to capture the reverse epistemological trend within and beyond the discipline of practical theology should not be mistaken as an argument for the demise of mind and the dominance of matter. This is neither likely nor desirable. It is not likely because modern science wields and will continue to wield immense power in today's university, corporate world, and government politics. But such a reversal is also not desirable, given the benefits of science, the value of critical reason, the weight of accumulated theory, and the positive freedoms and knowledge that have accompanied Western Enlightenment, all of which give me both means and voice to do the work of this essay itself. A dualistic and exclusivist approach serves neither side well, much less the good of life as a whole, as the last several centuries have already shown with the repression of "matter."

The misperception that the rise of one sort of knowledge inevitably means the demise of other kinds, however, is a fear common to all power relationships. So, for example, some men feared feminism as threatening a reverse oppression — female domination of men, matriarchy in place of patriarchy — and for some feminists this was the intent. But the aim of this chapter (and the book as a whole) has been to understand better the nature

165. Tracy, "A Correlational Model Revisited," pp. 52, 56.
166. See, for example, the conversation between Jaco Dreyer and me in the *International Journal of Practical Theology* 16, no. 1 (2012).

of practical knowledge in order to enrich knowledge as a whole and not to disparage unjustifiably or rule out completely certain kinds of knowledge. Perhaps the analogy with feminism is helpful again. Many feminists actually worked hard to dispel misreadings of feminism as a reverse domination, redefining feminism as a broader movement of transformation for people in all positions.

The task at hand, then, is to gain a better understanding of the rise of ways of knowing largely suppressed within modernity in all their complexity, benefits, and pitfalls. Instead of a reverse domination, I think we have discovered that the new proclivity to value matter represents a more complex reshuffling of knowledge and a reconstruction of human subjectivity and community that in the best scenario breaks down dualisms and questions triumph itself (of one kind of knowledge over another) as antithetical to genuine understanding.

The final section of this chapter on the last two decades speaks for itself. Building on the 1980s literature, it makes evident a primary thesis of the chapter — that practical theology functions as one of the most important contemporary movements exploring alternative ways of religious knowing, including the kind of wisdom or knowledge that chapters in Part 1 attempt to show. Efforts to understand *phronesis* as a distinct kind of theological knowledge in the 1980s made possible surprisingly fruitful ventures in the following two decades for a more intricate relationship between mind and matter and for creative encounters with new forms of knowledge and wisdom, partly paving the way for this book. The yearning for new ways of conceptualizing knowledge is evident in the growing list of action-oriented, quotidian-centered adjectives attached to theology — theology as practiced, lived, embodied, operative, everyday, ordinary, and popular. Immersion in context and materiality — whether in local congregations or locations of race, gender, orientation, religious identity, disability, and so forth — renders certain aspects of practical knowledge more visible through attention to bodies, relationships, emotion, place, and local communities.

The bigger question behind that of adjudicating among plural knowledges comes down to the matter of the wider telos or purpose for which knowledge is sought, whether as an end in itself or for some larger aim. If knowledge is sought for some larger purpose, whether a divine aim or more mundane but still lofty goals such as saving the earth, then certain kinds of theoretical knowledge remain insufficient for the job. When it comes to the question of telos, my account in the chapter as a whole reveals a shadow side — the ultimately unsatisfying nature of academic means, the almost-but-not-yet quality of intellectual discovery when it comes to Christian practical wisdom, the sense that theories almost get it right but not completely. Practical theologians have been attempting, through academic tools, to articulate something that seems essential to Christian life but has been hard to see and sustain precisely within the standard academic way of life. With some exceptions within professional schools of law, medicine, education, and so forth, the academy is necessarily and justifiably ruled by other important ways of knowing that, nonetheless, do not help Christian wisdom thrive as a way "to understand God truly," to borrow David Kelsey's words in his own contribution to the 1980s efforts to reconceive theological education.[167] As scholars, we have used the word *wisdom* in this book to stretch toward a way of knowing that encompasses but is more than information, knowledge, or understanding and includes a way of life and being that refuses to separate itself from practice. But the various dead ends in this chapter — whether with Browning, liberation theology, or even the more recent foray into materiality — suggest that we cannot quite get there through *disciplining* alone. This chapter shows how Christian practical wisdom has been both advanced *and lost* through the disciplining practices of academic discourse.[168]

So we reach once again what we might call "Fowler's paradox," which Hastings nicely paraphrases as *"reason trying to conquer reason by reason,"* a problem that Fowler says plagues even those who try to do theology on ground laid by philosophical critics of modern rationality — Gadamer, Heidegger, and Wittgenstein included.[169] Instead of getting "beyond the rationally self-grounded subject of the Enlightenment," Fowler says, "we inevitably end up worshiping before the altar of the sovereignty of method" on which rests the idol of critical reason.[170] The academic route to reviving

167. David H. Kelsey, *To Understand God Truly: What's Theological about a Theological School* (Louisville: Westminster John Knox, 1992).

168. Much more could be said about this by turning to Michel Foucault's work, including but certainly not limited to *Discipline and Punish: The Birth of the Prison,* trans. Alan Sheridan (New York: Pantheon Books, 1977), and *The Archaeology of Knowledge,* trans. A. M. Sheridan Smith (New York: Pantheon Books, 1972). I hope those who know his work well might take this up.

169. Hastings, *Practical Theology and the One Body of Christ,* p. 6; emphasis in original text.

170. Fowler, "Practical Theology and Theological Education," p. 57.

practical Christian knowledge — and even this chapter, which hopes to help its cause — has limits despite its gifts. As helpful as careful theorizing may be, it falls short of grasping the fullness of Christian wisdom. This chapter partly repeats the injury, earning legitimacy through erudition and review of theory while arguing that credibility belongs somewhere else, minimally in some of the realities depicted elsewhere in this book (and here I think especially of the "show" chapters of Part 1 and the two chapters that follow this one). This is not unlike the dilemma I face in teaching about bodies and situated knowledge in classrooms where movement is greatly restricted and at a serious distance from actual contexts, or in presenting a paper on embodied knowing in didactic theoretical abstraction (both experiences I have had recently). In all cases, I find myself falling back on the terrible parental adage — "Do as I say, not as I do" — that essentially tells children and adults to ignore practice and disregard what they really see and know at a deeper, intangible level. Or, to turn to Shakespeare, I am "hoist by my own petard."

Thus, I am glad this chapter is situated within this book as a whole and not read or measured on its merits alone. Each chapter in the book, in fact, needs the other chapters as additions, corrections, and reminders of the more encompassing telos that lies within and beyond Christian wisdom. The "tell" chapters of Part 2 especially need the "show" chapters of Part 1, regardless of their limitations and oddities. And there are missing chapters in both sections, chapters we cannot write because of who we are, chapter that others like Jennings or Walton have written or must write. In acknowledging that scholars can only get so far within the limits of critical reason and its usual methods, this chapter points toward, even demands, the chapters that follow in which my colleagues delve into other ways to grasp Christian practical wisdom — through scripturally funded living and spiritual disciplines that prize unknowing itself, an idea that goes almost completely against the grain for all those swimming in late-modern waters where we aspire to obtain knowledge. The following chapters respond, in one way or another, to Fowler's plea for "more radical trust, investment, and engagement in God's redemption."[171] They join Fowler in inviting others to contribute their own chapters on what is needed to live and know (and not know) as people of faith.

Wisdom depends on multiple means — story, embodiment, prayer,

---

171. A paraphrase of Fowler, "Practical Theology and Theological Education," p. 58.

imagination, humility, attunement, and inclusivity — that are hard to en-act when focused on the demands of the typical intellectual exercise. This is what leads my first-year advisee to lament the absence of Scripture as she knows it from faith practice in a required course on the Hebrew Bible focused on the history and social context of ancient Israel. Or middle-year students to wonder where God has gone in their studies, when they have come to school on a spiritual quest. Or the ministry graduate to revert to what he knows best and to preach as if he never went to seminary. Or the person in the pew to shut down when the newly minted minister does in fact preach like she is still in seminary. Or the doctoral graduate in New Testament to complain that she cannot pursue the kind of integration of knowledge she desires and still produce a respectable, narrowly focused dis-sertation that gets her a job and tenure. Doctoral candidates seldom focus on this kind of knowledge, as Cahalan's account of her own experience in "Swimming" reveals. But then, if they land jobs in seminary contexts, they have to make radical adjustments in their disciplinary expertise, honed for scholarly publication in specialized areas, as they respond to the needs of the students in their classes or the faithful in their religious communities.

As all these examples suggest, theological scholarship produced in con-ventional ways can be deadening for faculty, students, graduates, seminary teachers, ministers, and, of course, all the rest of the laity seeking to grasp the workings of God within their lives. If this chapter on the many and var-ious efforts to address this problem (and their failure to do so) is of any help in lightening the burden, raising the clarion call, and opening up Christian practical wisdom for those seeking it, then it has more than met its purpose.

imagining

BIBLICAL IMAGINATION AS A DIMENSION
OF CHRISTIAN PRACTICAL WISDOM
DOROTHY C. BASS

IN MODERNITY, AN "ECLIPSE" closely related to the diminishment of practical wisdom described in Christian Scharen's chapter "Eclipsing" radically
altered how Western Christians understood and envisioned the world.
Throughout most of the church's history, the Bible was received as a reliable account of reality, portrayed in a great story that moves from origins to
future fulfillment while enfolding and giving significance to the present age.
Between the seventeenth and nineteenth centuries, the theologian Hans
Frei has argued, theologians lost track of the encompassing narrative set
forth in the realistic prose of the Bible's central story line. Influenced by
modern epistemology, theologians' understanding of the "literal" sense of
scripture changed, causing them to search the text for historical accuracy
while neglecting the identity-shaping vision provided by scripture's realistic
(though not necessarily factual) narrative. The result was "the eclipse of
biblical narrative," the loss of a sturdy, irreducible description of the world,
from its origins to its end, capable of framing the church's vision.[1] The Bible began to be approached as a relatively inaccessible collection of texts

1. Hans Frei, *The Eclipse of Biblical Narrative: A Study in Eighteenth and Nineteenth Century
Hermeneutics* (New Haven: Yale University Press, 1974). Frei's assertion of the basic unity of
the Christian Bible, which is most strongly evident through the line of the overall narrative
within which the several parts make sense, emboldens me to speak in this chapter about "the
Bible" or "scripture" as an entity. Although this is common language in the church, most historically aware scholars (among whom I count myself as well) hesitate over such terms, given
the great diversity of texts within the Bible, which are now most often studied piece by piece.

that needed to be studied by rational subjects who thought of themselves as living in a much different world than the one biblical texts described. Some modern readers adopted an analytical distance, treating biblical texts as historical sources and then doing theological work that abstracted principles and themes for present-day application. Others tried to hold text and theology together by insisting on the Bible's historical accuracy. In Frei's view, both approaches weakened theology.

Struggles over how to interpret scripture and what to make of it amid the cultural mixing that characterizes every historical period have existed across the centuries. However, as analyzed by Frei in one aspect and by Charles Taylor more generally, modernity brought a more encompassing change. When readers approach the Bible as buffered, internally knowing selves — that is, when readers understand themselves as separate from the text and charged with analyzing it rationally — the Bible's overall standing in the church, theology, and culture is altered. Many a college or seminary student has had her communally formed knowledge of scripture shaken upon encountering the critical study of biblical texts in an academic setting. Some fundamentalists, recoiling, have constructed interpretations that are as rigidly rational in style as the research reports of pure historicists.[2] Meanwhile, many critically minded individuals are morally offended by what the Bible evidently or reportedly says and so determine that it is irrelevant or harmful. And all around, with religious knowledge both destabilized and pluralized, a larger culture comprised of many faiths and none sets up the "mutual fragilization" of every religious conviction.[3]

2. George M. Marsden's influential studies of Christian fundamentalism in modern America have interpreted fundamentalism as a distinctive appropriation of modernity's quest for universal certainty. Marsden views fundamentalist biblical interpretation as deeply shaped by modernity: it aims at fact-truth, uses Enlightenment methods of classification and citation, and fights (academic) science with (an alternative) science rather than shifting the conversation. See Marsden, *Fundamentalism and American Culture* (New York: Oxford University Press, 1980), and "The Evangelical Love Affair with Enlightenment Science," in his *Understanding Fundamentalism and Evangelicalism* (Grand Rapids: Eerdmans, 1991). A different set of Christian responses to modernity led to pietism, which reflected the sense of faith as a private, inward reality, emphasizing the "heart" rather than the "head" in a culture where religious "head" knowledge had become problematic.

3. This situation grew from a long process of historical change; see Charles Taylor on this process, *A Secular Age* (Cambridge: Harvard University Press, 2007); on "mutual fragilization," pp. 303-4; on the "buffered" self, pp. 300-302.

In this context, and persuaded of the intellectual and moral value of critical approaches to the study of the Bible, it is impossible to live, like fish in water, within "the world Scripture made," as premodern Christians did.[4] However, to abandon these depths is impossible as well, for the church's confession and long life with the Bible continue to shape its worship, understanding, and living. Disengaged knowledge of biblical texts is different from the practical wisdom Christians need for faithful living, much as Descartes's method differed from the engaged, contextual discernment expressed in the letters and actions of Elisabeth of Bohemia. If the contemporary church is to live wisely, it needs — as indeed it yearns for — an engaged, holistic, and embodied comprehension of scripture. It is to this end that key practices of the church supply and stir the ecclesial imagination with the language of scripture, in preaching, praying the psalms, performing narratives of Christ's death and resurrection, catechesis, hymnody, and discernment, as well as through academic studies that probe ancient texts for meaning. The ecclesial imagination bears fruit as it emerges, articulate and embodied, in a way of life.

Even though it is beleaguered in modernity, in fact I catch glimpses of this kind of biblical imagination all around me.[5] It is stirred when children hear stories of shepherds, angels, and an infant wrapped in swaddling clothes and lying in a manger; it grows through reading, criticism, educa-

4. This language of world-making is from an influential manifesto by Luke Timothy Johnson, "Imagining the World Scripture Imagines," in *Theology and Scriptural Imagination,* ed. L. Gregory Jones and James J. Buckley (Oxford: Blackwell, 1998), which incorporates essays first published in the journal *Modern Theology.* I appreciate Johnson's summons to theologians to "become less preoccupied with the world that produced Scripture and learn again how to live in the world Scripture imagines" (p. 3), though I think he overestimates the ease of full reimmersion in the latter world.

5. In spite of his negative assessment of the state of biblical imagination in academic theology (and this was his major concern and audience), Johnson believes that actual Christian communities are still imaginatively alive. The renewal of (academic) theology, he argues, depends on renewed appreciation for such communities: "Theology's recovery of a scriptural imagination must come from a relationship with Scripture that is mediated, not by a scholarly guild committed to historical reconstruction, but by a faith community whose practices are ordered to the transformation of humans according to the world imagined by Scripture — a world, faith asserts, which expresses the mind of God" (p. 9). To isolate the text in the ancient world is to treat it as an archaeological artifact, foreclosing its capacity to challenge, instruct, inspire, and guide contemporary communities. To read it attentively in the contemporary world is both desirable and possible, Johnson argues.

tion, and conversation; it works its way into bodies in the language, song, and movements of Christian liturgy. Biblical imagination is enriched and expanded when a congregation that has ears to hear attends to good preaching or struggles together over what to do with difficult passages. But it also lives beyond the sanctuary. I have friends who have helped me to see an ordinary meal as manna, a time of uncertainty as a wilderness journey, and an object of desire as a golden calf. Inspired orators, such as Dr. Martin Luther King Jr., help a people to reframe their history by placing it within biblical narrative. Novelists, poets, musicians, and visual artists continue to plumb and stretch the riches of biblical imagination as well.

For a more focused set of examples, consider the stories gathered in the first part of this book. For each of the five authors, certain texts simply came to mind in specific circumstances — not as proof texts grabbed to justify something after the fact, but through a kind of experiential resonance with biblical images that caused certain things to stand out in greater relief, as the three women who shared a blanket under the stars stood out for me one August night, or as the water in which she swam became for Kathleen Cahalan a sign of God's renewing presence. Moreover, the desires that drove the stories all five authors told — desires for healing, love, community, reconciliation, and truth — reached toward promises that we have learned to imagine most fully in biblical terms. In these cases (and surely in countless others that readers can call to mind) biblical texts shaped how we actually experienced our lives; if we had not known these texts, we would not have known ourselves and our world in the same way. Similar instances of resonance and reach can be heard in daily conversation in countless homes, congregations, workplaces, artistic venues, and public settings.

More importantly, these examples suggest why a scripturally funded Christian practical wisdom matters. In these stories, how to criticize or establish scripture's truth is not at issue. Instead, the authors are concerned about how to inhabit the world in a way that might help them to know and love God, self, world, and others more truly. They find help for that concern when they look through the lens of scripture at what is around and within them. Comprehending scripture in a way that shapes one's vision, then, is not an end in itself. Instead, it is a formative dimension of a way of life with God, in Christ, along a path that leads to God's new creation and offers foretastes of it along the way.[6]

---

6. Martin Luther reportedly wrote, "It is for Christ's sake that we believe in the scrip-

As a dimension of Christian practical wisdom, biblical imagination is a walking-around knowledge — not a map drawn from above that provides abstract rules but a journey along paths described by attentive participants who once walked these paths in other contexts, heading in the same direction even though that direction was sometimes difficult to discern, then as well as now.[7] In the first century CE, the story of Abraham's trusting response to God's call enabled the author of the letter to the Hebrews to imagine the ongoing journey of his own community, and since that time this letter has helped countless other communities to imagine the great cloud of witnesses surrounding them as they continue this journey in their own contexts. Walking this way, the author suggests, both requires and bestows a way of seeing the world that probes beneath the visible surface of things, through a faith that bears "the conviction of things not seen" (Heb. 11:1).

Biblical imagination is not a form of knowledge *about,* which depends on separating the subject (the reader, student, critic) from the object (the text), though, as we shall see, knowledge about (that is, critical knowledge regarding texts) is indispensable to biblical imagination in modernity.[8] Rather, biblical imagination is a knowledge *of,* which cannot be had without life-shaping embodied participation. Communities wrestle the text for meaning just as Jacob wrestled a stranger for a blessing, a struggle from which he emerged with both a limp and a new name (Gen. 32:22-32). Confident in "things hoped for," this kind of knowing emerges as perception and

tures; it is not for the scriptures' sake that we believe in Christ" (in Diane Jacobson, "Some Fun Quotations about the Bible from Martin Luther," at http://www.bookoffaith.org, accessed March 27, 2014). This website is part of a churchwide initiative of the Evangelical Lutheran Church in America to encourage members to read and discuss the Bible more often and more fluently. As a member of the ELCA, I very much appreciate this initiative, as well as the way in which this particular "fun quote" reminds me that the Word of God is first of all Jesus Christ, not the Bible through which we learn of Christ and our lives in Christ. While other quotations on this web page include full references, this one does not, and I cannot find its original source.

7. A rich and influential account of engaged knowing is Michel de Certeau, "Walking in the City," in his *The Practice of Everyday Life,* trans. Steven Rendall (Berkeley: University of California Press, 1984).

8. A book that prominently promotes the importance of biblical imagination is Jones and Buckley, eds., *Theology and Scriptural Imagination,* cited above as the source of Luke T. Johnson's influential essay. It is interesting that "scriptural imagination" seems to be most often invoked by those worried about its corruption or decline.

response, even when perception seems to be taking place through a dark piece of glass and when the ultimate effect of a response cannot be known. Further, it depends on a kind of desire that is best articulated in the language of scripture itself, a hungry love that knows deep down that "one does not live by bread alone, but by every word that comes from the mouth of the Lord" (Deut. 8:3; Matt. 4:4; Luke 4:4). In the ancient world, the longing of some to incorporate biblical substance into their lives was so strong that they refrained from eating in order to keep scripture's precious words on their tongues as long as possible.[9] And though less weird by twenty-first-century standards (perhaps), Christian liturgy today still guides worshipers into practices that involve tongues and bodies, as people gather to worship God in the language of the Bible.

Something like this is essential to the life of faith. And yet post-Enlightenment people do not have the unmediated access to biblical imagination of the holistic, world-defining kind that was available in premodern times. We do have maps — critical procedures, scientific theories, clarity about differences — that direct much of our journey through texts and through life. We want the facts. We have an individualized notion of reading as the solitary, inward act of an individual, whose mental work it is to extract meaning from a text by a process of inward cognition rather than shared discernment and appropriation. Further, we are suspicious. While scripture itself has always incorporated awareness of sin's distortions and been on guard against the evil imaginations of the heart, modernity has brought a critical spirit that leaves no authority unchallenged. A biblically informed practical wisdom, lodged in the hearts of the faithful, does not live easily in this context.

Critical thinking is now a given, as immersive for late modern people as an enchanted, biblically narrated world was for premodern Christians. Further, it is indispensable as we try to gain nourishment from the texts we love. This book's critique of overreliance on disengaged reason might seem to suggest that I attribute the decline of biblical imagination to the rise of higher criticism among biblical scholars. To the contrary, as I hope will

---

9. Blake Leyerle, "Monastic Formation and Christian Practice: Food in the Desert," in *Educating People of Faith: Exploring the History of Jewish and Christian Communities,* ed. John Van Engen (Grand Rapids: Eerdmans, 2004), explores the monks' understanding of the strong connection between fasting and the recitation of scripture.

be clear below, I believe that modern biblical scholarship contributes powerfully to contemporary biblical imagination. When some scholars place overriding value on disengaged reason in their work, I see their approach as a result of epistemological shifts that have impacted every aspect of culture rather than as a cause of problems in the ecclesial appropriation of scripture. Biblical imagination has been undermined by the overarching social imaginary, not by modern biblical scholarship as an independent force.

In what follows, therefore, I shall assume, rather than argue, the value of historical criticism and other critical approaches informing the contemporary academic study of scripture. Along the way, I shall draw on the work of a few of the many scholars who are working to close the gap between the Bible and contemporary life, who employ the disengaged reason of historical criticism as just one move within a larger hermeneutical process whose end is to discern an engaged and life-giving knowledge of scripture. In doing so, I reflect the fact that this entire book is by and for those who embrace life amid what Charles Taylor calls "modernity's cross-pressures," where assumptions about historical time and critical reason pervade intellectual discourse while at the same time epiphanies of transcendence persistently disrupt secular certainties.

The theologian David Ford inspires a lively intermingling of critical and imaginative perspectives in his work, which relies crucially on continual engagement with the Bible. He urges theologians — and here I believe he would include all Christians as they seek to live faithfully — not just to read scripture but to reread it and reread it again, drawing on multiple interpretive perspectives and continually listening for both the "cries" in scripture (most importantly, Jesus' cry from the cross) and contemporary cries of suffering and joy. Signaling the importance of imagination, he often integrates contemporary poetry into his reflections. Ford's sense of scripture's sheer abundance of meaning, and his declaration that Christians are to read it together in seeking wisdom for a way of life, encourage the eclectic and imaginative forays that comprise this chapter, and more importantly an approach to scripture aimed at the formation of Christian practical wisdom.[10]

10. David F. Ford develops an approach to scripture that attends to "cries" and advocates for "reading and rereading" in *Christian Wisdom: Desiring God and Learning in Love* (Cambridge: Cambridge University Press, 2007). He develops the theological concept of abundance in *Self and Salvation: Being Transformed* (Cambridge: Cambridge University Press, 1999), ch. 5. Both books incorporate and dialogue with the poetry of Michael O'Siadhail.

The imaginative turn to scripture I hope to encourage requires neither extensive knowledge of specialized biblical scholarship nor a systematic theory of scripture's place in belief and practice. At the same time, the insights of theorists of the imagination and the work of imaginative biblical scholars are extremely helpful as I attempt, in this chapter, to clarify, to advocate, and finally to portray biblical imagination as a dimension of Christian practical wisdom. Drawing on these, I plunge into the deep waters of scripture, not as a biblical scholar but as a historian, a practical theologian, and a member of the community that expects to be shaken and shaped by encounter with this set of texts, and that yearns someday to find them written on our hearts.

Imagination as a Way of Knowing

Distinctions between *poesis* and *phronesis* — the knowing that belongs to the artist and the knowing of the wise participant in society — began with Aristotle, and I make no claim that imagination and practical wisdom are identical. However, I do want to argue that the vision that imagination makes available and lodges in the heart is indispensable to the embodied, walking-around knowledge we are describing and advocating in this book. Imagination gathers language, bodily experience, concepts, desires, and dispositions into a life-shaping capacity to see reality in a certain way; in its absence, meaning, action, and relationship are impossible. Imagination belongs not to the mind alone but to the whole person. "Its impetus comes from the emotions as much as from the reason," the philosopher Mary Warnock writes, "from the heart as much as from the head."[11]

One dimension of imagination appears in the term "social imaginary," which, in Taylor's use, provides a preconscious understanding of what is real and possible, shaped by and embodied in the practices of a commu-

---

11. Here and elsewhere my understanding of the imagination is influenced by the work of Craig Dykstra in *Vision and Character* (New York: Paulist Press, 1981), and in his important work (which prepared the way for this book) on "the pastoral imagination"; see "Pastoral and Ecclesial Imagination," in *For Life Abundant: Practical Theology, Theological Education, and Christian Ministry*, ed. Dorothy C. Bass and Craig Dykstra (Grand Rapids: Eerdmans, 2008). Dykstra quotes Mary Warnock on p. 48. Whereas Dykstra's emphasis has been on pastoral imagination, I am especially interested in the broader imagination of the church, which Dykstra referred to as "ecclesial imagination" but did not develop at length.

nity.[12] Another dimension is suggested by Taylor's account of an important manifestation of resistance to the immanent frame: imaginative art and literature, understood in the secular age as the expression of human spirit and creativity over against this iron cage of modern rationalism. Imagination appears, thus, in two forms: as a deeply integrated vision that determines how human beings see reality, and as a force that bursts through the constraints of the taken-for-granted.[13] Christian practical wisdom relies on imagination of both kinds — deeply formed as habitus yet also transformatively eruptive as death and resurrection, Christ's and our own.

While seeking the kind of imagination that can serve Christian practical wisdom, we must acknowledge at the outset that not all "Christian" imagination is faithful. In a recent book whose title, *The Christian Imagination*, cuts like a two-edged sword, the theologian Willie Jennings shows how the occlusion of certain biblical narratives, notions of place and belonging, and accounts of human community contributed to a pervasive social imagination that sustained the enslavement of Africans. Imagination can do damage; it can go very, very wrong; it can kill. Jennings's analysis of a horrendously broken imagination is accompanied by, and grounded in, a proposed recovery of Christian imagination that draws on a chastened and renewed reading of scripture, for the sake of transformed communities. Constant chastening and renewal are crucial to any worthy Christian imagination.[14]

Imagination is as corruptible as every other human capacity, and also as open to repentance and redemption. Every occurrence of the English

---

12. Paul Ricoeur calls the social imaginary "the touchstone of the practical function of the imagination" in "Imagination in Discourse and in Action," in *From Text to Action: Essays in Hermeneutics II,* trans. Kathleen Blamey and John B. Thompson (Evanston: Northwestern University Press, 2007), p. 169. For Charles Taylor on the social imaginary, see *A Secular Age,* pp. 171-76; on imagination as resistance to modern abstract reason, pp. 355-61.

13. In a recent study of moral imagination, Richard Osmer and Ariana Salazar-Newton specify three forms of imagination: "primary," which corresponds roughly to my first meaning; "secondary," which is similar to my second form; and "mythic," which is close to the kind of imagination I shall develop through engagement with the work of Paul Ricoeur later in this chapter. "The Practice of Reading and the Formation of the Moral Imagination," *Ecclesial Practices* 1 (2014): 51-71. They ground these forms in contemporary neuroscience, cognitive psychology, and creativity studies, which are beyond the scope of this chapter.

14. Willie James Jennings, *The Christian Imagination: Theology and the Origins of Race* (New Haven: Yale University Press, 2010). Bonnie Miller-McLemore also discusses Jennings's work in the previous chapter, "Disciplining."

word "imagination" in the KJV and the NRSV refers to the constructions of sinners, who "prophesy out of their own imagination" rather than from God's word (Ezek. 13:2), for example, or who mistake the true God for "an image formed by the art and imagination of mortals" (Acts 17:29). H. Richard Niebuhr noted that the important question about imagination is "not whether personal images should be employed but only what personal images are right and adequate and which are evil imaginations of the heart."[15] As the philosopher Iris Murdoch cautioned, imagination can malfunction in ways that construct "a fantasy world of our own into which we try to draw things from the outside, not grasping their reality and independence, making them into dream objects of our own."[16] In providing access to reality that is quite different from what disengaged reason can attain, imagination both disrupts the limits of reason in life-giving ways and depends for its health upon the criticism that reason provides. Acknowledging the importance of the imagination, as such, is crucial to our task here, but it is the content of the imagination — the images it holds and the dispositions it fosters — that allows us to speak of a *Christian* practical wisdom.[17]

Voices within scripture continually try to shape the imagination of readers by imaginatively urging those with ears to hear to perceive reality as belonging to God. "Consider the lilies," Jesus says, and notice the widow giving two small coins (Matt. 6:28; Luke 21:1-4). In the Gospels, Jesus incarnates attentiveness to what is really there though unacknowledged by others: he notices a touch on the hem of his robe, the little children who are trying to come near, the thief dying beside him. He directs the gaze of disciples toward the outcast, toward those who are overlooked or on the margins.[18] Moreover, what he sees and how he responds are deeply informed by his own immersion in scripture. Isaiah's vision becomes real as Jesus heals the lame and declares jubilee. Later, the biblical imagination of the first Christians, including those

15. Oremus Bible Browser, accessed September 20, 2013. H. Richard Niebuhr, *The Meaning of Revelation* (1941; New York: Macmillan, 1960), p. 72.

16. Iris Murdoch, "The Sublime and the Good," *Chicago Review* 13, no. 3 (Autumn 1959): 52.

17. Garrett Green, *Imagining God: Theology and the Religious Imagination* (Grand Rapids: Eerdmans, 1989), pp. 110-11.

18. For a wonderful account of how Jesus instructed his disciples' gaze, see Matthew Myer Boulton's chapter, "Study," in *On Our Way: Christian Practices for Living a Whole Life*, ed. Dorothy C. Bass and Susan R. Briehl (Nashville: Upper Room, 2010).

who would write and share new texts we now read as scripture, would allow them to show the world who Jesus was and is. We see Philip interpreting Isaiah to the Ethiopian eunuch in Acts 8, for example, and Paul reinterpreting the Hebrew scriptures in light of Jesus' death and resurrection.[19]

In these examples of scriptural "seeing," we encounter a form of radical attentiveness that not only grants loving regard but also participates in a transvaluation that burns away false vision — don't touch that bleeding woman! — to perceive God-given reality: that woman is God's creation and already/not yet also part of God's new creation. Sometimes it even deploys scripture to turn scriptural expectations on their head, as when Jesus grudgingly agrees to learn something from the Syro-Phoenician woman, one who would have been granted little status in earlier versions of biblical imagination.[20] In Luke's Gospel, a father responds in joy to the sight of his long-absent son, seeing not his prodigality but his return (15:11-32). Peter is willing to eat with Gentiles because God has forced him to see in a new way the edible creatures he once considered profane, and his identity and relationships are thereby transformed (Acts 10). These stories, along with thousands of others, challenge readers to reimagine themselves and their world. "Go and do likewise," Jesus says at the end of one story (Luke 10:37). Subtly, unsystematically, the language of the Bible comes to lace Christians' speech. "I have been to the mountaintop," a young preacher proclaims, and the horizons of ancient and modern forms of liberation are fused. "This son of mine was lost and is found," an old man muses as he tries in vain to help his godson, an alcoholic who longs to return to the home he left as a child; the gravity of their failure is deepened by the fact that the author telling their story frames it with a parable of Jesus.[21]

In providing depth perception that discloses a transvalued vision of re-

19. See Richard B. Hays, *The Conversion of the Imagination: Paul and the Interpretation of Israel's Scripture* (Grand Rapids: Eerdmans, 2005).

20. The healing of the woman with hemorrhages is in Luke 8:43-48. Ellen F. Davis, "Critical Traditioning: Seeking an Inner Biblical Hermeneutic," *Anglican Theological Review* 82 (2000): 747-48, interprets the "remarkable story of the 'Canaanite' woman (Mt. 15:21; cf. Mk. 7:26, 'a Syrophoenician')," which, Davis notes, requires the hearer to learn "something previously unimaginable about the fundamentals of your life with God — and to learn it from 'the least of these.'"

21. The novelist Marilynne Robinson draws on the parable of the lost son (Luke 15:11-32) in *Gilead* and *Home* (New York: Farrar, Straus and Giroux, 2004 and 2008).

ality, biblical imagination is eschatological. It both points toward and participates in a telos of the fullness of God. In the words of the philosopher Caroline Simon, "imagination is a capacity to see people in light of the hope of wholeness that God intends for them."[22] Dietrich Bonhoeffer, whom Simon quotes in her study of love and imagination, gets at the Christology at the heart of the transvaluation of vision at stake here: "Self-centered love constructs its own image of other persons, about what they are and what they should become. It takes the life of the other person into its own hands. Spiritual love recognizes the true image of the other person as seen from the perspective of Jesus Christ. It is the image Jesus Christ has formed and wants to form in all people."[23] Being and becoming, formed and still being formed: this kind of seeing is eschatological, also, in its present incompleteness, which yearns toward future fulfillment. It happens through a mirror dimly, now, but in confidence of a face-to-face seeing, "then" (1 Cor. 13:12).

An imagination that has been broken open by God's eschatological promises also necessarily incorporates a shattering harshness that is quite different from the "imagination" of childhood fantasy and adult nostalgia. Walter Brueggemann's well-known work on "the prophetic imagination" has helped readers to listen deeply to the visionary poetry of the prophets and summoned them to reject the socially dominant imagination of the "royal court" in all its guises.[24] All the prophets of Israel paint pictures that shatter complacency, whether with judgment or with hope. At certain moments, their hearers or readers are forced to gaze upon the destruction they have themselves wrought. "I looked, and lo, there was no one at all, and all the birds of the air had fled. I looked, and lo, the fruitful land was a desert, and all its cities were in ruins before the Lord, before his fierce anger" (Jer. 4:25-26). At other points, the prophets insist that they gaze upon God's promise, healing, and peace. "The wolf shall live with the lamb, the leopard shall lie down with the kid, the calf and the lion and the fatling together. . . . They will not hurt or destroy on all my holy mountain" (Isa. 11:6, 9). But consistently in both voices, as biblical scholar Ellen Davis notes, the proph-

22. Caroline J. Simon, *The Disciplined Heart: Love, Destiny, and Imagination* (Grand Rapids: Eerdmans, 1997), p. 28.

23. Dietrich Bonhoeffer, *Life Together,* Dietrich Bonhoeffer Works 5 (Minneapolis: Fortress, 1996), p. 44.

24. Walter Brueggemann, *The Prophetic Imagination,* 2nd ed. (Minneapolis: Fortress, 2001).

ets "speak of, and to, the faculty they call *leb,* 'heart' — which is, in biblical physiology, the organ of perception and response." Here Davis draws on the work of theologian Garrett Green, who argues for a close link between "heart" and "imagination" in biblical anthropology.[25]

These musings on biblical imagination come from rummaging about in the treasure house of scripture. They offer a glimpse of what biblical imagination might be and what it might help one to see (though these few paragraphs can contain far less even than a glimpse, given the multiplicity and range of biblical texts). As noted earlier, however, attempts to integrate this kind of engaged, eschatological imagination into personal and communal life in the modern West face massive epistemological, ethical, and cultural challenges. Is it possible actually to trust the vision made accessible by scriptural imagination? Can moderns find here the kind of practical wisdom needed for life in the twenty-first century? I think I know some who do — not with premodern seamlessness, to be sure, but still in ways that inform lives of wise Christian practice. However, even when one shares Taylor's relatively optimistic view of the possibility of enjoying an engaged, embodied knowledge of transcendence amid the cross-pressures of our time, participatory engagement with the world of scripture cannot be taken for granted. It must be chosen, critically and postcritically.

Embracing Biblical Imagination in and after Modernity

One of the most generative twentieth-century approaches to life-shaping engagement with scripture was forged by the philosopher Paul Ricoeur, who pondered the questions addressed in this book (and many other questions as well) throughout his long and very prolific career. Like many other scholars in late modernity (as noted, for example, in the two previous chapters), Ricoeur resisted the exclusive claims of modern rationalism and noted the inability of empirical criticism to address some of humankind's most important existential questions. As he wrote in an oft-quoted declaration:

25. Ellen F. Davis, *Scripture, Culture, and Agriculture* (Cambridge: Cambridge University Press, 2009), p. 10. "Whether we call it the heart or the imagination," Green writes, referring to a range of biblical texts, "this human function is the anthropological locus, though not the substance, of revelation." What finally matters theologically, however, is not the imagination per se, but the images by which it imagines. Green, *Imagining God,* pp. 109-11.

"Beyond the desert of criticism we wish to be called again."[26] In the more verdant landscape into which his constructive work invites readers, imagination and engagement with sacred texts become indispensable ways of knowing. Crucially, they also foster transformative practice in the present day.

Ricoeur argued that modern people, who have irretrievably lost the "first naïveté" that upholds religious meaning in premodern cultures, could explore and claim a richer sense of their own identity and of the sacred "by taking up residence in the worlds of mythopoetic literature, such as the Bible." Driving this proposal, writes Mark I. Wallace, was "a fragile hope that in the borderlands beyond calculative reason there might be a world of transcendent possibilities (mediated through the text) that can refigure and remake the world of the reader."[27] Although Ricoeur did not limit his theorizing to Christian texts, the complex, life-shaping adherence of Christian communities to scripture provided an obvious and fruitful example of the hermeneutics he advocated. He insisted on (and evidently delighted in) the internal diversity of the biblical canon: its range of contrasting genres, its rich intertextuality, its superabundance of metaphor and meaning, its resistance to any effort to reduce its complexity.[28] Further, he was well aware of the diversity of interpretations to which this canon has given rise and the very different ways in which various historical communities have read this set of texts and imagined the world in relation to it, and he was alert

26. This sentence from the conclusion of Ricoeur's *The Symbolism of Evil* appears on the first page of two essays that have guided my own reading of Ricoeur: Mark I. Wallace, "Introduction," in Paul Ricoeur, *Figuring the Sacred: Religion, Narrative, and Imagination,* trans. David Pellauer, ed. Mark I. Wallace (Minneapolis: Fortress, 1995); and Lewis S. Mudge, "Introduction," in Paul Ricoeur, *Essays in Biblical Interpretation,* ed. Lewis S. Mudge (Minneapolis: Fortress, 1980).

27. Wallace, "Introduction," in *Figuring the Sacred,* pp. 1-2. Ricoeur's philosophy addressed a wide range of texts and communities and influenced disciplines across the humanities and social sciences. However, the implications of his work for theology became increasingly evident (to himself and others) as his life advanced.

28. Ricoeur showed both strong appreciation of exegetical scholarship and an awareness of its limitations. To make sense of the texts of the biblical corpus, he wrote, one must approach it as "a world of discourse where the metaphorical language of poetry is the closest secular equivalent." *Neither* "scientifically descriptive or explanatory" *nor* "apologetic, argumentative, or dogmatic" thought will disclose what these texts have to offer. André LaCocque and Paul Ricoeur, *Thinking Biblically: Exegetical and Hermeneutical Studies* (Chicago: University of Chicago Press, 1998), p. xvi.

to criticize harmful interpretations.[29] To think with Ricoeur about biblical imagination is not to grasp a single, commendable perspective on scripture, but rather to acknowledge human capacities of imagination and interpretation and to appreciate the ongoing, constantly renewed encounters with scripture these capacities make possible.

Human beings forge their experience and understanding of the world and of themselves — indeed, not only their understanding of themselves, but their very selves — through engagement with the signs, especially language, they encounter. In Ricoeur's account, "we see images only insofar as we first hear them"; words disclose realities we would not otherwise see and indeed have already shaped our taken-for-granted perception of the features of the world and our place within it.[30] Thus words that initially exist beyond the self (in communal traditions, cultural discourse, texts, and so on) come to shape the self by making certain experiences thinkable.[31] When language is impoverished by deafness to symbol and metaphor, as Ricoeur thought had happened in modernity, certain ultimate questions cannot even be asked, and the human ability to articulate and explore crucial aspects of reality is foreclosed. However, when human beings participate in deeply invested engagement with symbols — which are most fully and complexly available in narrative, poetry, myth, and such — human aspirations to fullness of life can be pursued.

Every text invites readers into the possibilities and limits of the world it portrays.[32] In reading a text, Ricoeur argued, "what has to be appropriated is the meaning of the text itself, conceived in a dynamic way as the direction of thought opened up by the text."[33] In other words, texts open a future even

---

29. E.g., in "Imagination in Discourse and in Action," pp. 182-85, Ricoeur identifies ideology and utopia as two forms of imagination that can become pathological. In ideology, a group refuses to see the actual distance that grows "between real practice and the interpretations through which the group becomes conscious of its existence and its practice." In utopia, "the field of the possible extends beyond that of the real," leading to certain harmful forms of "perfectionism" or "blindness."

30. Ricoeur, "Imagination in Discourse and in Action," p. 174.

31. Mudge, "Introduction," in *Essays in Biblical Interpretation*, pp. 8-9.

32. Ricoeur generally means rich, complex mythopoetic texts — "classics," great literature, sacred scriptures, and so on. However, it seems that in principle even simpler texts could be said to open certain (though more shallow) possibilities.

33. Ricoeur, *Interpretation Theory: Discourse and the Surplus of Meaning* (Fort Worth: Texas Christian University Press, 1976), p. 92.

while reflecting a past. By positing certain visions of what the world is, how it works, and what humans should hope and fear, they disclose possibilities and define limitations. They "project" a space "in front of the text," a space into which readers may be drawn and within which new ways of seeing and acting become available to them.

In upholding the disclosive power of texts, Ricoeur explicitly countered the modern suspicion that "a subject already mastering his own way of being in the world projects the *a priori* of his self-understanding on the text and reads it into the text." He also made it clear that interpretation, as he understood it, is quite different from the modern project of seeking knowledge for the sake of mastery. A subject engaged in the act of interpretation, Ricoeur argued, can discover something new and life-altering — something from beyond the self that may have the power to transform the self.

> [I]t is not the reader who primarily projects himself. The reader rather is enlarged in his capacity for self-projection by receiving a new mode of being from the text itself. Appropriation, in this way, ceases to appear as a kind of possession, as a way of taking hold of things; instead it implies a moment of dispossession of the egoistic and narcissistic ego.

When the subject's interpretation "complies with the injunction of the text," following the "arrow" of the sense and trying "to think accordingly," a "new self-understanding" can emerge.[34]

Although his grammar of argumentation often emphasized the reading, interpreting "self" (singular), Ricoeur was also deeply interested in the interpretation communities undertake. "It is in interpreting the Scriptures in question that the community in question interprets itself," he wrote in *Thinking Biblically,* a book coauthored with Old Testament scholar André LaCocque. "A kind of mutual election takes place here between those texts taken as foundational and the community we have deliberately called a community of reading and interpretation," the two scholars noted. For members of this community, the circle of relationship between community and text is not a vicious one in which each points equally to the other in a kind of stasis. Rather, the sacred text is taken to be "founding" while the community is understood as "founded." As with individual reading, this

34. Ricoeur, *Interpretation Theory,* p. 94.

claim addresses the suspicion of interpretation as self-authenticating projection. "The founding text *teaches* — this is what the word *torah* means. And the community *receives* instruction. Even when this relation surpasses that between authority and obedience to become one of love, the difference in altitude between the word that teaches with authority and the one that responds with acknowledgement cannot be abolished."[35]

This privileging of sacred texts arouses modern suspicions of a different kind, of course. Aware of this, Ricoeur emphasized that interpretation is an active, ongoing process that disrupts certainty and smugness. In "The Bible and the Imagination," he explored the imagination at work within biblical texts themselves, identifying such imagination as a key element in the texts' capacity to generate creative change in individual and communal readers. Through "fiction" — the strongest form being narrative — the text "redescribes" reality, depicting a world in which certain things are possible and true. A competent reader must attend closely to the text and its depiction of the world, but she "is not confined to repeating significations fixed forever." Instead, Ricoeur declared, "I would like to see in the reading of a text such as the Bible a creative operation unceasingly employed in decontextualizing its meaning and recontextualizing it in today's *Sitz im Leben.*" The imagination — a faculty characterized by "the union of fiction and redescription" — is the key to this creative operation.[36]

Ricoeur's hermeneutical theory is too extensive and complex to treat adequately here, but two further points are especially noteworthy for our purposes. The first is the fundamental importance of metaphor, which for Ricoeur is an expansive term incorporating various figures of speech. Metaphors redescribe reality by offering predicates that contradict expected meaning, as in *you are dust* or *the king is lying in a manger.* By posing odd and surprising — for Ricoeur, even "deviant" and "bizarre" — connections, metaphors disrupt certainty, raise questions, and provoke the dialectic of interpretation.[37] "Semantic innovation" frustrates the reader at the literal level and initiates an imaginative process that is funded, in part, by the rest of the text. "Strictly speaking," the homiletician Lance Pape points

35. LaCocque and Ricoeur, *Thinking Biblically,* pp. xvi-xvii.

36. Ricoeur, "The Bible and the Imagination," in *The Bible as a Document of the University,* ed. Hans Dieter Betz (Atlanta: Scholars, 1981), p. 50.

37. Ricoeur, "Imagination in Discourse and in Action," p. 172.

out, "metaphor is not the deviant predication itself but its rescue by the imagination of the reader."[38] As Ricoeur's student and interpreter John Wall puts it, "metaphors are not just alternative ways to represent concepts, but dialectical means by which particular new meaning is formed."[39] While Ricoeur undertook a particularly rich study of metaphor, the capacity of the imagination to reconfigure relations between one thing and another, one person and another, one historical plane and another, has been widely understood as the basis of human imagination and transformation. "Metaphoric construction is what enables human beings to engage in transformative action in the world as they create new conjunctions which allow them to apprehend existence in fresh ways," the practical theologian Heather Walton observes.[40] Closely related are similar uses of "analogy," as in theologian David Tracy's account of "the analogical imagination" and in the work of biblical scholars whose work we shall consider in the next section of this chapter.[41] Historically, "figural" interpretation enacted a similar dynamic, by allowing theologians to discern connections between the Old Testament and the New Testament, and between the world of the Bible and the present day. The loss of figural interpretation, Hans Frei believed, was central to the modern eclipse of biblical narrative as encompassing not only the past but also the present.[42]

These observations point to a second insight of particular relevance for the concerns of this book: Ricoeur's insistence that life-giving relationships can and do take place between ancient sacred texts and real contemporary life, as the imagination bridges the distance between one temporal field and another. The existential incommensurability between "now" and "then," presumed by disengaged historical criticism, can, through imagination, be

38. Lance B. Pape, *The Scandal of Having Something to Say: Ricoeur and the Possibility of Postliberal Preaching* (Waco: Baylor University Press, 2013), pp. 60-61. Pape also emphasizes that for Ricoeur metaphors link longer narratives and not only single words or phrases. "Extended poetic texts [also] create new meaning through the tensive redescription of the reader's possibilities in terms of the way of thinking made available in the text" (p. 75).

39. John Wall, "Phronesis, Poetics, and Moral Creativity," *Ethical Theory and Moral Practice* 6 (2003): 332.

40. Heather Walton, "Poetics," in *The Wiley-Blackwell Companion to Practical Theology,* ed. Bonnie J. Miller-McLemore (Oxford: Wiley-Blackwell, 2012), p. 179.

41. David Tracy, *The Analogical Imagination: Christian Theology and the Culture of Pluralism* (New York: Crossroad, 1981).

42. Frei, *The Eclipse of Biblical Narrative,* pp. 7-10.

transcended. The seamless integration of the premodern imagination is unavailable, to be sure, but for those who move beyond criticism through hermeneutics to a "second naïveté," embodied, life-shaping engagement in the world in front of the text is possible. Scripture's richest metaphors and narratives are thus extended beyond the text into life, where they impact present existence "by configuring the most tenacious and most dense human hope, and by rectifying traditional religious representations."[43] In this sense, Ricoeur's project is about far more than how to interpret scripture. It is about how readers come to live in the world it projects — not mechanically or as if they were premodern acolytes, but by recognizing how the itineraries of meaning that actually exist within these layered, imaginative texts have a "course," a projected line of possibility that runs all the way into the real world of the present day, and from here into the future. Thus is transformation engendered, not only in interpretation but also in life. To seek such meaning as readers, together, in context, is to take up a way of life that continues the course imagined in the text.

Imagining Practical Wisdom with Paul and the Philippians

Among the many places one might turn in scripture to study wisdom, Paul's letter to the Philippians provides an especially rich focus for reflection on practical wisdom and the imagination. Ten occurrences of words that share a root with *phronesis* have drawn the attention of scholars interested in practical wisdom in recent years,[44] and Paul's urging to "have this mind in you as was in Christ Jesus" makes it a crucial text for any account of Christian ways of knowing. In addition, the text is infused with affection

43. Ricoeur, "The Bible and the Imagination," p. 71.

44. Scholars who have discussed practical wisdom in Philippians include Susan Eastman, "Imitating Christ Imitating Us: Paul's Educational Project in Philippians," in *The Word Leaps the Gap*, ed. J. Ross Wagner et al. (Grand Rapids: Eerdmans, 2008); Stephen E. Fowl, *Engaging Scripture: A Model for Theological Interpretation* (Eugene, OR: Wipf and Stock, 2008), and Fowl, *Philippians* (Grand Rapids: Eerdmans, 2005); Wayne A. Meeks, "The Man from Heaven in Paul's Letters to the Philippians," in *The Future of Early Christianity*, ed. Birger A. Pearson (Minneapolis: Fortress, 1991); and Carolyn Osiek, *Philippians and Philemon* (Nashville: Abingdon, 2000). I appreciate Susan Eastman's acknowledgment of how intimidating it is to write about this oft-studied text (p. 428).

and familiarity; Paul speaks to the *leb,* the imaginative heart as the organ of perception and response, with palpable concern for persons he knows and loves, never becoming abstract or disengaged. What makes the letter most remarkable, however, is a rich intertextuality that creates multiple layers of metaphor, which the scholars I will draw on refer to as "analogies." The imaginative intensity of the analogies that provide its structure and project its lines of possibility, not only for the Philippians but also for later readers, exemplify what Ricoeur called "the productive imagination" of the biblical text.

First, a note on genre. To focus on a letter in this inquiry into imagination may be surprising, since narrative is the genre most prized, and surely most often explored, by those who ask how scripture forms the imagination and lives of its readers. However, a great narrative's encompassing depiction of the world is established partly by its capacity to deploy many voices and approaches in portraying a world whose shape and meaning can never be represented fully (as biblical narrative especially concedes). As David Ford argues, the genre of biblical narrative is closer to "drama" than to "epic," because drama is an open-ended form that incorporates many players and implicitly projects a next act at its apparent conclusion,[45] a dynamic clearly at work in Philippians. Moreover, this particular letter has at its heart a narrative that is at the same time its cosmic context: the narrative of Jesus Christ, incarnate, crucified, risen, and exalted. A narrative *within* the letter is also the narrative *within which* the letter and the lives of its ancient and modern readers make sense.[46]

Paul writes from prison to the young church in Philippi, a community he clearly loves and misses. In the face of opposition from without and division within the community, Paul urges the Philippians to "be of the same mind, having the same love, being in full accord and of one mind." This will require humility, as "each of you look not to your own interests, but to the interests of others" (2:2, 4). Paul then quotes a hymn, which scholars

45. David F. Ford, *The Future of Christian Theology* (Oxford: Wiley-Blackwell, 2001), p. 41.
46. In "The Bible and the Imagination," Ricoeur takes as his example of intertextuality and transformation through metaphor another brief narrative that both stands within and summarizes the encompassing Christian narrative of redemption, the parable of the sower (pp. 52-55, 68). A similar structure is at work in the letter to the Philippians' inclusion of the Christ hymn in 2:6-11.

believe was already in use in the community's worship, to show what such humility would look like.[47]

> [5] Let the same mind be in you that was in Christ Jesus,
> [6] who, though he was in the form of God,
> did not regard equality with God
> as something to be exploited,
> [7] but emptied himself,
> taking the form of a slave,
> being born in human likeness.
> And being found in human form,
> [8] he humbled himself
> and became obedient to the point of death —
> even death on a cross.
> [9] Therefore God also highly exalted him
> and gave him the name
> that is above every name,
> [10] so that at the name of Jesus
> every knee should bend,
> in heaven and on earth and under the earth,
> [11] and every tongue should confess
> that Jesus Christ is Lord,
> to the glory of God the Father.

Here, Christ is the exemplar of the unifying, other-regarding humility Paul urges upon the Philippians. Though Christ's position was unsurpassably high, he did not use it to his own advantage; rather, in obedience, he emptied himself, taking on the lowest social condition — an emptying undertaken for the good of others, as the Philippians already know because

---

47. This is a much-studied passage, and of course there are scholarly disputes, but as Carolyn Osiek notes, it has become "a tradition" (and in her view correct) to call 2:6-11, which is usually typeset as poetry, a hymn. Osiek, *Philippians and Philemon*, p. 56. Stephen Fowl grants that this formal designation is a "critical commonplace" but does not agree. Fowl, *Philippians*, pp. 108-13. I am not qualified to make a textual ruling on this matter. However, as an educator and practical theologian I see some practical wisdom in Paul's supposed incorporation of a liturgical text known to his readers. This adds another layer of imaginative analogy to Paul's argument for unity by linking it to the church's shared language and experience.

they have experienced this as the source of their own salvation. In context, the point of this hymn is not to establish doctrine but to integrate the narrative at the heart of Christian faith into believers' ways of seeing and living their own lives, for the good of the church and in mimetic cooperation with Christ's action for and among them. Paul narrates his own life as another example of the same pattern. See, he says at several points, my life also has a kenotic shape: "my desire is to depart and be with Christ, for that is far better; but [for me] to remain in the flesh is more necessary for you" (1:23-24); and "even if I am being poured out as a libation over the sacrifice and the offering of your faith, I am glad and rejoice with all of you" (2:17). Timothy and Epaphroditus are also praised for putting others before themselves (2:19-30). In urging the Philippians to adopt "the same mind," Paul asks them to extend the analogy with their own lives.

Wayne Meeks and Stephen Fowl have offered insightful readings of Philippians that trace these analogies throughout the letter. Paul's purpose in setting forth a procession of analogies, Meeks argues, is to teach "a Christian *phronesis,* a practical moral reasoning that is 'conformed to [Christ's] death' in hope of his resurrection." Meeks's proposed translation of 2:5, "base your practical reasoning on what you see in Christ Jesus," highlights this purpose. Fowl quotes Meeks approvingly, seeing the letter as Paul's effort "to form in the Philippians the intellectual and moral abilities to be able to deploy, by means of analogy, their knowledge of the gospel in the concrete situations in which they find themselves so that they will be able to live faithfully (or 'walk in a manner worthy of the gospel,' 1:27)."[48]

Although Fowl declares that the analogical extension at issue is "not a wooden sort of repetition, but a 'non-identical' repetition," the "practical reasoning" he advocates, drawing on Meeks, is primarily a cognitive operation.[49] In this rendering, the evocative, irreducible hymn of Christ's self-emptying and exaltation loses some of its narrative shape and power; it "functions as an exemplar, a concrete expression of a shared norm or rule from which Paul and the Philippians can make analogical judgments about how they should live."[50] In the end, this reading of Philippians never quite

48. Meeks, "The Man from Heaven," p. 332; Fowl, *Engaging Scripture,* p. 195.

49. The chapters "Disciplining" and "Unknowing" also note the tendency of many contemporary scholars to restrict the operation of *phronesis* to a cognitive process.

50. Fowl, *Engaging Scripture,* p. 191. In his more extensive theological commentary on Philippians (2008), Fowl offers a more expansive, embodied translation of *phronein* in 2:5:

addresses the complex, embodied formation of practically wise *people*. Its greater contribution (and apart from a few pages at the end, its stated goal) is to describe the practical reasoning necessary to interpret scripture and the practical reasoning portrayed in scripture.[51]

An imaginative reading of the letter to the Philippians by Susan Eastman offers a more embodied and emotionally rich understanding of Christian practical wisdom. In Eastman's account, "Imitating Christ Imitating Us," the metaphor at the heart of the letter expands, opening up connections to further layers of biblical narrative and Christian worship, in part by drawing on the imaginative repertoire of theater. As a result, the *mimesis* encouraged in the letter — Paul urges the Philippians to imitate him, as he imitates Christ — becomes more complex. Introducing a venerable analogy — Christ as the new Adam — Eastman imagines Christ as a player who "puts on" the human condition, deliberately donning "the mask of Adam."[52] This performance is the opposite of those enacted by prisoners forced to dress up like gods in the Roman arena, where the play would end with their humiliation. By reversing this dominant plot, Christ's *mimesis* of humanity reorders the structure of the stage itself, and thereby rescripts all social interactions. Those who enact this new script by "imitating Christ imitating us" become models "not of moral mastery and superiority, but of humble trust and solidarity." Paul, Eastman argues, is engaged in a countercultural pedagogy that replaces the cruel, hierarchical "upward mobility" of Roman *paideia* with the redemptive "downward mobility" of Christ and those who would "put on" the mask of Christ. In Paul's pedagogical use of these images, the terms of Roman *paideia* are in a sense acknowledged: students, it is understood, learn through embodied interaction with and imitation of their teachers. But these terms are also profoundly subverted. Like Meeks, Eastman sees Paul as seeking to teach the Philippians. However, in her reading the apostle teaches not only "moral reasoning" but also an embodied *mimesis* rich in the

---

"Let this be your pattern of thinking, acting, and feeling, which was also displayed in Christ Jesus" (p. 88). This commentary develops the moral ("acting") implications more fully as well, but Fowl's approach is still primarily cognitive.

51. The systematic theologian David H. Kelsey draws on the Meeks/Fowl thread in emphasizing the practical reasoning required to read scripture well in *Eccentric Existence,* vol. 1 (Louisville: Westminster John Knox, 2009), pp. 144-45.

52. As Eastman notes, an immense literature has debated this point (p. 441). Fowl rejects the Adam analogy in *Philippians,* pp. 114-17.

colors of popular culture. Eastman does not follow the itinerary of meaning projected by this text into the contemporary world, but if she did she might discover affinity in today's new monastic communities, which choose to "relocat[e] to the abandoned places of Empire," in solidarity with the poor.[53]

Such multiple layers of reference — in this case, a spiral of analogies drawing profound connections between Adam, Christ, Paul, the Philippians, and the Romans — display the imagination within the text, which is fueled by intertextuality within and between texts and surrounding cultures. Ricoeur called this "productive imagination" because of its "aptitude for engendering transformations." In encountering and living in front of such a text, readers are invited *by the imagination within the text* to extend a series of analogies into their own lives *through their own imaginations.* When they do so, Ricoeur declared, interpretation moves beyond concerns "internal to the text" and makes "the passage from text to life." Interpretation moves "from the semiotic phase to the existential phase."[54] The text comes to present life; it moves off the page to create new possibilities in the lives of its readers. This happens not through a mechanical process of repetition, as if one could specifically mimic either Jesus or Paul in the specific *Sitz im Leben* of the reader's present context. Rather, through imaginative (not mechanical) analogy, a continuing process of decontextualization and recontextualization occurs. The meaning thus appropriated never arrives at a final destination, always remaining open to new situations, but at the same time it is limited by and genuinely attentive to the codes within the text.

Power, Conflict, and Biblical Imagination

The itineraries of meaning projected by Philippians (or any text) do not open the same course of possibility in every situation. Recontextualization is not stable. Rather, it often becomes an arena of conflict, as communities that live in front of scripture struggle to imagine fully the world it projects into the present, in order to live more faithfully in the present. For example, the directional arrows of "humility" emerging in Fowl's reading

53. The Rutba House, ed., *Schools for Conversion: 12 Marks of a New Monasticism* (Eugene, OR: Cascade Books, 2005), p. xii.
54. Ricoeur, "The Bible and the Imagination," pp. 56, 71-72.

and "downward mobility" in Eastman's evoke quite different present-day analogies for people of privilege and for those who struggle for recognition or survival. Writing in *The Women's Bible Commentary,* Pheme Perkins notes the ambiguity of women's role in Philippians and cautions the oppressed not to follow the course projected by the narrative of Christ's self-emptying. "The poor in Latin America who are told to suffer like Christ rather than struggle for freedom, or abused women whose ministers tell them to submit to husbands, are not in the position to copy the Christ of this hymn," Perkins writes. "Its challenge is addressed to persons of some status and power, just as Christ had the status of God."[55] Similarly, Monya A. Stubbs's article on Philippians, in *True to Our Native Land: An African American New Testament Commentary,* grapples with the letter's difficult images of slavery and suffering, noting that "one can easily read Philippians and walk away with the sense that Paul encourages people to value the experience of suffering." She counters this reading by emphasizing Paul's summons to communal unity as solidarity in opposition to oppression and by relating it imaginatively, through an analogical connection that bridges the distance between temporal fields, to Dr. Martin Luther King Jr.'s emphasis on being "other-regarding" in the pursuit of justice.[56] Another reading, Elizabeth A. Castelli's *Imitating Paul: A Discourse of Power,* offers a postmodern critic's view of the trajectory of meaning projected by Paul's letters. Paul's discourse of *mimesis,* Castelli argues, served and serves to erase difference in order to rationalize and shore up a particular set of power relations within the early Christian movement and in the "destinations far beyond the first-century Mediterranean basin" where his letters have been, and still are, read.[57]

The theologian Sheila Briggs demonstrates the importance of imagi-

55. Reprinted from Carol A. Newsom and Sharon H. Ringe, eds., *The Women's Bible Commentary* (London: SPCK, 1992), in Janet Martin Soskice and Diana Lipton, eds., *Feminism and Theology* (Oxford: Oxford University Press, 2003), p. 200. In "Kenosis and Subversion," Sarah Coakley surveys the interpretation history of Philippians 2 and develops a different approach, offering "a defense of some version of *kenosis* as not only compatible with feminism, but vital to a distinctively Christian manifestation of it." *Powers and Submissions: Spirituality, Philosophy and Gender* (Oxford: Blackwell, 2002), p. 4.

56. Monya A. Stubbs, "Philippians," in *True to Our Native Land,* ed. Brian K. Blount (Minneapolis: Fortress, 2007), p. 377.

57. Elizabeth A. Castelli, *Imitating Paul: A Discourse of Power* (Louisville: Westminster/John Knox, 1991), p. 119. We should note that Castelli does not read Philippians as (her own) scripture, unlike the other authors cited here.

nation and analogy in constructing a life-giving reception of this text in situations of oppression in "Can an Enslaved God Liberate? Hermeneutical Reflections on Philippians 2:6-11." Because the experience of oppressed people at the time of the text's composition has been lost, Briggs discerns what this text may have meant to them by developing analogies between oppression now and oppression then. Tentatively but with clarity and conviction, she builds a hermeneutical bridge that relies on the imagination to articulate the direction of thought opened by the text, "fictionally" inhabiting the imagination of ancient readers in order to open lines of possibility for contemporary readers. Crucially, this method leads to her claim that "to be able to think the enslavement of God [Phil. 2:7] makes it possible to conceive of an inversion of the hierarchy of being and worth." Developing this kind of theological imagination, Briggs concludes, is "a theological task proper to the narrative creativity of biblical proclamation within the communities of the oppressed today."[58]

Thus the Christ hymn in Philippians, which I have presented as a rich example of the imaginative process of metaphorical transformation by which biblical texts shape the lives of the communities that treasure them, also provides a rich, if troubling, example of the fractured imagination of a conflicted church and a broken world. Academic arguments such as those summarized here clarify what is at stake in texts and their diverse interpretations, and they set forth historical or linguistic knowledge that clarifies the direction of thought emerging from a text (doing what Ricoeur called in another context the "semiotic" interpretation that prepares the way for "existential" appropriation). But argument also takes place within the ecclesial communities that live in front of the text and look to it for a life-giving word, sometimes in conversation with academic sources and sometimes not. Arguing — a commonplace of academic life, and also something church bodies and congregations do all the time — sounds like a routine activity. However, oppression, pain, and violence often frame or accompany arguments about the living meaning of texts. Even if we grant Alasdair MacIntyre's claim that argument is precisely what constitutes a valued tradition,[59] and even if

58. Sheila Briggs, "Can an Enslaved God Liberate? Hermeneutical Reflections on Philippians 2:6-11," *Semeia* 47 (1989): 149.

59. "A living tradition then is an historically extended, socially embodied argument, and an argument precisely in part about the goods which constitute that tradition." Alasdair MacIntyre, *After Virtue,* 2nd ed. (Notre Dame: University of Notre Dame Press, 1984), p. 222.

we understand that it is necessary in an always changing world, we should acknowledge its power to harm.

Today, interest in how ecclesial communities know scripture and live with the arguments it fuels is strong in some quarters of academic theology. In part, what we find in such work is attention to the actual imagining and interpreting that are already taking place, *de facto* and unsystematically, in every Christian congregation. A linguistic and imaginative world that at least includes the Bible, and that sometimes is heavily shaped by it, is inhabited before it is queried. As systematic theologians who are deeply interested in scripture's role in shaping the ways of life of contemporary communities and also alert to dynamics of power and the value of difference, Kathryn Tanner and Mary McClintock Fulkerson have probed this question especially thoughtfully.

Tanner argues that a "plain sense" of scripture exists in every congregation. This sense, which is functional rather than absolute, provides a basic common understanding of what the Bible means. Often, this "plain sense" barely needs to be articulated; it is the background against which certain things are possible, and thus is not primarily cognitive but embodied and imaginative. However, in times of change and conflict the plain sense may need to be disputed and renegotiated. When this happens, Tanner argues, the prior possession of a plain sense can in fact foster openness, change, and "exegetical ingenuity" within communities that accord the Bible authority. An element of scripture that many find constraining — the existence of a canon — becomes, in Tanner's view, a channel for innovation: "this limited body of unrevisable texts . . . of crucial relevance to my life now as a Christian whatever my particular circumstances" forces communities to come up with revised readings over time. That the plain sense is, overall, a narrative fosters open-ended interpretation, since narrative "does not itself specify communal practice . . . in the way a catechetical plain sense would." Together, Tanner argues, these features create the "discursive conditions for a tradition of appealing to texts that is inherently self-critical, pluralistic, and flexible."[60]

Before moving to the second theologian, I want to suggest that a narrative plain sense is necessary to most on-the-ground appropriation of scripture, including in Christian practical wisdom. In fact, assumptions about a kind of plain sense pervade many of my uses of biblical language and story

60. Kathryn Tanner, "Theology and the Plain Sense," in *Scriptural Authority and Narrative Interpretation,* ed. Garrett Green (Minneapolis: Fortress, 1987), pp. 72-75.

in this chapter. This plain sense is informed by my own lifetime of study and worship and by my expectations regarding the imaginative repertoire of this book's readers. For instance, I refer to the prodigal son or to the thief dying beside Jesus without employing any critical apparatus at all; I assume familiarity. The plain sense is in this regard more literary than historical, even though in a different context I would be eager to bring critical historical perspectives to bear on the texts I seem here to cite rather casually. At the same time, if someone called what I now take to be the plain sense into question, for instance by pointing out ambiguities in the story or by showing me how differently others understand its meaning, I would be impelled to search for revised interpretations, and my biblical imagination would shift and, I hope, expand. Indeed, good sermons, novels, and works of theology often require of me exactly this response.

In an ethnographic study of a United Methodist congregation, the theologian Mary McClintock Fulkerson also remarks on the powerful presence of assumed meanings — the frames or "pre-texts" gained from prior instruction and experience — in how parishioners understand scripture. However, her extended, participatory investigation of what she calls the "biblical practices" of this congregation enables her to draw a more finely grained portrait than Tanner's thematic account provides.[61] Three different approaches, each socially embodied in a specific Bible study group, were at work in this one congregation, overlapping at times but readily distinguishable. In the first, the Bible was taken as the only reliable source of guidance for believers' lives; as persons whose lives were marked by risk, vulnerability, and a sense of shared struggle to be disciples in a hostile world, the readers in this group were drawn to texts about the overall shape of their existence with God and neighbor. Association and mutual help, rather than conflict over specific issues, fueled their imaginative reading and appropriation of scripture. Another group, which converged when homosexuality became an explicit congregational issue, also assumed the Bible's authority, but its members were uninterested in vulnerable conversations or encompassing accounts of Christian life. "Biblical citing" was their mode of interaction, shutting down

---

61. Mary McClintock Fulkerson, *Places of Redemption: Theology for a Worldly Church* (New York: Oxford University Press, 2007). In "Disciplining," Bonnie Miller-McLemore lifts up Fulkerson's work as an example of the turn to bodies and place in recent theological scholarship.

conversation and prioritizing the search for specific rules. Fulkerson's guiding theological concern is for place and community rather than imagination, but as I read her accounts of these groups with a concern for imagination, I conclude that a simple form of biblical imagination (analogically generative, even though naïve in Ricoeur's sense) was at work in the first group, while the rules logic of the second group foreclosed the imaginative process.

One other group — a Bible study for women, most of whose members were African or African American — shimmered with imagination, although Fulkerson depicts the group's imaginative process as relatively unbound from scripture. This group used as a study guide Renita Weems's *Just a Sister Away: A Womanist Reading of Women's Relationships in the Bible,* in which an Old Testament scholar writing for African American women "combines feminist biblical criticism's directive for recovery of women's stories with 'the best of the Afro-American oral tradition, with its gift for storytelling and its love of drama.'" Fulkerson's description of Weems's book recalls Sheila Briggs's advocacy of imagination in a hermeneutic for the oppressed, as well as other aspects of the imagination developed in this chapter.

> This study guide is explicitly aimed at *recreating* the text, not discovering its "real meaning." Given how little information the biblical text provides about women's lives, Weems acknowledges that hers is necessarily creative fiction. But it is just this kind of imaginative portrayal that can show how life struggles of biblical women and women of today are analogous. The stories create a "common thread of sacred female experiences" between ancient and contemporary women.[62]

As Fulkerson tells it, Weems's chapters provided jumping-off points, but the women were often unwilling to pursue the points about race and gender that Weems sought to address (perhaps because their leader, Fulkerson, is white). Longing for a less "negative" account of their situation, the women developed a hermeneutic that looked to the wisdom of their own group as their "primary interpretive grid." In response to stories that "mirror their exclusions and oppressions," they laughed about what the Bible would say "if women wrote it," responding to texts with their own creatively imagined

---

62. Fulkerson, *Places of Redemption,* pp. 169-70; her quotations are from Renita Weems, *Just a Sister Away* (Philadelphia: Fortress, 1988), pp. viii-x.

stories. As Weems had reimagined biblical narratives, so they reimagined Weems. "Their 'readings' were artful practices that moved effortlessly between the stories of the biblical text and contemporary storied lives with a freedom that recreated the text in ways reminiscent of oral traditions of 'telling and retelling' of African American and African cultures." Because of their narrative shape and their part in these cultural traditions, these readings were "funnier and explicitly freer [than those of the other groups], offering open-ended possibilities for identification and elaboration." Imagining scripture, these women refused to be bound by scripture, choosing instead to pursue stories and images that they believed would provide hope that dealt honestly with the sufferings of their lives.[63]

While the imaginative process necessary to the faithful appropriation of scripture today includes an important role for rational criticism, this process will never provide the clear and certain knowledge prized by either modern rationalists or confessional biblicists. As a dimension of *practical* wisdom, biblical imagination, as I mean it, is always unfinished and dynamic, always coming newly to life in response to the needs of new situations. Further, it always includes a dimension of unknowing, as developed in Kathleen Cahalan's chapter "Unknowing." But these features do not render it utterly indeterminate.[64] If biblical imagination is to be "productive" — if its capacity to engender transformation is to be fulfilled — it needs to be constantly renewed by honest encounters with the text as the word of God, as the language of an Other who we trust knows us far better than we know ourselves, and whom we long to know.

Practicing Biblical Imagination

In the preceding sections, I have necessarily and gratefully relied on the work of scholars who specialize in the study of biblical texts. I am deeply

63. Fulkerson, *Places of Redemption*, pp. 172, 185-92.

64. The character of the Bible's normative role for theology is a huge topic that exceeds the scope of this chapter. However, I am intrigued by David Kelsey's proposal to explore this role by referring to a *phronesis* that disciplines the study of biblical texts as Holy Scripture. Following Garrett Green, he argues that a key element in such *phronesis* is a "paradigmatic imagination" that discerns in scripture constitutive patterns of how God relates to all that is not God. *Eccentric Existence*, pp. 142-47.

indebted — in this chapter, in other work, and in my life as a person of faith — to those who shape and reshape the imagination of the church through such scholarship. I will never forget an evening in 1970 when I heard Phyllis Trible lecture for the first time on Genesis 2–3, which revolutionized my sense of gender as a dimension of Christian existence.[65] I imagine the created world differently because I have read books by Terence Fretheim, Ellen Davis, and William Brown.[66] I celebrate the capacity of historical-critical study to deconstruct readings that undergird unjust power relations, as in the work by Monya Stubbs and Pheme Perkins quoted above. I am amazed by the eloquence of many of the scholars who write in this field; much of their work is moving as well as instructive, and full of the kind of literary and theological imagination that inspires wise practice. Further, I fully support efforts to make the findings of academic studies of scripture more widely accessible to all Christians.

At the same time, those who study the Bible academically are not the primary keepers of the biblical imagination. At the most basic level, it is through the proclamation and practices of the church that the biblical text is acknowledged as Holy Scripture. To modern eyes, it is obvious that a particular set of texts is not intrinsically authoritative, and some in the contemporary academic and literary worlds studiously avoid treating with any special regard the books that Christians call canonical. Yet in worshiping communities the special status of these pages is performed in countless ways. Liturgical practices of procession, elevation, placement, and public reading and interpretation embody a worshiping community's confession that this book is received from God as Holy Scripture.[67] The language of liturgy is by and large a series of quotations from this same book. Selected passages are memorized, explained, sung, and cited in virtually every part of the church's common life, and they also inform the lives of many members after they have dispersed to their homes and places of work. The stories

65. This path-breaking lecture was eventually published in Phyllis Trible, *God and the Rhetoric of Sexuality* (Philadelphia: Fortress, 1978).

66. For example, Fretheim's *God and World in the Old Testament: A Relational Theology of Creation* (Nashville: Abingdon, 2005); Davis's *Scripture, Culture, and Agriculture* (Cambridge: Cambridge University Press, 2008); and Brown's *The Seven Pillars of Creation: The Bible, Science, and the Ecology of Wonder* (New York: Oxford University Press, 2010).

67. Ron Anderson, "Practicing Scripture, Unsealing the Book," *Wesleyan Theological Journal* 46, no. 2 (Fall 2011).

within the Bible, and sometimes the overarching narrative to which they belong as well, are told to children and adults, providing the substance of education and the focus of preaching. Further, some of these narratives are explicitly and repeatedly reenacted by communities that gather around the Word (Jesus Christ) who is known through the Word (Holy Scripture), as happens in weekly celebrations of the Lord's Supper and annual observances of Holy Week. Groups read together in congregations such as the one studied by Fulkerson, and individuals read alone (though still surrounded by a communion of saints, as we have seen in Kathleen Cahalan's discussion of *lectio divina* in "Swimming"). Throughout the life of the church, both gathered and dispersed, Holy Scripture enters the ears, the mouths, the hands, the feet, the thinking, and the vocabulary of embodied persons, young and old. This is not to say that worship or the larger life of the church is faithfully attuned to the Word in most enactments or that each encounter with scripture is either honest or transformative. However, this does mean that the church is the primary keeper of the biblical imagination needed for Christian practical wisdom.

In *Imagining the Kingdom: How Worship Works,* the evangelical theologian James K. A. Smith emphasizes the centrality of embodied participation in worship for "Christian formation," which he understands as "a conversion of the imagination effected by the Spirit, who recruits our most fundamental desires by a kind of narrative enchantment — by inviting us narrative animals into a story that seeps into our bones and becomes the orienting background of our being-in-the-world."[68] Part of Smith's agenda is similar to that of this book: to urge those who overemphasize what he calls an "intellectualist" approach to faith to recognize the crucial role of the body and the imagination in shaping Christian people. Because human beings are "kinaesthetic" and "poetic," Smith argues, that which is most meaningful to us takes on, first, the "incarnate significance" of embodied knowing, and, second, the deep orientation provided by story and imagination. "Liturgies are formative," he asserts, "because they are both kinaesthetic and poetic, both embodied and storied."[69] Although his argument seems at first

---

68. James K. A. Smith, *Imagining the Kingdom: How Worship Works* (Grand Rapids: Baker, 2013), pp. 14-15.

69. Smith draws on Bourdieu in arguing for the importance of "teaching the body." His advocacy of the important role of the imagination is very helpfully expanded by his prolific references to works of fiction throughout his argument.

to be more about liturgical than biblical imagination, Smith's Reformed theology is deeply attentive to scripture, which provides the substance, and importantly for Smith the norm, of the imagination he commends. In a section that draws appreciatively on Jewish scholar Peter Ochs's account of the formative power of liturgical practices, Smith summarizes the hope he says is central to his book: "for Christian teachers and learners to imagine how liturgical practices informed by our own scriptural tradition could transform and repair our habits of judgment, our patterns of discernment, and our openness to divine wisdom."[70]

As we ponder the imagination that undergirds and frames how Christians perceive and respond to situations, it is wise to recall scripture's own warning against "the evil imaginations of the heart," as well as the deformations of biblical imagination unmasked by Willie Jennings and other contemporary scholars and prophets. Some of these lurk nearby in the supposedly innocuous form of biblical blockbusters produced by Hollywood, or in the careless or manipulative use of biblical imagery in public life. Other deformations work more subtly and insidiously, coopting our very sense of what it means to be redeemed. As Smith notes, "disordered secular liturgies, ordered to a rival telos [such as consumerism or war], also work on the imagination."[71]

Smith's book belongs to a wave of enthusiastic assessments of how liturgy shapes Christian imagination, identity, and ways of living in the world. For example, *The Blackwell Companion to Christian Ethics,* edited by Stanley Hauerwas and Samuel Wells, is based entirely on this assertion. In my own tradition, liturgical scholars such as Gordon Lathrop and Benjamin Stewart have written and taught extensively on this point. Drawing on perspectives affirmed by the Second Vatican Council, Roman Catholic theologians William Cavanaugh, Vincent Miller, Richard Gaillardetz, and others have found in the Mass a powerful imaginary that shapes people for Christian living.[72] However, another group of scholars has recently been insisting on

70. Smith, *Imagining the Kingdom*, p. 166.

71. Smith, *Imagining the Kingdom*, p. 140.

72. Stanley Hauerwas and Samuel Wells, eds., *The Blackwell Companion to Christian Ethics* (Oxford: Blackwell, 2004); Gordon Lathrop's influential series *Holy Things: A Liturgical Theology; Holy People: A Liturgical Ecclesiology;* and *Holy Ground: A Liturgical Cosmology* (Minneapolis: Fortress, 1993, 1999, 2003); Benjamin Stewart's effort to forge important connections between liturgy and formation for environmental sustainability in *A Watered Garden:*

testing such claims, arguing that theologians' assertions about liturgy and its power to form imagination, identity, and action need to be described more carefully and assessed more critically. Mary McClintock Fulkerson's study of a congregation, discussed above, exemplifies this approach, as does Christian Scharen's study of how the liturgies of three congregations from different traditions shaped their distinctive social presence and witness in downtown Atlanta. Under the banner of "ecclesiology and ethnography," these and other scholars argue that theology and social science can and must work together in discerning how living imagination and its ethical fruits actually emerge within the messy, culturally complex worlds of Christian people.[73] Generally, they do discern formative power, but they are eager to disclose as well its complex and provisional character under current conditions, in countless specific contexts and amid overarching cultural multiplicity. Ultimately, such scholarly proposals may contribute to the formation of biblically informed practical wisdom by helping leaders better to understand — and thus more effectively to serve and teach — actual communities.

In the part of North American Christianity where I have made my home (what used to be called "mainline Protestantism"), worry about inadequate lay knowledge of the Bible has been strong among church leaders for at least two generations. For some, the main problem is the lack of basic knowledge about the Bible's content.[74] Others, more troubled by the hold of harmful

---

Christian Worship and Earth's Ecology (Minneapolis: Augsburg Fortress, 2011); William T. Cavanaugh's *Theopolitical Imagination* (Edinburgh: T&T Clark, 2003), and other books; Vincent J. Miller's *Consuming Religion: Christian Faith and Practice in a Consumer Culture* (New York: Continuum, 2005); and Richard R. Gaillardetz's *Transforming Our Days: Spirituality, Community, and Liturgy in a Technological Culture* (New York: Crossroad, 2000).

73. Fulkerson, *Places of Redemption,* and Christian Scharen, *Public Worship and Public Work: Character and Commitment in Local Congregational Life* (Collegeville: Liturgical, 2001). An international network of scholars founded the journal *Ecclesial Practices* in 2013 as the flagship of what is already a strong scholarly movement. Significant early publications include Pete Ward, ed., *Perspectives on Ecclesiology and Ethnography* (Grand Rapids: Eerdmans, 2012), and Christian B. Scharen, ed., *Explorations in Ecclesiology and Ethnography* (Grand Rapids: Eerdmans, 2012), which also includes an article coauthored by our colleague James R. Nieman and another coauthored by James K. A. Smith, who is a friend of this approach in spite of what I see as the somewhat idealizing qualities of *Imagining the Kingdom.*

74. For example, the "narrative lectionary" movement originating from a group of scholars at Luther Seminary advocates changing the Sunday readings to a series that will teach

misreadings and simplistic forms of biblicism, emphasize the urgency of bringing criticism to bear.[75] Of course, it is quite possible (and justifiable) to be concerned on both counts. My sense is that for many lay people the two approaches are necessarily linked: modern readers cannot leave their critical habits of mind at the door when they approach scripture, and many are helped in embracing scripture by gaining a better understanding of its history. It is unfortunate when the learning ends there, however, without proceeding beyond the semiotic to the existential. Failing to address either lack diminishes the biblical imagination of the church and thus the capacity of Christian people to perceive and respond to the world through the lens of scripture, renouncing evil imaginations and embodying the possibilities God is opening, through this text, in the distinctive contexts of their own lives.[76]

Helping Christian people to perceive these possibilities and respond to them in faith is one of the chief concerns of the church's ministry, and also a guiding concern for practical theology in its several dimensions. Practical theology's most visible way of pursuing this concern within the theological curriculum of the nineteenth and twentieth centuries focused on the various practices of ministry, such as Christian education and homiletics.[77] Contem-

---

the overall narrative of scripture, as a way of enhancing a form of "biblical fluency" these scholars take to be indispensable to the life of faith. In a lecture at Valparaiso University's Institute for Liturgical Studies, April 30, 2014, David Lose argued vigorously that widespread lay ignorance of scripture presents a crisis for the church. I offer this simply as one concrete example of a diagnosis held by many church leaders.

75. I see the work of Marcus Borg, which has a large following in mainline Protestant circles, as an effort in this direction.

76. Many denominations, publishing houses, and educational programs are working to address both needs. For example, the Evangelical Lutheran Church in America and Augsburg Fortress Press have developed an extensive array of print and online resources in a "Book of Faith" initiative, which aims to renew the place of the Bible in the lives of the church and its members. This initiative both encourages greater familiarity with the Bible's content and teaches several approaches for reading and rereading the texts, including devotional reading, historical-critical interpretation, literary study, and theological interpretation informed by key themes in Lutheran theology.

77. This curricular understanding of "practical theology" persists today, helpfully bringing attention to important ministerial practices but often limiting the reach of its epistemological insights, as noted by Bonnie Miller-McLemore in "Disciplining." See, for example, Paul Ballard and Stephen R. Holmes, eds., *The Bible in Pastoral Practice: Readings in the Place and Function of Scripture in the Church* (Grand Rapids: Eerdmans, 2005), which assembles articles by historians, biblical scholars, systematic theologians, and (the largest group) practical

porary practical theology, as described by Bonnie Miller-McLemore in her chapter "Disciplining," also envisions an approach to theology, available to scholars and students in other curricular areas, whose purpose is to serve embodied Christian faith that is oriented toward abundant life — an approach that some biblical scholars, historians, and systematic theologians are already adopting, as I hope this chapter shows. At the same time, lay people, artists, community leaders, parents, and many others who are not professional religious leaders are engaged in a related form of practical theology when they seek to live faithfully in front of the biblical text, when they chew on it, puzzle over it, pray it, recontextualize it — that is, when they help one another in trying to embody the possibilities God is opening, through this text, in the distinctive contexts of their own lives. The Christian practical wisdom so urgently needed today will be strong and resilient insofar as it draws on and draws in all these communities of reflection, in church, academy, and society.[78]

Seeing and Being Seen

The British theologian David Ford has observed that American Christians are often so concerned about how to read the Bible that they do not consider how the Bible reads them and their world.[79] Ford's claim suggests a shift

---

theologians in this modern curricular sense to address "a chasm opened up between those engaged in Biblical studies and those in Practical Theology, whose function is the teaching of the theory and skills in pastoral care" (p. xiv), by which they mean the full spectrum of pastoral work.

78. These three forms of practical theology are identified by Bonnie Miller-McLemore in "Practical Theology," in *Encyclopedia of Religion in America,* ed. Charles Lippy and Peter Williams (Thousand Oaks, CA: Congressional Quarterly Press, 2010), p. 1741. She also describes a fourth form that would include the work of scholars such as the authors of this book. Practical theology, she writes, "refers to an *activity* of believers seeking to sustain a life of reflective faith in the everyday, a *curricular area* in theological education focused on ministerial practice, an *approach* to theology used by religious leaders and by teachers and students across the curriculum, and an *academic discipline* pursued by a smaller subset of scholars to sustain these three enterprises." Miller-McLemore develops this framework further in the introduction to and structure of *The Blackwell Companion to Practical Theology.*

79. Ford made this comment at a conference sponsored by the Valparaiso Project on the Education and Formation of People in Faith at Yale Divinity School, April 3, 2003.

in emphasis that is entirely in keeping with what I am attempting to do in this chapter and with what this book as a whole seeks to commend. If the perception and response at the heart of Christian practical wisdom are to be vital and well formed, we must allow scripture to read us and our world, so that we might discover and take up our parts in the narrative that unfolds within and from and in front of the text.

I recently encountered an imaginative invitation that expresses this reversal of perspective a little differently but in a way I find quite intriguing. Here the supposition is not that scripture reads us but that God reads us through scripture (an amendment I suspect Ford would see as a friendly one). Imagine, a wise and imaginative pastor recently suggested, that the Bible is like a tree, and we are like Zacchaeus. We climb up into the branches of scripture hoping to catch a glimpse of Jesus, only to find that we ourselves have already been seen by him.[80] Our purpose in climbing is not to determine the tree's species, classify its leaves, or prune its dead branches. Instead, desire for God and God's gifts is what impels the climb. Pondering this invitation, it occurred to me that, in many ways, the story of Zacchaeus (Luke 19:1-10) exemplifies the kind of biblical imagination that belongs to Christian practical wisdom. Imagination active within the text can be productive, fostering transformed imagination on the part of readers.

Many English-speaking children first meet Zacchaeus in a song about a "wee little man." There is wisdom in setting this story for children, who are themselves wee, unable to see over the heads of grownups, and fond of climbing trees. More important, children want to see Jesus, a desire the

---

80. The pastor, Susan Briehl, attributed this image to the Canadian Lutheran theologian Jann E. Boyd Fullenwieder, who wrote, "Like Zacchaeus of old, we climb up into the scriptures, a great tree of life grafted to the Crucified One's cross, that we might see Jesus. There we discover that we, too, are seen, named, invited, and welcomed to share the life of God, whom we spy through the branches and leaves of scripture, even as Christ has already spied us." From "Proclamation: Mercy for the World," in *Inside Out: Worship in the Age of Mission,* ed. Thomas H. Schattauer (Minneapolis: Augsburg Fortress, 1999), p. 29. Without invoking Zacchaeus, Serene Jones has similarly written of "the 'eyeglass' power" of scripture, noting that "the bible functions authoritatively when it reads us as we read it." Serene Jones, "Inhabiting Scripture, Dreaming Bible," in *Engaging Biblical Authority,* ed. William P. Brown (Louisville: Westminster John Knox, 2007), p. 78. Jones and Ford were both students of Hans Frei, whose thesis about the eclipse of biblical narrative opened this chapter; their use of scripture in systematic theology demonstrates that Frei's concerns have not gone unaddressed.

song stirs and affirms. Zacchaeus's story assures them that Jesus wants to see them, too. How delightful to imagine Jesus spying them in a tree, calling them by name, helping them down, and inviting himself over — "to *your* house, today." Jesus can see you, little children; he wants to visit you and eat with you, just as he visited wee Zacchaeus. Indeed, it is possible, even likely, that when Zacchaeus climbed up he joined a child or two or three already up in the branches, becoming himself like a child.

To adult eyes, this rich man appears far from childlike. As a chief collector of Roman taxes, Zacchaeus is despised by his neighbors as a collaborator and extortionist. But when we meet him he is already laying aside the dignity of the powerful: he is running through the city streets and climbing a tree, as the desire to see Jesus overwhelms the constraints of his social role. Perched among the leafy branches, he is not only observing but also hiding, perhaps from the hostile gaze of the townspeople, perhaps from Jesus himself. Tomas Halik, a Czech theologian, likens Zacchaeus to those in secular Europe who are drawn to faith but who cannot bring themselves to walk publicly into a church because they feel doubtful, unworthy, or wary of acceptance. They want to look from a distance.[81] This approach contrasts sharply with that of the blind man in the previous passage (Luke 18:35-43), who shouts "Son of David, have mercy on me! Lord, let me see again!" Zacchaeus, who may hate himself as much as the local taxpayers hate him, longs to see the Messiah, but he cannot risk being seen.

In his exploration of how the grace of God enters and changes human lives, the theologian W. H. Vanstone offers Jesus' call to Zacchaeus as "a shining example." Jesus did not shame Zacchaeus for his misdeeds. Instead, he "healed and saved Zacchaeus by asking a kindness of him — his hospitality for the night," like a parent healing the "shame and misery" of a naughty child by asking a small favor, which the child "gladly" performs as a sign that reconciliation has been accomplished.[82] As we shall see, more than this is going on in the salvation of Zacchaeus, but Jesus' practical wisdom in approaching this particular sinner in this particular way is worth noticing. Together, Jesus and Zacchaeus perform actions that embody assurance of God's grace (Jesus) and longing for God's coming realm (Zacchaeus) in

81. Tomas Halik, *Patience with God: The Story of Zacchaeus Continuing in Us,* trans. Gerald Turner (New York: Doubleday, 2009).
82. Vanstone, *Fare Well in Christ* (London: Darton, Longman and Todd, 1997), pp. 60-63.

actual situations, in the right way and at the right time. Further, Jesus takes what Zacchaeus may have hoped would be a secret action and performs it publicly, in front of murmuring townspeople who judge him harshly as a result. By going to Zacchaeus's house, he takes Zacchaeus's sin upon himself. This encounter in Jericho is one more step in Jesus' journey to Jerusalem, where he will be judged again and put to death. The encounter is both a harbinger and an instance of Jesus' mission to lay down his life for others. This short narrative summarizes the longer one in which it is embedded.

And what of Zacchaeus's joyful response? As in so many biblical narratives, the language is spare, and motives remain unarticulated. At the same time, it is clear that Zacchaeus's desire is strong — desire for the Messiah, for righteousness, for reconciliation with the God of his ancestors. The exchange between the two men is swift and direct. There is no time for Zacchaeus to add up sums or for Jesus to provide ethical instructions. Zacchaeus simply declares that he will give half of his possessions to the poor, and that he will pay fourfold restitution to anyone he has defrauded. Then Jesus announces, "Today salvation has come to this house, because he too is a son of Abraham. For the Son of Man came to seek out and to save the lost."

Zacchaeus's promise of fourfold restitution shows that he already lives in front of the biblical text (Exod. 22:1). Indeed, the entire scene is imagined as taking place on the stage of God's covenant with Israel. The offering that springs from his repentance is not a matter of rigid adherence to a predetermined code, whether of Torah or a new covenant, but erupts as one immediate, situated response within a series of responses to God. Luke places Zacchaeus's story shortly after that of the rich ruler, who is saddened by Jesus' call to give all that he has to the poor, one of several of Luke's suggestions that discipleship requires all one's wealth (Luke 14:3; Acts 2:44-45). The biblical scholar Luke Timothy Johnson argues that in Luke/Acts sharing possessions "is a mandate of faith, for clinging to what one has is incompatible with faith in God and an expression of idolatry. But the shape of the mandate . . . is as diverse as life's circumstances and requires not an ideology but hard thinking about the inevitable symbolic shape of our lives."[83] Taken as a rulebook on sharing possessions, Luke/Acts is inconsistent and contradictory, Johnson argues, even though every page bears good news for the

83. Luke T. Johnson, *Sharing Possessions: What Faith Demands* (Grand Rapids: Eerdmans, 2011), p. 133.

poor and encourages the rich in openhanded, openhearted faith. Johnson's own reading and discernment lead him to commend almsgiving, rather than the renunciation of private property in favor of communal ownership, as a fitting way for contemporary Christians to share their possessions, in part because the Jewish community's ongoing, centuries-old practice of reflection and discernment about almsgiving provides a helpful and appropriate source of practical wisdom for Christians.

Zacchaeus's spontaneous pledge embodies his glad repentance and joyful faith. It does not establish a new rule. Instead it exemplifies one wealthy person's personal, extravagant response to the call of Jesus. It exemplifies practical wisdom in much the same way as the Good Samaritan's act of compassion does, in Charles Taylor's reading. That Lukan parable, Taylor notes, is a foundational narrative of the universalist moral consciousness of the West. Following Ivan Illich, Taylor insists that this story works not by establishing a new rule (such as "help a stranger in need, even if he is not of your tribe") but rather by disclosing a new and transformative way of seeing and inhabiting the world. "What the story is opening for us," Taylor argues, "is not a set of universal rules, applying anywhere and everywhere, but another way of being. This involves on one hand a new motivation, and on the other, a new kind of community."[84] The new motivation is a deeply personal response to another's need. The new community is the church, not as an institution but as a network of compassion that overcomes encoded divisions of tribe and class, operating not by rules but by embodied practical wisdom in countless specific circumstances. What Taylor is pointing to sounds very much like what the authors of this book identify as Christian practical wisdom.

Seen in isolation, Zacchaeus may indeed be only a "wee little man" — though this is no small thing, since it has fixed him in the imaginations of generations of children who want to see Jesus. Beyond this, however, Zacchaeus has taken up residence in the church's memory, where he lives as a person encountered by Jesus on his way to Jerusalem, restored to the family of Abraham, and remembered as an example of repentance and generosity. He thus continues to stir the church's imagination — more so or less, and in different ways, depending on the other practices of given communities. In an address to a United Nations group drafting goals for sustainable global

84. Taylor, *A Secular Age*, p. 738.

economic development, Pope Francis pointed to Zacchaeus as an example of one who made "a radical decision of sharing and justice," adding that "this same spirit should be at the beginning and end of all political and economic activity."[85] A London-based charity addressing poverty issues caused by unfairness in the legal and benefits systems bears Zacchaeus's name, as does a Catholic house for homeless men in transition on the south side of Chicago.[86] A family I know sets aside money in what it calls "the Zacchaeus account" and decides together each year where to contribute it for the sake of justice and mercy.

That said, I don't recall ever hearing a sermon on Luke 19:1-10. In the lectionary used in all the congregations I have attended in adulthood, this passage is assigned to the Sunday between October 30 and November 5 — a span that always includes either Reformation Sunday or All Saints' Sunday, whose texts preempt the succession of readings from Luke's Gospel in Year C of the Revised Common Lectionary. Thus, for Lutherans at least, Zacchaeus has gone missing outside the children's program. By contrast, he has a prominent place among the Orthodox, who hear his story annually on Zacchaeus Sunday, one of several that prepare the community for Lent: Jesus' command to "come down" becomes a summons to humility, and Zacchaeus's responses of repentance and almsgiving become models of Lenten discipline. When I asked a friend who is Orthodox about Zacchaeus, he said that Zacchaeus is a very minor figure in the tradition — but then proceeded to speak of him for several minutes as one whose insignificance is like our own. Though Zacchaeus was little and lost, he did all he could to get close to Jesus, and his efforts were rewarded.

The church as I know it has not yet figured out what to do with Zacchaeus. However, he will continue to surface as long as Luke's Gospel is read. As successive generations encounter Zacchaeus and his story in a wide range of situations, the imagination within this text may continue to stir their wise

---

85. "Address of Pope Francis to the UN System Chief Executives Board for Coordination," meeting in Rome on May 9, 2014; http://w2.vatican.va/content/francesco/en/speeches/2014/may/documents/papa-francesco_20140509_consiglio-nazioni-unite.html (accessed July 3, 2014).

86. The Zacchaeus 2000 Trust, http://z2k.org/ (accessed July 3, 2014); Zacchaeus House, http://www.zacchaeushouse.com/ (accessed July 3, 2014). There are many other examples; regrettably but predictably, some of these attach Zacchaeus's name to causes I see as contrary to Luke's Gospel.

and imaginative engagement in their own contexts. They may imagine Jesus calling by name those who feel small, doubtful, and unworthy, and so they may look more carefully into the branches where those who are despised observe and hide, waiting to be noticed and called by name. They may imagine meals that include those who once were banished from the table where the "good" people eat. They may imagine the rich loosening their grip on their wealth, sharing it generously and offering restitution for wrongful acquisition. And some among these may suddenly realize that they are the ones who have been seen, welcomed, and redeemed by Jesus, and respond in extravagant repentance, generosity, and joy.

The story of Zacchaeus narrates a relationship that begins in the heart and is played out in perception and response. It incorporates many features of Christian practical wisdom. Its plot is driven by radical attentiveness and the disruption of boundaries. It presents a way of being in relationship that rejects rigid rules. It shows a person who lives in front of one text becoming an actor within another, by his own imaginative appropriation of his people's traditions. It both incorporates and points ahead to the narrative of cross and resurrection. At the same time, by itself it is incomplete, offering just a glimpse of redemption. It paints a vision of Jesus' realm coming into existence in a modest, penultimate way in the life of Zacchaeus and his community.[87]

I long to hang out in the tree of scripture for the rest of my life, celebrating its sturdiness and imagining what I might see of the world from within its branches. And indeed I fully intend to do just that, even though I am well aware by now that I will not in this life know all I long to know, and that the knowledge of the scholars who probe texts critically and the pastors who preach from these texts is limited as well. Further questions will continue to

---

87. This story's narration of God's gracious abundance and a human being's situated, penultimate response reminds me of one of David Ford's descriptions of the relationship between imagination and action, and thus of the Christian practical wisdom that unites both: "The Christian imagination, fed by Jesus' teaching and parables on the Kingdom of God" — and, I would add, by narratives like Luke 19:1-10 — "is intoxicated by the abundance of God's compassion, generosity, and love." Knowing such fullness and abundance, Ford declares, "allows an ultimate vision of church and society taken up into the fullness of love and of God. This in turn encourages modest, responsible, thankful, joyful, penultimate action in the present, creating with others in church and society signs of hope in the abundance of the Kingdom of God." Ford, *The Future of Christian Theology*, p. 129.

arise, among scholars and also in the midst of life, and at times unknowing may overwhelm me. Yet I am grateful for the multiple ways in which those of us who live amid modernity's cross-pressures are able to read and reread scripture, critically and imaginatively. I am grateful that when one of my young grandchildren hears an already-familiar creation story from Genesis and asks "but what about the dinosaurs?" I will have an answer that will not require her to renounce her fascination with the natural world or to choose between studying the evolution of reptiles and puzzling over the serpent in the primordial Garden. I am grateful for the decades of intensive scholarly investigation of the Gospels' accounts of Jesus' passion, which has delegitimized anti-Semitic interpretations and allowed me and those with whom I worship to understand and move beyond the anti-Judaism of the texts we hear each Holy Week.[88] I am grateful for historical scholarship on the Psalms as well — though it seems more important to notice, here, that their very existence and continued use demonstrates that the long practice of prayer is much, much bigger than our present understanding of the psalter.

While confessing the unknowing that will always surround biblical imagination, I trust, with Gabriel Marcel, that "wisdom is in a sense indistinguishable from the pursuit of it."[89] I also trust, thanks be to God, that I pursue wisdom not alone but in the company of sisters and brothers in Christ who both share my questions and raise new ones I could not have conceived. Most important, I am grateful that they and others beyond the Christian community remind me again and again that the point is not to stay in the tree but to come down from it, like Zacchaeus, in response to Christ's summons and in imitation of Christ's own self-emptying for the sake of the world. "We use our imagination not to escape the world but to join it," Iris Murdoch declared.[90] We read scripture because we are called to live wisely in the beautiful, endangered, broken world that opens in front of this text today.

88. See, for example, Mary C. Boys, *Redeeming Our Sacred Story: The Death of Jesus and Relations between Jews and Christians* (New York: Paulist, 2013).

89. Gabriel Marcel, *The Decline of Wisdom,* trans. Manya Harari (London: Harvil, 1955), p. 40.

90. Murdoch, *The Sovereignty of Good* (New York: Routledge & Kegan Paul, 1970), p. 88.

unknowing

SPIRITUAL PRACTICES AND THE SEARCH FOR
A WISDOM EPISTEMOLOGY

KATHLEEN A. CAHALAN

CONTEMPORARY DISCUSSIONS OF PRACTICAL WISDOM build on Aristotle's definition of *phronesis* as "right reason about things to be done." Indeed few Western thinkers have escaped this formulation. For Aristotle *phronesis* relates to knowledge needed for practical affairs, as distinguished from the kinds of knowledge that stem from theory or contemplation, a distinction that has led to an unfortunate separation between practical and theoretical knowing. In today's most influential epistemologies, the practical has been disregarded, even degraded; we are, as William Sullivan and Matthew Rosen note, steeped in the "triumph of abstract theory and criticism over formation and action."[1]

Yet, as this volume demonstrates, practical reason and wisdom are gaining attention among academics as well as practitioners in a variety of fields. Many realize the limits of technical rationality and abstract reason and seek to understand and educate for other ways of knowing, particularly in the face of global social, environmental, and political challenges. For example, scholars of professional education such as Patricia Benner, a nursing educator; William Sullivan, a philosopher; and Don S. Browning, a practical theologian, have each in quite different spheres critically appropriated Aristotle's concept of *phronesis,* arguing for the importance of a kind of practical knowing that is neither below nor opposed to abstract or theoretical

1. William M. Sullivan and Matthew S. Rosin, *New Agenda for Higher Education: Shaping a Life of the Mind for Practice* (San Francisco: Jossey-Bass, 2007), p. xix.

knowledge. Each author argues that theoretical knowledge is one important and necessary dimension of practical knowledge, to be sure, but all agree that it has for too long eclipsed the wisdom that resides in practice. Practical reason, as these thinkers understand it, also includes narrative, imagination, discernment, perception, communal wisdom, and moral vision as indispensable aspects of human knowing that inform intention and action.

Aristotle's *phronesis* points to a particular kind of knowledge that is gained from experience in particular situations and accumulates over time. It is progressive and developmental, following a trajectory in which time and circumstance shape what is known while the particularities of situations are considered in light of other cases as well as the norms and principles that guide decision making. For Benner, the expert practitioner is able to draw on a wide range of experience, and for Sullivan, practical reason functions through comparison, analogy, and synthesis of many kinds of experience. To know well means to know more, not just by accumulating more data or information, but by collecting a repository of similar cases on which a practitioner can draw in subsequent situations. As Bent Flyvbjerg, an economic geographer who teaches development and planning, notes, "Common to all experts is that they operate on the basis of intimate knowledge of several thousand concrete cases in their areas of expertise."[2] In a sense, practical wisdom is a storehouse where accumulated narratives, insights, information, and comparisons are gathered.[3] Because practical wisdom requires a particular kind of knowledge based on experience and learning over time, Aristotle argued that the young cannot possess it.[4]

The current interest in practical wisdom is an important corrective to modernity's more narrow epistemologies, and one necessary for professional judgment today. However, it fails to establish practical wisdom as other than a form of cognitive rationality. These scholars, like many others,

2. Bent Flyvbjerg, "Five Misunderstandings about Case-Study Research," *Qualitative Inquiry* 12, no. 2 (April 2006): 222.

3. Benner et al. argue that teaching nurses to develop a sense of "salience," the capacity to recognize what really matters in a situation, requires that "the student increases her cognitive capacities to think in relation to the particular demands of the situation." Patricia Benner, Molly Sutphen, Victoria Leonard, and Lisa Day, *Educating Nurses: A Call for Radical Transformation* (San Francisco: Jossey-Bass, 2010), p. 94.

4. *Nicomachean Ethics* 1142a, in *Introduction to Aristotle,* 2nd ed., ed. Richard McKeon (Chicago: University of Chicago Press, 1973).

retain certain assumptions that permeate the philosophical and theological traditions of the West. Often when *phronesis* is being retrieved it is presented as a function of the mind. For example, Browning notes regarding Aristotle that "the specific task of *phronesis* is to discern and apply the rational principle that would supply the mean between the excesses."[5] In spite of hints toward its embodied, intuitive, and affective dimensions, *phronesis* remains, as Bonnie Miller-McLemore points out, a mental process internal to the mind geared toward cognition, verbal interpretation, and morality.

The widespread intellectualization of *phronesis* may also result from a sense that it is necessary to elevate *phronesis* above *techne,* the third kind of knowledge described by Aristotle. *Techne* is the knowledge belonging to making, as in crafts or skilled labor. Some professional educators are worried that *techne* is prized over both practical wisdom and theory, to the detriment of professional practice and judgment.[6]

While Aristotle's legacy contains much wisdom regarding how to exercise *phronesis,* it carries us only so far. The Christian spiritual tradition holds other ways of understanding practical wisdom that have largely been obscured or even lost but that can greatly expand our sense of this indispensable kind of knowing. Christian practical wisdom arises from how one lives and prays in relationship to the ultimate goal of loving communion with God and neighbor. The pursuit of God through spiritual practice is not aimed at acquiring knowledge *about* something; nor is it aimed at living a better life as such. Rather, the proximate aim has been described as *metanoia,* purity of heart, selfless love, and service to the poor. These are what lead us toward life in and with God in everyday life. Spiritual practice entails the remaking of the self for the sake of the self-in-communion.

In this book we are seeking to articulate a more expansive epistemology as it relates to practical wisdom and to retrieve a kind of knowing that has been part of the Christian tradition though not readily recognized

5. Don S. Browning, *Fundamental Practical Theology: Descriptive and Strategic Proposals* (Minneapolis: Fortress, 1991), p. 176. In this book, see Bonnie Miller-McLemore's chapter "Disciplining."

6. Donald Schön argues that technical rationality has become the dominant epistemology of professional practice, what he calls the "high ground overlooking a swamp" in which "research-based theory and technique" can be applied to problems. *Educating the Reflective Practitioner: Toward a New Design for Teaching and Learning in the Professions* (San Francisco: Jossey-Bass, 1987), p. 3.

or emphasized. My contribution is to turn to the spiritual tradition and ask: What kind of knowing arises from spiritual practice, and what do this knowledge and practice reveal to us about practical wisdom? The breadth of this question is more than I can adequately explore here, and so I have chosen to focus on three dimensions of early Christian spiritual practice that illuminate features of practical wisdom not found in Aristotle or in contemporary discussions: the virtue of discernment, the virtue of humility, and the encounter with unknowing.[7] In particular, I want to examine the practice of praying with scripture and how it gave rise to these dimensions of practical wisdom in early desert Christian spirituality. I hope to show the ways in which virtue and formation took shape through a particular practice, and also the ways in which practical wisdom was indispensable to a way of life capable of supporting and sustaining this practice. The practice I describe laid the foundation for particular kinds of knowledge to emerge — knowledge of the self, which begins in the struggle to overcome sin and acquire virtue; knowledge in community for the sake of community; and knowledge of God, which eventuates in unknowing. Together with other features of early Christian desert spirituality, prayer with scripture shaped a distinctive Christian practical wisdom — an epistemological approach manifesting a wisdom way of knowing.

I have selected discernment, humility, and unknowing for several reasons. First, they offer aspects of practical wisdom that are neglected in today's conversation about knowledge and practice. They are not part of Aristotle's legacy, and though they can be found in other religious traditions, the forms I shall describe are particular to Christian practice. Further, these dimensions of spiritual practice are suggestive for contemporary reflection on professional education, since they are forged in community and passed on by expert practitioners to novices.

Second, the spiritual practices that gave rise to these virtues and experiences were lost for centuries, even among Christians, and have only recently been retrieved and appreciated. Those who desire to cultivate practical wisdom today need to take seriously the practices that gave rise to it in the past — something only now becoming possible, owing to recent scholarship

---

7. I tread lightly here since I am not a historian of Christianity and I recognize that even experts of early Christian texts are challenged to sort out the biblical, philosophical, and theological influences on Christian practice from Jewish, Hellenistic, and other cultural sources.

on ancient and medieval Christianity and to a contemporary renewal of monastic practice and widespread interest in spiritual practices.

Third, discernment, humility, and unknowing provide important counterpoints to contemporary epistemologies. According to Charles Taylor, the dominant cultural sources in modernity for understanding the self are derived from two major philosophical streams, one from Descartes in the form of disengaged reason and the other from Romanticism in the form of expressive individualism.[8]

The first of these epistemologies spurs modern technical society, while universities strive to accumulate greater bodies of knowledge to master and possess nature. A bottom-line mentality and prospects of material abundance lure us toward ever more flattened and utilitarian kinds of knowledge, at the expense of human and natural life.

The second stream — Romanticism — informs the explosion of spiritual practice in the past few decades that leans toward "expressivism," the belief that each person has an inner nature, truth, or self that drives toward expression.[9] Within the social construction of the "immanent frame," with its singular focus on human well-being within the horizontal plane of time and space, attempts to embark on a spiritual path readily become programs for self-improvement.[10] In some cases, this is valuable, as in contemporary critical retrievals of spiritual practices that have corrected the tradition's degradation of the body. At the same time, however, bodily practices that are deeply connected to particular religious traditions have been severed from spiritual teachings and become self-focused. Take yoga, for example, or fasting, when they are rendered as weight loss and self-enhancement programs. Meanwhile, dissatisfied selves engage in various forms of romantic revolt. Humility and unknowing have little value in the drives for certainty and escape that such epistemologies promote. Absent from both rationalism and Romanticism is a wise telos for the good of society. Humility and unknowing have little value in the drive for certainty or self-actualization that modernity promotes.[11]

8. See Charles Taylor, *Sources of the Self: The Making of the Modern Identity* (Cambridge: Harvard University Press, 1989).

9. Taylor, *Sources of the Self*, pp. 374-75.

10. For a discussion of Taylor's view of the immanent frame in modernity and how it shapes our perspective, see the chapter "Framing," above.

11. See Christian Scharen's discussion of Descartes's view of the drive for certainty through abstract and universal reason in "Eclipsing."

These three aspects of spiritual practice — discernment, humility, and unknowing — shed important light on the relationship between the knowing comprised in practical wisdom and God's transformation of that knowledge. Wisdom, this tradition insists, emerges through participation in a set of *spiritual* disciplines that radically remake the self through the gospel. I want to show that there is a particular kind of knowing that arises within Christian spiritual practice, a knowing of God that emerges through the intentional, disciplined practice of attending to God through scripture, in which the scriptures act back upon the self.[12] Further, I want to take seriously the ancients' insistence that it is only through rigorous practice that one becomes discerning, humble, and able to comprehend the limits of all knowledge. Through continual practice, this tradition asserts, a kind of knowing emerges that goes beyond ordinary forms of knowing, beyond mastery or self-expression. And only through practice can one encounter this, entering a kind of (un)knowing that moves beyond language and thought.

To examine the virtues of discernment and humility, I will turn to the work of John Cassian (360-435 CE), a late patristic figure noted for his profound achievement in bringing Eastern (Greek) monastic practices to the Latin West. After extensive travels in Egypt and Syria during which he learned what he could from monastic desert practitioners, he returned to Europe and founded monasteries in Marseilles. There he authored two major works, *Conferences* and *Institutes*.[13] I will draw primarily from the *Conferences,* a set of dialogues that take place between Cassian, his companion Germanus, and several important Egyptian figures on the nature of coenobitical, that is, communal, practice.[14]

12. On appropriating scripture, see also Dorothy Bass's account in "Imagining."

13. Cassian's primary concern is pedagogical, and thus both works are devoted to teaching the basics of monastic life to new communities he was establishing in Gaul. The *Conferences* pertain to the "inner disposition of the one who prays and the nature of prayer itself, especially as unceasing," and the *Institutes* focus on the basic rules of monastic life and the eight principal faults. For an overview of both works, see Columba Stewart, *Cassian the Monk* (New York: Oxford University Press, 1998), p. 31.

14. The *Conferences* are conversations between an elder and the two travelers, John Cassian and Germanus, which follow a classical dialogue, or *erotapokriseis,* question-and-answer format. In Cassian's writings, he is the narrator, Germanus the interlocutor, and an Egyptian monk the speaker. See Stewart, *Cassian the Monk,* p. 30. Pierre Hadot discusses the Socratic dialogue as a communal spiritual practice in which the interlocutor comes to "know thyself

I have selected Cassian because he is considered a practical thinker of his time, less concerned with systematizing doctrine and ideas and more focused on passing on the teachings of wise elders for the sake of sound practice.[15] I will explore his understanding of practical and spiritual knowledge, examining in particular three aspects of his teaching on discernment: his reliance on Aristotle's understanding of the mean as the guide of virtue; his emphasis on discernment as the sorting of one's thoughts; and the practice of memorizing scripture to replace afflictive thoughts with God's Word.[16]

To examine unknowing, I will turn to a work by Gregory of Nyssa (ca. 335-395 CE), noting particularly his evocative use of prayer with scripture. His writings would influence Pseudo-Dionysius (ca. 500 CE) and, later, the author of one of the only Christian texts that explains how to practice unknowing, the medieval classic, *The Cloud of Unknowing* (ca. 1350 CE). I will conclude the chapter with reflections on what I see as the key points we can draw on today in our own practice as Christians, as theologians, and as educators.

Retrieving spiritual practices from earlier eras is risky. Deeply embedded in the texts and practices are assumptions about the human person, God, and the goals and purpose of the spiritual life, including a host of problems — dualisms of flesh and spirit, emotion and mind, action and contemplation, sense experience and reason, female and male, *cataphatic* and *apophatic* — that contemporary theologians have attempted to overcome.[17] Understanding the experience and practice of early Christians — and, further, gleaning from them help for our own path — is exceptionally challenging.

... as someone *on the way toward* wisdom." Pierre Hadot, *Philosophy as a Way of Life: Spiritual Exercises from Socrates to Foucault,* ed. Arnold I. Davidson (Cambridge, MA: Blackwell, 1995), p. 90.

15. See Bernard McGinn, *Foundations of Mysticism: Origins to the Fifth Century* (New York: Crossroad, 1994), p. 219, and Stewart, *Cassian the Monk,* p. 37.

16. I wrote of my own experience with afflictive thoughts and their spiritual antidote in the memorization of scripture in my chapter "Swimming" in the first part of this book.

17. Philip Sheldrake reminds us that "'spirit' and 'spiritual' are not the opposite of 'physical' or 'material' (Greek *soma,* Latin *corpus*) but of 'flesh' (Greek *sarx,* Latin *caro*) in the sense of everything contrary to the Spirit of God." See *A Brief History of Spirituality* (Malden, MA: Blackwell, 2007), p. 3. For further discussion, see Walter H. Principe, CSB, "Broadening the Focus: Context as a Corrective Lens in Reading Historical Works in Spirituality," in *Minding the Spirit: The Study of Spirituality,* ed. Elizabeth A. Dreyer and Mark S. Burrows (Baltimore: Johns Hopkins University Press, 2005), pp. 42-48.

A conversation between past and present of the kind I will attempt must be done with what I call critical empathy. As we proceed, we shall need a deep appreciation for the wisdom gained by earlier spiritual practitioners who lived in worlds quite different from our own, and also judicious alertness to the distortions embedded in their worldviews.[18] I turn to these texts because they constitute an important part of the wisdom tradition of Christianity.[19] As we struggle to find a wisdom epistemology for our time, we need to be open to discovering in ancient sources important elements of discernment, humility, and unknowing that are otherwise unavailable in the twenty-first century.

Practicing and Knowing

As is commonly recognized by scholars of early Christianity, "the ascetic life in Christianity was a direct continuation of the contemplative life of Greek philosophy."[20] Pierre Hadot, in *Philosophy as a Way of Life,* demonstrates that early Christians drew upon the spiritual exercises *(askesis)* of Hellenistic and Roman schools of philosophy in shaping their way of life: "Both idea and the terminology of *exercitium spirituale* are attested in early Latin Christianity, well before Ignatius of Loyola, and they correspond to the Greek Christian term *askesis.* In turn, *askesis* — which must be understood not as asceticism, but as the practice of spiritual exercises — already existed within the philosophical tradition of antiquity."[21] Neither philosophy nor theology was considered a set of ideas discovered in rational systems or "abstract theory — much less in the exegesis of texts — but rather in the art of living."[22] The philosophers' spiritual exercises aimed at conversion, the complete shift in one's understanding of the self, society, and the cosmos —

18. On "critical distance and participative engagement," see Douglas Burton-Christie, "The Cost of Interpretation: Sacred Texts and Ascetic Practice in Desert Spirituality," in Dreyer and Burrows, eds., *Minding the Spirit,* pp. 100-107.

19. See Valerian John Odermann, OSB, "Interpreting the *Rule of Benedict:* Entering a World of Wisdom," *American Benedictine Review* 35, no. 1 (March 1984): 33ff.

20. Abraham J. Malherbe and Everett Ferguson, "Introduction," in *Gregory of Nyssa: The Life of Moses* (New York: Paulist, 1978), p. 3.

21. Hadot, *Philosophy as a Way of Life,* p. 82.

22. Hadot, *Philosophy as a Way of Life,* p. 83.

"a profound transformation of the individual's mode of seeing and being." Their aim was wisdom. Without embodied engagement in such practices as paying attention, meditating, memorizing a rule of life, keeping short maxims "at hand," and preparing to die, the philosopher could not attain the knowledge necessary to ascend to wisdom, the truth of existence beyond all other knowledge.[23] Spiritual exercises provided not so much a code for moral conduct as, more importantly, a way of being that engaged the totality of the person. Their goal was for the divine element in the soul (the *nous*) to return and be united with its source, the Absolute Good (or, for Plotinus, the One).[24] The *nous* ascends through purification of the passions *(askesis)* and the rise and development of virtue, from forms of sense knowledge to, finally, the contemplative vision *(theoria)* of the Good, a kind of knowledge inexpressible in human words.[25]

Influenced by neo-Platonic teaching regarding the soul's ascent to the Good, Christian patristic writers proposed similar stages of the spiritual life: the purification of desire, the acquisition of virtue, and the soul's contemplation of the Divine.[26] We find this pattern in early monastic writers such as John Cassian. The *Conferences* begin with a discussion of a goal Cassian considered paramount in monastic life — purity of heart (Matt. 5:8), which is an intermediate and proximate goal that stands in relationship to an ultimate telos:[27] "But our point of reference, our objec-

23. Hadot notes that there are no systematic treatises on the spiritual exercises, but he does identify several of the practices, including remembrance of good things; intellectual activities such as reading, listening, and research; self-mastery; therapies of the passions; and indifference to indifferent things. *Philosophy as a Way of Life,* pp. 82-109.

24. Andrew Louth notes that *nous* in Greek is not mind or intellect as moderns understand those terms; instead, *nous* refers to "an almost intuitive grasp of reality," more "like an organ of mystical union." See Andrew Louth, *The Origins of the Christian Mystical Tradition: From Plato to Denys,* 2nd ed. (New York: Oxford University Press, 2007), pp. xiv-xv.

25. For a discussion of *theoria* in Greek and patristic texts, see Dorothy Emmet, "Theoria and the Way of Life," *Journal of Theological Studies* 17, no. 1 (April 1966): 38-52.

26. For an overview of the development of these stages in Christian spirituality and the problem it poses see Karl Rahner, *Theological Investigations III: The Theology of the Spiritual Life* (Baltimore: Helicon, 1967), pp. 3-23.

27. Stewart points out that purity of heart is the "centerpiece" of Cassian's theology and a term that embraces many other metaphors of perfection such as "tranquility," "contemplation," "unceasing prayer," "chastity," and "spiritual knowledge." Cassian's notion of purity of heart is indebted to Evagrius's concept of *apatheia,* the state of "passionlessness." For a discus-

tive, is a clean heart, without which it is impossible for anyone to reach our target."[28]

To become pure of heart Cassian taught that one must attain two kinds of knowledge — practical and spiritual — which are integrally related to each other.[29] Practical knowledge "is achieved through the correction of one's moral acts and through the purging of sin" as well as learning "the means of curing them" by acquiring virtue through the practice of ceaseless prayer.[30] And it can be lived out in any number of ways, not solely by desert monastic practice. He notes that some will find it through care for the sick and "wretched and the oppressed," or teaching, or "help to the poor."

The second kind of knowledge is *theoria,* that is, "the contemplation of things divine and the awareness of very sacred meanings."[31] As the monk (his reader and main concern) becomes disentangled from the seduction of afflictive thoughts and unruly passions, he or she will experience a kind of tranquility that allows contemplation to emerge. Contemplation is spiritual knowledge that allows one to see and know God in a completely new way, providing a "foretaste of heaven."[32]

We can see from this one example how the Greek distinction between *phronesis* and *theoria* influenced early Christian spirituality. Over time, unfortunately, the distinction would become a wedge, even a barrier between the two kinds of knowing, but that is another story. This was not true for Cassian, who adopted the two-part schema in order to show the "peda-

---

sion of Evagrius's concept of *apatheia* and Cassian's concept of purity of heart, see Stewart, *Cassian the Monk,* pp. 11-12 and 42-47; and Owen Chadwick, "Introduction," in *John Cassian: Conferences,* trans. Colm Luibheid (Mahwah, NJ: Paulist, 1985), p. 4; forthwith *Conf.*

28. *Conf.* 1.4. All quotations from the *Conferences* are taken from the Luibheid translation unless otherwise noted.

29. For a discussion of the two kinds of knowledge, see Stewart, *Cassian the Monk,* pp. 50-55, and Antony D. Rich, *Discernment in the Desert Fathers: Diakrisis in the Life and Thought of Early Egyptian Monasticism* (Carlisle: Paternoster, 2007), pp. 87-93.

30. *Conf.* 14.1; 14.3.

31. *Conf.* 14.1. Influenced by the leading theologians of the Alexandrian School, Clement (ca. 150–ca. 215) and Origen (ca. 184–ca. 253 CE), Stewart claims, Cassian associates contemplation *(theoria)* with knowledge *(gnosis),* which is closer to "wisdom" than to "learning." This kind of wisdom is "a matter of insight or perceptiveness rather than literary education." Stewart, *Cassian the Monk,* p. 48.

32. Stewart discusses the neo-Platonic view of contemplation that Cassian adopts in *Cassian the Monk,* pp. 47, 49.

gogical and progressive interaction" of knowledge in relation to different aspects of practice.

Both kinds of knowledge emerge through the spiritual practice of reading scripture. Cassian follows Origen's method of biblical exegesis in reading the text on two levels, one literal, or historical (what the text is about), and the other spiritual, in which the hidden meaning is found in allegory and symbols; this includes the "spiritual insight" of tropology, moral and practical teaching, allegory, events that prefigure or symbolize a great mystery, and anagogy, which leads up to higher realms such as the heavens.[33] Practical knowledge emerges through memorizing and repeating biblical texts, as I will discuss below, as a way of driving out thoughts and inclinations that fuel the passions toward sin. Spiritual knowledge emerges when the biblical text takes hold of one's consciousness, one's way of seeing the self and the world, where the imagination is filled with its "images and dispositions."[34] Over time, as the biblical text "reduces the inner chaos" of the mind, another kind of knowledge emerges, a spiritual knowing of God beyond all knowing. As the historian Douglas Burton-Christie notes,

> As the heart is purified, as one grows in self-knowledge, the contemplative awareness of God's presence becomes more and more vivid. And as the experience of contemplation grows, the mysteries of Scripture are revealed and these texts take on more meaning. Finally, from this more profound appropriation of Scripture, the monk is led ever deeper into contemplation. Thus Scripture, self-knowledge and contemplation are all part of a single, evolving process.[35]

Cassian does acknowledge that wordless silence beyond the text, which he describes as a "fiery outbreak, indescribable exaltation, an insatiable thrust of the soul," is the highest form of prayer, though he does not have much to say about it.[36] His two major works are taken up primarily with

33. *Conf.* 14.8. Regarding Origen's method, see Bernard McGinn, "The Language of Inner Experience in Christian Mysticism," in Dreyer and Burrows, eds., *Minding the Spirit,* p. 137.

34. See Dorothy Bass on biblical imagination in "Imagining."

35. Douglas Burton-Christie, "Scripture, Self-Knowledge and Contemplation," in *Studia Patristica,* vol. 25, ed. Elizabeth A. Livingstone (Leuven: Peeters, 1993), p. 344.

36. *Conf.* 10.11. See also *Conf.* 10.5 and 9.25.

teachings that address the practical knowledge of monastic life. I can only hazard to guess at two reasons.

First, Cassian's writings are aimed at the formation of new communities, and novices must start from the beginning. The *Conferences* distill teachings that Cassian acquired and refined from his travels and conversations with Eastern monastics; he and Germanus encountered these teachings as the students of great masters, not as teachers themselves. As the two friends discuss the practices in the *Conferences,* they are depicted as model novices who display their eagerness to learn what to do and how to do it.

Second, Cassian, unlike other early authors, believed that the majority of the Christian life was lived in the long, hard struggle to disengage from afflictive thoughts and acquire virtue, which took years of prayer and *askesis.*[37] Spiritual knowledge does not simply follow or replace the practical. As Cassian biographer Columba Stewart notes, Cassian did not have successive stages or a linear sense of the spiritual life: "What one contemplates at the summit of the monastic journey is what one began to memorize and recite on the first day of the monastic life: the Word of God. And, for Cassian, the spiritual knowledge of the divine realities of Scripture is the means of entering *now* into the Kingdom of God, the end of the Christian journey."[38] Thus, prayer with the scriptures forms the integral relationship between practical and spiritual knowing. Cassian may have found, like many others, that what emerges as wordless prayer is finally impossible to speak about. Whatever his experience of this dimension of prayer was, it does not seem to have taken place apart from the encounter of God through the scriptures.

Spiritual knowing, then, is entirely dependent on practical knowing through disciplined practice; it cannot be reached in any other way.[39] One

---

37. *Conf.* 14.3.

38. Stewart shows how the structure of the *Conferences* moves back and forth in discussions of practical issues and the goal, thus establishing a sense that one learns this practice over a lifetime and never ceases in its practice. The organization "echoes his pedagogical intention." Columba Stewart, OSB, "Scripture and Contemplation in the Monastic Spiritual Theology of John Cassian," in Livingstone, ed., *Studia Patristica,* vol. 25, pp. 459-61.

39. Sarah Coakley makes a similar observation in her discussion of the threefold path of the "purgative," "illuminative," and "unitive" way in the spiritual tradition. See Sarah Coakley, "Deepening Practices: Perspectives from Ascetical and Mystical Theology," in *Practicing Theology: Beliefs and Practices in Christian Life,* ed. Miroslav Volf and Dorothy C. Bass (Grand Rapids: Eerdmans, 2002), p. 84.

may achieve the "practical mode" independent of contemplation, but "in no way can contemplation be arrived at without the practical."[40] For Cassian, then, the spiritual life consists in engaged practice that leads to different kinds of knowing, each with a purpose and goal. Through the *askesis* of desert practice, particularly sustained reading of the biblical text over time, a practical knowing of the self emerges, the goal of which is purity of heart. One comes to the knowledge that passionate thoughts, especially those leading to sin, must be relinquished in order that God's grace may allow growth in virtue. As I will discuss below, the central practice for Cassian is replacing afflictive thoughts with the biblical text.

Practice, Virtue, and the Knowledge of God

The novice must begin with rigorous moral formation, the uprooting of sin, and the implanting of virtue. For Cassian, the two central virtues to be acquired at this stage are discernment and humility. To acquire discernment, the novice must learn two practices. The first is discernment in regard to the proper use of life's basic necessities, such as food, sleep, clothing, sexual desire, and material goods. Here Cassian relies on Aristotle's virtue of *phronesis* as the mean between two extremes. The second practice is discernment of one's thoughts, the desires, inclinations, and passions that drive one to act.[41] One learns discernment as *phronesis* through practices of daily life, following a rule, and observing the practice of others. One learns discernment through recognizing the source of one's thoughts and keeping vigilant attention toward thoughts of God. Humility is a virtue born of renunciation, both renunciation of food, sex, and money and the arduous struggle to relinquish desires that lead one away from God. Practical wisdom, for Cassian, was knowing what was proper in both cases. As they adopted the virtues from Greek thought, Christians also brought their own interpretations, and in this section I will explore Cassian's understanding of the virtues of discernment, as *phronesis* and as sorting the thoughts, and humility.

---

40. *Conf.* 14.2.

41. Rich discusses three uses of discernment in the New Testament: distinguishing good from evil (Heb. 5:14), distinguishing between spirits (1 Cor. 12:10), and passing judgment (Rom. 14:1). Rich, *Discernment in the Desert Fathers,* pp. 6-7.

*Discernment: "The Mother, the Guardian,
and the Guide of All the Virtues"*

Cassian relates how he and his companion, Germanus, traveled through the
Holy Land and the Egyptian desert in the late fourth century to inquire of
renowned monastics how to pray without ceasing.[42] Abba Isaac admonished
them to begin with "a complete removal of all concern for bodily things"
and "worldly cares."[43] The ascetical life, he explained, includes renunciation
as well as spending long hours in the solitude of one's cell, performing all-
night vigils, engaging in manual labor, reading and memorizing scripture,
and meeting for spiritual guidance with a wise elder.

With our postmodern sensibilities, we shudder at the rejection of the
body, of sexual desire, and of the material world and the unquestioning
obedience to a religious authority; yet these practices, as Cassian notes, are
not an end in themselves.[44] He was also not an extremist, as some desert
practitioners were prone to be. Rather, he believed that taking up such a rule
of life would in fact change him for the good. Renunciation, discipline, and
constraint were the means by which virtue is born and the heart purified.
For Cassian, "The beginning of our salvation and the preserving of it is the
fear of the Lord. For by this the rudiments of conversion, the purgation of
vice, and the preserving of virtue are acquired by those who begin and are
schooled for the way of perfection."[45] Here the Christian desert practice
finds its direct link to its Hellenistic context, as Hadot notes:

> In the view of all philosophical schools, [the] principal cause of suffering,
> disorder, and unconsciousness were the passions: that is, unregulated desires
> and exaggerated fears. . . . Philosophy thus appears, in the first place, as a
> therapeutic of the passions. . . . Each school had its own method, but all

42. In the writings of John Cassian, the models and companions are male monastic figures. For insights on similar teachings from the desert *ammas,* see Mary Forman, *Praying
with the Desert Mothers* (Collegeville: Liturgical, 2005). See also Shawn Carruth, OSB, "The
Monastic Virtues of Obedience, Silence, and Humility: A Feminist Perspective," *American
Benedictine Review* 51, no. 2 (June 2000): 121-47.

43. *Conf.* 9.3; 9.5.

44. *Conf.* 1.7.

45. See *John Cassian: The Institutes,* trans. Boniface Ramsey, OP (Mahwah, NJ: Newman,
1997), 4.39.1; forthwith, *Inst.*

linked their therapeutics to a profound transformation of the individual's mode of seeing and being.[46]

Acquiring virtue, *arete,* is the first step in the spiritual journey.[47] Despite the fact that it is not a primary concept in scripture, this Hellenistic idea significantly influenced Christian moral thought.[48] By the late patristic era, the Stoic virtues — prudence, temperance, courage, and justice — had been wedded to the three Christian virtues — faith, hope, and love.[49] But early desert authors did not create a system of the virtues; rather, they retained the Greek category as a way of understanding the dynamic interplay of unrestrained passion and vice that leads toward sin, on the one hand, and the goodness and charity that are planted in the soul through the power of the Holy Spirit, on the other.

Cassian retains Aristotle's understanding of *phronesis* as the chief virtue, "supreme and master over them all," and "the mother, the guardian, and the guide of all the virtues."[50] Discernment is necessary for the other virtues to develop, it provides the norm by which to exercise virtue properly, and it unites the virtues as one. For Aristotle, there are two kinds of virtues, theoretical and practical; prudence is a practical virtue because it aims at good

46. Hadot, *Philosophy as a Way of Life,* p. 83.

47. Virtue is an approach to ethics that is based on the pursuit of the good life, rather than an ethics rooted in principle or law. While virtue or *arete,* which means "excellence," had various interpretations in ancient Greece, by the fifth century it generally referred to becoming a good citizen of the polis and reaching some level of success in public life, such as politics or law. See Raymond J. Devettere, *Introduction to Virtue Ethics: Insights of the Ancient Greeks* (Washington, DC: Georgetown University Press, 2002).

48. See Jaroslav Pelikan, *Christianity and Classical Culture: The Metamorphosis of Natural Theology in the Christian Encounter with Hellenism* (New Haven: Yale University Press, 1993), pp. 140-46. Pelikan notes that Christian *aretai* is rooted in Greek understandings, notably Aristotle's teaching on the mean. The term *arete* appears in the New Testament four times, as well as in the Septuagint and in the Apocrypha.

49. Later the four cardinal virtues figured prominently in the great medieval systems, most notably Aquinas's *Summa.* See Thomas Aquinas, *Summa Theologica,* trans. Fathers of the English Dominican Province (New York: Benziger Brothers, 1947), I-II, qq. 55-67.

50. See *Conf.* 2.26; 1.23; and 2.4. Discernment is called "mother of all virtues" more than thirty times in Hellenistic and patristic writings. Christians refer most often to temperance, humility, *discretio,* sobriety, *continentia,* obedience, justice, and love. See Harry Hagan, OSB, "The Mothers of Virtues and the Rule of Benedict," *American Benedictine Review* 60, no. 4 (December 2009): 371-97.

action, but it is also intellectual in the sense that it has to grasp the good toward which action aims. The virtues need the guidance of prudence in order for persons to act rightly, to avoid the extremes of excess and defect, and to assure that their feelings and actions occur at the right time, about the right things, toward the right people, for the right reason, and in the right way. Prudence is right reason, the rational part of the soul that directs the nonrational part of the soul (appetites, emotions, and desires.) The virtuous person, according to Aristotle, develops the capacity to identify the mean within a range of moral possibilities, particularly its extremes — for example, to be courageous rather than either timid or foolhardy. Knowing the mean enables one to judge and choose the action that is fitting and right in a particular situation.[51]

Similarly, Cassian counsels a middle way. He discourages both fasting too much, which leads to sluggishness, and having no regard for the fast, which leads to gluttony.[52] The same idea is found in numerous early Christian texts. For example, Gregory of Nyssa, who portrays the path to God as the path of "perfection according to virtue," uses Aristotle's definition of virtue as the mean, coupling it with Philo's understanding of "the royal way." He writes, "This teaching lays down that virtue is discerned in the mean. Accordingly, all evil naturally operates in a deficiency of or an excess of virtue.... Wisdom holds to the mean between shrewdness and simplicity ... the disposition which closely unites these two by the mean that is virtue." Aristotle's understanding of virtue as the mean is wedded to the biblical idea of perfection ("Be perfect as your heavenly Father is perfect"; Matt. 5:48). But in Gregory, the royal way is "narrow and hard."[53] Following this same idea of moderation, Abba Moses counseled that the general rule to follow is to "take cognizance of the state of one's strength and body and age and allow oneself as much food as will sustain the flesh but not satisfy its longings." He warned that excessive eating is dangerous, as is extreme restraint, which can make the "spirit, brought low by lack of food," unable to maintain the "vigor of its prayerfulness."[54] Abba Moses explained to his two listeners that holding to this rule requires some flexibility, especially when "hospitality

---

51. See *Nicomachean Ethics* 1139a-1141b, in McKeon, ed., *Introduction to Aristotle*.
52. *Conf.* 2.16.
53. Gregory, *Life of Moses* 2.287.
54. *Conf.* 2.22.

and fraternal concern" demand that the monks offer food to a visitor. In such a case, Abba Moses suggested, they should eat with the guest, adapting their discipline of fasting and their "allotted measure of food" as needed. Echoing Aristotle, he taught that "life must be lived with due measure, and with discernment for a guide, the road must be traveled between the two kinds of excess."[55]

Many reports of self-destructive practice establish that monks sometimes failed to discern the mean. Abba Moses told the story of two monks traveling across the desert; "by a lapse of discernment," they resolved that "the only food they would take would be whatever the Lord Himself offered them." Hungry and weak, they came upon people known to be cruel and savage, who, surprisingly, "rushed with bread" to feed the two starving men. One of the monks, "moved by discernment, accepted with joy and blessing the food offered him, as if it were the Lord Himself who was giving it." The other refused the food and died. Both, Abba Moses said, made the wrong discernment at the outset, vowing not to eat, since it was foolish to travel across the desert with no food, but one man, "with the help of discernment," was able to see God's gift and change his mind.

Realizing that discernment is "the source and root of all virtues," Cassian and his companion, Germanus, asked, "How can we recognize something to be true and from God or false and from the devil?"[56] It would have been easy for the wise elders they visited to give the two seekers a rulebook to follow. But following an external rule is not discernment as practical wisdom. Rules are a guide, the elders taught, but cannot be applied to all individuals and all situations in the same way. *Phronesis* is discerning the best course of action given the situation. As the patristics scholar Anthony Rich points out, discretion is not a "legalistic tool by which an individual judges which 'rule' applies in a given situation, but rather an intuitive sense of how to behave appropriately."[57]

Abba Moses offered the seekers a general rule, based on the practices of the elders. In regard to eating food and keeping the fast, the general rule is moderation; this must be applied according to one's age, physical condition, and the work one needs to do. The particularities of the situation require at-

55. *Conf.* 2.16.
56. *Conf.* 2.9.
57. Rich, *Discernment in the Desert Fathers*, p. 91.

tention as a monk discerns what is right and proper to eat. Discernment also requires the counsel and wisdom of others: one can learn from the examples of both those who lack and those who have discernment. Thus, one comes to know the "measure of his own strength" in assessing what is appropriate and fitting in terms of eating food, a site of desire and passion encountered every day. Discernment is necessary in order to decide and judge what is needed to reach one's goal.[58] Any practical discipline pertaining to the body "should be observed thoughtfully according to the occasion, place, method and time, so that they would be beneficial rather than harmful."[59]

Thus Cassian retains and modifies key elements of Aristotle's understanding of *phronesis*. On the one hand, virtue is natural, requiring deliberate effort. As Rich notes, Cassian's description is akin to "gymnastic exercise, individual practice and wearing oneself out." Discernment could be "acquired through constant human effort and means; it is not exclusively a spiritual gift." This notion can be found in Hebrews 5:14, in which discernment is used "for the more mature and advanced in faith" who have experience and "a skill born of practice" that gives them "the sensitivity and ability to distinguish . . . what is morally good and evil." Discernment is a "skill exercised in the mind as well as a spiritual gift as indicated in Scripture elsewhere."[60] This kind of practical wisdom is a matter of trial and error, as one comes to self-understanding about what best fits one's circumstances in order to reach one's goal. And yet Cassian also departs from Aristotle on this point. As much as Cassian emphasizes the intense effort required in the development of discernment, he also believes that discernment is a gift of God that cannot "be seized anywhere merely by human effort."[61] Christian discernment, for all of its commonality with *phronesis,* is a gift of the Holy Spirit.

58. Cassian notes that many try strenuous ascetical practices, forgoing food and practicing nightly vigils, but lack of food and sleep will not lead to one's goal; rather, only discernment of the proper amount of food and sleep can lead to virtue. *Conf.* 2.2.

59. Rich, *Discernment in the Desert Fathers,* p. 88.

60. Rich, *Discernment in the Desert Fathers,* p. 7.

61. *Conf.* 2.1. Cassian became known for his part in the debates about free will and grace (see *John Cassian: The Conferences,* trans. Boniface Ramsey, OP [Mahwah, NJ: Newman, 1972], *Conf.* 13). Like most Eastern monastics, Cassian agreed with Augustine's critique of Pelagius, but did not concur on the idea that persons had no responsibility for an "initiative of faith." See Stewart, *Cassian the Monk,* pp. 19-22 and 76-81. Unfortunately, this debate led to suspicion of Cassian's theology; despite this setback, he was a primary influence on the early sixth-century texts *Rule of the Master* and *Rule of Saint Benedict.*

Perhaps by effort and "a natural sense" Cassian means the way a novice begins to learn a practice, through aligning one's intention and motivation with one's ability and bodily skill. A novice must apply great effort to pay attention and do an action repeatedly, until it becomes a habit and does not require full conscious attention. Perhaps it is only later that Cassian realized that this early effort of the will is also completely dependent on God, but in the initial experience it feels as though one is doing it "naturally," by one's own exertion. Theologian Sarah Coakley offers a similar explanation: "One starts from practices one might be tempted to regard as entirely self-propelled; but they are joined over time by practices that involve deeper and more demanding levels of response to divine grace and that uncover by degrees the implications of our fundamental reliance on that grace as initiated at baptism."[62] Through one's effort, the practice itself reveals the divine source.

Discernment as *phronesis* is practical knowledge about practical affairs in the world. Without it, one's practice can become foolish, even destructive. Finding the mean of one's daily needs, living without excess, allows bodily, personal, and community needs to be met; but excessive and persistent attention to such needs distracts one from prayer. Thus, Cassian counsels a further practice of discernment, sorting one's thoughts, knowing their derivation, and uprooting the most afflictive ones through practices of reading and memorizing the words of scripture.

Discerning Thoughts, Remembering the Word

For Cassian, discernment shapes practice. To acquire the practical knowledge necessary to live faithfully, as we have seen, it is necessary to develop the capacity of discernment that guides, forms, and directs ascetical practices through acquiring insight into the mean. Beyond this, however, discernment is also the capacity to sort out the kinds of thoughts, motives, emotions, and intentions that intrude on or sustain the life of prayer. As Rich notes (using the Latin term), "while *discretio* is necessary for the right use of outward practical disciplines it also has an inward dimension and as such forms a bridge between the inner and outer life of the monk, binding

62. Coakley, "Deepening Practices," p. 80.

them together and enabling him to perfect *virtutes* and advance towards his goals."[63] Three aspects of this inward dimension of discernment must be learned: recognizing and diagnosing the problem of the thoughts, engaging a new practice to counter the problem, and sustaining the practice at all times.

The problem for Cassian and Germanus, as for any beginner in the spiritual path, was that when they sat to pray, they grew frustrated since their thoughts would "slip away from spiritual contemplation and run here and there." Their minds would whip about like a "shipwreck," "forever wandering," "tossed in all directions, like a drunk."[64] When reading the scriptures or sitting in silence, they found that their thoughts would come rushing in, thoughts about getting something to eat, or finding a more comfortable bed or a sexual companion. Even if these were let go, others would arise — anger at an old friend, dejection that one's life is worthless. Even after much practice in silent meditation, they found, the mind can stray to thoughts against God or thoughts of one's own fame and glory. Each realized that his mind was "unable to keep its grip on holy thoughts."[65] I am referring here to the experience of the eight thoughts, first described by Evagrius Ponticus and borrowed by John Cassian — thoughts about food (gluttony), sex (lust), money and material goods (avarice), anger, dejection, apathy (acedia), vainglory, and pride.[66] The eight thoughts referred not to ordinary ideas or feelings, but uncontrolled passion, demonic suggestion, or self-will — thoughts that were constant, repetitious, or uncontrollable in which the self loses the capacity to consent or reject.[67] Such thoughts rise in the mind in five "moments," as Mary Forman explains: thoughts begin as a "suggestion" or "simple idea"; the suggestion then "couples" with something ("to do it or

63. Rich, *Discernment in the Desert Fathers*, p. 87.

64. *Conf.* 10.8.

65. *Conf.* 9.7.

66. See *Evagrius of Pontus: Talking Back; A Monastic Handbook for Combating Demons*, trans. David Brakke (Collegeville: Liturgical, 2009); Evagrius Ponticus, *The Praktikos and Chapters on Prayer* (Kalamazoo: Cistercian, 1972); *Conf.* 5, in *Cassian: The Conferences*, trans. Ramsey. For a discussion of discernment and the thoughts, see Rich, *Discernment in the Desert Fathers*, pp. 93-99.

67. For a discussion of how demons play a psychological and theological role in monastic literature, see Columba Stewart, OSB, "Evagrius Ponticus and the Eastern Monastic Tradition on the Intellect and the Passions," *Modern Theology* 27, no. 2 (April 2011): 265-66.

not?"); this becomes "mental consent" to something that is forbidden and can become a sin; consent moves to "inner struggle" and finally "captivity"; the passion "becomes 'a vicious habit' as a result of a long series of assents. These thoughts are mulled and brooded over until they take root like weeds in the soil of one's heart and eventually manifest themselves as uncharitable behavior of all kinds."[68]

Discernment, then, guides the practitioner in identifying the sources of the thoughts by examining whether they are from God, the devil, or one's self. Thoughts from God come as an "illumination of the Holy Spirit, lifting up and opening the mysteries of God." Thoughts from the devil lure one by the "attractiveness of sin," in which evil appears as good. Thoughts from the self are "natural" and pertain to "what we do or have done or have heard."[69] The discernment of thoughts is essential to spiritual practice for Cassian because of the great danger of evil thoughts.

> We must therefore keep a close eye on this threefold scheme of our thoughts and we must exercise a wise discretion concerning them as they surface in our hearts. Right from the beginning, we will scrutinize their origins, their causes, their originators, deciding our necessary reaction to them in the light of who it is that suggests them.[70]

Once one grasps whether thoughts are good or are temptations, one can choose to "permit them entry or drive them away." If we are careless about our thoughts, Abba Moses taught, "we give ourselves over to dangers and useless chattering."[71] Consenting to thoughts rooted in evil leads to one's demise; contemplating thoughts rooted in good leads to virtue. Next is to "identify the vice with which [the monk] struggles most, then concentrate a watchful mind on it, use the practical disciplines against it and when it is overcome go on to defeat other lesser thoughts that remain."[72]

How could the monk keep such persistent thoughts at bay? Like most novices of spiritual practice, Cassian and Germanus had to learn a method

68. Forman, *Praying with the Desert Mothers,* p. 60.

69. *Conf.* 1.19.

70. *Conf.* 1.20. See also Benedicta Ward, "Foreword," in Rich, *Discernment in the Desert Fathers.*

71. *Conf.* 1.18.

72. Rich, *Discernment in the Desert Fathers,* p. 93.

for responding to them. "Keep the thought of God always in your mind," a wise elder told them, introducing them to the practice of unceasing prayer. "You must cling totally to this formula for piety: 'Come to my help, O God; Lord, hurry to my rescue' (Ps 69:2)." The text, repeated continually — during the day, when at work, while eating, and during sleep — will disable other thoughts from crowding one's consciousness. Once this thought is firmly rooted in consciousness, the novice has taken the first step in learning to pray.

Drawing on this tradition, Cassian made the repetition of short prayers central to the monastic practice he brought to the Latin West.[73] This practice is a way to counter, uproot, and cast aside thoughts arising from distracting desires and passions. For Cassian, we can acquire thoughts that are "holy and spiritual" or "earthly and of the flesh," but the key is "regular reading and continuous meditation on Scripture so that a spiritual turn be given to our memory. The constant singing of the psalms is designed to produce a persistent compunction within us so that the mind, slimmed down, may not have a taste for the things of the earth but will turn, instead, to behold the things of heaven."[74]

Discernment, then, begins to mean more than judgment in a particular instance about practical affairs, and begins to "express a spiritual critical faculty that enables believers to develop their spiritual life."[75] According to Rich, this marks a shift in the meaning of discernment: "*discretio* takes on a more general sense of discernment needed by everyone in every aspect of the spiritual life, rather than an extraordinary spiritual gift occasionally used, and a more specialized sense for facilitating the mystical search for God."[76]

The third dimension of the practice was to sustain it at all times, to be vigilant in turning away from thoughts rooted in evil and toward thoughts of God. As Cassian points out, when the "mind is occupied" with God's word it is not prone to the "snares of dangerous thoughts."[77] It renders the heart pure of inclinations that drive against love of God and neighbor. Cassian taught that the psalm "should be turning unceasingly in your heart," to

73. Stoics and Epicureans practiced repeating a short saying as an exercise of meditation. See Hadot, *Philosophy as a Way of Life,* pp. 85-87, 133.

74. *Conf.* 1.17.

75. Rich, *Discernment in the Desert Fathers,* p. 11.

76. Rich, *Discernment in the Desert Fathers,* p. 121.

77. *Conf.* 14.10.

the point that "you get in habit of repeating [it] even in your slumbers" as well as at rising in the morning. By repetition it can "accompany you in all your works and deeds. . . . You will write it upon the threshold and gateway of your mouth, you will place it on the walls of your house and in the inner sanctum of your heart. It will be a continuous prayer."[78] Over time, the practice replaces afflictive thoughts with God's Word and becomes unceasing.

The use of short prayers, as well as the memorizing and repeating of scripture aloud, primarily the psalms, became a central desert practice, and later became the practice of *lectio divina*. The practice kept the mind free from the distractions of afflictive thoughts, but furthermore it meant that the text would shape one's identity, consciousness, and intentions. Duncan Robertson describes the spiritual benefits:

> Reading aloud transforms prayer. Pronouncing the words under one's breath, one can quite literally "taste" them in the mouth and more profoundly "in the mouth of the heart." . . . Sounding words out loud engages the sense of hearing and opens the ethical dimension of the listening attitude. By these means, the reader discovers the emotional inflections contained in the meaning of the words and acts out the protagonist's role. . . . Having memorized the texts and having placed them in the context of one's own experience, the reader re-authors them and makes them in effect his or her own.[79]

The use of this exercise in the silence of the desert revealed at least two dimensions of self-knowledge. First, one becomes aware of one's consciousness, particularly the thoughts that can lead one to sin, away from the goal of seeking God. Second, through the practice of *not* consenting to a thought by replacing a thought with a biblical text, a new consciousness begins to form. As the text becomes the conscious thought, the self comes to be known in and through the narrative, to such an extent that the words of scripture become one's own words. As Dorothy Bass notes in her chapter "Imagining," "words that initially exist beyond the self . . . come to shape the self." In Cassian's account, Abba Isaac made a similar point:

78. *Conf.* 10.10.

79. Duncan Robertson, *Lectio Divina: The Medieval Experience of Reading* (Collegeville: Liturgical, 2011), p. xiv-xv.

The zeal of his soul makes him like a spiritual deer who feeds on the high mountains of the prophets and the apostles, that is, on their most high and most exalted teachings. Nourished by this food, which he continually eats, he penetrates so deeply into the thinking of the psalms that he sings them not as though they had been composed by the prophet *but as if he himself had written them,* as if this were his own private prayer uttered amid the deepest compunction of heart. Certainly he thinks of them as having been specially composed for him and he recognizes that what they express was made real not simply once upon a time in the person of the prophet but that now, every day, they are being fulfilled in himself.[80]

Acquiring spiritual knowledge through scripture leads to a new understanding of the self, wherein the person is "revealed, heart and sinew. . . . [T]he meaning of the words comes through to us not just by way of commentaries but by what we ourselves have gone through."[81] Burton-Christie points to the "sophisticated hermeneutical circle" in which this "self-knowledge and contemplation are all part of a single, evolving process."[82] Who does one become through this process? What happens when one repeats the phrase: "O God come to my assistance, Lord, make haste to help me"? Cassian, and these desert practitioners, understood that scripting the biblical text on one's consciousness was akin to "taking on the mind of Christ."[83] In this way the virtue of humility is born. The Christian follows one who himself is humble.

Humility: "The Teacher of All the Virtues"

While early Christians such as Cassian retain Aristotle's focus on acquiring virtue and finding the mean in one's action, they part company with the philosophical tradition in which virtue lies at the heart of the virtuous life. For Aristotle, practical wisdom is at the center, but for Christians, charity

80. *Conf.* 10.11; emphasis added.
81. *Conf.* 10.11. In fact, Cassian and Germanus were surprised to find out that this method reveals that "no one is shut off from perfection because of illiteracy." No further training is required to acquire this self-knowledge. *Conf.* 10.14.
82. Burton-Christie, "Scripture, Self-Knowledge and Contemplation," p. 344.
83. See Dorothy Bass's discussion of Philippians 2:1-11 in "Imagining."

becomes the root of all virtue — related to faith and hope but greater than they, according to Saint Paul. When Cassian holds that the goal of monastic practice is purity of heart, he means: "the high point of love."[84] From purity of heart, love is born. "When virtue abounds purity of heart is acquired. With purity of heart the perfection of apostolic love is possessed."[85] Yet even though love is primary, it is not easily achieved. Charity cannot be acquired until discernment and humility are operative, for it is through these virtues that the heart is rid of selfish and evil intentions and charity emerges. Benedicta Ward notes, "Certainly the early writers connect discernment and love, admitting that great love can give someone particular sensitive insight into another, but as everyone knows, love is not enough. There is a distorting lens in the eye of the soul which sends the most loving gesture awry without discernment."[86] One passes from "sleeplessness and fasting to chastity, from chastity to knowledge, from knowledge to patience, from patience to kindness, from kindness to a spirit of holiness to the rewards of genuine love."[87] Different virtues emerge along the path toward spiritual maturity.

Cassian claims that humility, like discernment, is the virtue that must precede other virtues; it is also called the "mother of all virtues."[88] When Cassian calls humility a virtue, he is concerned with the experience and practice of what the monastic scholar André Louf refers to as "the original sense of the Greek word *tapeinosis* — the state of abasement, or in Latin: *humilitas/humus* — the condition in which one finds oneself flatly on the ground. A state which is absolutely indispensable in order that a virtue (in Greek we would call this *tapeinophrosune*) might be born."[89] Humility takes

---

84. *Conf.* 1.7.

85. *Inst.* 4.43. McGinn notes that the "positive pole" of Cassian's "practical science is less easily schematized" than the negative task; he "emphasizes humility and discretion as the primary guiding forces in virtuous action . . . recognizing that it is the acquisition of *puritas cordis* and *caritas* that gives meaning to all moral effort." McGinn, *Foundations of Mysticism*, p. 219.

86. Ward, "Foreword," in Rich, *Discernment in the Desert Fathers*, p. xiv.

87. *Conf.* 14.16. See also Stewart's discussion of purity of heart and love (*Cassian the Monk*, p. 44).

88. *Conf.* 19.2, in *Cassian: The Conferences*, trans. Ramsey.

89. Louf is interested in retrieving "the traits embodied in concrete experience which is both connected to particular situations and properly scriptural — an experience that the early monks actually lived out and described as an essential stage of Christian living." André Louf, OCSO, *The Way of Humility*, trans. Lawrence S. Cunningham (Kalamazoo: Cistercian, 2007), p. 10.

root through experiencing many obstacles to the goal of purity of heart, especially the thoughts that render one helpless. Only through struggle, temptation, and even failure does the monk learn absolute dependence on God's grace and arrive at the state we would call "giving up control."

Humility, according to Cassian, is not a "natural" virtue, acquired by human effort. It arises as a person is able to "look at the succession of obstacles to be overcome . . . to unload all our vices and rid our souls of the wreck and rubble of passion."[90] As one faces the power of afflictive thoughts and desires, one grows in the knowledge that one can do little to overcome all that stands in the way of seeing God. Just as discernment arises in practice, so does humility. In repeating scripture as the thoughts rise up, one is able to more firmly grasp "human nature" and all that it contains.[91] The scriptures that become one's conscious thoughts lead one first to humility — a truthful sense of the self before God.

The scriptures also give many examples of humility as a significant quality of the faithful and righteous person. In the Hebrew Bible, humility is associated primarily with low socioeconomic status, those who must rely completely and totally on YHWH for life, sustenance, and deliverance. Their total dependence is a mark of their special attention. But humility is also related to Moses as one who is pious (Num. 12:3) and to the messiah (Zech. 9:9). In the wisdom literature it refers to fitting into the cosmic order (Job 22:29; Prov. 3:34), having the right estimate of one's self (Eccles. 10:28), and being afflicted (Ps. 22:26; 25:9; 147:6). In the New Testament, humility appears thirty-four times in the Gospels and in Paul's letters as a characteristic of the true disciple. Aspects of humility include being like a child (Mark 10:15), being poor in spirit (Matt. 5:3), and being last and not first. Mary's *Magnificat* expresses the humility (*tapeinōsis,* meaning "abasement" or "lowliness") of God's servant (*doulē* or "slave"). Humility is a chief characteristic of Jesus: "for I am meek and humble of heart" (Matt. 11:29), expressed in table fellowship with sinners and the washing of his disciples' feet (John 13:14-15). Paul proclaims that Jesus is the one who "humbled himself, becoming obedient to death, even death on a cross" (Phil. 2:8) and

90. *Conf.* 9.2.

91. *Conf.* 10.10. As an example, Cassian demonstrates how Psalm 69:2 (70:1) can be used in relationship to all eight thoughts. This one verse applies to "every condition" and "every danger," conveys a sense of "our frailty, the assurance of being heard, the confidence in help that is always and everywhere present."

links humility and love (1 Cor. 10:24; 13:4), forging Christian humility with selflessness.

To be humble is to know one's self in relationship to God as creature, as sinner, as poor, and as in need of God. It is the opposite of pride, arrogance, and self-reliance, all qualities which God overthrows while lifting up the lowly (1 Sam. 2:7; Luke 1:48-51). The outward sign of humility, in desert practice, was compunction, a feeling of deep sorrow for sin, accompanied by profound joy for God's goodness and mercy, expressed in tears.[92]

Humility, then, like discernment, is a form of self-knowledge — the self-knowledge of what one cannot do and achieve on one's own.[93] It is for Cassian the "teacher of all the virtues."[94] In the desert tradition, humility relates to obedience, as the Philippians text expresses, "to the point of death." Obedience in the desert tradition meant submitting one's self to a wise elder. It is in the context of seeking an elder that Cassian calls humility "the mother of all the virtues."[95] According to Abba Moses, "The first evidence of this humility is when everything done or thought of is submitted to the scrutiny of our elders."[96] Thus, the relationship between the virtue of discernment and humility is essential: "True discernment is obtained only when one is really humble." As Rich notes, "Experienced monks exercised *discretio* up to a point, judging themselves and their own inner state, but were also willing to submit themselves in humble obedience to the *discretio* of others when they discerned the need to do so." According to Rich, "*discretio* is thus a natural partner with obedience and humility."[97]

It is through Cassian's teaching that humility became an indispensable dynamic of the spiritual life.[98] But despite its importance in monasticism,

92. Cassian states that at the "thought of my own sins my tears have flowed and at the coming of the Lord this unspeakable joy has so revived me." *Conf.* 9.28. Compunction combines the Greek words *penthos,* meaning sorrow, and *katanysix,* meaning "a sudden shock, an emotion which plants deep in the soul a feeling, an attitude, or a resolution." See Irénée Hausherr, *Penthos: The Doctrine of Compunction in the Christian East,* trans. Anselm Hufstader, Cistercian Studies 53 (Kalamazoo: Cistercian, 1982), p. 8.

93. On *discretio* and self-knowledge, see Rich, *Discernment in the Desert Fathers,* pp. 99-101.

94. *Conf.* 15.7.

95. *Conf.* 19.2, in *Cassian: The Conferences,* trans. Ramsey. See also *Inst.* 4.30.1 on obedience.

96. *Conf.* 2.10.

97. Rich, *Discernment in the Desert Fathers,* p. 118.

98. Cassian was the first to enumerate degrees of humility (*Inst.* 4.39), which were

humility as a virtue held an ambiguous place in Christian thought. For the Greeks, humility was not a virtue. The term *tapeinos* and its cognates were used in a pejorative sense; to be humble was to be "lowly, servile, mean, insignificant."[99] Because of the centrality of humility in the New Testament, Louf shows how the attempt to make it a virtue was tried and won, but also compromised. Origen, for example, explained "that the ancient philosophers recognized this virtue under the name of *metriotes* (measure), which was to become in Latin 'moderation' *(mediocritas)*."[100] As the four cardinal virtues became the central moral categories, humility was incorporated into the virtue of temperance.

Humility, then, like discernment, lost its foundation in spiritual practice and experience. In my brief examination of humility in Cassian's thought we see how humility is forged in practice, becoming an essential disposition, a virtue that is fundamental to the Christian life. It is crucial to the next component of practical wisdom that I will discuss — unknowing. Unknowing was never defined as a virtue, though it may well have been since it does entail a method and a practice. But it is directly linked to humility since only the truly humble encounter the God beyond all knowing. In other words, through practice one's consciousness is free from inner chatter and conflict so that one can stand before God in humble waiting. Most of what the tradition says about unknowing suggests that it is a kind of spiritual knowledge revealed beyond effort. Unknowing comes to be known through encounter.

Unknowing

Cassian demonstrates that practical knowledge arises from spiritual practice over time — from relinquishing vice, dismantling afflictive thoughts, discerning right practice, memorizing scripture, and purifying one's heart. Only after concerted practice can a further kind of spiritual knowledge emerge; as the scholar Dorothy Emmet notes, there was "no *theoria* without a way of life."[101]

---

adopted and expanded by Benedict (480-547) in the *Rule,* and later by Bernard of Clairvaux (1090-1153) and Ignatius of Loyola (1491-1556).

99. Lawrence Cunningham, "Introduction," in Louf, *The Way of Humility*, p. viii.

100. Louf, *The Way of Humility*, p. 7.

101. Dorothy Emmet, "Theoria and the Way of Life," *Journal of Theological Studies* 17,

Spiritual knowledge, as understood in this tradition before the wedge between practice and theory emerged in the West, is not an abstract esoteric knowledge, but one born of "practical moral wisdom" that moves "towards union with the God whom 'no man has seen.'" Spiritual knowledge, in Christian thought, derived from the Greek understanding of *theoria,* which means "to see" (in Latin, *contemplatio*), and *gnosis,* which means "knowledge" that "illuminated the soul."[102] Spiritual knowing referred to seeing and knowing God as God. "The knowledge of Christ needs, not an intellectual soul, but a seeing soul," declared Evagrius. Emmet points out that for Gregory of Nyssa this meant "participating in [Christ], through the formation of his image in us, restored through 'purity of heart.'" Christian contemplation came to refer to knowing in which the mind is passive and receptive, yet active in love. To contemplate meant to seek "wholeness" and integrity that could only be found in seeing, or knowing, the divine.[103] In this receptivity, the God of unknowing emerges.

The transcendence and unknowability of God, according to the historian Bernard McGinn, is "a central element in all the religious literature of the second and third centuries CE, both the properly philosophical and the mysteriosophical," which includes the Middle Platonists, Gnostics, and Christian theologians, especially those of the Alexandrian School (which included the teachers who most influenced Cassian).[104] The monastic em-

---

no. 1 (April 1966): 38. The meanings of *theoria,* contemplation, and *gnosis* underwent many changes in Hellenistic and early Christian thought.

102. Emmet, "Theoria and the Way of Life," p. 46.

103. Emmet, "Theoria and the Way of Life," p. 44.

104. McGinn, *Foundations of Mysticism,* p. 43. R. T. Wallis claims that the first explicit Western spiritual references to "unknowing" or "ignorance" can be found in two Gnostic texts, the *Apocryphon of John* (a Christian mythological gnosis) and *Allogenes* (a non-Christian text), both first- or second-century texts. Wallis summarizes their main claims: "(1) the Supreme God utterly transcends knowledge, language, and indeed existence (being termed 'nonexistent' or 'preexistent'). (2) What partial knowledge humans can have of him is conveyed through an intermediary or intermediaries; (3) yet even the latter are very imperfectly knowable; hence (4) humans must rest content with knowing the Supreme by 'ignorance' and 'silence.'" Wallis summarizes further: "We reach God by turning our energies within and ascending by stages from self-knowledge to the One who is known only by ignorance. We must cease seeking the incomprehensible and receive the supreme revelation in silence and without effort." "The Spiritual Importance of Not Knowing," in *Classical Mediterranean Spirituality: Egyptian, Greek, Roman,* ed. A. H. Armstrong (New York: Crossroad, 1986), p. 468.

brace of the encounter of unknowing insisted that it does not take place in isolation from practical knowledge. It is not an experience, by and large, set apart from practice. Rather, according to McGinn, it takes place within an "ecclesiological setting, scriptural matrix, and sacramental practice."[105] Unknowing as encounter appears first in patristic pedagogical manuals on spiritual practice, only later finding its way into systematic theological treatises. In the patristic period and well into the Middle Ages, spiritual practice and theology were not distinct discourses; rather, theology grew out of spiritual practice or was expressed in and through spiritual practice.[106] By the time of high scholasticism, however, the claims about God's unknowability had become a doctrine in a system.

Four characteristics of unknowing are especially relevant to this chapter. The first three reveal that experiences of unknowing are passive, ineffable, and noetic — that is, they display the key features of mysticism described by William James in *The Varieties of Religious Experience*.[107] I am especially interested in how Gregory of Nyssa's *The Life of Moses* (roughly 390 CE) demonstrates several ways in which the noetic characteristic — that is, its capacity to convey knowledge — is expressed. The fourth feature of unknowing is, paradoxically, that it can be practiced, or at least that practice predisposes one to it, which is the focus of the famous spiritual text *The Cloud of Unknowing*.

Practice beyond Virtue, Speech beyond the Speakable

Gregory of Nyssa, the youngest of the three Cappadocian fathers, contributed significantly to the effort to draw Hellenistic thought and the Bible into a coherent theological worldview.[108] He was highly influenced by Origen's

---

105. McGinn, *Foundations of Mysticism*, p. 64.

106. Louth claims that mystical and dogmatic theology "are fundamentally bound up with one another." "The mystic is not content to know *about* God, he longs for union with God." *The Origins of the Christian Mystical Tradition*, pp. x, xiv.

107. James discusses four marks of mysticism — ineffability, noetic quality, transiency, and passivity. William James, *The Varieties of Religious Experience: A Study in Human Nature* (New York: Longmans, Green and Co., 1902), pp. 380-81.

108. For a discussion of the epistemology of the Cappadocians, see Pelikan, *Christianity and Classical Culture*, pp. 57-73.

approach to reading the scriptural text discussed above.[109] In *The Life of Moses,* Gregory first recounts Moses's encounter on Mount Sinai as history, reflecting on the literal events of Moses's life. In the next section, entitled "Contemplation on the Life of Moses," he reads these same events symbolically, as stages in Moses's ascent to God: enslavement, plagues, the parting of the Red Sea, the cloud, desert, wilderness, mountain, darkness and light, and the ark and the tabernacle. Three great movements give shape to Gregory's interpretation: the experience of purification and illumination told through the story of the burning bush; the Christian's separation from the world, told through the story of passing through the desert led by the cloud; and the encounter of contemplative knowing and unknowing through darkness, told in the story of Moses's encounter with God on Mount Sinai. Like Cassian, Gregory believed that acquiring virtue through ascetical practices is the beginning of the spiritual life and that its substance is a movement away from sin and toward virtue along the path to right knowledge, the encounter in which one sees God as God.

First of all, this encounter is passive. What is experienced cannot be constructed or planned. The quality of passivity, for James, points to the givenness of the experience: it occurs beyond "preliminary voluntary operations" such as "fixing the attention" or other acts of practical *askesis.*[110] For Gregory, the spiritual life begins in the practical exercises that shape the life of virtue, but once virtue is established, the mind can ascend to know God in further ways. The encounter with God at the burning bush (Exod. 3:1-6) and in the darkness and cloud over the mountain (Exod. 19:16-25) could not be constructed or determined by Moses; all he could do was make progress up the mountain toward his goal.[111] The encounter was entirely "given" and could only be "received."[112]

A second characteristic of unknowing encounters is their ineffability.[113]

---

109. See Malherbe and Ferguson, "Introduction," in *Gregory of Nyssa: The Life of Moses,* pp. 5-9.

110. James, *The Varieties of Religious Experience,* p. 381.

111. Most descriptions of mystical encounters claim that the encounter is "radically different from that found in ordinary consciousness" or through regular religious activities such as prayer, sacraments, and rituals. McGinn claims that such encounters take place in "what lies 'between' these necessary mediations." McGinn, *Foundations of Mysticism,* pp. xix-xx.

112. McGinn, *Foundations of Mysticism,* p. 125.

113. Though the concept of unknowability can be found throughout Greek thought,

The mystical encounter, McGinn notes, "defies conceptualization and ver-
balization, in part or in whole." Moses is "led to the ineffable knowledge of
God."[114] Gregory writes,

> For leaving behind everything that is observed, not only what sense compre-
> hends but also what the intelligence thinks it sees, it keeps on penetrating
> deeper until by the intelligence's yearning for understanding it gains access
> to the invisible and the incomprehensible, and there it sees God. This is the
> true knowledge of what is sought; this is the seeing that consists in not see-
> ing, because that which is sought transcends all knowledge, being separated
> on all sides by incomprehensibility as by a kind of darkness.[115]

Unknowing is beyond language, and yet such experiences seek to be
expressed through language. McGinn notes that such an experience

> can only be presented indirectly, partially, by a series of verbal strategies
> in which language is used not so much informationally as transformation-
> ally, that is, not to convey a content but to assist the hearer or reader to
> hope for or to achieve the same consciousness. Even those mystics who
> have paradoxically insisted on "strong" ineffability have tried to use all
> the resources of language — and often to create new ones — to assist this
> transformative process.[116]

Gregory, whom McGinn calls the first systematic negative theologian in
Christian history,[117] begins the long tradition of recounting in language
the experience of God beyond language. Even when words are attempted,
however, it is understood that this kind of knowing "plunges into the truly
mystical darkness of unknowing," as stated by the sixth-century theologian
Dionysius the Areopagite, who was influenced by Gregory. And he goes

---

R. T. Wallis notes that accounts of experiences of unknowability are limited: "Our knowledge both of such nonphilosophical experiences and of the external preparations for them is
generally limited." Wallis, "The Spiritual Importance of Not Knowing," p. 460.

114. McGinn, *Foundations of Mysticism*, p. xvii; *Life of Moses* 2.152.

115. *Life of Moses* 2.163.

116. McGinn, *Foundations of Mysticism*, p. xvii. For a discussion of *apophatic* theology as
a "theory of language," see Pelikan, *Christianity and Classical Culture*, pp. 40-56.

117. McGinn, *Foundations of Mysticism*, p. 141.

on to note that "What is to be said of it remains unsayable; what is to be understood of it remains unknowable."[118]

The third characteristic of unknowing — that it is a kind of knowledge — follows from the paradoxical claims of ineffability and articulation in language. McGinn explains that the inner "experience" of God that mystics attempt to account for becomes

> concrete and communicable by being fixed within modes of symbolic discourse that are presented as forms of affective intentionality. . . . [I]nsofar as mystical self-consciousness seeks to constitute itself as communicable, if always imperfectly, to others, it often does so by utilizing language that tries to fuse feeling and knowledge — *amor ipse intellectus est,* as a well-known expression of medieval Latin Christian mysticism put it.[119]

Beyond the experience of unknowing, there comes a kind of knowing, a way of knowing that shapes all knowledge. This claim reflects James's view that mystical encounters have a noetic quality, that is, something is known through them:

> Although so similar to states of feeling, mystical states seem to those who experience them to be also states of knowledge. They are states of insight into depths of truth unplumbed by the discursive intellect. They are illuminations, revelations, full of significance and importance, all inarticulate though they remain; and as a rule they carry with them a curious sense of authority for after-time.[120]

The knowledge of unknowing has been described in numerous ways and is still a matter of intense theological concern. For instance, Gregory's encounter of unknowing is akin to David Tracy's notion of "limit-questions" and "limit-situations." Tracy suggests that

> reflection upon limit-questions and limit-situations does disclose the reality of a dimension to our lives other than the more usual dimensions:

118. Dionysius, quoted in McGinn, *Foundations of Mysticism,* p. 182.
119. McGinn, "The Language of Inner Experience in Christian Mysticism," p. 135.
120. James, *The Varieties of Religious Experience,* pp. 380-81.

a dimension whose first key is its reality as limit-to our other every day, moral, scientific, cultural and political activities; a dimension which, in my own brief and hazy glimpses, discloses a reality, however named and in whatever manner experienced, which functions as a final, now gracious, now frightening, now trustworthy, now absurd, always controllable limit-of the very meaning of existence itself. I find that, although religiously rather "unmusical" myself, I cannot deny this reality.[121]

When faced with questions of limit in science and morality, "we may find ourselves turning to the limit-languages of religion in order to see how they try to re-present that 'other,' that limit dimension of our lives." Tracy describes how common human experiences of the everyday as well as "scientific, aesthetic, and moral experience" disclose a "properly religious horizon."[122] "Boundary" situations such as guilt, anxiety, illness, or death, and "ecstatic" experiences such as joy, love, and nature are "all genuine limit-situations . . . both positive and negative, wherein we both experience our own human limits (limit-to) as our own as well as recognize, however haltingly, some disclosure of a limit-of our experience."[123]

For Gregory, the primary reason we cannot know God as God resides in the natures of God and humanity. God "is beyond all knowledge and comprehension" and has no boundary.[124] Similarly, Tracy argues that all "authentically religious experience and language" displays an "ineluctably limit-character."[125] The quality of limit "acknowledges that there is a language, an experience, and even a knowledge which correctly be-speaks, dis-closes, and e-vents that limit as a final limit-of dimension of all our existence."[126] Here we see that the apophatic tradition, to which unknowing belongs, has what McGinn identifies as two dimensions: the subjective, which asserts that "God is said to be unknowable and ineffable to our mode of perception and expression," and the objective, which claims that God cannot be known in God's self. McGinn distinguishes between "unknowability,

121. David Tracy, *Blessed Rage for Order: The New Pluralism in Theology* (Chicago: University of Chicago Press, 1996), p. 105.

122. Tracy, *Blessed Rage for Order*, p. 93.

123. Tracy, *Blessed Rage for Order*, p. 105.

124. *Life of Moses* 2.164; 2.236.

125. Tracy, *Blessed Rage for Order*, p. 132.

126. Tracy, *Blessed Rage for Order*, p. 133.

which relates to the mind, and inexpressibility, which relates to the mind's ability to communicate what it knows."[127]

Thus, unknowing is often expressed in terms of contrasts — what it is not — rather than by noting similarity or likeness. In *The Life of Moses,* for example, Gregory contrasts light and darkness in two apparently contradictory ways, expressing both his subjective and his objective apophaticism. At the beginning of the path to virtue, "religious knowledge comes at first to those who receive it as light"; here, darkness is that which is opposed to God. But the images reverse as one progresses up the mountain, where darkness becomes the primary way of "seeing" God. He writes, "But as the mind progresses and, through an ever greater and more perfect diligence, comes to apprehend reality, as it approaches more nearly to contemplation, it sees more clearly what of the divine nature is uncontemplated."[128] From this perspective, darkness is to unknowing as light is to simpler kinds of knowledge.[129]

Such contrasts also disclose a dialectical kind of knowledge, exemplified in "positive" and "negative" experiences of presence and absence in Christian spirituality. According to McGinn,

> because of the incommensurability between finite and Infinite Subject, Christian mystics over the centuries have never been able to convey their message solely through the positive language of presence. The paradoxical necessity of both presence and absence is one of the most important of all the verbal strategies by means of which mystical transformation has been symbolized.[130]

127. McGinn, *Foundations of Mysticism,* p. 31.

128. Gregory, *Life of Moses* 2.162.

129. Other descriptions of contrasts abound in experiences of unknowing. Like Gregory, Dionysius holds to the movement of ascent in the spiritual life, from the affirmative on to the negative. He uses several terms for *apophatic* knowing. *Aphaeresis* is the removal of all analogies and symbols, the point at which one can accept "the denials" rather than the "assertions" about God. This leads to *agnosia,* which is not a knowing about what is, such as a concept about something, but, as McGinn describes, "more like a state of mind, . . . the subjective correlative to the objective unknowability of God. It can only be spoken about through paradoxical assertions of contraries: *agnōsia* is the only true *gnōsis* of God." McGinn, *Foundations of Mysticism,* pp. 174-75.

130. McGinn, *Foundations of Mysticism,* p. xviii.

The Life of Moses exemplifies both: the cataphatic use of the provocative and imaginative interpretation of Exodus, and the apophatic encounter in which Moses understands that there is no name that fully captures who God is.[131]

The dialectic between knowing and unknowing is later captured by Dionysius.[132] Like Gregory, he offers a fully developed cataphatic theology in his teachings on the many names of God and the beauty of the universe. However, he also contends that the knowledge expressed in names, creation, symbols, and texts "can dialectically attain the negation of representations necessary for discovering that God is always more than we can conceive." As the soul appropriates knowledge of God through "the positive symbols of scripture and liturgy," it progresses through a dialectic in which the "shock of dissimilar symbols" leads it to surpass the "material level to reach the conceptual level of meaning." Through concepts, "we ascribe names to God," but we also realize that all "conceptual signification must be abandoned in order to appreciate the real depths of the dissimilarity that leads to God."[133]

A final aspect of the noetic character of unknowing relates to the affections, and particularly to the intensity of desire and love for God. The affections are not denied in the encounter of unknowing; instead, the encounter directs them toward their ultimate purpose. McGinn notes that the knowledge of the mystic is a knowledge that "fuse[s] feeling and knowledge," a knowledge that intensifies feeling and desire for God. He points out that Gregory describes this as "passionless passion," a "paradoxical state" in which every enjoyment of God is also "the kindling of a more intense and unfulfilled desire, and in which every knowing of God is also a grasping of his transcendental unknowability."[134]

Where does this sublime unknowing finally lead? As Gregory recounts the story, Moses is a symbol of the one who by God's deliverance overcomes sin and lives virtuously, who withdraws from the world through solitary

131. *Life of Moses* 2.165.

132. See McGinn's discussion of Dionysius, *Foundations of Mysticism*, pp. 157-82.

133. Quotes taken from McGinn, *Foundations of Mysticism*, p. 174. McGinn also quotes Dionysius as saying, "God is therefore known in all things and as distinct from all things. He is known through knowledge *(gnōsis)* and through unknowing *(agnōsia)*. . . . This knowing through unknowing is the heart of Dionysius's negative theology."

134. McGinn, "The Language of Inner Experience," p. 136.

movement toward God, and who then in the darkness encounters the One who is unknowable. After that, however, Moses must descend the mountain. He must "return to society for service," of which Gregory unfortunately does not tell us much. Here is where we would like to know what difference the encounter of unknowing makes once ordinary life returns. Gregory holds Moses up as a "pattern of beauty" that "each one of us might copy" by "imitating his way of life."[135] Because of Moses's perfection, he is called the "servant of God" and a "'friend of God' by God himself."[136] *The Life of Moses* concludes that the movement from practical to spiritual knowledge is preparation for the life of service. In this text, at least, contemplation is not an end in itself. There is a return to daily life where discernment and humility are essential. But how does unknowing impact these virtues?

A Practice Not of Labor but of Love

Claiming that encounters of unknowing are passive and ineffable does not necessarily lead to the conclusion that there is no method that predisposes a person to this encounter. Gregory does not teach his reader a method of contemplative prayer, but the author of a later text in the same contemplative tradition does. The anonymous author of *The Cloud of Unknowing*, which draws from both Gregory and Dionysius, describes a kind of knowing that surpasses all conceptual knowledge.[137] This unknowing is born of love, not concepts. As the author famously states, "But no man can think of God himself . . . because [God] can certainly be loved, but not thought."[138]

 The Cloud of Unknowing is a practical manual that teaches a contemplative-apprentice a way of prayer through a basic "exercise," which the author considers the highest and most perfect prayer, the "easiest exercise of all," and

135. *Life of Moses* 2.319. For Gregory, as for Cassian, "practical philosophy must be joined to contemplative philosophy" (*Life of Moses* 2.200). In the wonderful saying (unattributed), "After the vision, the laundry." See Stewart, "Scripture and Contemplation," p. 460.

136. *Life of Moses* 2.317; 2.319.

137. *The Cloud* is influenced in both the affirmative and the negative way of knowing by Gregory and Dionysius. See William Johnston, "Introduction," in *The Cloud of Unknowing and The Book of Privy Counseling*, ed. William Johnston (New York: Doubleday, 1973), pp. 24-28.

138. *The Cloud of Unknowing*, ed. James Walsh (Mahwah, NJ: Paulist, 1981), p. 130.

"the shortest possible of all exercises."[139] The exercise consists of two main elements: emptying the mind of all thoughts and images, and filling the heart with the desire of love. The first part requires considerable learning and effort, for not only is one to relinquish thoughts that may lead to sin, as in the desert teaching, but one is even to give up thoughts of God's creatures, saints, and all good and holy things, including thoughts of God. What the apprentice must realize is that what one can know through intellectual study or the imagination must be forgotten; the exercise is not to think about God or God's wonders, but to love God with no thought. The practitioner's work is undertaken "with the help of grace," is to keep thoughts under the cloud of forgetting. The filling with the "impulse of love," the desire for God above all else, is the "work of God alone."[140]

Love is the second element of the exercise: the apprentice is told to "lift up your heart to God with a humble impulse of love; and have himself as your aim, not any of his goods. . . . [A]void thinking of anything but himself so that there is nothing for your reason or your will to work on."[141] Following this instruction is not easy. The author warns:

> Whoever hears this exercise read or spoken of may think that he can or ought to achieve it by intellectual labour; and so he sits and racks his brains how it can be achieved, and with such ingenious reasonings he does violence to his imagination, perhaps beyond its natural ability, so as to fashion a false way of working.[142]

Such a person is "perilously deluded." "Take care in this exercise and do not labour with your senses or with your imagination. . . . [T]his exercise cannot be achieved by their labour." The author goes on to explain that those who can exercise no thought, only a desire to love God, will find themselves in a darkness or cloud.

139. *The Cloud of Unknowing*, p. 121. In the active and contemplative life, there is the first part, which is corporal works of mercy and charity; the second part, which is "spiritual meditations on wretchedness and passion and heaven"; and the third part, which is the "dark cloud of unknowing." "First is good, second better and third best of all." *The Cloud of Unknowing*, p. 164.

140. *The Cloud of Unknowing*, p. 174.

141. *The Cloud of Unknowing*, pp. 119-20.

142. *The Cloud of Unknowing*, p. 127.

I call this exercise a darkness or a cloud; do not think that it is a cloud formed out of vapours . . . [or] a darkness such as you have in your house at night, when your candle is out. . . . When I say "darkness," I mean a privation of knowing, just as whatever you do not know or have forgotten is dark to you, because you do not see it with your spiritual eyes. For this reason, that which is between you and your God is termed, not a cloud of the air, but a cloud of unknowing.[143]

All other thoughts and desires are to be "hidden in a cloud of forgetting." In this experience, the person is between the cloud of unknowing, which is above, "between you and your God," and the cloud of forgetting, which is beneath.

The author is not opposed to knowledge in other circumstances and understands that in general the disciple will find it necessary and good to think about God's creation and the "kindness and worthiness of God."[144] In this exercise, however, "it is of little or no profit to think." Discernment and moderation are not needed in this practice. The object of the prayer is to encounter God as God is, and this cannot be achieved by thinking of God, only by love. "He can be taken and held by love but not by thought."[145] Although one can know through reason that God is the source of all there is, relinquishing one's thoughts about God teaches more: that God's wisdom, thoughts, goodness, and beauty cannot be known because they are categorically different from human wisdom and thoughts. We cannot acquire this knowledge through study, nor is it contained in books or attained by effort. We can only live in such a way as to purify ourselves from sin and exercise contemplative stillness that surpasses our senses and intellect to receive the pure light of God, which is received as darkness, in a cloud.[146]

---

143. *The Cloud of Unknowing*, pp. 127-28.

144. *The Cloud of Unknowing*, p. 130.

145. *The Cloud of Unknowing*, p. 130.

146. The "dark knowledge" that one comes to know through this practice has three elements, according to Johnston: faith, of which the cloud is a symbol; love, the "naked intent of the will, [which] rises from this faith and goes directly to God"; and wisdom, which is the fruit of this work. William Johnston, *The Mysticism of "The Cloud of Unknowing"* (St. Meinrad, IN: Abbey Press, 1975), p. 59. Two other aspects are humility (*The Cloud*, pp. 147-51) and discernment (*The Cloud*, pp. 198-201). Of humility, the author speaks of two kinds: an imperfect humility that focuses on one's "wretchedness and weakness" from sin, and a perfect humility

As with all practices (spiritual and otherwise), learning requires some tips and a few rules. When thoughts rise up beyond the cloud of forgetting and "continue to press in," *The Cloud* teaches the apprentice to deal with these thoughts firmly, by saying "Go down again" or by lifting up a "sharp dart of longing love" to the cloud of unknowing. If it is necessary, the author counsels using a single word of one syllable, such as "God" or "love," as a "shield" and "spear" to strike down thoughts and to "beat upon the cloud and this darkness above you." The short word expresses the intention of love toward God and the letting go of all other thoughts.[147] The author also offers other techniques to help the beginner. Thus, even in what was considered the highest realms of spiritual knowledge, some practical help is warranted.[148]

The Cloud's method of prayer is not aimed at unknowing. Unknowing is neither the method nor the goal. Instead, the goal is a quality of experience that defines both the human person and the Divine. Why pursue the cloud of unknowing? For one reason alone: true charity. Readers should attempt this prayer in order to love God above all else and to love one's neighbor by showing no partiality and considering every person, even stranger and enemy, as kin and friend.[149] What we do not know from *The Cloud* is how this encounter of unknowing changes how one loves the neighbor or makes one wise. Here the wedge between practical and spiritual knowing begins to be felt in the Christian tradition.

"All Serious Theology Should Be Practical"

I turned to the spiritual practices of John Cassian, Gregory of Nyssa, and *The Cloud of Unknowing* not because I think we can simply embrace their

---

that is "the superabundant love and worthiness of God." Of discernment, the author states that one should use discretion in terms of eating, sleeping, prayer, and conversation, but for this exercise none applies, since one should always be preparing for the exercise or doing the exercise. The fruit of this exercise will be discretion in all things: "Work at this exercise without ceasing and without moderation, and you will know where to begin and to end all your other activities with great discretion" (p. 200).

147. *The Cloud of Unknowing*, p. 134.
148. *The Cloud of Unknowing*, p. 181.
149. *The Cloud of Unknowing*, pp. 169-70.

practices. I have certainly come to "know a subject by loving it," as Burton-Christie says.[150] But I also recognize the problem of looking back hoping to find a clear answer. I also mostly agree with Louis Dupré when he says that it is a mistake,

> and one frequently made by those who undertake this spiritual journey, to believe that the solutions to all our problems lie buried in old masters and ancient monasteries. The doctrines, life-styles, and methods of a previous age were conceived within the reach of a direct experience of the sacred. This has for the most part ceased to exist. . . . A confrontation with the past may be necessary, but the shape of the spiritual life in the future will be entirely our own.[151]

While modernity has in many ways eclipsed religious experience and the kind of knowing gained from a life of spiritual practice, what in fact I think these practitioners show us (and Dupré seems to lack confidence in) is that such experience lies within the realm of practice. We must, it seems, practice our way to it.

For me, these Christians had a sense of embodied, situated, imaginative, communal, participatory knowing that had direct bearing on the concrete realities of everyday life and that embraced their whole life, not some part of it. While Cassian gives us a sense of what those decisions constituted in terms of eating, for instance, it would be helpful for us if he, as well as Gregory of Nyssa and the author of *The Cloud,* had shown us how the kinds of knowing that emerge from spiritual practice — discernment as *phronesis,* as knowledge of one's motives and intentions, humility as a true sense of one's self and of God, and unknowing as the encounter of the limits of all knowledge — matter in the daily realities of family life, camping trips, raising children, teaching class, listening to music, and forming communities. But this is where the wedge appeared.

150. "This is, I believe, an important epistemological statement: we begin to know a subject by loving it. Everything else follows from this, including the hard critical work of deepening our understanding of it." Burton-Christie, "The Cost of Interpretation: Sacred Texts and Ascetic Practice in Desert Spirituality," in Dreyer and Burrows, eds., *Minding the Spirit,* p. 101.

151. Louis Dupré, "Spiritual Life in a Secular Age," in *Religion and America: Spiritual Life in a Secular Age,* ed. Mary Douglas and Steven Tipton (Boston: Beacon, 1982), p. 13.

Fortunately, we have many practitioners and scholars retrieving and remaking spiritual practice today in light of both the desert monastic tradition and *The Cloud*.[152] And there are exciting communities of practice that are forming around these and other spiritual practices. Thus, it is not my agenda to propose a program for the spiritual life; rather, by way of conclusion, I would like to examine the twofold problem of relating practical wisdom and spiritual practice today and glean a few lessons from this historical examination.

As I mentioned at the outset of this chapter, practical wisdom, as it is being reconceived today, lacks the rigor of the spiritual exercises, and the retrieval of spiritual practice is largely disconnected from practical wisdom, the kind of wisdom we need in our daily lives. What do we need to be aware of as we try to draw these two closer together?

Retrievals of practical wisdom among professional educators largely focus on Aristotle's *phronesis*, which is crucial to practical wisdom, especially in developing a "sense of salience," what Christian Scharen describes as "concrete, as well as universal; timely, as well as timeless; a kind of knowing rooted in a capacity to understand situations with reference to their type and to hear their call, that is, the need to which one's action responds."[153] But we are missing in these proposals and discussions a wisdom epistemology that includes the sorting of the thoughts (or motivations), humility, and unknowing. What would professional education look like if we taught practices of identifying one's intentions and motivations underneath or inside the practice? How might we form ways of knowing through humility and unknowing? These are certainly not the only aspects of wisdom to be found in spiritual texts. We could also look to the practices of forgiveness, nonviolence, justice, or healing. The point is that practical wisdom requires engaging in spiritual exercises that remake the self so that it will flourish in a more robust, holistic way. There is widespread interest in expert practice among researchers, which is often equated with a kind of wisdom, but unfortunately this equates to the ability to do things, particularly physical ac-

152. On the practices related to early desert practitioners, particularly John Cassian, see Mary Margaret Funk, OSB, *Thoughts Matter: The Practice of Spiritual Life* (New York: Continuum, 1998). For a contemporary retrieval of the practice of unknowing, known today as centering prayer, see Thomas Keating, *Open Mind, Open Heart: The Contemplative Dimension of the Gospel* (New York: Amity House, 1986).

153. Scharen, in his chapter "Eclipsing," p. 172 above.

tivities, with great speed and accuracy.[154] But spiritual practice often entails a movement in the other direction — toward slowness, passivity, waiting. What if professional education taught this kind of knowing?

What is needed in professional education is an even wider epistemology, one that embraces unknowing. What flies in the face of modern forms of knowing more than the claim that unknowing is critical to practical wisdom? Such practical wisdom is a kind of knowledge that cannot be learned or known by reason alone, and certainly not by modernity's constricted notions of reason. As discussed throughout this book, modernity's disengaged, disembodied, and abstract reason has in fact limited human capacities, leading to the domination of peoples and the natural world. As Charles Taylor has shown, disengaged reason remains severed from a moral telos. Yet many fields of study remain afflicted with a mechanized view of the world that supports the notion that there is no limit to human knowing. Scientific knowledge is not rooted in the pursuit of wisdom, nor is wisdom required to pursue it.[155] Academic theology, too, has absorbed these perspectives, prizing systems of rational discourse and argumentation more than the knowledge that arises from spiritual practice.[156] Thus, a primary kind of knowing and experience is lost in our epistemologies. For Christians, by practicing unknowing we place ourselves in relationship to a telos that is beyond what we can know. Knowledge of ourselves and of God are reframed when we know the power of this unknowing.

The traditions of spiritual practice I have considered here contend that we cannot study our way to the kind of wisdom and knowledge born of life in God. What can be known through analytical reason is important, even

154. See, for example, K. Anders Ericsson, "Enhancing the Development of Professional Performance: Implications from the Study of Deliberate Practice," in *Development of Professional Expertise: Toward Measurement of Expert Performance and Design of Optimal Learning Environments*, ed. K. Anders Ericsson (Cambridge: Cambridge University Press, 2009), pp. 405-31.

155. Peter Harrison, "Disjoining Wisdom and Knowledge: Science, Theology and the Making of Western Modernity," in *Wisdom or Knowledge? Science, Theology and Cultural Dynamics*, ed. Hubert Meisinger, Willem B. Drees, and Zbigniew Liana (New York: T&T Clark, 2006), p. 61.

156. Practical theology, Claire Wolfteich notes, has rarely engaged mystical texts, generally preferring hermeneutics, social science, and ethics as dialogue partners, while "mysticism generally falls outside the scope of the discourse." Claire Wolfteich, "Practices of 'Unsaying': Michel de Certeau, Spirituality Studies, and Practical Theology," *Spiritus* 12 (2012): 161.

essential, and is not to be rejected; but it is limited. Beyond it, there is still more to know. While there is little place in our epistemologies, pedagogies, or ethics for the stance of unknowing, there may be nothing more crucial at this point in our history.

If the first problem is that discussions of practical wisdom lack attention to spiritual practice, the second problem arises in the widespread interest in spiritual practice that is not linked to discussions of practical wisdom and that lacks connection to a broader social ethic. Spiritual practice can be caught in the cultural trajectory of expressive individualism as a means of developing and improving the self. Again, it is exciting to see that practices of meditation are growing (and being studied by social scientists), but I fear that the aim of some of this is self-enhancement that lacks the rigor and discipline to remake the self and our communities.

Consider a research project at the University of Chicago, entitled "Wisdom Research." Scientists across several institutions are engaged in a multidisciplinary study that is exploring "big questions in the field that have the greatest potential of influencing research, education, policy and professions: What is the relationship between expertise and wisdom? How does experience increase wisdom? What is the relationship between cognitive, social and emotional processes in mediating wisdom?"[157] Every time I receive their e-newsletter I am both excited and disappointed.

While there is significant insight to be gained from studies of wisdom and expert practice, much of it misses the point. Ursula M. Staudinger, a pioneer in the field of wisdom studies, defines wisdom as "self-insight; the ability to demonstrate personal growth; self-awareness in terms of your historical era and your family history; understanding that priorities and values, including your own, are not absolute; and an awareness of life's ambiguities."[158] Self-knowledge is certainly part of practical wisdom, but, as *New York Times* writer David Brooks says in another post on the Wisdom Research website, "the real problem is the 'self' part."[159] What in Staudinger's definition of

157. See http://wisdomresearch.org/. Accessed June 30, 2014.

158. Quoted in Gregory Beyer, "Wisdom Isn't What You Think It Is, and It Doesn't Always Come with Age," http://wisdomresearch.org/blogs/news/archive/2014/05/05/wisdom-isn-t-what-you-think-it-is-and-it-doesn-t-always-come-with-age.aspx#sthash.dDUgO2G6.dpuf. Accessed June 30, 2014.

159. David Brooks, "The Problem with Confidence," http://wisdomresearch.org/blogs/news/archive/2014/05/16/the-problem-with-confidence.aspx. Accessed June 30, 2014.

wisdom does not fall into the category of expressive individualism or the autonomous self? The danger of these discussions of practical wisdom in the sciences is that they fail to realize how culturally bound are their assumptions about the self and wisdom. They rarely raise the question about communities of practice that shape the wise person. And they have little interest in religious practice, except for nontheistic meditation practices.

But spiritual exercises are not an end in themselves. They orient us to ever-deeper relationship, and in the Christian tradition that means a direction toward our neighbor that is grounded in the Holy Mystery we know through Christ. For the desert practitioners, an ethic of hospitality shaped their communal life, and it is one we can learn from, but it is not enough in our time. We require a robust social ethic that is alert to the systemic distortions and violence our institutions perpetuate, the threat posed by ways of life that destroy human life as well as nature. Recently practical theologians have called for greater attention to spirituality. David Tracy, for example, argues that "all serious theology should be practical (praxis-determined) as both ethical-political (prophetic) and aesthetic meditative, even mystical."[160]

The ancient practices I have examined here demonstrate that practical wisdom is born in the concreteness of daily, bodily, economic, communal life. They require commitment and discipline in a community of practice. We have to be careful since spiritual practice today can become too episodic, a matter of personal taste and choice. What our practice today can mask is the real demands required of exercise, the rigorous following of a way of life, the need for teachers who are wise and discerning, the need to become humble in the face of the unknowable God.

My goal has been to lift up a few examples of how spiritual practice relates to practical wisdom in the Christian life, as spiritual practice both draws upon Aristotle's *phronesis* and goes beyond it. Although this is only a modest beginning in our search for a wisdom epistemology, it does provide some lessons that point a way forward.

First, we have seen that wisdom is born of practice and that those who

---

160. David Tracy, "A Correlational Model of Practical Theology Revisited," in *Religion, Diversity and Conflict,* ed. Edward Foley (Münster: LIT Verlag, 2011), pp. 49-60. See also Claire Wolfteich, "Animating Questions: Spirituality and Practical Theology," *International Journal of Practical Theology* 13, no. 7 (2009): 121-43.

desire it must practice their way to it. In retrieving older forms or adopting new ones, we need embodied spiritual exercises that teach us discernment through *askesis*. Moral virtue arises from orienting our daily actions away from evil and toward the highest good, the gracious presence of God as Holy Mystery. By this grace, Christians claim, we are remade; wisdom requires such a rebirth, a rejection of both pride and lack of self-worth (as feminist theologians have shown), and a turning toward our neighbor in generosity, reconciliation, and love. Practice predisposes us to this kind of knowing. But, as we have seen, practice thrives only when it is undertaken in relation to a clear and compelling telos. A renewal of *askesis* will require discernment of a telos that incorporates practical wisdom regarding what is necessary and good for ourselves, our communities, and the natural world — our proximate goal — as we seek to know God truly.

Second, in addition to discernment, practice gives rise to humility, and humility opens out to encounters of unknowing. In the examples above, we see how humility is born of the struggle and failure to live by a rule. The point, of course, is that one cannot live a disciplined life on one's own, without either community or God's gracious presence. The path of humility may begin with learning one's weakness and dependence, but it eventuates in having a "right estimate of one's self," both as *anawim* and as *imago dei,* as one in need of God's mercy and guidance and, at the same time, as one graced with God's power and gifts. We need to learn and to follow the "directional arrows of 'humility'" projected by biblical texts.[161] Humility reminds us of what can be known and what remains unknown. It is a disposition toward knowledge of any kind; it teaches us that knowledge is not to be mastered, that we are not to conquer all that can be known, and that gaining more and more knowledge is not a wise telos. Humility invites us not to cling to knowledge for its own sake, but to discover a wisdom that draws from the practices of unknowing. By opening a space within ourselves that claims we cannot and do not know, we dispose ourselves to the God of unknowing. Humility is an active virtue; it is being awake to the God of unknowing.

Finally, such wisdom can be taught, but only in the midst of shared practice. Theological teaching today, grounded in a wisdom epistemology, must arise from the spiritual practice of teachers and must seek to foster

161. See Dorothy Bass's chapter "Imagining," above.

the spiritual practice of students. All of the spiritual authors I cited have in common that they are teachers of a practice. Their writings are pedagogical in character. Cassian is writing for new communities embarking on the monastic life.[162] Gregory of Nyssa is recounting the life of Moses for Caesarius, a "man of God," in order that he might imitate this life so as to become a servant and "friend of God."[163] The author of *The Cloud* is writing a letter to a twenty-four-year-old disciple who is beginning to learn contemplative prayer. The disciple is most likely in a community informed by Dionysian theology, where such letters commonly circulated among members.

In each case the authors' writings are not meant to be systematic discourses. Rather, these are the works of master practitioners who are teaching novices how to practice.[164] They are not teaching the virtues or theories of the virtues; rather, they are teaching a practice by which to acquire virtue, unknowing, and wisdom. In fact, we cannot say we fully understand their teachings by reading their texts alone; we would first have to practice what they teach in order to fully engage and critique their methods. Cassian notes that to teach discernment one must have discernment. And he warns his students that they should neither seek out a teacher who lacks knowledge derived from spiritual practice nor teach what they themselves have not practiced.[165]

162. For a discussion of Cassian's pedagogy see Stewart, *Cassian the Monk*, pp. 37-38; on the teacher-disciple relationship, see Rich, *Discernment in the Desert Fathers*, pp. 114-19.

163. Malherbe and Ferguson point out that the *Life of Moses* has the "form of a logos," a formal treatise that "may have been designed for reading aloud in a household of ascetics." The two main sections, the *historia* and the *theoria*, were common forms of catechetical instruction. Since it is addressed to Caesarius, it may have been written as a response to a request for guidance in living the virtuous life. "Introduction," p. 3.

164. Hadot notes that the philosophers' aim in writing was to teach spiritual exercises — not to set out a system of ideas, but to present a "reflection of pedagogical, psychagogic, and methodological preoccupations." He argues that contemporary scholars misunderstand this literature because they see contradictions in a "system" that does not exist; the different ways of presenting ideas are due to context and the "spiritual level of the audience to which the commentary is addressed" — that is, beginners or more sophisticated practitioners. *Philosophy as a Way of Life*, pp. 105-7.

165. *Conf.* 14.9; 14.16.

part three

collaborating

AN INVITATION TO EXPERIMENT,
AN EXPRESSION OF THANKS

IN THIS BOOK WE HAVE LIFTED UP a kind of knowing that emerges as embodied human beings experience the world, engage in practices, live imaginatively before texts and traditions, and acknowledge the limits of their knowing. We assume that those who read this book already possess this kind of knowledge to some degree, as we believe we five authors also do. However, this kind of knowing is by its very nature difficult to articulate, encourage, and hold up for theological scrutiny. As we offer this book to readers and invite you to consider its implications, we want to share some of the unexpected moves we found necessary as we tried to explore Christian practical wisdom in ways that take seriously its embodied, adaptive, immersive, imaginative, and reverent character. How we go about learning and knowing — how we interact, talk, read, write, and engage one another — can itself become its own exercise in the pursuit of practical wisdom, as we discovered and as we hope others may find as well.

We invite collaboration and conversation because we believe that appreciating and fostering practical wisdom matters immensely for faithful, generative living in our broken world. As a way of knowing that enables people to embody love of God and love of neighbor within the countless situations they encounter, practical wisdom is indispensable to all Christians, and understanding and fostering it should be a strong concern of those called to lead, teach, and serve others. And so our invitation is broad. At the same time, we especially want to encourage approaches that go deep, that is, approaches that honor and embody the creative engagement that characterizes Christian practical wisdom itself. Such approaches require a willingness to explore the terrain where academic, ecclesial, and quotidian experience meet and diverge. Those attuned primarily to texts and theories will miss crucial dimensions of practical wisdom if they examine it only abstractly, while those formed in hands-on activity can forgo crucial opportunities for reflection if they avoid the thinking we hope to encourage.

As we hope this book demonstrates, Christian practical wisdom can be manifest in every sphere of life and also debated in complex regions of thought. Those who would understand it will do best if they bring their whole selves, together with others, to explorations that are themselves exercises in practical wisdom. This is what we have tried to do, though it took us some time to realize what we were doing and why. Investigating and advocating for the kind of knowing we call *Christian practical wisdom* led this book's five authors into forms of writing and collaboration that are notably different from what we had previously done. We share an account of our own work together not to provide a rigid or definitive model but to prompt others to imagine their own experiments in learning. Making space for the kind of knowing we lift up in this book calls for new and creative forms of engagement.

An Experiment in Learning

Our collaboration developed through meetings on the grounds of Saint John's Abbey and University, a Benedictine community in a beautiful part of central Minnesota. When we first began to work together, following up on issues in *For Life Abundant,* we naturally adopted the usual scholarly procedure of reading one another's individual research and discussing common readings. In spite of our shared and urgent concern about the plight of practical knowledge, we did not know with certainty that we would write a book. At first some found this openness to being unproductive liberating, while others found it frustrating. Looking back, we agree that it proved to be generative, in part because it built a foundation for work that truly moved beyond individual authorship.

During this time, Chris Scharen suggested that we consider a rather radical form of collaboration that was being proposed in the field of anthropology. In *Designs for an Anthropology of the Contemporary,* anthropologists Paul Rabinow, George Marcus, James Faubion, and Tobias Rees had recently argued that old modes of research limit, rather than allow, the sort of scholarship that is most needed to study the shifting, globalizing societies of the present day. Individual projects driven by interpretive and authorial virtuosity could never get at the broad, rapidly changing contours of the phenomena anthropologists long to understand. Collaboration within a common workspace similar to the design studio (from architecture, for instance) or the laboratory (from the sciences) would be far more likely to contribute to the development of knowledge in their field, they proposed.[1] Inspired by their ideas, Chris suggested that we invite one another into our research and writing in a similar manner, to see what common ground would emerge. In an email he wrote, "Actually thinking together about how to be more intentional about a common space for sharing thoughts on concept formation, methodology, research, and writing might be extraordinarily productive." He also noted that we were already in the habit of gathering in an appropriately generative place, "amidst the rhythm of prayer and silence and natural beauty Saint John's provides."

To some of us, the proposal set forth by Rabinow and his colleagues seemed a little preposterous. The perception of collaborative work as lesser is deeply embedded in the promotion practices of the academy, something our pre-tenure members felt acutely. Moreover, the logistical and ideological challenges of studio or laboratory experimentation are daunting. One

1. Paul Rabinow and George Marcus, with James Faubion and Tobias Rees, *Designs for an Anthropology of the Contemporary* (Durham: Duke University Press, 2008). The book not only proposes but also displays a collaborative model by setting forth a transcribed, edited conversation among the authors. One odd feature is the two-tier attribution of authorship, with the names of two prominent senior anthropologists preceding those of their students Faubion and Rees. While Rabinow's and Marcus's voices dominate the transcribed conversation, it appears that Rees did the lion's share of planning and editing, and the internal table of contents attributes the introductory and concluding chapters to him. This particular articulation of shared authorship may be just and proportional in this case, but the adoption of such a distinctive articulation also confirms just how complicated collaboration can be, both while it is being done and in how it is valued. Like this team of anthropologists, all five authors of *Christian Practical Wisdom* claim authorship of our book, even though each of us maintains individual authorship of specific chapters. However, even these chapters were written in the midst of ongoing contact with and criticism from the others within a model of full mutuality. We also present the first and last chapters as jointly written based on long conversations about our process, aims, and hopes.

of us had already participated in a coauthored book project with five authors that did not turn out so well because orchestrating the completion of the book proved difficult, political differences became hard to manage, and seniority among authors in rank and finances ended up controlling the argument. The idea of this alternative mode of working fell to the wayside. Or so it seemed. However, almost without recognizing it until near the end of our process, this is in essence what we have done. We share the anthropologists' proposal here not because it consciously shaped us — as far as we were aware at the time it did not — but because we now see that their proposal articulates well much of what we came to value in our own collaboration. Further, their proposal may point to a growing awareness more broadly that individualistic scholarship cannot adequately explore a range of intriguing theological questions or foster the kind of knowledge needed to address them.

A collaborative space such as an architectural design studio, Rabinow, Marcus, Faubion, and Rees argue, acknowledges in its very structure the diffuse character of authorship as it is formed through conversations, borrowed concepts, and exposure to colleagues' work on related topics. In the studio or laboratory setting, authorship is a "problem" because lines of authorship (and thus ownership) are blurred, in contrast to familiar academic forms outside the sciences such as contributions to journals, conferences, and most multi-author books. However, certain kinds of much-needed work can be generated much more readily in collaborative settings. The authors of *Designs for an Anthropology of the Contemporary* made their proposal at a moment when their discipline was at a turning point. They noted that its emerging focus on the multiple, fluid appearances of "the cultural" in the contemporary world meant that future research would always be, by its nature, "unfinished." No single researcher could fruitfully work alone, as anthropologists did when they traveled to isolated settings with the goal of describing "a culture" as a "bounded whole."[2] Individual contributors would continue to be indispensable, to be sure, but their learning and that of their teachers, peers, and readers would need to be enhanced by mutual criticism, negotiation, and breakthroughs along the way.

In retrospect, the anthropologists' proposal helps us to see that collaborative, disciplined scholarly practice over time offers practical theology

2. Rabinow et al., *Designs for an Anthropology of the Contemporary*, pp. 106-9.

and theological education a way of adaptive learning that may be just what the church and its academic leadership need in these challenging, complex times. Although individual names are linked to most of the chapters in our book, these chapters are what they are only as a body of work together, elicited by each other, written in companionship, and honed by conversation and by detailed and sometimes sharp feedback. Each of us has generated work that each of us needed to do, in areas where we have distinctive expertise and experience. But each of us also moved in new intellectual directions encouraged by each other and our shared aim of learning more about Christian knowing, and we opened ourselves and our chapters to far more than the usual criticism and revision, a process sustained in large part by mutual affection, trust, and respect. Most of us had to discard or do extensive rewriting on early drafts, discovering only by failing what it was we wanted to say.

Further, in a process of this kind, life's limitations, competing vocational demands, and finitude itself complicate collaboration and impose certain costs. One colleague at early meetings simply could not be absent from his home institution as frequently as this endeavor demanded. Another decided not to continue because of a commitment to be present for young children. A job change on the part of one who did continue meant that we lost a valuable chapter. And as we finished this work, the final crafting of the opening and concluding chapters fell more heavily on a few of us. Even so, we five authors insist that the flexibility and forbearance required for this kind of work were necessary if we were to pursue our topic wisely and well. We took time and made space to discuss the complex realities of faith and ministry, not as, say, discrete problems for preaching or leadership but as connected to many aspects of daily life. We found ourselves naming the difficulty of the hard work that was required and also loving it when this work was done in community. We brought a common focus to the usually disparate work of those in various sub-areas of practical theology and, indeed, in the specialized disciplines of theological studies at large. Similar to the anthropologists' focus on "the cultural" rather than on a variously contained "culture," we found ourselves more engaged by "the theological" than by a bounded entity called "theology." We experimented with genre, searching for a form appropriate to our subject matter.

In a sense, our "laboratory" was also an "oratory" — a fact that encouraged many of the unusual moves just described. We came to care deeply about one another and to attend to the moments of bereavement, celebration, illness, or vocational transition that came to each of us during these years, and we took time at each meeting to tell of these things, understanding that they were occasions that required Christian practical wisdom. Sometimes we joined the monks in prayer; sometimes we prayed in our own small group. We lived in simple quarters, surrounded by plain but beautiful furniture built in the Abbey woodshop from trees harvested on neighboring grounds. We shared many good meals, especially cherishing hospitality and renewal around the hearth and table of one of our members. We rested, walked, and talked for hours in a sunlit room with floor-to-ceiling windows overlooking a lake. Meeting within a contemplative space permeated with scripture and a longing for communion with God, rather than an airport hotel, say, mattered greatly. As we received the hospitality of the Benedictine community, we found insight in the argument of a Benedictine theologian that Benedict's *Rule* itself "takes its stand with the wisdom literature" by showing concern for every aspect of quotidian life and by placing itself within a wider set of texts and an ongoing, generations-spanning community of readers who seek to embody its teaching in new contexts.[3]

Ultimately, what set our imagination and curiosity afire and laid the ground for this book were our "field trips" — a series of encounters with exemplary practitioners who began to disclose to us what the intelligence of practice can be when embodied at a high level of excellence. On one occasion, we learned from a young woman who helps to tend the three-thousand-acre Saint John's Arboretum about the ongoing human care and restraint that make the lake, meadows, and forests thrive. More than once, we visited the exhibits of the Saint John's Bible, watching as new vellum pages of the first handwritten, illuminated text of Christian scriptures to be created in five hundred years arrived in Collegeville. From a generous guide, we learned how the illuminator who did the calligraphy used his whole body to perform his work, his knowledge going "from toes to head." We saw how imagination, discipline, skill, and body-knowledge fostered wise judgments about both theology and budgets, about the juxtaposition of word and image, and about the interactions between medieval, modern, devotional, and liturgical approaches to scripture.

3. Valerian John Odermann, OSB, "Interpreting the *Rule of Benedict:* Entering a World of Wisdom," *American Benedictine Review* 35, no. 1 (March 1984): 42.

A similar interweaving of *techne, phronesis,* and *theoria* shapes the work at Saint John's Pottery, where we drank tea as guests of an internationally acclaimed potter who offers hospitality to interested inquirers every afternoon. Richard Bresnahan works within traditions learned during his artistic formation in Japan, using clay from local ground, glazes from the ash of local plants, and mixers from recycled machine parts. Under his guidance, apprentices learn how to shape and fire objects that will please the eye, meet human needs, sustain traditions of craft, and (not incidentally) enable them to earn a living. As we talked, they worked at wheels nearby, using tools they had made themselves and asking one another for help as needed. Once an apprentice has thrown at least eight hundred pieces of a single design, the master potter told us, consciousness falls away, and the know-how is in her hands. Our conversation in the pottery studio brought to mind the insights of nursing scholar Patricia Benner, who argues that "a wealth of untapped knowledge is embedded in the practices and the 'know-how'" of expert practitioners. This knowledge is not easy to capture in words, and this "lag in description contributes to the lag in recognition and reward." Further, Benner argues, "adequate description of practical knowledge is essential" to the advance of theory.[4]

Thus instructed by many practitioners, we began to see more clearly the mission of the theological work that lay before us. As others pick up this work, we encourage robust communities of collaboration to carry it forward. We hope that the various chapters will suggest a multitude of ways for readers to do so. In particular, we urge readers to be creative in crafting collaborative conversations. Such learning communities can create spaces where members read together without being pressured to produce, where prayer and conversation take place around tables of intellectual, spiritual, and physical nourishment, and where rest and beauty foster personal renewal. Further, we believe that such communities can be crafted in financially and personally sustainable ways by gathering at retreat centers, monasteries, church camps, or parks. The point is to be both practical and wise when seeking to study or to foster practical wisdom, and to be prayerful when discerning how it shapes ministry and the life of faith. The mode of inquiry must to some degree match the subject itself.

---

4. Patricia Benner, *From Novice to Expert: Excellence and Power in Clinical Nursing Practice* (Menlo Park, CA: Addison-Wesley, 1984), p. 11.

With Gratitude

One thing would have made our gatherings at Saint John's even better: the full collaboration of our colleague, teacher, and friend, Craig Dykstra. Craig is the one who got us started along the intellectual paths that led to this book. His own work as a practical theologian has been influential in renewing interest in the kind of knowing that is both needed for practice and acquired in the midst of practice. His articulation of "pastoral imagination" has brought attention to the complex intelligence that belongs to the wise and excellent practice of ministry. As the foremost theological educator of his generation, he has helped many people understand how indispensable lifelong learning that encompasses every dimension of a pastor's personhood is to the flourishing of the church and the world.

In addition, it is Craig who gave us the gift of collaboration, an art form of which he is the most adept practitioner we know. Over the past quarter century, he has invited each of us to share in various ways in the work of strengthening the religious lives of American Christians through the multiple creative endeavors he guided as Senior Vice President of Lilly Endowment. As a result, each of us has discovered and developed dimensions of our vocations as teachers, scholars, and disciples that might otherwise have gone unnoticed. Across many years of highly visible and influential grant-making, Craig brought Christian practical wisdom fully into play each day as he discerned, with others, how to help pastors, scholars, and other leaders to use their gifts in response to God's active presence for the life of the world.

At several crucial points during the development of this book, Craig met with us to discuss its concerns and review some of its early drafts. We are grateful for his characteristically incisive questions on those occasions, as well as for his encouragement to continue our efforts to advocate for Christian practical wisdom. Even more, however, we are grateful to him for exemplifying that way of knowing, which we have seen embodied in his action not only during those conversations but on many occasions across many years. Generosity has been Craig's daily work — institutionally, as a steward of the resources of Lilly Endowment, and also personally, as a Christian minister, disciple, and scholar who has offered gracious non-financial support to countless pastors, scholars, students, and friends. His capacity to reflect, criticize, and teach in each new situation is extraordinary. With Craig, Christian practical wisdom is no abstraction but an actual, embodied response to the grace of God poured out abundantly for the life of the world in Christ. Craig's generosity flows from his gratitude to God, his collegiality from love of neighbor and awareness of the overflowing abundance of God's grace toward us all, and his remarkable generativity from his hope in God's future.

We hope that he will receive this book as a testimony to the affection and respect in which we hold him.

THE AUTHORS

Dorothy C. Bass is director emerita of the Valparaiso Project on the Education and Formation of People in Faith.

Kathleen A. Cahalan is professor of theology at Saint John's University School of Theology and Seminary and director of the Collegeville Institute Seminars.

Bonnie J. Miller-McLemore is E. Rhodes and Leona B. Carpenter professor of religion, psychology, and culture at Vanderbilt University Divinity School and Graduate Department of Religion.

James R. Nieman is president of the Lutheran School of Theology at Chicago.

Christian B. Scharen is vice president for research at Auburn Seminary.

INDEX

on Cassian's positive/negative tasks,
299n85
on characteristics of mystical
encounters, 305n111, 306, 307,
308–9, 310
on expression of experience of
unknowing, 309
on transcendence and unknowability
of God, 303
on unknowing as practice, 304
mean
as guide of virtue, 281, 290, 291
phronesis as, 277, 287
mediocritas, 302
Meeks, Wayne, 253
Mellott, David, 28, 29
Merleau-Ponty, Maurice, 172, 174
Merton, Thomas, 51
metanoia, 277
metaphor
in exegetical scholarship, 245n28
intertextuality and, 251–53, 251n46,
254–55
transformative power of, 248–49,
249n38, 251n46
metriotes, 302
"middle axioms," 209, 209n109
Milhaven, John Giles, 33, 42
Miller, Donald, 206
Miller-McLemore, Bonnie, 23–44,
175–231
bodily knowing, 23–25, 32–33
on curricular understanding of
practical theology, 266n77
in *For Life Abundant,* 11, 12
forms of practical theology, 267n78
on *phronesis vs.* embodied knowing,
277
teaching of pastoral care, 35–37,
213–14
works on embodied knowing in
theology, 41
mimesis, 254, 256
"mind over matter," 177, 178, 217. *See*

also practical wisdom, eclipsed by
disengaged reason
ministry, bodily knowledge in, 40–41
Modern Theology journal, 183
Moschella, Mary Clark, 223–24
Moses, 305, 306, 310–11
Mozart, 131–32
Murdoch, Iris, 84, 241, 274
mysticism, 304, 304n107, 305n111,
317n156

Nanko-Fernandez, Carmen, 209
narrative
community enactment of, 263
in conventional practical thinking,
195
eclipse of biblical, 232, 249
in everyday practical wisdom, 69, 75
fictional, 115, 248
as formative, 46, 250, 253, 261
as genre, 251
plain sense reading of scripture based
on, 258–59
power differentials and, 240, 256–57
in Ricoeur's thought, 69, 86, 249n38
self-knowledge through, 297–98
in study of congregations, 115–16, 223
"narrative lectionary" movement,
265n74
natural philosophy, 151
Niebuhr, H. Richard, 241
Nieman, James, 88–118
career influenced by upbringing,
113–14
in *For Life Abundant,* 11
on learning to recognize communal
wisdom, 96–99, 107, 112–13, 114–16
resources recommended by, 116–18
study of theology in congregational
contexts, 224–26
noetic quality of unknowing, 304,
307–10
nous, 283, 283n24
Nouwen, Henri, 51

interpretation *vs.* mastery-driven
  knowledge, 247
Thatamanil, John, 226
theological education. *See also* academic
  theology
  body work in, 35–39
  collaborative spaces for, 328–29
  vs. embodied knowing, 226
  focus on *phronesis,* 316
  goals and conflicts in, 54–57, 58, 61
  identity and integrity in teaching,
    60, 61
  incorporating spiritual practice in.
    See under spiritual practices
  narrow context for, 230–31
  practice in teaching, 61–62
theological histories of practice, 166–67
theology. *See* academic theology;
  practical theology
Theology of Liberation, A (Gutiérrez), 219
theoria
  Aristotle's inclusion of, 173
  biases behind hierarchy of, 200
  dominance in modern Western
    thought, 1–2
  in early spiritual exercises, 283
  gnosis and, 284n31
  phronesis and, 196, 284–85
  purity of heart and, 284
  spiritual knowledge and, 303
  way of life and, 302
Thinking Biblically (LaCocque,
  Ricoeur), 247–48
Thirty Years' War, 146, 154, 156, 173
thoughts
  afflictive. *See* afflictive thoughts
  in contemplative prayer, 312–14
  countering problem with new
    practice, 294, 295–96
  "eight thoughts," 49, 50, 294
  five "moments" in rise of, 294–95
  recognizing and diagnosing, 291,
    294–95
  sorting of, 281, 287, 293–95, 316
Tillich, Paul, 196

Tompkins, Jane, 56
Toulmin, Stephen
  on Plato, 173
  reason and reasonableness, 3, 147
  on recovery of practical philosophy,
    179–80
  theoretical knowledge–practical
    wisdom balance, 3, 146
Tracy, David
  on analogical imagination, 184,
    184n28, 249
  contribution to practical theology as
    discipline, 184–85
  influence on Browning, 196, 198n74
  "limit-questions" and "limit-
    situations," 307–8
  "logical spectrum" of academic
    theology types, 184, 184n28
  on recovery of fragmented
    theological knowledge, 227
  on separations in modern Western
    culture, 226
Traina, Cristina, 32, 43
Transforming Practice (Graham), 211
Trible, Phyllis, 262
tropology, 285
Turnbull, Paula Mary, 84

U2, 134–38, 141
unknowing
  author's exploration of, 278–79, 280,
    281
  characteristics of, 304, 311–14
  as dimension of biblical imagination,
    261, 273–74
  as dynamic of practical wisdom, 10
  as encounter, 302–4, 303n104, 304
  ineffability of, 304, 305–6, 311
  method for practice, 304, 311–14
  modern devaluation of, 279, 317
  noetic quality of, 307, 308–11,
    309n129
  passivity of, 304, 305, 311
  in theological education, 316, 317
  unknowability of God, 303, 303n104